Conservation and the Law
A Dictionary

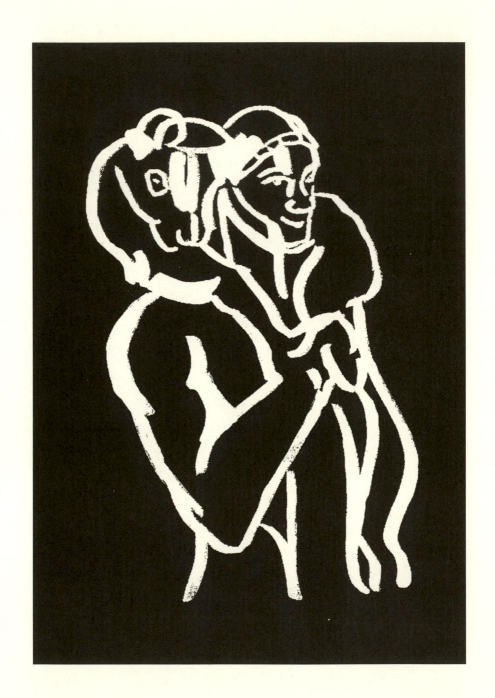

CONTEMPORARY LEGAL ISSUES

Conservation and the Law

A Dictionary

Debra L. Donahue

ABC CLIO

Santa Barbara, California Denver, Colorado Oxford, England

Library of Congress Cataloging-in-Publication Data

Donahue, Debra L.
Conservation and the law : a dictionary / Debra L. Donahue
     p. cm.
  Includes bibliographical references and index.
  1. Conservation of natural resources—Law and legislation—United States—Dictionaries, Juvenile.   I. Title
KF5505   A68D66   1998

ISBN 0-87436-771-9 (alk. paper)

03 02 01 00 99   10 9 8 7 6 5 4 3 2   (cloth)

ABC-CLIO, Inc.
130 Cremona Drive, P.O. Box 1911
Santa Barbara, California 93116-1911

This book is printed on acid-free paper ∞ .

To J.D.L., with deep appreciation for his unflagging support.

Contents

Preface

The conservation of natural resources is a subject that concerns all human beings—Americans and citizens of developing countries, adults and children, the current generation and ones to come. If the human population continues to grow, the rate of resource consumption will need to be curtailed, and/or substitutes for resources found, if humans are to maintain accustomed lifestyles and economic status. Conservative use of resources not only prolongs the availability of commodity resources, but can help ensure that the natural environment remains healthy and continues to function normally. This, in turn, will contribute to the sustainability of resource supplies, but it will also enhance the quality of life for all earth's inhabitants. On the other hand, if natural ecological processes are disrupted—by pollution, abuse of the land, elimination of species or habitats—conservation efforts based simply on limiting the consumption of resources will be doomed to failure.

While there is considerable disagreement about the resiliency of the environment to withstand and recover from human-caused disturbances, most ecologists concur that limits do exist. Moreover, most would concede that man's ability to replicate natural systems is, at best, highly uncertain. Thus, if we do not protect the natural systems that produce the resources on which we depend, we are likely to lose that capacity for production, while simultaneously losing many amenities that make our lives more enjoyable—clean rivers, thriving forests, healthy wildlife populations.

Conservation is a job for everyone—scientists, lawmakers, landowners, administrators, parents, students. Similarly, the law of conservation affects all of us, directly or indirectly. It influences how we manage and use our private lands, how and where we spend our leisure time, the quality and kinds of products we buy and how much they cost, even the beauty of our surroundings. Conservation law is an amalgam of local, state, and federal requirements, interlaced and strengthened by policies and social goals that go far beyond the actual words of statutes or ordinances or regulations. The value in everyone knowing something about how conservation law works is that it will work more successfully. Harvard entomologist and conservation biologist Edward O. Wilson believes that "familiarity will save ecosystems," because the values that people place on species and natural systems will increase as human knowledge of them grows. Thus, "the better an ecosystem is known, the less likely it will be destroyed." Wilson concludes that the "wise procedure is for law to delay, science to evaluate, and familiarity to preserve." (Wilson 1992) The utility of the law, of course, goes beyond delaying actions whose consequences are not yet known. Once the value of an ecosystem or one of its components is appreciated, the law can help ensure that value is preserved. If the goal of the law and the mechanisms it employs to promote that goal are generally understood, the law is much more likely to be effective.

This book is designed to help the reader understand what the law of conservation encompasses and how it works. It begins with an overview, which defines conservation, describes briefly the origins and history of the conservation movement, and outlines the contours of modern conservation law—the legal processes, players, and principles. The bulk of the book consists of individual entries on significant conservation law-related topics. These include statutes and cases, organizations and people, and terms. Coverage is extensive, rather than intensive. Most entries are followed by cross references to other, related entries in the book. Additional reading is suggested in the bibliography. Following the entries and the bibliography, readers will find tables listing the cases, statutes, and regulations referred to throughout the book, and a list of some of the (many) common acronyms used by practitioners and others associated with the field of conservation law. A general subject index is also included for the reader's convenience.

Readers may profit from this book without having any experience in or knowledge of the law; all that is needed is an interest in the subject. Students at all levels—high school, college, and postgraduate—should find the book useful, as will anyone with an interest in land use and resource conservation. The book is comprehensive, but far from exhaustive. Readers will not become experts in the field, but they will acquire a solid foundation in conservation law and, it is hoped, the motivation to explore this important subject further.

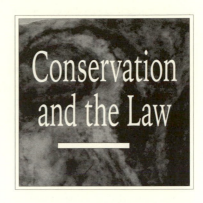

Conservation and the Law

CONSERVATION AND THE LAW

Natural resources, it is commonly said, come in two varieties: renewable and nonrenewable. Nonrenewable resources are exhaustible; they may be permanently depleted, used up. Fossil fuels and precious metals are familiar examples. Renewable resources—water and trees, for instance—are replenishable, but even they are available only in finite quantities at any given time. In either case, resource use, to be sustained, must be planned and managed; that is, resources must be "conserved."

The previous paragraph seems to assume that natural resources must or will be "used." It suggests that resources have significance or value only if, and to the extent that, they have utility to human beings. A distinguished professor of wildlife biology points out that the textbook definition of "natural resources" is "objects and substances in nature that have value to humans." This is also the implication of Webster's Third New International Dictionary's definitions of "resource" and "natural resources." "Resource" is characterized as "a new or reserve source of supply or support; a fresh or additional stock or store available at need; something in reserve or ready if needed." "Natural resources," in turn, is defined as "capacities...or materials (as mineral deposits and water power) supplied by nature." Both definitions connote something of value to or needed by people. The definition of "natural resources" is particularly illuminating. The example it offers is not water but water *power*. Humans *use* water to *produce* power to serve their domestic and industrial needs. Strictly speaking, a flowing river or a waterfall is itself an example of water power, but it is unlikely that the authors of Webster's had either of these in mind when they wrote *"materials...supplied* by nature."

But "natural resources" seems to take on additional meaning in the context of "conservation," which Webster's defines as:

1

deliberate, planned, or thoughtful preserving, guarding, or protecting...; preservation; ...planned management of a natural resource to prevent exploitation, destruction, or neglect...; the wise utilization of a natural product esp. by a manufacturer so as to prevent waste and ensure future use of resources that have been depleted; a field of knowledge concerned with coordination and plans for the practical application of data from ecology, limnology, pedology, and other sciences that are significant to preservation of natural resources....

In other words, conservation is a field of applied science, which incorporates the notion of "use" as well as the seemingly contradictory idea of "preservation." "Preserve" would seem an inappropriate word choice if the scope of the term were limited to management of the supply of resources simply in order to continue to be used by people.

Because this book is about the law that relates to conservation of natural resources, the reader needs to have an idea of what both terms encompass. Most scholars agree that President Theodore Roosevelt and the first chief of the U.S. Forest Service, Gifford Pinchot, coined the term "conservation" near the turn of the century. Pinchot himself wrote that Roosevelt's administration "originated, formulated and laid before the American people and the world the Conservation idea—the greatest good for the greatest number for the longest time, the development and use of the earth and all its resources for the enduring good of men—both on a national and international scale." According to Pinchot:

> Conservation is the application of common sense to the common problems for the common good. Since its objective is the ownership, control, development, processing, distribution, and use of the natural resources for the benefit of the people, it is by its very nature the antithesis of monopoly....
>
> The Conservation policy then has three great purposes.
>
> First: wisely to use, protect, preserve, and renew the natural resources of the earth.
>
> Second: to control the use of the natural resources and their products in the common interest, and to secure their distribution to the people at fair and reasonable charges for goods and services.
>
> Third: to see to it that the rights of the people to govern themselves shall not be controlled by great monopolies through their power over natural resources.

Pinchot's description includes the term "preserve," but not very prominently. In fact, Pinchot broke sharply with others of his own era (notably

John Muir) over whether resources should ever be preserved for their own sake. Pinchot maintained adamantly that they should not.

John Muir was the original preservationist. He founded the Sierra Club and served as its president until his death in 1914. Muir was Pinchot's contemporary and a close friend until 1896, when they split over the damming of Hetch Hetchy Valley in Yosemite. Muir believed firmly in the value of wilderness, of preserving at least some forests that would not be cut and watersheds that would not be grazed. He saw the healthy forest and watershed as having value apart from their ability to provide trees or forage for man's use; they are beautiful, and beauty has value in its own right. To Muir, the natural world did not exist solely to be *used for* man's benefit; indeed, it must be *protected from* man and from his government. In 1965, *Time* magazine called Muir the "real father of conservation." The tension between these two brands of conservation persists today on the political scene, within the resource agencies, and in the law.

The concept of conservation and our understanding of it were expanded greatly a generation later by wildlife ecologist and writer Aldo Leopold. Leopold, whose own thinking on the subject evolved dramatically over the course of his career, described conservation as "a state of harmony between men and land." He wrote: "Conservation is our effort to understand and preserve" land health, which he defined as "the capacity of the land for self-renewal." Leopold advocated the need for a land ethic, urging people to "quit thinking about decent land-use as solely an economic problem. Examine each question in terms of what is ethically and esthetically right, as well as what is economically expedient," he exhorted. "A thing is right when it tends to preserve the integrity, stability, and beauty of the biotic community. It is wrong when it tends otherwise." According to Leopold, the "evolution of a land ethic is an intellectual as well as an emotional process. Conservation is paved with good intentions which prove to be futile, or even dangerous, because they are devoid of critical understanding either of the land, or of economic land-use."

This combination of science/philosophy and intellect/emotion can be found in the thinking of many modern-day conservationists, particularly conservation biologists. One of the better known is Harvard entomologist Edward O. Wilson. Suggesting the roles that science, education, and the law ought to play in the task of conservation, Wilson wrote:

> I am willing to gamble that familiarity will save ecosystems, because bioeconomic and aesthetic values grow as each constituent species is examined in turn—and so will sentiment in favor of preservation. The wise procedure is for law to delay, science to evaluate, and

familiarity to preserve. There is an implicit principle of human behavior important to conservation: *the better an ecosystem is known, the less likely it will be destroyed.*" [Emphasis in original]

The writings of Leopold and Wilson clearly reveal that it is *the whole* with which conservation is concerned—the land itself, or ecosystems—not (or not simply) the component "resources" of that whole. Scientists, land managers, and legal scholars increasingly subscribe to this view, even though the law "on the books" largely reflects the outdated notion of natural resources as component parts. One statute, the 25-year-old Endangered Species Act, purports to take a broader view, declaring that its purposes are "to provide a means whereby the *ecosystems* upon which endangered species and threatened species depend *may be conserved.*" [Emphasis added] Nonetheless, the mechanisms prescribed by this act focus less on ecosystems than on their "components": individual species or populations of organisms.

Still, this country's approach to conservation, including the manner in which current law is applied, is broadening. The entries in this book reflect this phenomenon.

THE SCOPE OF CONSERVATION LAW

Considered most broadly, conservation law includes state, federal, tribal, and international legal regimes concerned with the use and preservation of natural resources. Each of these regimes is comprised of statutes, regulations, common law (court decisions), administrative decisions, and/or treaties. Conservation law deals with common resources, such as air and water; privately or publicly owned natural resources, such as minerals and forests; and more intangible values or amenities, such as wilderness and biodiversity. The vast diversity of natural resources themselves, the breadth of potentially relevant law, and the variation among states' and local communities' approaches to the regulation of lands and resources necessitate some limits on this book's scope.

Although other limits could have been selected, this book emphasizes the conservation of federal public lands and the natural resources and values on those lands. The principal federal laws and policies are examined, as are current issues relating to the conservation of these public lands and resources. A secondary focus is on federal policies concerning the conservation of private lands. The two categories of private lands that receive the greatest federal attention are wetlands and agricultural lands. Finally, where possible the book also addresses selected state and local issues and laws pertaining to the conservation of privately or publicly owned natural resources and amenities. Conservation easements and land trusts are examples. These land protection tools are creatures of state law, but are sufficiently common that the relevant law can be summarized, and important enough that they should not be overlooked in any discussion of conservation. This book does *not* treat international or tribal law, nor is it concerned with environmental laws concerning air or water pollution or solid/hazardous waste management. Readers interested in these topics are encouraged to consult *Environment and the Law: A Dictionary*, a companion text in this series.

Despite its emphasis on federal law, this book may be perceived as exhibiting a "western states" bias. Any such bias is unintentional; rather, it is a function of the disproportionate amount of public lands and natural resources located in the western United States.

Among the categories of federal lands discussed in this dictionary are national forests, Bureau of Land Management lands, national parks and monuments, wilderness areas, and national wildlife refuges. The individual natural resources addressed include fish and wildlife, range/grazing, timber, recreation, water/watershed, minerals, wilderness, soil, and wetlands. Some of these resources, such as timber or minerals, which have economic value, are called commodities. Certain other resources might be considered amenities: They contribute to our quality of life, and their value is noneconomic or can't readily be measured. Amenities include scenic beauty, ecosystem services, recreation benefits, solitude, and open space. Finally, some of these resources are assemblages of traditional, component resources. Wilderness is an aggregate of many resources and values: vegetation, wildlife, water, topography, scenic beauty, geology, etc. Likewise, ecosystems, watersheds, communities, and biological diversity can all be considered resources although each consists of many parts.

Many natural resources have both economic and amenity value. Wildlife, for instance, supports tremendous recreational and tourism-based industries, but wild animals also perform vital functions in maintaining healthy, functioning ecosystems. It may be difficult or impossible to measure the latter value, let alone assign a dollar amount to it. (Having said that, however, a group of scientists recently assigned a monetary value of $33 *trillion* annually to 17 of nature's "ecosystem services," such as water purification, food production, and carbon dioxide regulation. This figure is nearly double the world's gross economic product.) Many conservationists argue that humans' inability to measure the dollar value of some resource doesn't lessen its importance; resources also have intrinsic worth. This perspective derives from a biocentric, rather than a homocentric, view of the Earth, and is promoted by many philosophers, ethicists, and environmentalists. They maintain that a spiderwort or a meadow vole or a tree fungus has value simply because it exists. This view, of course, is at odds with the utilitarian approach to natural resources taken by Pinchot and many others.

HISTORY OF CONSERVATION LAW

The advent of the conservation movement coincided with the "custodial" era in federal public land law. This era was preceded by periods during which the federal government acquired a vast territory from foreign countries and Native American tribes and then engineered the disposal of much of it, both by granting tracts to states, homesteaders, railroads, and others, and simply by permitting its resources (timber, minerals, grass for fattening livestock) to be exploited by settlers and other users. The federal laws that provided for disposal of the lands had little or nothing to say about "conservation." Even where statutes did limit the amount of land or resources available to the recipient of a grant, or set conditions on the grant, these limitations were often circumvented; fraud and other abuses were widespread.

Meanwhile, forests from the Atlantic coast to the Missouri River were cut down and the land converted to farms. Western forests were "tie hacked"—raided for wood to make railroad ties. In many areas, wood for fuel and building material soon became scarce. Wildlife was slaughtered; western ranges were trampled to dust and stripped of their grasses by hordes of cattle and sheep. Reservoirs filled up with silt spilled by logged and overgrazed watersheds. "Sodbusters" plowed up fragile soils in the Great Plains, and when the droughts came, the ever-present winds blew the soil away. The government literally gave away public oil reserves, and miners ravaged mountainsides and streams for mere ounces of gold. The perception grew that publicly owned resources, once considered inexhaustible, were being wasted and depleted. Many people were outraged at the lack of government regulation and by the abuse of the few regulations that did exist.

These circumstances, along with a growing concern that the American wilderness was vanishing, led to the dichotomy between utilitarian and preservationist resource philosophies. Pinchot's turn-of-the-century policies had some success on the forest reserves (the predecessors of today's national forests), where he began to limit grazing (requiring a permit and a small fee) and restrict logging in sensitive watersheds. But the law that gave Pinchot his authority (the 1897 Organic Act) did not apply outside the forests, and Pinchot's brand of conservation was not adopted elsewhere. Although use of the public domain remained essentially unregulated, the federal government—Congress and the president—began a haphazard practice of preserving areas considered to possess important resources or values. These preserves included Yellowstone National Park (in 1872, the world's first national park), Yosemite National Park, and dozens of bird refuges. Even the Forest Service (after Pinchot departed) began to set aside administratively established wilderness and primitive areas. The president and then Congress (in 1920) made oil, previously free for the taking, off-limits under the General Mining Law of 1872. Congress passed the Antiquities Act, which authorized the creation of national monuments, and a few years later, the National Park Service Organic Act. Apart from these, most federal resources were still free for the taking—by miners, homesteaders, and livestock owners. In 1930 the federal government attempted to give to western states all nonmineral, unreserved federal lands (often simply referred to as the western range), but the states refused. One of the numerous reasons states gave for declining the offer was the lands' condition—generally abused and in need of rehabilitation, an expense that the states could ill afford.

The Taylor Grazing Act of 1934 can be seen as a turning point in western history and in conservation law. Its purposes were to "stop injury to the public lands by preventing overgrazing and soil deterioration, to provide for [the range's] orderly use, improvement, and development, and to stabilize the livestock industry." The Taylor Act (as amended and supplemented by executive orders) "closed the public domain;" that is, all unreserved public lands became unavailable for homesteading or disposal under other laws unless and until the Secretary of the Interior classified them as best suited to that purpose. The act also ended free, unrestricted grazing of the public domain. Henceforth, grazing would be by permit only and subject to a fee.

The Taylor Act gave the Interior secretary considerable discretion, however, and itself imposed no regulations on the public lands. The process of establishing grazing preferences and levels of permitted use took many years. In the meantime, little of the public domain's condition improved; rather, many lands continued to deteriorate. World War II intervened, distracting the nation's attention from these problems and increasing the demands on all domestic supplies of natural resources. The aftermath of the war brought a surge in highway construction, with accompanying increases in demands for resources and energy supplies; more roads and better automobiles made Americans more mobile and led to increased interest in outdoor recreation and sight-seeing. The nation's population boomed, adding to the demand for resources, and suburban sprawl led to losses of agricultural lands and open space.

Americans' environmental awareness grew in the 1960s. Important federal conservation legislation during this period included the first endangered species protections; the first statutory provisions for acquiring and administering lands for wildlife refuges; the Wilderness Act of 1964; the Land and Water Conservation Act of 1964; the Forest Service's Multiple-Use, Sustained-Yield Act of 1960; the Bureau of Land Management's (BLM) Classification and Multiple-Use Act of 1964 (expired 1970); the Wild and Scenic Rivers Act and National Trails System Act, both of 1968; and, at the end of the decade, the landmark National Environmental Policy Act (NEPA). The first Earth Day was 22 April 1970, and environmental and conservation legislation continued to burgeon in the 1970s. Major statutes included the Wild, Free-Roaming Horses and Burros Act of 1971; Alaska Native Claims Settlement Act of 1971; Endangered Species Act of 1973; Federal Land Policy and Management Act of 1976; National Forest Management Act of 1976; and Public Rangelands Improvement Act of 1978. Section 404 of the Federal Water Pollution Control Act Amendments of 1972 provided the foundation for a federal regulatory program for conserving wetlands.

The proliferation of conservation legislation continued during the 1980s and 1990s. Some legislation consisted of adjustments, or fine-tuning, of laws passed during the previous 20 years. Other measures were limited geographically, such as the Alaska National Interest Lands Conservation Act of 1980 and numerous statewide wilderness bills. Congress also passed three Farm Bills between 1985 and 1996, reflecting significant new federal policies concerning agricultural subsidies and conservation of soils and wetlands. Agency regulations multiplied, and the courts took an increasingly active role in land-use disputes—a reflection of Americans' litigiousness and the growing number of national, state, and local public interest groups.

The local face of conservation law also changed during this period. The American population became increasingly urban, and population growth resulted in urban and suburban sprawl, with migrations chiefly west and south. High property and estate taxes and the lower profitability of existing land uses (e.g., agriculture) led to the development of (or pressure to develop) vacant lands and the devouring of open space. Much of the growth occurred in areas with no or inadequate planning or zoning controls. States became increasingly concerned about protecting wildlife habitat, private landowners sought ways to keep family lands within the family, and conservation groups wanted to preserve unique lands, species diversity, and open space. These forces combined to produce greater use of conservation easements, the establishment of land trusts, and the formation of partnerships to promote conservation objectives.

Plainly, the dimensions of the conservation movement have evolved dramatically since Pinchot and Muir's day. Government's involvement has skyrocketed; legislatures, local governments, administrative agencies, and the courts all take active parts. The field today is more organized, more heavily statutory/regulatory, and involves a wider range of players: government, private property owners, and a variety of public interest groups (environmental, sportsmen, animal rights, preservationist, recreational, individual rights). As our population has grown, so have demands on our land and natural resources. In turn, these demands have led to increasing—and increasingly rancorous—conflicts, as well as to innovative approaches to resolving such disputes.

PRINCIPAL THEMES OF MODERN CONSERVATION LAW

Conflicts between public and private interests are among the more common features of natural resource policy debates and legal controversies, especially on public lands but on private lands as well. The public always has an interest, whether expressed or not, in how publicly owned resources are developed, usually by private contractors or permittees. Local publics may also have concerns about how private lands are used, for instance, whether logging on privately owned forests will affect the water quality of local streams or how a proposed subdivision will impact open space or wildlife habitat. Such concerns are expressed before planning commissions, state or federal permitting agencies, city councils, state legislatures, and sometimes in the courts. Related issues include conflicts between preservation and use—sometimes characterized as choices between the environment and the economy—and between the needs and demands of current and future generations. The tradeoffs embodied in all these choices complicate, even polarize, discussions of land and resource policy.

Other recurring themes and issues in natural resources conservation law include the impacts on land values where demand exceeds supply and use is not (or not adequately) limited or allocated. Overuse of parks and other recreational areas is a common example. How to make choices among uses and users on multiple-use lands when conflicts arise is the subject of ongoing debate. This issue becomes more prevalent and heated as population pressures on public resources grow, and many agency heads and interest groups criticize the lack of guidance in the current law. The propriety of government subsidies—whether they encourage resource use or conservation—is an issue of growing concern in fiscally tight times. And sustainable development—what does it mean and how can we plan for it?—is attracting increasing interest among landowners and policy makers alike. Finally, a perennial issue of increasing moment is that of states' rights. Especially in the West, where federal lands are most abundant, state and local governments often express frustration at being left out of resource planning and decision making. States and counties employ various tactics—including collaboration, litigation, and even civil disobedience—to address perceived problems.

MAJOR PLAYERS IN CONSERVATION LAW

Conservation law is shaped not only by the law itself and the lawmakers, but by their constituents and those in a position to influence policy and decision making. As noted earlier, conservation law consists of constitutions, statutes and ordinances enacted by legislative bodies, regulations and decisions rendered by administrative agencies, executive orders and proclamations, and judicial decisions. Congress has the ultimate authority over the federal lands, but many state laws also apply. State legislatures have primary authority to regulate state and private land use within their respective borders. County commissions and city councils or equivalent bodies establish local land-use policies.

Both state and federal administrative agencies with land management or environmental responsibilities perform a variety of functions. They promulgate rules to implement the authority delegated to them by statute, issue permits and licenses, perform land-use planning, and decide contested cases (e.g., between applicants for a permit) and challenges to their rules. Major agencies with conservation and land-use functions include the U.S. Forest Service, BLM, National Park Service, Environmental Protection Agency, state fish and game agencies, state land boards, and planning and zoning boards.

Courts are the final arbiters of the meanings of statutes or regulations and the rights and responsibilities conferred by the law. They settle disputes among resource users or landowners, decide challenges to statutes and regulations, and enforce the law. The cases they hear may be based on common-law (i.e., judge-made law) claims, such as nuisance, or on statutory or regulatory causes of action. The latter categories of cases include citizen suits, in which a private group or individual acts as a "private attorney general" to enforce a state or federal law, as well as direct challenges to agency action by those adversely impacted by the decision.

The processes of formulating, implementing, and adjusting resource policy involve many other actors. Congressional committees and their staffs play major roles in drafting legislation and steering it through the legislative process—or preventing its passage. At the national level, the Department of Justice's Land and Natural Resources Division is responsible for enforcing federal wildlife laws and protecting wetlands. The Interior Solicitor advises the Interior secretary and issues legal opinions concerning public land and resource issues on all federal lands managed by Interior agencies. The Interior Board of Land Appeals decides a variety of public land-related legal disputes. Conservation organizations and other public interest groups—at local, state, regional, and national levels—help shape public policy by watchdogging government agencies, commenting on environmental impact statements and other planning documents, challenging agency decisions, and bringing citizen suits to enforce adherence to the laws. They also participate in certain important litigation, not as a party, but as an *amicus curiae*, or "friend of the court." Public land user groups, commodity interests, private landowners, and government entities all play similar roles. In addition, all of these interests lobby Congress and state legislatures to pass new statutes, amend existing laws, and fund favored programs.

Natural resource litigation is often "three-cornered"—that is, it involves a government agency and two or more private parties (individuals or public interest organizations). For instance, a conservation group concerned about preserving old-growth forests and a timber company may both challenge the harvest level established by the Forest Service in a forest plan. Occasionally, disputes involve two government entities, as when the United States sues a county to enjoin illegal road-building activities on federal lands, or when a state challenges federal authority within its borders. But most resource and land-use disputes pit private interests against a government policy or regulation.

CONTEMPORARY CONSERVATION ISSUES AND FUTURE DIRECTIONS

As indicated earlier, conservation law has changed dramatically in the past 100 years, and even in the past ten. Endangered species protection efforts are expanding to encompass biodiversity conservation—nonendangered species, genetic diversity, entire communities. Land management efforts are increasingly directed at ecosystems or watersheds, and ecosystem management includes managing for human communities and cultures. Government agencies work with private landowners and other local stakeholders to resolve or avoid land-use problems, for example, to avoid habitat fragmentation, retain or create biological corridors or linkages, or preserve open space. A variety of mechanisms for achieving these objectives is available, including partnerships, land exchanges, conservation easements, land trusts, and transferable development rights.

Conflicts between levels of government, and between government and private property owners and advocates, over resource policy and land-use regulation have given rise to the Wise Use and County Supremacy movements and the Sagebrush Rebellion in the West, and to nationwide campaigns in support of property and other individual rights. Fiscal conservatives and environmentalists concerned about the degradation and depletion of natural resources decry government (chiefly federal) subsidies, and call for government to obtain a fair return for public resources and services. In particular, they urge reforms of federal grazing, logging, and mining laws, and agricultural programs.

Many of these and other contemporary resource issues can be resolved within the current legal framework. Agencies have considerable latitude in interpreting and implementing the mandates they receive from Congress or state legislatures, and in responding to public opinion. In some cases, however, new legislation is needed, either because agency initiatives require statutory authorization or because cooperative or voluntary efforts fail to produce adequate results. For example, several federal land management agencies are implementing ecosystem management under existing statutory mandates that are silent about "ecosystems." Many commentators argue that more explicit statutory authority is needed to ensure that these efforts are consistent and successful. Similarly, biodiversity conservation efforts now being made under the Endangered Species Act may fail unless the act is amended, or additional legislation is enacted, to specifically authorize these programs.

On the other hand, because numerous regulatory programs are already in place, many politicians and citizens resist the suggestion that additional "command and control"-type laws or regulations are needed. Consequently, attention has shifted to other approaches to achieving conservation objectives: incentives, collaboration, better coordination of agency functions, and integrating resource policy with other (e.g., tax) laws.

CONCLUSION

No one can dispute that land and the resources it provides are in limited supply. If the Earth's population continues to grow—and all indications are that it will—humankind's overall demands for resources will also grow, unless the *rate* of our consumption significantly subsides. Public opinion polls continue to show that Americans favor environmental protection and conservation of public lands and resources, even if it costs them more. Still, political and fiscal constraints—both real and perceived—may dictate other outcomes. Furthermore, Third World countries aspire to the quality of life most Americans have achieved and believe that the way to accomplish this goal is to exploit their resources as we have used ours. To say the least, it will be problematic to attempt to discourage such behavior by others when the United States has reaped the benefits of profligate resource consumption for more than a century. Resolution of this dilemma will require greater self-discipline by Americans and will challenge the United States to set an example with innovative and equitable approaches to conserving resources.

Resource conservation can be reduced to a few basic principles: supply, demand, ethics, and sustainable use. The United States has been and will remain a leader in the use of the law to promote conservation of resources and sustainable use. Nevertheless, development of a true conservation ethic cannot be legislated or otherwise imposed. Whether a conservation ethic becomes widely embraced, therefore, will depend on the continued efforts of writers, scientists, policy makers, and teachers to educate Americans, and on individual Americans accepting responsibility for their actions and for the well-being of all the Earth's inhabitants, both present and future.

Administrative Procedure Act (APA)

ADMINISTRATIVE PROCEDURE ACT (APA) Enacted in 1947, the APA governs various actions of federal administrative agencies. The act defines what constitutes an agency subject to its provisions, categorizes the kinds of actions in which agencies engage (e.g., making rules, hearing appeals), and prescribes the procedures that agencies must follow in undertaking certain actions. Although each federal agency also establishes its own specific procedural regulations, all federal agencies discussed in this volume are subject to the APA's broad requirements. For instance, the act specifies which actions require public notice and opportunity for public comment, and sets forth procedures for agencies to satisfy those provisions; it establishes procedures for administrative hearings and outlines the bases upon which an agency decision may be challenged and reversed upon appeal; and it provides for agency policies, interpretative guidance, and meetings. The APA also established the function of the administrative law judge.

The APA provides that a "person suffering legal wrong because of agency action" is entitled to seek judicial review of that action. Assuming that preliminary requirements, such as standing, ripeness, and exhaustion of remedies, are met, courts presume that agency decisions are reviewable unless a statute specifically provides otherwise. Such statutes are rare; thus, nearly all final agency decisions affecting the use or conservation of federal lands or resources are subject to judicial review under the standards set forth in the APA. In general, this means that a court may overturn agency actions that are arbitrary, capricious, or not supported by substantial evidence; exceed agency authority; fail to adhere to required procedures; or are otherwise contrary to law. However, the burden is on the plaintiff to show that an agency decision is arbitrary or unlawful, and because courts are generally deferential to agencies carrying out their statutory missions, prevailing in a case against an agency is seldom easy.

Most states also have a statute governing administrative procedures; many of these are patterned on the federal APA.

See also **Deference; Exhaustion of Remedies; Ripeness; Standing.**

15

ALASKA NATIONAL INTEREST LANDS CONSERVATION ACT (ANILCA)

A complex statute, passed in 1980 and taking up 181 pages in the U.S. Statutes at Large, whose purpose is to preserve for present and future generations of Americans federal lands in Alaska containing nationally significant values. The 56 million acres of wilderness areas created by the statute comprise two-thirds of the national system. In addition, ANILCA designated millions of acres of national parks, monuments, and wildlife refuges and 13 new wild or scenic rivers in Alaska; established a preference for rural residents to engage in subsistence hunting and fishing on federal lands; made specific provisions for mineral development in the state; and contained numerous other provisions relating to public lands and resources within Alaska. One of its provisions, recognizing a right of access across national forest lands to enclosed private lands, has been held by several courts to apply not just to those within Alaska, but to all national forests.

Several provisions of ANILCA have proved controversial. For instance, the act established a quota for the harvest of timber from the Tongass National Forest, which was eventually amended by the Tongass Timber Reform Act of 1990. ANILCA's recognition of valid, existing mineral rights on those lands included in the federal conservation systems has also given rise to controversy, particularly in Alaska's national parks, where many hardrock mining claims regulated by the National Park Service are viewed as threatening other park values. Still another section of the statute called for an assessment of the resources of the Arctic National Wildlife Refuge (ANWR) coastal plain, including the area's potential for oil and gas development, but prohibited oil and gas production unless and until specifically authorized by a subsequent act of Congress. No such legislation has yet been passed, and ANWR's future remains a subject of continuing and heated debate.

See also **Arctic National Wildlife Refuge; Subsistence Hunting and Fishing; Tongass National Forest.**

ALASKA NATIVE CLAIMS SETTLEMENT ACT (ANCSA)

A federal statute passed in 1971 whose purposes were to resolve claims of Alaska natives to federal lands within the state and to provide for their future economic well-being. Following statehood in 1959, Alaska natives asserted claims to much of the territory that was then almost entirely federally owned; these claims threatened to interfere with management of the land and impede land selections by the state of Alaska, authorized by the state Enabling Act. ANCSA addressed these problems by extinguishing Alaska natives' "Indian title" (or aboriginal title) and providing for compensation.

Unlike Native American tribes in the lower 48 states, Alaska natives had not entered into any treaties with the federal government, nor had any reservations been established for them. Although the U.S. Constitution did not require compensation to native inhabitants, most people agreed that the nation was morally and politically obligated to provide some form of compensation. Accordingly, ANCSA authorized Alaska natives to select 44 million acres of lands. Half of this land was to be transferred to about 200 village corporations established by the act, 16 million acres were selected by 12 regional corporations, and the remainder was reserved for townsites, native allotment applications, and other purposes. ANCSA also provided for a fund of nearly $1 billion, payments from which are made to the regional corporations and then transferred to their stockholders and to villages. Every Alaska native alive on the date the act was passed was allotted 100 shares in a regional corporation, and could also be eligible to hold shares in a village corporation.

ANCSA further provided for state land selections to resume, and it authorized the secretary of the Interior to withdraw from development or disposition under other resource laws up to 80 million acres of federal lands that might merit inclusion in one of the "national interest" land conservation systems (parks or monuments, forests, wild rivers, and wildlife refuges). The latter provision, known as the "d(2)" provision, was the authority for the withdrawals made by Interior Secretary Andrus in 1978; those withdrawals were ultimately enacted into law via the Alaska National Interest Lands Conservation Act (ANILCA) in 1980. ANCSA extinguished aboriginal hunting and fishing rights, and Alaska native hunting and fishing are now subject to provisions of state law, ANILCA, and the Marine Mammal Protection Act.

See also **Alaska National Interest Lands Conservation Act; Marine Mammal Protection Act.**

AMERICAN RIVERS   A nonprofit, tax-exempt organization dedicated to protecting and restoring American rivers and fostering a river stewardship ethic. Formed in 1973 as the American Rivers Conservation Council, today the group claims 15,000 members and credit for the protection of 20,000 miles of river and 5 million acres of riverside habitat. It staffs regional offices in Seattle and Phoenix.

American Rivers' six priority program areas are: protection of wild rivers, reform of federal hydropower policies, protection of endangered fisheries and associated habitats, reform of policies that result in dewatering western U.S. streams, cleanup of drinking water supplies, and restoration of urban ("hometown") rivers. Campaigns listed in its strategic plan for 1997-2001 include blocking the New World Mine in Montana; reforming mining law and practices; protecting wild and scenic rivers; restoring dammed, urban, and flow-impaired rivers; and developing a model watershed agreement and a model water trust.

To further these objectives the group lobbies, litigates, facilitates the formation of partnerships, encourages grassroots river protection efforts, and educates the public. Recent lobbying efforts focused on federal hydropower reforms; litigation includes a suit attempting to block a U.S. Army Corps of Engineers flood-control project on the lower Mississippi River that would destroy 11,300 acres of forested wetlands, and an Endangered Species Act challenge to operation of federal dams on the Columbia and Snake Rivers. One of the most notable partnerships instigated by the group is the Big River Partnership, a consortium of upper Missouri River interests, including government agencies, business and industry leaders, and conservation groups. This group has formed several teams to explore research needs and possible restoration projects that meet both economic and environmental needs of the river and river-based communities.

American Rivers publishes a newsletter, a citizens' guide to hydropower, an annual list of the nation's most threatened rivers (the Missouri topped the list in 1997), and a guide to wild and scenic river designation. Its website, RiverWeb, is being developed to connect and provide information to local, regional, and national river advocacy groups, with the ultimate goal of establishing a geographically based information system.

See also **Geographic Information System; Partnerships; Wild and Scenic Rivers Act of 1968.**

ANADROMOUS FISH   Fish that migrate from salt or brackish water to fresh water to spawn, typically in the same stream or lake in which the fish were hatched and reared. Several species of salmonids (salmon and trout) are anadromous. After hatching, these fish spend several months to several years in their natal (birth) stream or lake before migrating to the ocean, a stage of life during which they are called smolts. Smolts develop into adult fish, and adults may remain in the ocean for up to three or four years, and travel thousands of miles, before returning to their natal waters to spawn and die.

The Decline of Salmon

Anadromous fisheries, particularly in the Pacific Northwest (northern California, Oregon, Washington, Idaho, and Montana), are in crisis. Not only are salmon numbers in decline, but salmon and the Endangered Species Act of 1973 (ESA) may be on a collision course. Even though it is widely believed that protection under the ESA will be necessary to save the declining runs of salmon and steelhead (anadromous rainbow trout) from extinction, listing additional species as endangered or threatened has been actively avoided, at least until 1997, because of fears that listing additional stocks could have major repercussions for reauthorization of the ESA.

Pacific salmon stocks have been drastically reduced, from estimated historical runs of 10 to 16 million fish per year to recent averages of 2.5 million or fewer. Harvests have declined steadily since 1883, when more than 80 million pounds of chinook (king) salmon alone were taken. Current total harvests for all salmon species and steelhead are only 5-8 million pounds annually. The Snake River sockeye provides a dramatic example: These fish migrate from the Pacific Ocean up the Columbia, Snake, and Salmon river systems to Redfish Lake (named for this species) in central Idaho. In the past ten years the number of adult sockeyes returning to Redfish Lake to spawn have ranged from a *high* of 16 in 1987 to a low of 0 in 1990.

Several factors are to blame for the plight of Pacific salmon. Undoubtedly, the chief culprits are dams—more than 450 major dams in the Columbia River Basin alone. In addition to destroying at least 55 percent of the salmon's historical spawning habitat, dams obstruct or interfere with fish migration up- and downriver, kill smolts in their hydroelectric turbines, and render the young fish more susceptible to disease and predation in the reservoirs behind the dams. Other factors include the depletion of river flows by diversions for agriculture and other purposes; pollution of waters by clear-cut logging, livestock grazing, mining, use of pesticides and fertilizers, urban runoff, and other land-use practices; and overfishing of stocks for many years.

Attempts to Resolve the Crisis

In the 1970s it became impossible to disregard the warning signs. A number of legal strategies were implemented to address the problem of declining stocks and increasing competition. Several court decisions, notably the famous "Boldt decision" in 1974 by Federal Court Judge George Boldt, upheld native tribes' treaty rights to half the salmon harvest. In 1976 the Magnuson Fishery Conservation Act was passed, and in 1977 the Columbia River Inter-Tribal Fish Commission (CRITFC) was formed. CRITFC represents four major Columbia River fishing tribes and coordinates their efforts and resources in dealing with anadromous fishery concerns. It has amassed considerable expertise and respect in the areas of fishery ecology, population biology, hydrology, and economics, and was influential in the passage of the Pacific Northwest Electric Power Planning and Conservation Act of 1980.

This 1980 statute called for rigorous energy conservation efforts in the region—which has the cheapest energy costs in the country and, not surprisingly, the highest per capita rates of energy usage—and mandated that anadromous fish be a "co-equal partner" with energy production. The act's express goal was to "protect, mitigate and enhance" Pacific salmon. The statute also created the Northwest Power Planning Council, a unique administrative entity to be comprised of two representatives of each of the four affected states (Oregon, Washington, Idaho, and Montana) and charged with developing programs to govern federal energy development and enhance the salmon runs. The council thus was given responsibility for planning functions previously exercised by the old-line federal power authorities: the U.S. Army Corps of Engineers, Bureau of Reclamation, Bonneville Power Administration, and Federal Energy Regulatory Commission. Two key elements of the program subsequently developed are: (1) a "water budget," which establishes times for extra releases of water from dams (flushing flows) designed to assist downstream smolt migrations, and (2) a requirement that agencies develop fish passage plans to enable fish to bypass the dams (methods include barging smolts, installing screens over turbine intakes, and constructing diversion channels). The council designates protected areas—portions of free-flowing rivers set aside as wildlife habitat—although these designations are not necessarily binding on regulatory or land management agencies.

By the time the United States and Canada signed a treaty in 1985 that settled rights to fish stocks migrating between American and Canadian waters, it was widely, if cautiously, believed that legal and political structures were then in place that would arrest the downward spiral of Pacific salmon stocks. Nevertheless, three years of below-average runoff, followed by an especially dry year in 1989, caused the runs to hit new lows. The Shoshone-Bannock Tribe in Idaho then petitioned the Fish and Wildlife Service to list the Snake River sockeye under the ESA. In 1997, competition between the American and Canadian commercial fishing industries led Canadian fishermen to seize an Alaska state ferry in Prince Rupert, British Columbia, for several days.

The Endangered Species Act of 1973 (ESA)

A 1990 scientific report seemed to confirm the fears of the Shoshone-Bannocks and others. The report listed 214 native stocks of Pacific salmon, 101 of which were considered at high risk of extinction, 58 at moderate risk, and 54 of special concern. Yet, at that time only one species of salmon, the threatened Sacramento River winter-run chinook, had been listed under the ESA.

Another last-ditch effort to avoid listing salmon stocks as threatened or endangered was the so-called "salmon summit" of 1990. Essentially all the interested parties were seated at the table: hydropower interests, the states, commercial and sport fishing groups, federal land management agencies, the government of Canada, and several Indian tribes. The participants put together a short-term recovery plan and also succeeded in encouraging the Northwest Power Planning Council to implement stronger measures. But the effort may have been too little, too late. By 1992, the Snake River sockeye and two other subspecies—the fall and spring-summer runs of Snake River chinook—had been listed as threatened. (Their status was subsequently revised to endangered.) Since then, the National Marine Fisheries Service (NMFS) has received several petitions to list additional species, but listings were blocked during 1995-1996 by congressional moratoria.

The logjam broke in 1996. In that year the NMFS listed as endangered the Umpqua River cutthroat trout, some of which are anadromous, and the next year it designated critical habitat for the species. In 1997, NMFS listed as endangered two evolutionarily significant units (ESUs) of steelhead (in southern California and the Columbia River of Washington) and three steelhead ESUs as threatened (in central California and in the Snake River Basin of Idaho, Oregon, and Washington). Also in 1997, a coho salmon ESU in southern Oregon and northern California was listed as threatened. The agency further proposed to list Klamath River (Oregon) bull trout as endangered, and Columbia River bull trout as threatened. Although these two populations are not anadromous, some bull trout are, and most populations of this species are considered at risk. In addition, NMFS reopened comment in 1997 on its proposal to list as threatened anadromous Atlantic salmon in seven Maine rivers in order to allow the public to consider a conservation plan submitted by the state of Maine under ESA section 4(d). Maine urged NMFS to find that the listing was no longer warranted in light of the habitat protections outlined in its plan. NMFS was sued in late 1997 by several fishing and conservation groups who claim that all chinook salmon in Oregon, Washington, and California should be listed as endangered.

The fear persists that a Congress disinclined to favor the environment at the perceived expense of local economic concerns will retaliate against additional listings by amending and severely weakening the ESA. In 1997 a congressional hearing was held on the NMFS's salmon management, which was under fire from nearly all sides. The NMFS had been holding discussions with all major stakeholders, but some parties, including the state of Montana and four Indian tribes, had walked out of the talks. The House Resources subcommittee, which held the hearing, suggested that federal legislation might be needed to resolve salmon management, and that perhaps NMFS should be removed from the process.

Also in late 1997, the Federal Energy Regulatory Commission, which is responsible for regulating hydroelectric projects, proposed for the first time that an *operating* dam (the Edwards Dam in Maine) be removed to promote salmon recovery. The Interior Department had previously called for the removal of two dams on the Olympic Peninsula of Washington, and two members of the Washington congressional delegation supported legislation authorizing removal, but no funding has yet been authorized. Many other dams, mostly in the Pacific Northwest, are the targets of unofficial removal proposals, heightening the stakes—and the tensions—in the debate over ESA reform.

See also **Endangered Species Act of 1973; Listing.**

ANIMAL DAMAGE CONTROL (ADC)   The federal program for control of predators and animal pest species, formerly housed in the U.S. Department of the Interior and now part of the U.S. Department of Agriculture's Animal and Plant Health Inspection Service. Federal predator and pest control efforts date to the early 1900s when the Bureau of Biological Survey first undertook to eradicate (from both public and private lands) wolves, coyotes, and other species considered injurious by farmers and livestock owners. The ADC program has been extremely controversial. Environmentalists criticize it as a subsidy to agricultural interests and contrary to conservation interests in conserving wildlife species. The program is also coming under increasingly heavy fire from animal rights groups for its methods (especially trapping) and for killing nontarget animals (individuals or species that are not the object of the control measures, but which are inadvertently killed). From 1937 through 1983, the federal ADC program was responsible for killing approximately 26,000 bears, 500,000 bobcats, 3.7 million coyotes, 50,000 red wolves, 1,600 gray wolves, and 8,000 mountain lions. ADC kill statistics for 1991 alone revealed that more than 150,000 nontarget animals of 23 species were destroyed.

See also **Animal Rights Movement.**

ANIMAL RIGHTS MOVEMENT   An umbrella term for individuals and organizations advancing the proposition that humans have a moral, legal, and/or custodial duty to treat animals humanely. "Animal rights" has no precise definition. Peter Singer, whose book *Animal Liberation* is often credited with articulating the philosophical basis of the current humane movement, prefers the term "animal liberation" because it is "less legalistic." Animal rights groups include traditional humane organizations, such as the American Society for the Prevention of Cruelty to Animals; more confrontational groups, such as People for the Ethical Treatment of Animals; and groups dedicated to changing the legal status of animals, such as the Animal Legal Defense Fund. In addition, specialty groups form around specific issues, for example, ending factory farming or the use of animals in biomedical research, and many communities have local groups focused on local issues.

Animal rights theory rests substantially on the premise that animals, like humans, suffer when mistreated. As philosopher Jeremy Bentham argued in 1789, "The question is not can [animals] reason? nor, can they talk? but, can they suffer?" Still, many animal rights theorists also point to other similarities between animals and humans, including their capacity for communication, reasoning, self-consciousness, and social structure. On the other hand, some advocates contend that it is the *differences* between humans and other animals that give rise to humans' unique moral obligation to treat animals humanely.

Animal rights advocates differ widely in their view of what humane treatment entails. Some would end all exploitation of animals for the benefit of humans, including animal testing, sport hunting, and meat production. Others would continue to allow the use of animals to benefit humans, while seeking to end mistreatment, including specific practices like factory farming, "puppy mills," unnecessary and repetitive animal testing, and "canned" sport hunts. Animal rights proponents further differ in their tactics. Many lobby for stronger legislation, more vigorous enforcement of existing animal cruelty laws, and stricter inspections of research laboratories, pet stores, zoos and similar attractions, and meat production facilities. Others boycott manufacturers that engage in animal testing or sell animal products, such as furs; sponsors of events like coyote hunts or pigeon shoots; and even states (Alaska was boycotted as a travel destination by several groups after announcing that it would resume aerial hunting and "control" of wolves). More radical groups have been implicated in vandalizing animal testing labs and freeing research animals. In response to the tactics of certain animal rights advocates, a few states have recently passed laws prohibiting anyone from interfering with the lawful pursuit of game under state hunting laws.

See also **Animal Damage Control; Hunting.**

ANTIQUITIES ACT OF 1906   A federal statute authorizing the president of the United States to designate national monuments. The act provides for designation of "historic landmarks, historic and prehistoric structures, and other objects of historic or scientific interest" that are located on federal lands. It further provides for reservation of "the smallest area compatible with the proper care and management of the objects to be protected." Despite this narrow, apparently limited language, national monuments encompassing thousands and even millions of acres have been designated. Most notable are the 56 million acres designated in Alaska in 1978 by President Jimmy Carter, the 270,000-acre Grand Canyon monument set aside by Theodore Roosevelt in Arizona in 1908, and Franklin Roosevelt's 220,000-acre Jackson Hole monument in Wyoming in 1943. The latter two designations have withstood court challenges. Nearly every president has exercised his power under the Antiquities Act to designate national monuments.

National monuments and national parks are managed under the National Park Service Organic Act of 1916 to promote their fundamental purpose: "to conserve the scenery and the natural and historic objects and the wild life therein and to provide for the enjoyment of the same in such manner and by such means as will leave them unimpaired for the enjoyment of future generations." Monuments are administered by the National Park Service or the original land management agency. Management varies according to the type of area and its resources, and the compatibility of other resource uses with the area's fundamental purpose.

See also **Grand Staircase-Escalante National Monument; National Park Service Organic Act of 1916; Reservation.**

ARCTIC NATIONAL WILDLIFE REFUGE (ANWR)

Known as "America's Serengeti," ANWR (pronounced an´war) is a 19-million-acre refuge in Alaska bordering the Arctic Ocean, home to musk oxen, Dall sheep, polar bears, caribou, nearly 150 species of birds, and—potentially—billions of barrels of oil. Since passage of the Alaska National Interest Lands Conservation Act (ANILCA) in 1980, ANWR has been the subject of ongoing wrangling between the state of Alaska and Congress, Congress and the president, citizens of Alaska and residents of the lower 48 states, and environmentalists and the oil industry.

ANILCA directed the U.S. Department of the Interior to determine whether oil and gas development on the 1.4-million-acre coastal plain of the refuge is advisable. Debate has since raged over whether the coastal plain should be opened to oil and gas drilling or designated a wilderness area (or otherwise put off-limits to such development). Bills to accomplish both objectives are perennially introduced in Congress. By mid-1997 a House bill that would grant wilderness status to the coastal plain had more than 100 cosponsors. Also in 1997, The Wilderness Society included ANWR in its list of the ten most endangered wild lands.

Projecting that drilling in ANWR would produce revenues of $1.3 billion that could be used to offset the federal deficit, Republicans in the 104th Congress made opening the ANWR coastal plain a key component of their budget bill—and President Clinton singled it out for criticism when he vetoed the bill in December 1995. He called the revenue projection an "estimate based on wishful thinking and outdated analysis." Interior Secretary Babbitt also refuted the deficit-reduction claims, pointing out that no one knows how much oil lies beneath the Arctic coastal plain. Environmentalists argue that the chance of finding developable reserves is less than 20 percent, but in 1991 the Bureau of Land Management revised its prediction of the possibility of a major oil find from 19 to 46 percent. Oil discoveries in the Prudhoe Bay area west of ANWR in 1997 provided additional ammunition for proponents of oil and gas development. (Exploratory drilling is being allowed in the Beaufort Sea, just three miles off ANWR's coast.) Babbitt cautioned that projected federal leasing revenues from ANWR are predicated on unrealistically high predictions of the price of oil in the year 2000, and that they ignore the possibility that the state, not the U.S. Treasury, will reap as much as 90 percent of that income. Moreover, Babbitt says, energy conservation programs, which the Republican-dominated 104th Congress sought to eliminate from the Department of Energy, "would save more oil than we could ever pump out of [ANWR]."

One of the chief objections to development of the coastal plain is concern about the possible impacts on the Porcupine caribou herd. These animals are one of the world's last, large migratory herds of caribou; the plain provides both summer home and calving grounds.

Congressman Don Young and Senator Frank Murkowski, both Republicans from Alaska, have long supported drilling in ANWR and staunchly oppose wilderness designation for the area. Hoping to gain wider congressional support for drilling, they announced in 1995 that Alaska would settle for 50 percent of the leasing revenues from ANWR, rather than the 90 percent the state receives from other areas (and which it had long insisted it should receive from ANWR as well). In 1997 they suggested that provisions for leasing the coastal plain be included in both a stand-alone bill and as an amendment to an omnibus budget bill.

In 1996, 8 million acres of the refuge encompassing the Brooks Range were renamed the Mollie Beattie Wilderness Area, honoring the recently deceased director of the U.S. Fish and Wildlife Service.

See also **Alaska National Interest Lands Conservation Act; Murkowski, Frank H.; Senate Appropriations Committee; U.S. Fish and Wildlife Service; Young, Don.**

BABBITT, BRUCE Secretary of the U.S. Department of the Interior, appointed by President Bill Clinton in 1992. Babbitt, an attorney from a ranching family, was governor of Arizona from 1978 to 1987, and described in *The Almanac of American Politics* as one of the United States' "brainiest and most original governors." He helped change Arizona groundwater use practices and was instrumental in implementing the Central Arizona Project and curbing air pollution from southern Arizona copper smelters. Babbitt also served as Arizona's attorney general from 1975 to 1978. He was a Democratic candidate for president in 1988, president of the League of Conservation Voters from 1991 to 1992, a former partner in the Phoenix law firm Steptoe & Johnson, and a founding member of the Grand Canyon Trust. He has a B.A. degree in geology from Notre Dame, an M.S. degree in geophysics from the University of New Castle, England, and a law degree (LL.B.) from Harvard.

Environmentalists hailed Babbitt's nomination and appointment as Interior secretary, and greeted with enthusiasm some of his early moves, such as filling an assistant secretary slot with a former president of The Wilderness Society and proclaiming that the federal Bureau of Reclamation must be "destroyed." But Babbitt's record—like environmentalists' reaction to it—has been mixed. Babbitt may be best remembered for his repeated attempts to reform public land grazing regulations, implement the Endangered Species Act to protect ecosystems and provide greater certainty to landowners, and achieve legislative reform of the General Mining Law of 1872. He is also known for trying to develop wide-scale, consensus-based resource management efforts, such as grazing reform, and environmental restoration projects, such as the Florida projects to restore the Everglades and Florida Bay and the San Francisco Bay-Delta Accord. Babbitt played important roles in the Clinton administration's Northwest Forest Management Plan, reintroduction of wolves to Yellowstone, dramatically increased use of habitat conservation plans to implement Endangered Species Act protections, increased funding for some national parks, and passage of the California Desert Protection Act. In 1993, he established the National

Biological Service to coordinate Interior Department research and inventory functions (though Congress subsequently renamed this bureau and relocated it to the U.S. Geological Survey).

In speeches in 1985 and 1990, Babbitt called for replacing the old "unworkable" multiple-use concept with a "concept of public use." He argued that the "next step in the evolution of public land-use policy is to replace multiple-use management with a new concept—dominant public use—that gives priority to recreation, wildlife, and watershed uses." Other topics he has chosen to address in public speeches while leading the Interior Department include the interagency "Bring Back the Natives" fish-restoration program, federal fire policy, and protection of the Arctic National Wildlife Refuge. Babbitt has served as chair of the National Groundwater Policy Forum and the U.S. Nuclear Safety Oversight Committee. Reportedly a top contender for a vacancy on the U.S. Supreme Court in 1993, Babbitt was passed over for Ruth Bader Ginsburg.

See also **Biodiversity Conservation; Department of the Interior; Endangered Species Act of 1973; General Mining Law of 1872; Habitat Conservation Plan; League of Conservation Voters.**

BABBITT V. SWEET HOME CHAPTER OF COMMUNITIES FOR A GREAT OREGON (1995)

A landmark U.S. Supreme Court decision and one of the Court's most recent interpretations of the Endangered Species Act of 1973 (ESA, or act). The respondents—a group of landowners, logging companies, and others dependent on the timber industry in the Southeast and Pacific Northwest—challenged a regulation issued by the U.S. Fish and Wildlife Service (USFWS). They argued that the rule, which prohibits any person from modifying the habitat of a threatened or endangered species in a way that would actually kill or injure any individuals of the species, exceeded the USFWS's authority under the act. The Supreme Court rejected the challenge.

The Act

Section 9 of the ESA prohibits any person from taking any endangered species of fish or wildlife. Section 3 defines "take" to mean "harass, harm, pursue, hunt, shoot, wound, kill, trap, capture, or collect, or to attempt to engage in any such conduct." Regulations issued by the USFWS extend the taking prohibition to all listed species, threatened as well as endan-

gered, and define the term "harm," used in the statutory definition, to include "significant habitat modification or degradation where it actually
kills or injures wildlife by significantly impairing essential behavioral patterns, including breeding, feeding or sheltering." The respondents (plaintiffs in the district court case) objected to the rule because it effectively
limited logging and other activities on private forests occupied by the endangered red-cockaded woodpecker in the Southeast and the northern
spotted owl in the Northwest.

The Parties' Arguments

The respondents argued that the act's prohibition against taking endangered animals applies only to the direct or willful application of force to
animals, such as shooting or trapping them, not to the modification of a
species' habitat on private property. They contended that Congress never
intended the ESA to affect private landowners' ordinary use of their property; rather, in section 7 of the act, Congress had placed on federal agencies
the responsibility for conserving the habitat of threatened and endangered
species. The respondents also pointed to the provision in ESA section 5,
which authorizes certain federal agencies to acquire private property in
order to preserve important habitat for listed species. This section, they
argued, is the only option available to the government where it seeks to
prevent modification of habitat on private land.

The government and other parties who supported the USFWS rule argued that the respondents' interpretation would lead to absurd results.
For example, they said, a landowner could lawfully cut down an endangered bald eagle's nest tree as long as the nest was unoccupied at the time.
They argued that Congress was well aware when it enacted the taking prohibition that habitat loss was a chief cause of species' decline and extinction; thus, Congress must have intended to include habitat loss or
destruction in the term "harm."

The Court's Reasoning

The Supreme Court, in a 6-3 decision, upheld the USFWS regulation.
The Court decided that both the ordinary meaning of "harm" and the legislative history of the ESA supported the USFWS interpretation, and it rejected the argument that harm must involve direct or intentional action.
The Court conceded that the rule was written broadly and that it might
be applied in a particular case to forbid conduct that Congress had not

intended to regulate, but the Court stated that such issues would have to be decided if and when they arose. (In this case, respondents had challenged the rule "on its face," rather than as it applied to a specific set of facts.) The Court further held that the USFWS regulation was a reasonable interpretation of an ambiguous statutory provision, and thus under the rule established in *Chevron U.S.A., Inc. v. Natural Resources Defense Council* (1984), it must be upheld. Finally, the Court noted that Congress had amended the ESA in 1982 by adding section 10, which authorizes permits for the "incidental" (and unintentional) "taking" of endangered species. This provision, the Court said, suggests that Congress believed that section 9 prohibits "indirect as well as deliberate takings," and that indirectly harming a species, such as by modifying its habitat, is unlawful unless permitted under section 10.

Three justices (Rehnquist, Scalia, and Thomas) dissented, on several grounds. They reasoned that the word "harm" in the statutory definition of "take" should be interpreted in light of the other terms used in the definition and accordingly should apply only to direct, intentional conduct. In their view, the rule violates accepted legal principles of foreseeability and proximate cause by making people strictly liable for many ordinary activities, such as farming or logging, that "fortuitously injure protected wildlife, no matter how remote the chain of causation and no matter how difficult to foresee." Rejecting the majority's interpretation of Congress's intent in the ESA, the dissenters agreed with the respondents that Congress meant to make the public in general, not individual private landowners, responsible for conserving protected species' habitat.

The Upshot of *Sweet Home*

The effect of the harm regulation, as ratified by *Sweet Home,* is to subject private property owners to the ESA's civil and criminal penalties (fines or imprisonment or both) for using their land in ways that degrade habitat, thereby killing or injuring listed species. If, as the majority assumed and most commentators have concluded, traditional notions of causation and foreseeability will apply when the USFWS seeks to enforce the harm regulation, the rule will not have the unfair or absurd results envisioned by the dissenters and respondents. Indeed, the USFWS's enforcement of the rule depends partly on its ability to prove that a taking has occurred. For instance, draining the only wetland where an endangered amphibian is known to live almost certainly would take the protected animal by harming its habitat. On the other hand, allowing irrigation water containing pesticides to flow off cultivated lands, contributing to downstream concentrations that pose risks to a threatened fish, probably could not be shown to actually kill or injure wildlife. The need to prove harm, as defined by the rule, helps to assure that the USFWS will not bring cases involving long or tenuous chains of causation. Furthermore, the USFWS's proposed policy, exempting individual homeowners and certain small landowners from compliance with section 9, would help alleviate the burden on private property owners. However, as of late 1997 this policy had not been finalized.

Despite these assurances, *Sweet Home* has been received with widespread apprehension. According to one writer, the case serves as the "poster child" for the campaign to reform the ESA. Even without *Sweet Home*, the ESA was expected to be a principal target of the 104th Congress's legislative reform efforts. Although that Congress's accomplishments fell far short of the dire predictions, private property rights remain a rallying point in the Wise Use Movement, in the conservation and environmental arenas generally, and among most Republicans. Thus, the ESA—and *Sweet Home*—will continue to attract attention and generate heat. Even so, until Congress amends the ESA, *Sweet Home* confirms that all landowners—private, state, and federal—share responsibility for conserving threatened and endangered fish and wildlife.

See also *Chevron U.S.A., Inc. v. Natural Resources Defense Council* (1984); **Endangered Species Act of 1973; Incidental Taking; Scalia, Antonin; Section 7 Consultation; Take;** *Tennessee Valley Authority v. Hill* (1978); **U.S. Fish and Wildlife Service.**

BALDWIN V. FISH AND GAME COMMISSION OF MONTANA (1978)

A U.S. Supreme Court decision (6-3) that upheld a Montana law imposing substantially higher license fees for hunting elk and other game species on nonresidents than residents. The Court ruled that the law did not violate either the Equal Protection or the Privileges and Immunities Clause of the U.S. Constitution. Hunting is merely a sport, not a means to a nonresident's livelihood, the Court held, and thus not a fundamental right protected by the Privileges and Immunities Clause. Furthermore, the Court ruled that the state law was a rational economic measure for protecting the state's finite supply of game animals; therefore, it met the Court's test for complying with Equal Protection requirements.

Although *Baldwin* provides support for state laws that distinguish between resident and nonresident hunters, it was later held not to justify a

Wyoming law requiring persons to be residents of that state in order to obtain a Wyoming hunting guide license. The Wyoming Supreme Court held in *Powell v. Daily* (1986) that the state law violated the Privileges and Immunities Clause because it impacted a fundamental right of nonresidents, the right to earn a living.

Baldwin has enduring significance because all western states charge differential fees for resident and nonresident hunting and fishing. A more recent federal appeals court decision, *Clajon Production Corporation v. Petera* (1995), reexamined some of the issues in *Baldwin* and reached the same result. But the *Clajon* court also addressed a Commerce Clause claim, which was not raised in *Baldwin*.

See also **Clajon Production Corporation v. Petera (1995); Commerce Clause;** *Hughes v. Oklahoma* **(1979); Hunting.**

BEAN, MICHAEL J.   Environmental attorney and chair of the Environmental Defense Fund's wildlife program since 1977. Bean is the author of *The Evolution of National Wildlife Law* (2d ed. 1983) and coauthor of the recently published third edition, considered the foremost treatise on the subject, and numerous law review and popular articles. Bean has participated in litigation involving the wildlife and other natural resource programs of several federal agencies and lobbied for reforms to the Endangered Species Act, Marine Mammal Protection Act, and National Wildlife Refuge System. He has also participated in numerous international conventions on endangered species protection and whaling, and has consulted on or been involved in implementation of international treaties on the protection of migratory species.

Bean, who helped draft the 1982 amendments to section 10 of the ESA, has been called the "dean of endangered species protection in the United States." He has also been criticized for that same role by those who see section 10 habitat conservation plans as losing propositions for threatened and endangered species. He has called for further amendments to the act to incorporate additional incentives for private landowners.

BELOW-COST TIMBER SALES   An imprecise term used to describe timber sales on national forests that net less to the U.S. Treasury than they cost federal taxpayers. The Government Accounting Office reported that for fiscal years 1992–1994 only 10 percent of receipts from U.S. Forest Service (USFS) timber sales were deposited in the U.S. Treasury, and those deposits amounted to less than 25 percent of the agency's expenditures to prepare and administer the sales. In 1992, timber sales on more than two-thirds of all national forests lost money. Such below-cost sales are most common in the Rocky Mountains, Alaska, the Appalachians, and the Lake States. In the first admission of its kind by an administration, the president's Council of Economic Advisors announced in 1997 that the U.S. Forest Service spent $234 million more than it made on national forest timber sales in 1995.

The National Forest Management Act of 1976 contains a general requirement that the USFS consider economics in its resource management activities. The act further requires the agency to identify lands "which are not suited for timber production, considering physical, economic, and other pertinent factors," and prohibits timber harvesting (with some exceptions, such as salvage logging) on those lands for ten years. These provisions do not expressly forbid below-cost sales, however, and the agency has considerable discretion in deciding whether and where to log national forests. Indeed, the Forest Service never receives bids for timber at its appraised price.

Closely related to the issue of below-cost sales are issues regarding road-building in the national forests. Timber harvesting generally requires road access; road construction costs are the largest cost component of timber sales and thus contribute to below-cost sales. Annual federal appropriations for USFS road construction from 1980 through 1990 ranged from $173 million to $250 million; in addition, purchaser road credits paid to logging companies varied from $83 million to $255 million annually. Roads also have negative effects on many forest resources: they fragment habitat, contribute substantially to erosion and siltation of streams, and can adversely impact forest wildlife in other ways, such as disrupting migration and other behavioral patterns or promoting poaching by increasing access. The national forests contain more than 380,000 miles of roads, eight times the length of the federal interstate highway system. For all these reasons, environmental groups and others oppose additional road building in forests, and expenditures for road construction have declined significantly in the past 15 years.

One road-related concern relates to purchaser road credits, which President Clinton proposed to eliminate in his 1997 and 1998 budgets. Under this complicated system (which has exceptions not described here), USFS timber contractors are given financial credit for any roads they must build to access and remove the timber covered by a sale contract. The credits, which are the equivalent of short-term, interest-free loans to the timber purchasers, are applied to the cost of the timber sold or to some future sale on the same forest. Clinton's plan would require timber buyers to build—and pay for—their own roads.

Critics, including environmentalists and many in Congress (particularly fiscally conservative Republicans), favor the elimination of purchaser road credits. They charge that the system is complicated and encourages fraud and abuse; they estimated that eliminating the system would save the federal government $55 million in 1998. Supporters, including the forest products industry, defend purchaser credits as an effective means of financing road construction, and point out that the new roads serve other forest purposes, such as recreational access and fire fighting. Some observers predict that eliminating the credits would not increase revenues to the Treasury because timber companies are likely to compensate by lowering their bids on timber sales. In 1996, the House came within one vote of eliminating the purchaser road credit system; in 1997, a vote in the Senate failed by an even closer margin—and the result would have been different had Vice President Gore been present to break the tie.

See also **Clear-Cutting; Knutson-Vandenberg (K-V) Fund; Salvage Logging.**

BENNETT V. SPEAR **(1997)**   The most recent U.S. Supreme Court decision concerning the Endangered Species Act of 1973 (ESA) and standing. In *Bennett,* a unanimous Court ruled that ESA's citizen suit provision, § 11(g), which authorizes "any person" to sue to enforce the act, authorizes persons claiming economic harm resulting from application of the act to sue for damages.

The plaintiffs were Oregon ranchers and irrigation districts who sued to prevent the federal Bureau of Reclamation from limiting water releases from the Klamath irrigation project to protect two endangered species of fish. The ranchers claimed that the water restrictions would cost them $75 million in damages. Two lower courts had ruled that the ranchers did not have standing under the ESA because their economic interests were not within the "zone of interests" protected by the act. But the Supreme Court reversed, holding that the zone-of-interests test was inapplicable given the act's "any person" language; no basis existed for restricting the right to sue under the ESA to those who claimed environmental harm. Even plaintiffs such as Bennett, who sought to *prevent* application of the ESA's environmental protections, were entitled to sue.

Commodity groups hailed the decision as a victory, while environmental groups played down its significance. Environmentalists have long favored lenient standing requirements; thus, it was not surprising that they did not participate in the case or urge the Court to close the courtroom door to economic interests. Moreover, as environmental officials explained, ESA plaintiffs (including the ranchers in this litigation) still must demonstrate actual harm in order to prevail in their suits.

Nevertheless, many observers expect *Bennett* to result in the filing of at least some additional cases. Moreover, because the ESA citizen-suit provision is very similar to the language of counterpart provisions in other environmental statutes, such as the Clean Water Act and Clean Air Act, any impact *Bennett* might have probably will not be confined to endangered species litigation.

See also **Citizen Suit; Endangered Species Act of 1973; Standing.**

BIODIVERSITY CONSERVATION   Literally, the conservation of the Earth's biological resources. Biodiversity has three facets: species, community, and genetic diversity.

The Problem of Extinctions

Approximately 1.4 million species of organisms have been identified by scientists; the total number of species on Earth may be as high as 100 million. Although we lack an accurate inventory, we are losing the stock. Worldwide, species are being lost at an unprecedented rate—perhaps 30,000 per year. Some local rates—for instance, in the Amazon River Basin—are even higher. Of the 9,000 known species of birds, 6,000 are in decline and 1,000 are threatened with extinction. At current rates of habitat loss (the chief cause of extinction), 20 percent of all presently existing life forms will have disappeared by the year 2020. A recent assessment by The Nature Conservancy determined that one-third of the United States's 20,439 species are vulnerable or in peril. Most at risk are inhabitants of freshwater ecosystems.

Although habitat loss and fragmentation are the chief causes of declining biological diversity, another major threat, globally as well as in the United States, is the introduction of nonnative, or "exotic," organisms. These introductions may be intentional or inadvertent. For instance, many state game and fish agencies have purposefully introduced wild turkeys or various species of fish to areas never formerly occupied by these species. Certain predatory animals have been introduced as a means of eliminating or reducing the population of some unwanted pest, especially in the past. On the other hand, many organisms are introduced accidentally, particularly through interstate and international commerce activities. Insects "stow away" in the packing materials of imported goods, seeds of nonnative plants arrive via shipments of hay or grain or in the livestock to which they have been fed, and the ballast water of ships often contains fish and shellfish larvae and plankton. Even foreign travelers contribute to the problem by picking up a parasite or becoming infected by a bacterium or virus and transferring it to another country. Still another pathway involves animals bought or captured in other states or countries (for use as pets or for commercial purposes) that escape after being imported.

Many exotics do not survive in their new environs, but of those that do, an estimated 10 percent ultimately cause some major ecological effect. In the case of exotic animals, these effects range from competing directly with local fauna for food or other habitat needs, to infecting susceptible native wildlife with exotic diseases or parasites, to interbreeding with closely related local species. Exotic plants compete with native plants for water and nutrients, and may alter a community's tolerance to drought, fire, or grazing pressure, or they may concentrate salts or toxic trace elements out of the soil. Microorganisms can have myriad effects; among them are altering soil chemistry processes and introducing diseases. Individual effects may combine to work cumulative damage or interact to produce synergistic effects. As a result, the stability of ecological processes and communities, even ecosystems, may be undermined.

The Value of Diversity

Conservation biologists' thinking has been inspired by the philosophy of Aldo Leopold, who wrote that the first rule of intelligent tinkering is to save all the parts. Leopold also admonished: "A thing is right when it tends to preserve the integrity, stability, and beauty of the biotic community. It is wrong when it tends otherwise." Whereas species were once categorized (even by Leopold himself) as good or bad, useful or injurious, most if not all ecologists today believe that each species has a role to play in communities and ecosystems. Many believe that even species considered redundant, or functionally nonessential, nevertheless have value—moral, aesthetic, inherent value.

Economists generally favor incorporating some sort of benefit-cost analysis in decision making, but this is problematic in decisions concerning biodiversity conservation. Weighing the costs and benefits of protecting biodiversity is an anthropocentric, utilitarian approach; it considers only how much species are worth to humans and ignores species' inherent (nonuse) value. The approach is further hampered by humans' inability to predict the costs of their actions to biodiversity and the difficulty of quantifying the benefits of preserving species or communities. Even if it could be predicted that the cumulative impact of development in a given area would extirpate a local population of birds, the implications for either the survival of the species or the functioning of the ecosystem will usually be unknown. Moreover, while some may consider the bird valuable only to the extent that it is *used*, for example, by hunters or bird-watchers, others may believe that it has *nonuse* (existence) value. If the bird were lost, a potential source of medicine or scientific knowledge might disappear along with it, or society might suffer because the landscape was rendered less diverse and thus less pleasing aesthetically. Even if these and other relevant questions and uncertainty about *this* bird could be resolved, similar questions will arise for other species—a squirrel, an earthworm, a fungus. Biologists and policy makers thus wrestle with the questions: *What* should we try to measure, *how* do we measure it, and *what do we do* with the data we generate?

Global Efforts to Conserve Biodiversity

An international Convention on Biological Diversity was finalized at the 1992 Earth Summit in Rio de Janeiro, Brazil, where it was signed by 157 countries, including the United States. The convention became effective at the end of 1993, and by early 1996 had been ratified by well over 100 nations. Although the U.S. Senate Foreign Relations Committee passed it by a wide margin, ratification by the 104th Congress was blocked on the Senate floor by Senators Jesse Helms (R-NC) and Robert Dole (R-KS).

The convention defines biological diversity as "the variability among living organisms from all sources, including...terrestrial, marine and other aquatic ecosystems and the ecological complexes of which they are a part; this includes diversity within species, between species and of ecosystems." The convention confirms each nation's sovereign authority over, and its responsibility for, its biological resources. Signatories to the convention agree to: develop national strategies for ensuring the conservation and sustainable use of biological resources; establish protected areas, restore degraded ecosystems, and control exotic species; ensure fair treatment of indigenous peoples who contribute their knowledge about species and conservation; establish biodiversity-related education and research programs; assess the impacts on diversity of any proposed development project before carrying it out; recognize and protect rights in genetic resources; and give financial aid to developing countries for implementing the convention.

Biodiversity Conservation in the United States

No coordinated "law of biodiversity" exists in this country, but provisions in many existing federal and state statutes can be employed to promote biodiversity conservation. Usually cited are the Endangered Species Act of 1973 (ESA), National Forest Management Act of 1976 (NFMA) (specifically its diversity provision), National Environmental Policy Act, Clean Water Act, and various programs for conserving wetlands. In addition to the NFMA, other federal statutes governing conservation system lands—for example, the Wild and Scenic Rivers Act of 1968 and Wilderness Act of 1964—may also promote species conservation, depending on how they are implemented. Conservation easements and land trusts are state law mechanisms that can be useful in conserving species by protecting their habitats. Many state laws also contribute to the goal of conserving biodiversity. A 1996 report prepared jointly by the Center for Wildlife Law and the Defenders of Wildlife surveyed and compared all 50 states' laws, policies, and programs for conserving species and habitats.

Some legal means exist to protect against the dangers of exotics, but they are not consistent among states nor well coordinated. State laws generally prohibit the possession of game and other protected animals and also regulate the importation of some species, but many animals are not covered by these regulations, and enforcement is spotty or infeasible. The ESA implements the United States's obligations under the Convention on International Trade in Endangered Species (CITES), which prohibits imports of endangered animals and provides mechanisms for discouraging other countries' trade in such animals. The Lacey Act makes it a federal crime to transport an animal taken illegally in one state into another state and forbids the importation of certain listed species. Other tools for addressing the problems posed by exotics, either by preventing such invasions or combating them after they have occurred, include the use of still other nonnative organisms to control the targeted exotic organisms (although such measures themselves pose many of the same potential problems), stepped-up customs inspections, and regulations concerning boat maintenance and transportation of agricultural products.

See also **Biosphere Reserve; Contingent Valuation; Ecosystem Management; Endangered Species Act of 1973; National Forest Management Act of 1976; The Nature Conservancy.**

BIOLOGICAL OPINION   The document produced by the U.S. Fish and Wildlife Service (USFWS) as a result of a consultation process required by section 7 of the Endangered Species Act. If a threatened or endangered species is likely to be affected by an action proposed by a federal agency, that agency is required to consult with the USFWS, which then studies the probable effects of the proposed action and prepares its biological opinion concerning those effects. This opinion is often part of an environmental assessment or environmental impact statement concerning the project. Biological opinions take one of two general forms: a so-called "jeopardy opinion," if USFWS finds that the proposed project would jeopardize the species or destroy or adversely modify its critical habitat, or a "no jeopardy opinion," if USFWS believes that no such effects would result. In the event of a jeopardy opinion, the proposed action may not proceed unless USFWS suggests an alternative that would avoid the prohibited, adverse consequences. Even if USFWS issues a no-jeopardy biological opinion, it still may require the acting agency to take steps to mitigate the project's impacts.

See also **Endangered Species Act of 1973; Section 7 Consultation; U.S. Fish and Wildlife Service.**

BIOSPHERE RESERVE   Land preserves designated under the auspices of the United Nations' Man and the Biosphere Program within the UN Educational, Scientific and Cultural Organization (UNESCO). Established in 1968, the biosphere reserve network consists of 324 reserves in 82 countries worldwide, including 47 in the United States.

Reserves are nominated by the locality and country in which they are located, and accepted by UNESCO for inclusion in the system based on three general criteria. These criteria resemble those advocated by conservation biologists for establishing biological reserves: a core protected area, surrounded by a buffer zone supporting low-intensity development or uses, and beyond that, transitional areas where cooperative efforts toward sustainable development are carried on. Reserves can be removed from the system by the home country at any time.

The biosphere reserve program aims to protect a broad array of representative biotic communities; foster ecosystem management, ecosystem-oriented research, and education; and ensure continued economic opportunities for people living in the vicinity of reserves. To promote the latter objective, comparative work is encouraged to determine how various biological systems can be used productively while maintaining their ecological integrity. Reserves are often centered around some already-protected tract of land, such as a national park, but may also encompass adjoining multiple-use or unprotected lands, including private lands. In the United States, the National Park Service considers the reserve designation an appropriate approach to regional resource management, but the U.S. Forest Service reportedly views the program as a "threat to its autonomy." [Grumbine 1988, cited in Bates 1993] There are 12 biosphere reserve parks in the United States, including Yellowstone National Park and Glacier Bay National Park and Preserve. Although the biosphere concept is meant to protect an ecosystem, reserve boundaries generally coincide with a park's borders and thus have no true relation to ecosystem limits.

The biosphere reserve designation does not result in legally enforceable management requirements, nor does it give UNESCO or any other entity jurisdiction over the reserve. Since 1984, however, participating countries have agreed to UNESCO's "Action Plan": a "minimum set" of research, education, planning, and management activities that "should be implemented in each biosphere reserve." In 1997 the House passed a bill introduced by Congressman Don Young (R-AK), which would limit the area that could be designated biosphere reserves and require congressional authorization to place lands on the World Heritage List. Some western congresspersons and governors question the motives behind the program and even criticize reserve designations as impinging on state and federal sovereignty (which they clearly do not).

See also **Ecosystem Management; Sustainable Development.**

Bureau of Land Management (BLM) A federal land management agency within the U.S. Department of the Interior. The BLM manages approximately 270 million surface acres and 570 million subsurface acres of mineral estate. The surface interests alone amount to 41 percent of all federal land holdings, more than those of any other federal agency.

History and Mandate

The agency was established in 1946 by combining the General Land Office (the entity formed in 1812 to oversee the disposal of federal lands through homestead patents, railroad grants, etc.) and the Grazing Service (an agency formed in 1934 to oversee livestock grazing on unreserved federal lands). For 30 years this heritage largely dictated the BLM's character and principal functions. Not until 1976, with the passage of BLM's organic act, the Federal Land Policy and Management Act (FLPMA), did BLM obtain full authority to actively manage its extensive land and resource holdings. Its multiple-use mandate is similar to that of its counterpart, the U.S. Forest Service (USFS), encompassing recreation, range, fish and wildlife, cultural, forestry, and watershed resources; it also manages wild horses under authority of the Wild, Free-Roaming Horses and Burros Act of 1973. The BLM is responsible for minerals management on all federal lands, not only its own.

The BLM also manages 2.6 million acres in northern California and Oregon under the Oregon and California Revested Lands Sustained Yield Management Act of 1937. These lands were granted to the Oregon & California Railroad in 1869 and returned in 1913 (pursuant to a court order) to the General Land Office. Although managed for multiple uses, they are subject to legal requirements not applicable to other BLM lands under FLPMA. Heavily timbered, the "O&C" lands account for 10 percent of annual federal timber sales. They were included in 1994 in the Clinton administration's Northwest Timber Management Plan.

Structure and Organization

Although the BLM employs far fewer persons per acre managed than the USFS, it is an extensive organization. Its 9,600 employees work out of more than 200 offices. The BLM's traditionally hierarchical structure includes a Washington, D.C., headquarters and 12 state offices, all but one of which are in the West, contrasting with the Forest Service's organization by multistate regions. These state offices provide support services to approximately 59 district offices and 130 resource area offices (roughly analogous to the Forest Service's national forests and ranger districts, respectively). Each state office is supervised by a state director; with few exceptions, district and resource area offices are headed by district and resource area managers.

BLM has seen some profound organizational and cultural changes in recent years, and these changes are ongoing. Its former management approach, based on individual multiple uses and commodities, such as grazing and minerals, has been replaced with an interdisciplinary, ecosystem-oriented strategy. In fact, BLM's "Blueprint for the Future" asserts five agency goals, the first of which is to maintain healthy ecosystems. The others relate to serving its publics, working for "collaborative leadership," and improving BLM's business and personnel practices. Similarly, its historical line-staff, program-based administrative and operational structure has been traded in for an interdisciplinary approach using teams.

Until recently, each office was organized by resource or administrative specialty—operations, range, recreation—as was BLM's budget, which once included line items for as many as 60 different programs. Thus, wildlife biologists and wilderness specialists and geologists could be found at each administrative level—national, state, and district. As part of the Clinton-Gore "reinventing government" initiative, however, this structure is changing. BLM transferred more than 200 of 700 targeted positions from state and district offices to the resource areas, and expected to decrease its supervisory ratio from 1:6 in 1993 to 1:13 by 1998. The agency intends to offset staffing reductions by simplifying administrative procedures, achieving greater efficiency, and cooperating more closely with other resource agencies. For instance, BLM is working with the USFS to develop shared grazing regulations, and the two agencies share a new field office.

The new management strategy at the state office and field levels is based on interdisciplinary teams. All BLM employees will be trained in team skills, and teams will be given greater management authority and held accountable for their performance. Each of the 12 state offices will be allowed to tailor its structure to meet local and resource needs. The new field organization itself has been flattened by reducing its hierarchical structure. One example is the Glenallen District in central Alaska, which recently decided *not* to fill its vacant district manager position. The office's 15 employees constitute a self-managing team, with each employee taking more responsibility for decision making. BLM headquarters personnel also have been formed into interdisciplinary groups that will eventually become self-managing. The agency claims it is relying more heavily on professional and scientific input. Some constituency groups initially objected that their interests would be diluted by the new team approach, but it is too early to assess whether such fears may be realized.

The current BLM director, Patrick Shea, was nominated and confirmed in 1997. He replaced Michael Dombeck, who served as acting director for nearly three years but was never nominated because of fears that western Republicans would scuttle his confirmation by the Senate. (Dombeck is now USFS chief.)

Resource Issues

Most of the important land issues facing the BLM today are described elsewhere in this book. They include reform of the 1872 Mining Law, rehabilitation of rangelands and reform of the agency's grazing program, resolution of rights-of-way claims under the antiquated "R.S. 2477" law, wilderness designations, wild horse management, oil and gas exploration and development, and relations with counties, states, constituency groups, the public, and Congress. Numerous proposals have been made over the years to transfer title and/or management of BLM lands to the states, including as recently as 1996, but have met with mixed or lukewarm responses from the states and stiff opposition from environmentalists and recreation interests.

See also **County Supremacy Movement; Federal Land Policy and Management Act; Grand Staircase-Escalante National Monument; Mining Law Reform; Multiple Use; Organic Act of 1897; Privatization; Range Reform; R.S. 2477; Sagebrush Rebellion; Shea, Patrick; Wild, Free-Roaming Horses and Burros Act; Wilderness; Wise Use Movement.**

BUREAU OF RECLAMATION (BOR) A federal land management agency within the Department of the Interior. The BOR is the largest supplier of water in the 17 western states. In 1992, BOR facilities delivered 10 trillion gallons of water for municipal, agricultural, industrial, and domestic purposes. BOR reservoirs and other projects provide flood control, hydropower, fish, wildlife, and recreation benefits. One of Bruce Babbitt's early goals as Interior secretary was to, as he put it, "destroy" the BOR, whose "practices have been the most environmentally destructive of all the public land agencies." Babbitt was referring to the BOR's mission to implement federal "reclamation" policies earlier in the century. These policies led to inappropriate cultivation of desert lands, water projects with devastating environmental consequences, and the subsidization of corporate agriculture in the name of the "small family farmer." Babbitt indicated that options for reforming the agency ranged from abolishing it and transferring its river management functions to interstate river basin councils, such as the Northwest Power Planning Council, to eliminating its construction budget and authority to build new projects and using current project revenues to fund a new reclamation policy. That policy, according to Babbitt, should be centered around facilitating market water transfers (e.g., transferring water used for agriculture to needy cities or other industries). Western cities need water and will continue to raid public land water sources and depletable groundwater supplies if they can't get it from agriculture, which uses more than 80 percent of all water in the West. Due in large part to administrative reforms undertaken during Babbitt's tenure at Interior, the BOR's current water management philosophy emphasizes balancing the increasing demands on water with the need to better protect natural resources.

See also **Anadromous Fish; Corps of Engineers.**

CALIFORNIA COASTAL COMMISSION V. GRANITE ROCK CO. (1987)

A U.S. Supreme Court decision in which the Court distinguished between land-use planning and environmental regulation, and reaffirmed a state's authority to impose its own *environmental* requirements on activities conducted on federal lands with federal permission. The U.S. Forest Service (USFS) had approved Granite Rock's operating plan for mining its unpatented mining claims in the Los Padres National Forest in California. Subsequently, the California Coastal Commission notified Granite Rock that it must obtain a coastal development permit. Rather than apply for a permit, the company filed suit in federal court, arguing that the state permit requirement was preempted by federal law.

The Court rejected Granite Rock's contentions, holding that USFS regulations actually contemplate that mining in national forests will be conducted in compliance with state and local environmental laws. Thus, the Court said, there was no federal intent to preempt state environmental regulation of mining in national forests. Nor was the Coastal Commission permit requirement an impermissible attempt to regulate land use within the national forest. Granite Rock had sued to enjoin California from enforcing its permit requirement before the company knew what requirements the state intended to impose, and no evidence existed to indicate that the state would deny a permit. Therefore, Granite Rock was foreclosed from arguing that the state was attempting to *prohibit* a land use authorized by the federal government. California could use the permit requirement as a means to obtain compliance with its environmental regulations, the Court ruled. It could regulate, though not prohibit, mining on federal lands.

The Court conceded that the line between land-use planning and environmental regulation "will not always be bright." But it observed that "the core activity described by each phrase is undoubtedly different. Land use planning in essence chooses particular uses for the lands; environmental regulation...does not mandate particular uses of the land but requires only that...damage to the environment is kept within prescribed limits." So long as a state seeks only to regulate the environmental impacts of activities

45

conducted on federal lands, and not to exercise final approval over the choice of land uses themselves, the state law may stand.

See also **Land-Use Planning; Preemption; Zoning.**

CALIFORNIA DESERT PROTECTION ACT OF 1994   Federal legislation that created the Mojave National Preserve, converted Death Valley and Joshua Tree National Monuments to national parks and expanded them, and created 69 wilderness areas on Bureau of Land Management (BLM) lands. The California Desert Act was the single largest expansion of the national wilderness preservation system since the addition of lands in Alaska in 1980 and the largest ever in the lower 48 states.

Although the act as a whole was hailed as an environmental victory by many conservationists, others criticized the compromises in the decision to make the Mojave area a national preserve rather than a park. Three desert ecosystems converge in this 1.4-million-acre area—the Mojave, Sonoran, and Great Basin—and the area is home to 300 species of animals and 800 plants. However, it is an "urban desert" in Los Angeles's and Baker's backyards, and remains open to livestock grazing, off-road vehicles, and mining and mineral prospecting, as well as a variety of recreational uses. The National Park Service has taken over management of the area from the BLM, and is formulating a land-use plan for the area with input from a 15-member planning advisory group appointed by Interior Secretary Babbitt. Congress's failure to provide adequate funding until 1997, however, prevented the agency from hiring personnel, constructing facilities, or making much progress on the plan, now scheduled for completion in late 1998.

See also **Wilderness.**

CHAFEE, JOHN H.   Republican senator from Rhode Island since 1976 and chair of the Senate Environment Committee since 1995. Considered a moderate, Chafee advocates reauthorization and reasonable reforms to the Endangered Species Act, reform of the General Mining Law of 1872, and reasonable, scientifically sound changes to federal wetlands law. In 1996, Chafee blocked proposed wetlands legislation that he believed went too far in reforming the law. In 1997 he introduced estate-tax-relief legislation designed to reduce urban sprawl. A budget bill signed by President Clinton in 1997 included a provision offered by Chafee allowing a 40 percent estate tax exemption for land devoted to conservation purposes, applicable to land within 25 miles of designated metropolitan areas, national parks, or wilderness areas, or within 10 miles of urban forests. Chafee was considered instrumental in securing passage of the 1990 amendments and reauthorization of the Clean Air Act, including its provisions regarding acid rain, and in the amendments and reauthorization of the Endangered Species Act in 1988.

See also **Endangered Species Act of 1973; Senate Environment Committee.**

CHECKERBOARD A land ownership pattern of alternating sections, or square miles, of privately and publicly owned land that, as depicted on a land status map, resembles a checkerboard. A vestige of western land disposal and expansion policies of the mid-1800s, checkerboard areas occur along railroad rights-of-way. As an inducement to build track, especially transcontinental routes, the federal government granted to railroad companies every other section within 10 or 20 miles on each side of the proposed line. Railroads received the odd-numbered sections, and the United States retained the even-numbered sections. The United States also reserved the minerals under the lands conveyed to the railroads. Promoters of the scheme believed that as the railroad advanced the land would be settled and become more valuable. Railroads could help finance construction by selling their parcels, while the government could allow homesteading on the retained parcels. The strategy was also a means of avoiding direct government subsidization of railroad construction, which some viewed as unconstitutional.

The railroads were built, but the legacy of the checkerboard land grants is a host of management problems that continue to this day. The railroad's sections are still private, owned by the railroads themselves or private parties to whom they sold. Likewise, the intervening sections have remained in government ownership for the most part. Thus, 20- to 40-mile-wide swaths of intermixed private and federal lands exist along most major railroad lines throughout the West. This ownership pattern presents access problems for and interferes with the efficient use of both private and federal lands. Public purposes such as recreation are not easily accommodated, fences and gates proliferate, and wildlife habitat may be fragmented. Moreover, in this arid and semiarid country where large tracts of land are required to support livestock, grazing is feasible only if the livestock operator has access to several sections of private and federal lands.

Public access problems in checkerboard areas are fairly common, although over the years the federal land management agencies, principally the Bureau of Land Management (BLM), have entered into agreements with private landowners, purchased easements, or made other provisions for access in many areas. One of the most important disputes over access made it to the U.S. Supreme Court. *Leo Sheep Co. v. United States* (1979) involved a disagreement between the BLM and ranchers in the checkerboard area along the Union Pacific railroad in south-central Wyoming. BLM had built and improved roads across the ranchers' (formerly, the railroad's) private sections to provide public access to Seminoe Reservoir; the ranchers objected. The Court held that when the government granted land to the Union Pacific Railroad Company, it did not retain an implied easement that would now allow the public motorized access across private land in order to reach and use public sections for recreation. (Also, the Union Pacific Act of 1862 contained no express provisions relating to access.) The Court intimated that agency personnel could cross the private land to access federal lands for administrative purposes, and it left open the questions of public access by foot or for purposes other than recreation.

One tool the government occasionally uses to resolve such problems is land exchange. "Blocking up" ownership (consolidating private and public sections) would seem to make good land-use sense for all concerned.

See also **Bureau of Land Management; Land Exchange.**

CHEVRON U.S.A., INC. V. NATURAL RESOURCES DEFENSE COUNCIL (1984) An important administrative law decision. This 1984 U.S. Supreme Court case established a two-part test for reviewing agency regulations promulgated to implement a federal statute. The Court stated that it must first determine whether the intent of Congress, as expressed in the statute, is clear. If it is, "that is the end of the matter; for the court, as well as the agency, must give effect to the unambiguously expressed intent of Congress." If the statute is *not* clear with respect to the precise issue, the Court will defer to any reasonable interpretation by the agency responsible for administering the statute. The issue in *Chevron* involved an Environmental Protection Agency rule implementing the federal Clean Air Act. The *Chevron* holding is consistent with an earlier Supreme Court opinion, *Udall v. Tallman* (1965), a case involving the withdrawal of national wildlife refuge lands in Alaska from mineral leasing. The *Tallman* Court held that interpretations of presidential and secretarial orders by the respective agency or its officers are entitled to substantial deference; furthermore, an agency's interpretation of its own regulations should be accorded even greater weight. *Tallman* is still sometimes cited in the public land law context instead of *Chevron*.

See also **Deference.**

CITIZEN SUIT   A lawsuit brought by an individual or group against another person, company, or agency, alleging that he or it has violated some law or regulation. Many environmental statutes contain specific provisions authorizing citizens to sue, as well as conditioning the exercise of that right. Others, including most of the laws discussed in this encyclopedia, do not provide for citizen suits per se. Many contain no provisions for seeking judicial review; the Federal Land Policy and Management Act, on the other hand, states simply that it is federal policy that "judicial review of public land adjudication decisions be provided by law." [43 U.S.C. § 1701(a)(6)] In addition, many decisions of federal agencies are subject to the National Environmental Policy Act (NEPA), and courts have long held that agency decisions pursuant to NEPA are reviewable in court.

Courts presume that agency decisions are judicially reviewable, so long as no statute clearly precludes it and provided that the citizen plaintiff meets all threshold requirements, such as standing, ripeness, and exhaustion of remedies. Agencies cannot be sued to compel them to bring an enforcement action, however. The courts have analogized this to prosecutorial discretion, and grant agencies wide latitude in making such choices for themselves.

See also **Administrative Procedure Act; Exhaustion of Remedies; Ripeness; Standing.**

CLAJON PRODUCTION CORPORATION V. PETERA (1995)   A decision by the U.S. Court of Appeals for the Tenth Circuit that upheld the state of Wyoming's hunting license scheme against claims that it violated the Commerce, Taking, and Equal Protection Clauses of the U.S. Constitution. *Clajon* is probably most important for its implications for future Commerce Clause challenges to hunting license allocation systems.

Wyoming law limits owners of 160 acres or more to two supplemental hunting licenses in addition to an individual personal license, and establishes separate pools of licenses for residents and nonresidents; 84 percent of elk and 80 percent of deer licenses are reserved for residents. The plaintiffs, Wyoming landowners who supplied outfitting services to out-of-state clients, claimed that the law violated the "dormant Commerce Clause" in that it discriminated against interstate commerce by favoring resident hunters.

The court ruled that the plaintiffs lacked standing to challenge the resident-nonresident license pool system because they failed to show that they suffered any injury caused by the system. That is, they failed to present evidence that the license allocation system "interferes with their ability to provide commercial outfitting services to out-of-state residents." The court suggested, however, that if the plaintiffs could demonstrate that the ratio of resident licenses to resident applicants was higher than the ratio of nonresident licenses to nonresident applicants, the plaintiffs might succeed in challenging the law.

Noting that a lesser burden applies to a claim that a regulation merely *burdens* commerce, as opposed to actually *discriminating* against commerce, one commentator suggests that a plaintiff in a similar position in a future case might be able to succeed in challenging rules like Wyoming's. The plaintiffs in *Clajon* alleged only that the regulations were discriminatory; thus, the court did not decide whether they excessively burdened commerce. Applying the balancing text used in the latter type of cases, this commentator suggests that outfitters' interests in supplying services to nonresident hunters, which are impacted by both the relatively small number of licenses issued and the uncertainty of nonresidents "drawing" licenses, could outweigh Wyoming's interest in giving a political advantage to resident hunters. Furthermore, alternatives exist. The writer points to allocation systems used in other states, which strike a balance more favorable to nonresidents. If a court were to agree with this analysis, it would strike down rules like Wyoming's as violating the dormant Commerce Clause.

Not surprisingly, the court also held that limiting large landowners to two licenses does not constitute an unconstitutional taking of their property because it does not destroy all beneficial use of their property. Furthermore, Wyoming's regulation advances legitimate state purposes, namely, conserving the state's big game animals and ensuring residents a reasonable opportunity to hunt.

See also *Baldwin v. Fish and Game Commission of Montana* (1978); Commerce Clause; *Hughes v. Oklahoma* (1979); Hunting; Taking.

🏛 **CLEAN WATER ACT SECTION 404** Regulates the discharge of dredged or fill material into waters and wetlands. Although section 404 regulates all waters of the United States—and mentions "wetlands" only once—it has evolved principally into a wetland protection program. In keeping with the overall goals of the Clean Water Act and of the past two presidential administrations, the administering agency, the U.S. Army Corps of Engineers (Corps), is guided in implementing section 404 by the goal of "no net loss of wetlands."

The Regulatory Scheme

Under Corps regulations, persons may lawfully dredge and fill "waters of the United States" only after obtaining a section 404 permit. Failure to obtain a 404 permit or to comply with its terms may lead to civil or criminal penalties. The Corps has defined "waters of the United States" broadly to include nearly all waters, lakes, streams, intermittent streams, playas, mudflats, and wetlands adjacent to such waters, as well as isolated wetlands, in certain circumstances. This broad definition has been approved by the courts and Congress; one court rejected an attempt by the Corps to tighten the definition, thus excluding certain waters previously regulated. [*United States v. Riverside Bayview Homes* (1985)]

On the other hand, Congress expressly exempted in section 404, and the Corps has interpreted section 404 to exempt, certain activities from the permit requirement. These activities include normal farming, silviculture, and ranching; maintenance of structures, such as dikes, dams, levees, and bridges; construction and maintenance of irrigation and drainage ditches; construction of temporary sedimentation ponds at construction sites; and construction of roads for farm, forest harvest, or mining use (*if* they use best management practices and their construction will neither impair nor change waters). These exemptions are not absolute. Section 404 dictates that exempted activities can be "recaptured" and regulated if they impair the quality or reach of surface waters.

The Corps has further determined that certain categories of dredge-and-fill activities pose only minimal adverse environmental effects and may be permitted under nationwide "general" permits (issued for five years and renewable). For instance, nationwide permit (NWP) #28 allows for certain modifications to existing marinas. (Expansion and dredging of existing marinas, however, requires an individual 404 permit.) NWPs are established through a formal rulemaking process. Of the 36 NWPs, 13 are self-executing. However, the person seeking to dredge and fill is responsible for obtaining the appropriate permission; thus, a prudent person will contact the Corps to ensure that the proposed activity indeed falls within an NWP. Failure to do so may result in a violation of section 404 and civil or criminal enforcement actions. Further, the Corps can overrule an NWP in specific circumstances if the waters have been identified by local, state, or federal authorities as having special importance, or if the Corps determines that the values of the Clean Water Act would be better served by an individual permit.

All activities not covered by a general permit, or NWP, are subject to individual permitting. The Corps reviews permit applications under section 404(b)(1) and regulatory guidelines to determine whether any "practicable alternatives" to the proposed activity exist. The applicant must show that his proposed activity is the least environmentally damaging. Activities deemed non-water-dependent, such as filling in wetlands to build shopping malls, are presumed to have practicable alternatives. The burden is on the applicant to show that an upland site either will not accommodate the project or is not available. The applicant must survey all practicable alternatives, even those which would entail using land not owned by the applicant. The CWA provides for states to assume section 404 authority, but to date only two—Michigan and New Jersey—have done so. The reasons cited include the complex procedures for assumption, costs of running the program, and the continued involvement of federal authorities.

The Permit System in Practice

Implementing the section 404 permit requirement requires input from applicants, other agencies, and the public. Applicants must provide the Corps with detailed information about their plans and can manipulate the agency's review by characterizing projects narrowly. This strategy limits the possible alternatives to the project, thereby enhancing the likelihood of permit issuance. For instance, an applicant might characterize a marina/golf course/hotel as one development, thus narrowing the options for alternative sites. Although the project could be viewed in two or three parts—

i.e., the golf course and hotel could be separated from the marina, thus allowing many more alternatives—the courts require the Corps to accept the applicant's characterization of the project. The Corps also must consider the applicant's financial resources and mitigation plan. However, the Corps cannot evaluate the application solely on the basis of either economics or the applicant's plan. The agency must conduct an independent assessment of the proposed project's environmental effects.

The permit application is further subject to public notice and comment and, potentially, to a public hearing. In determining whether to grant or deny a permit, the Corps must take into account any timely public comments. The Corps also must consult with other agencies, including the Environmental Protection Agency (EPA) and the U.S. Fish and Wildlife Service (USFWS) in the Department of the Interior. These agencies' comments may be the basis for rejecting an application.

In fact, under Clean Water Act section 404(c) EPA wields a veto power over 404 permits. However, it rarely exercises this authority. Between 1972 and 1994, the EPA vetoed Corps permitting decisions only 14 times; nearly all of these cases involved large public water projects. Still, the veto threat provides an incentive for the Corps to consider carefully EPA comments regarding permit applications. The responsibilities of the USFWS under the Endangered Species Act can also resemble a veto power. The Corps must consult with the USFWS if a proposed project might adversely affect threatened or endangered species. An affirmative decision may slow or prevent issuance of a 404 permit.

The Corps has come under attack by environmental groups and others in recent years because of its high rate of permit approval. According to the Corps, more than 80 percent of 62,000 permit applications in 1995 were approved under general permits; fewer than 8 percent were required to go through the individual permitting process. Only 274 (0.5 percent) applications for individual permits were denied. Furthermore, although applicants must adopt a mitigation plan to minimize environmental harms, one study (of a limited area in Ohio) suggested that the results of mitigation plans are mixed at best and probably lead to an overall loss of wetlands. Another source suggested that the Corps's 404 program effectively regulates only about 20 percent of the activities causing wetlands losses. According to William Reilly, EPA administrator in the Bush administration, only 40,000 acres of the 290,000 acres of wetlands being lost annually in the 1980s were reviewed under the 404 program. In large part this was due to exemptions and to the law's failure to address drainage of wetlands. Nationwide permits also take a toll—between 1988 and 1996 80,000 acres of wetlands were impaired by the NWP program.

Reforming the 404 Permit System

Recent administrative changes in the 404 permitting program alternately strengthen and weaken protections of our nation's wetlands. In December 1996 the Corps announced a list of 30 new or revised NWPs and further revealed that it would phase out (by 1999) NWP #26, which authorizes discharges in headwater streams and isolated waters less than 10 acres in size. (The agency plans to replace NWP #26 with several activity-based permits.) In the interim, the Corps advised, NWP #26 will not be available for projects affecting more than three acres or 500 linear feet of a stream. Headwater streams (defined as nontidal waters with flow rates of less than 5 cubic feet per second) are often extremely important to water quality, and isolated waters encompass many ecologically critical wetlands. Yet some authorities estimate that as many as 25,000 acres of these wetlands were lost in the last decade, and that NWP #26 has been responsible for widespread and serious environmental effects.

The National Association of Homebuilders filed suit in March 1997, arguing that requiring individual permits for activities in these wetlands will impose too onerous a burden on their development activities (individual permitting is also more time-consuming), and claiming that the Corps's action improperly ignored Administrative Procedure Act requirements for public notice and comment. The outcome of this legal challenge to the Corps's authority to eliminate NWP #26 will be watched closely by Congress, environmentalists, and the regulated community. (In fact, Congress has been urged by the National Wetlands Coalition, an industry group representing principally oil and gas exploration and real estate interests, to examine the Corps's decision to phase out NWP #26.) Meanwhile, several environmental groups have sued the Ohio Environmental Protection Agency to force it to stop applying NWP #26 to headwater streams and isolated wetlands *now*. These plaintiffs argue that, otherwise, developers will rush to begin construction under the NWP in the two years before it is ultimately terminated.

The Corps faces a legal challenge to yet another nationwide permit—NWP #29. Enacted in 1995, this NWP authorizes discharges of dredged or fill material for the purpose of building or improving single-family homes, if the fill affects no more than one-half acre of wetland. The permit requires preconstruction notification to the Corps—for instance, a homeowner who wants to put in a swimming pool must first notify the Corps before filling the low spot in the backyard. NWP #29 can be used only once on any parcel of land and cannot be "stacked" with other NWPs to avoid individual permitting. Several environmental and public interest organizations have sued, arguing that NWP #29 does not meet the criteria for nationwide permits, specifically, that single-family homebuilding does not constitute a category of similar activities with minimal adverse environmental effects. According to the plaintiffs, NWP #29 was simply a political tool designed to placate critics of environmental regulation.

Section 404 has received broad congressional scrutiny in recent years; in fact, wetlands protection has been a key issue in ongoing attempts to reauthorize the Clean Water Act, with factions arguing for enhanced or relaxed regulation of development in these areas. Some lobbyists and members of Congress believe that wetlands regulation should be removed from the Clean Water Act and dealt with in separate legislation. Even some Republicans believe that a strong federal law designed specifically to protect wetlands is needed. On the other hand, the chair of the House Resources Committee vowed in 1997 to sponsor legislation to force the Corps to establish an administrative appeals procedure for contesting 404 permit decisions. Another reform proposal is to exempt Alaska from the section 404 program, or to delay 404 enforcement there until 1 percent of the state's wetlands have been lost.

See also **Dredge and Fill; Mitigation; Mitigation Banking; Swampbuster; Corps of Engineers;** *United States v. Riverside Bayview Homes* **(1985).**

CLEAR-CUTTING   The common silvicultural, or timber harvest, practice of removing all trees in a given area, ranging from a few to occasionally hundreds of acres. Clear-cutting has economic and environmental advantages and disadvantages. Clear-cutting, as opposed to selective cutting, may be necessary to ensure regeneration of certain shade-intolerant tree species, notably Douglas fir. In addition, it may be the least costly method of harvesting timber, require fewer roads to access the timber, and stimulate new growth of shrubs and forbs favored by certain species of wildlife, such as deer, black bears, and ruffed grouse. However, clear-cutting displaces interior-dwelling forest species; it may open up the forest to greater use—and thus disturbance—by humans, lead to erosion, and have long-term effects on forest nutrient cycles that are as yet poorly understood.

For these and other reasons, clear-cutting has been highly controversial, especially in the national forests. In fact, adverse public reaction to clear-cutting practices in eastern hardwood forests was a major factor leading to passage of the National Forest Management Act (NFMA) in 1976. [*See West Virginia Division of Izaak Walton League, Inc. v. Butz* (1975).] Despite Congress's attempt to address the issue in the NFMA, the controversy continues. In 1994, the Sierra Club published an influential photo essay entitled *Clearcut*, to which the American Forest and Paper Association responded with *Closer Look: An On-the-Ground Investigation of the Sierra Club's Book*, Clearcut. Today, the propriety of clear-cutting as a silvicultural technique attracts the most attention in old-growth forests and roadless areas in the West.

The NFMA provides that clear-cutting and "other cuts designed to revegetate an even-aged stand of timber will be used as a cutting method on National Forest System lands only where [certain conditions are met]." One condition is that clear-cutting must be determined to be "the optimum method" of harvesting. In addition, cuts must "shaped and blended" with the natural terrain, and harvesting must be carried out in a manner that protects soil, watershed, fish and wildlife, recreation, and aesthetics and will ensure the regeneration of the timber stand within five years. [16 U.S.C. § 1604(g)(3)(E)-(F)]

Conservation biologists and environmentalists blame clear-cutting for fragmenting wildlife habitat and leading to declines in regional biodiversity. They also question whether old-growth forests can ever be reestablished after a stand is clear-cut. Clear-cutting practices can also contribute to serious erosion problems, particularly in areas of steep slopes and naturally unstable soils coupled with sudden precipitation events. [*See National Wildlife Federation v. U.S. Forest Service* (1984).] In many parts of the West, forests regenerate slowly if at all after clear-cutting.

See also **Below-Cost Timber Sales; Biodiversity Conservation; National Forest Management Act of 1976; Old Growth; Roadless Area.**

CLINTON, WILLIAM JEFFERSON   Forty-second president of the United States, elected in November 1992 and reelected in 1996. Clinton was governor of Arkansas from 1979 to 1980 and 1983 to 1992. He served as Arkansas's attorney general from 1976 to 1978 and, prior to that, taught law at the University of Arkansas-Fayetteville. He ran unsuccessfully for Congress in 1974. Clinton received a B.S. degree in international affairs from Georgetown University and a law degree from Yale University in 1973. He also attended Oxford University in England on a Rhodes Scholarship.

The Clinton administration's record on conservation and the environment is spotty, and his relations with environmental groups have been stormy. His election in 1992 was greeted with great optimism, in large part simply because the 12 years of Presidents Reagan and Bush had been bleak ones for the environment and everyone expected more from a Democrat. By Clinton's second campaign in 1996, they were less sanguine. The League of Conservation Voters gave Clinton a C- for his first term. David Brower, founder of Friends of the Earth, a Sierra Club board member, and a long-time environmental activist, wrote in 1996 that Clinton had "done more to harm the environment and weaken environmental regulations in three years than Presidents Bush and Reagan did in 12 years." On the other hand, polls showed that the American public generally trusted Clinton to protect the environment.

In his first term, Clinton signed the salvage logging rider, which conservationists deplored, and he attempted to abolish the Council on Environmental Quality (CEQ). The CEQ is an executive agency established by the National Environmental Policy Act (NEPA) in 1969, charged to "formulate and recommend national policies to promote the improvement of the quality of the environment." CEQ's guidelines for implementing NEPA, including preparing environmental impact statements, are binding on all federal agencies. Although Clinton created the White House Office on Environmental Policy to replace the CEQ, intending this step to be the first toward creating a cabinet-level Department of the Environment, many were suspicious and critical. Ultimately, Clinton abandoned the plan.

Conversely, the Clinton administration deserves credit for several conservation efforts and accomplishments. First-term successes include the Northwest Forest Management Plan and strategy for protecting the northern spotted owl, which was the first cooperative ecosystem management effort (upheld by a federal court in 1994); reintroduction of wolves to Yellowstone National Park and central Idaho; passage of the California Desert Protection Act, which created 3 million acres of new national parks and wilderness; initiating a major effort to restore the Florida Everglades; and signing the international Convention on Biological Diversity. Clinton backed efforts to reform rangeland management, regulation of mining activities, and implementation of the Endangered Species Act of 1973 (including development of an administrative "no-surprises" policy for landowners who participate in habitat conservation plans). He also took strong stands on agency funding for environmental and conservation programs, and he threatened to veto such antienvironment measures as the so-called "takings" bills and proposals to transfer Bureau of Land Management lands to the states. His administration created the National Biological Service and convened an Interagency Working Group on Federal Wetlands Policy.

Far and away the major accomplishment of Clinton's second term has been his designation of the Grand Staircase-Escalante National Monument in Utah. He also has been negotiating a land exchange or buyout to prevent development of the New World Mine on Yellowstone National Park's northern border. Clinton has not yet been able to make good on promises to reform federal mining law or raise public land grazing fees.

In 1997, Clinton announced his American Heritage Rivers program (formalized by executive order in late 1997). This nonregulatory initiative is intended to "support communities' efforts to realize their goals of economic prosperity, a healthy environment, and historical and cultural preservation." Rivers were to be nominated by the end of August; the president pledged to designate ten rivers with significant economic, natural, and cultural values to the history and future of the United States. Communities along the rivers would receive federal recognition and assistance, including access to federal technical resources and assistance in obtaining funding and other resources. The Council on Environmental Quality will oversee the program.

Some western Republicans object to the American Heritage Rivers program; Idaho's Congresswoman Chenoweth announced that she would attempt to block any federal funding for it. She was quoted in *Public Lands News* as claiming that the administration was attempting to "usurp individual water rights, private property rights, and state sovereignty." No evidence for such intent can be found, however; as Clinton said, the program involves no federal mandates, regulations, or restrictions on property.

See also **Endangered Species Act of 1973; Grand Staircase-Escalante National Monument; Northern Spotted Owl; Salvage Logging.**

COASTAL ZONE MANAGEMENT ACT (CZMA)

Established federal policy for land use in coastal areas. Passed in 1972 and significantly amended by the Coastal Zone Act Reauthorization Amendments (CZARA) of 1990, the CZMA encourages states to establish their own management plans by authorizing federal financial aid and other assistance in implementing coastal programs. The act was prompted by Congress's recognition of the national interest in coastal zones; the myriad resources of coastal zones—"natural, commercial, recreational, ecological, industrial, and esthetic"; the "increasing and competing demands upon the lands and waters" of these areas; and the fact that "ecological, cultural, historic, and esthetic values in the coastal zone which are essential to the well-being of all citizens are being irretrievably damaged or lost." According to the act, in 1972 half the U.S. population lived in coastal areas. The coastal population was predicted to grow to 127 million by 2010, with population densities among the highest in the nation.

The CZMA is not a regulatory statute, like the Clean Water Act or Endangered Species Act of 1973, nor a federal land management statute, such as the National Forest Management Act of 1976. Rather, it establishes a federal-state cooperative scheme for developing policies, standards, and processes for dealing with significant land and water issues in the coastal zone. Its principal mechanisms are the coastal management plan (CMP), which coastal states are encouraged to adopt, and a requirement that all federal actions conducted within or affecting the coastal zone be "consistent" with any applicable CMP. All proposed federal activities that might affect the coastal zone must be reviewed for consistency; unless the state concurs with the consistency determination, no federal license or permit may be issued to the proposed activity. The CZMA also provides for financial and technical assistance to states in developing and implementing CMPs.

A CMP must meet certain minimum requirements in order to receive federal approval and qualify the state for federal financial and technical assistance. For instance, CMPs must identify permissible land uses within coastal zones and set priorities for those uses, designate areas of particular concern, identify the means available to the state for controlling land uses, and establish planning processes for providing public access to beaches and other high-value areas, preventing erosion, and siting energy facilities. The state must demonstrate that coastal land uses can be regulated through the establishment of standards, government review of development proposals, coordinated application of existing law, or other means. The act requires an opportunity for any interested party—federal and state agencies, local governments, port authorities, individuals, and organizations—to participate in developing and implementing CMPs. Regulations guiding the development and implementation of CMPs have been promulgated by the National Oceanic and Atmospheric Administration (NOAA), within the U.S. Department of Commerce.

As a result of CZARA, coastal states with approved plans are also required to submit a coastal nonpoint-source pollution control program for approval by NOAA. Failure to submit an approvable program will cause a state to lose grants for which it would otherwise be eligible under the CZMA and the Clean Water Act. By 1994, all but 6 of the 35 coastal states were participating in the CZMA program.

See also **Clean Water Act Section 404; Wetland.**

COGGINS, GEORGE CAMERON   Professor of law at the University of Kansas School of Law. Professor Coggins is the principal author of the most comprehensive treatise on public land law, *Public Natural Resources Law*. A prolific writer, he is also coauthor of the number one public land law casebook used by law schools in the United States (*Federal Public Land and Resources Law*), and has written numerous articles on public land law topics, notably grazing management, multiple use, and watershed. He contends that public land grazing law is outdated and improperly subsidizes federal grazing permittees. He has also argued that multiple-use land management requirements, while vague, could be enforced more strictly by the courts to curtail arbitrary or biased agency management policies. A colorful public speaker, Coggins is not known for mincing words; he frequently takes politically unpopular positions on public land management issues.

See also **Multiple Use.**

COMMERCE CLAUSE   The Commerce Clause of the U.S. Constitution (article I, section 8, clause 3) provides that "Congress shall have Power...to regulate Commerce...among the several states." Federal environmental regulatory power derives principally from the Commerce Clause; federal authority to regulate natural resources and public lands derives from the Property Clause and treaty power, as well as the Commerce Clause.

The power conferred by the Commerce Clause is extremely broad. Indeed, until the U.S. Supreme Court decided *United States v. Lopez* (1995), it was considered by some observers practically limitless. The *Lopez* Court struck down a federal law prohibiting the possession of a gun in a school zone as having no connection with interstate commerce and therefore exceeding federal authority. Although *Lopez* reveals that the clause does have limits, and that the Court is capable of defining them, most observers expect the opinion to have little if any effect on federal environmental legislation.

The flip side to federal power under the Commerce Clause is a limitation on state authority. From the clause's express terms authorizing Congress to regulate interstate commerce, the courts have implied a "dormant Commerce Clause," which prohibits state action adversely affecting interstate commerce, even *in the absence of* congressional regulation. Exceptions to the dormant Commerce Clause prohibition, however, allow states to enact health and safety regulations even if the rules incidentally burden commerce, regulate commerce with Congress's express approval, and regulate an area of commerce in which the state is a "market participant."

Courts will strike down a state regulation if it actually discriminates against interstate commerce, that is, if a state law favors in-state over out-of-state economic interests, *unless* the state can show that it has a legitimate reason for the regulation and that no nondiscriminatory alternatives exist that would achieve the state's purpose. A state law is also considered discriminatory if its practical effect is to burden interstate commerce; even a nondiscriminatory state law may be invalid if its burden on commerce is excessive in relation to the state purpose behind the law. In such cases, the court balances the interests of the state against the interests of the person challenging the law.

See also *Clajon Production Corporation v. Petera* (1995); *Hughes v. Oklahoma* (1979); **Property Clause.**

COMMON LAW   Judge-made law, in contrast to law contained in statutes, regulations, and ordinances. The United States's common law derives from English law, imported to this country with the colonists in the 1600s and 1700s. It continually evolves, though generally slowly. American courts apply, and make, common law every time they hear and decide a case and then publish their opinion.

CONSERVATION EASEMENT A voluntary land conservation tool that consists of a legal agreement between a landowner and a land trust, other organization, or government agency. A conservation easement permanently protects the land's conservation values while allowing the owner to retain ownership and some use of the land. For instance, a ranch owner might retain the right to live on and operate his land as a ranch, but donate or sell (often at a discounted price) the right to subdivide or otherwise develop it. In other cases, an easement might prohibit all development or commercial use of the property. Selling or donating a conservation easement reduces the appraised value of land, thus reducing the owner's property, gift, and/or estate taxes. Conservation easements can enable a landowner's heirs to avoid a federal estate tax burden (as high as 55 percent) that would otherwise require them to sell the land to pay the tax. Conservation easements are recorded in a county's land records. When land burdened by a conservation easement is sold, it remains subject, in perpetuity, to the easement's limitations on development or use.

Conservation easements qualify as tax-deductible charitable contributions for federal income tax purposes if donated to tax-exempt organizations and if they serve significant conservation purposes. The federal Internal Revenue Service requires an appraisal and inventory of the property to claim the deduction. The value of a conservation easement donation is the difference between the pre- and post-donation appraised values of the property. The landowner may deduct the donation from his annual income, up to 30 percent of his adjusted gross income per year for six years, up to the full dollar value of the donation. Where the amount of the donation would exceed the allowable tax deduction (as in the case of a rancher with a relatively low income), the owner may sell the land to a wealthy "conservation buyer," who then donates the conservation easement to a land trust. The new, wealthier owner can usually take full advantage of the tax deduction and often retains the prior owner to stay on and manage the land. In other cases, the conservation buyer may acquire a parcel of the overall tract in exchange for purchasing the development rights on the whole tract.

Conservation easements are tailored to the particular needs and desires of the parties, and to the peculiarities of the land. The easement might forbid all development or only certain kinds; it may be designed to protect seasonal wetland habitat or the habitat of a threatened or endangered resident species. Conservation easements are an increasingly popular land protection and tax-avoidance mechanism. One of the best-known conservation easements covers 107,000 acres of Ted Turner's southwestern Montana ranch and is held by The Nature Conservancy. The Rocky Mountain Elk Foundation is another organization whose conservation mission relies heavily on conservation easements. Landowners interested in the benefits of conservation easements should seek advice from a lawyer, accountant, and tax adviser. Land trusts often offer such advice, and numerous publications are available. [*See* Bibliography.]

A 1997 federal budget law contained estate tax relief for persons who dedicate conservation easements on certain lands in proximity to metropolitan areas, national parks or wilderness areas, or urban forests.

See also **Land Trust; The Nature Conservancy; Rocky Mountain Elk Foundation.**

CONSERVATION RESERVE PROGRAM (CRP)   Farm Bill program that, in essence, pays farmers not to cultivate marginal lands. Established by the 1985 Food Security Act, the CRP's purposes are to "reduce water and wind erosion, protect our long term capability to produce food and fiber, reduce sedimentation, improve water quality, create better habitat for fish and wildlife through improved food and cover [and] curb production of surplus commodities." Under the CRP, the federal government, acting through the U.S. Department of Agriculture's Farm Service Agency, enters into contracts with landowners to remove highly erodible lands from agricultural use for 10-15 years in exchange for rental payments. Lands are identified on the basis of five factors: surface water, groundwater, air, soil, and wildlife habitat. Initially, Congress determined by the appropriations process how many of acres of land could be admitted into the program. Between 1986 and 1992, 36.4 million acres were enrolled at a cost to the government of $20 billion; erosion was reduced on enrolled lands from 21 tons per acre per year to less than 2 tons. The 1996 Farm Bill extended the CRP through 2002, and converted it and other conservation programs to mandatory spending programs, thus eliminating the need for annual appropriations. Initial enrollments began expiring in 1996; all prior contract holders must compete with new applicants for enrollment in the program.

The CRP was amended in 1990 to include a Wetlands Reserve Program (WRP), one of two major federal programs for agricultural wetland protection; the other is Swampbuster. The WRP authorizes the government to negotiate with farmers (owners, operators, or lessees) for restoration of wetlands converted to agricultural use before 1985. In this way, the WRP supplements the provisions of the Swampbuster program, which regulates only those wetlands converted *after* 1985. The parties may negotiate permanent or 30-year easements in exchange for government payments based on the land's reduction in value, or enter into ten-year cost-share arrangements under which the government pays 50 to 75 percent of the cost of restoration. The private party, in conjunction with the FSA, prepares and submits a restoration plan for the area. No agricultural commodity may be produced on enrolled lands, nor may they be grazed or otherwise harvested.

To be eligible for the WRP, converted wetlands must have been planted for at least two years during the period 1992-1996 and under cultivation at the time of enrollment. All such areas are potentially eligible, but by regulation the government has identified "priority wetland areas," such as important estuaries or mountain wetlands, and attempts to target the "more environmentally sensitive acreage" for participation. CRP-enrolled lands can be transferred to the WRP program if they qualify as wetlands. Until 1996, enrollment in the WRP was limited to just under 1 million acres; farmer interest consistently exceeded available funding. The 1996 amendment, which made the CRP a mandatory spending program, should alleviate this problem.

The Worldwatch Institute called the CRP a model of "an active approach to ending abuse of agricultural resources." The program has been criticized, however. A 1995 *Wall Street Journal* editorial protested the practice of paying American farmers not to farm, pointing to the 36 million acres idled under CRP, 22 million of which the writer claimed could be farmed safely using conservation tillage practices. Similarly, two Government Accounting Office (GAO) reports questioned the cost effectiveness of the program, noted that results are only temporary, and concluded that the same results might be achieved while removing much less land from production if farmers made greater use of buffer strips along waterways. The GAO conceded, however, that the whole-field (as opposed to a buffer-strip-only) approach has wildlife habitat benefits. Chiefly for this latter reason, most conservation organizations support the CRP program. Farmers and others question why more lands cannot be enrolled, and why enrollment criteria and rates seem to vary from state to state.

See also **Clean Water Act Section 404; Conservation Easement; Farm Bills; Swampbuster; Wetland.**

CONTINGENT VALUATION   An economic tool for assessing the passive-use or nonuse values of species, resources, or ecosystems. The method involves the use of survey techniques to evaluate a population's willingness to pay to preserve a species or a landscape. It can form the basis for assigning value to something that has no market value, that is, something not bought, sold, or traded. For instance, the researcher or survey technician might ask whether a person would vote for a property tax increase of $20 per year if the additional revenues would be used to reduce by 30 percent the likelihood that some endangered species would become extinct over the next 50 years. Contingent valuation allows researchers to estimate "option," "existence," and "bequest" values by asking questions such as "How much is it worth to you to protect the Grand Canyon, even if you might never visit it?" or, "How much would you pay to help preserve wilderness areas for future generations?"

Contingent valuation has been approved for use by both the Department of the Interior's U.S. Fish and Wildlife Service and the Department of Commerce's National Oceanic and Atmospheric Administration. Each agency incorporates the methodology in its regulations for assessing natural resource damages due to oil or hazardous substance spills. These rules were issued to implement provisions of the federal Clean Water Act; Oil Pollution Act; and the Comprehensive Environmental Response, Compensation, and Liability Act (CERCLA, or Superfund). In fact, contingent valuation measures were used to assess the damage to beaches, marine life, and other natural resources caused when the *Exxon Valdez* oil tanker ran aground and spilled 11 million gallons of crude oil into Alaska's Prince William Sound in 1989.

The methodology has been widely criticized, however. Anthony Scott, an economist writing 30 years ago about the use of the technique to value wildlife resources, said: "Ask a hypothetical question, get a hypothetical answer." Contingent valuation is hypothetical in that it asks people to put a monetary value on something they have never bought nor have any direct experience in assigning value to. Furthermore, they do not expect to be asked to pay the money, only to answer the question. Thus, they might answer several willingness-to-pay questions without considering the potential cumulative impact on their pocketbooks if, later, they were indeed asked to "ante up."

Some method is needed to place a value on nonmarket goods, though. In referring to the value of land, Aldo Leopold, advocate and author of

"The Land Ethic" wrote: "By value, I of course mean something far broader than economic value; I mean value in the philosophical sense." Some modern conservation biologists and environmental ethicists argue that economic measures are inappropriate for valuing biological resources, which have inherent value—moral, ethical, aesthetic—far beyond their worth in monetary terms. Nevertheless, a group of scientists recently assigned a monetary value to 17 of nature's "ecosystem services," such as water purification, food production, and carbon dioxide regulation. The bottom line? Their value totaled $33 *trillion* annually, nearly double the world's gross economic product.

See also **Biodiversity Conservation; Natural Resources Damages.**

CORPS OF ENGINEERS (CORPS)   A federal agency within the Department of the Army, whose responsibilities include regulating activities in wetlands; providing engineering, management, and technical support to the Department of Defense and other agencies; and planning, building, and administering projects for flood control, navigation, water supply, hydropower, environmental restoration, and wildlife habitat and recreation. The Corps employs 37,000 persons and is organized into 11 divisions, 40 districts, and hundreds of area and project offices in the United States and abroad.

The Corps is responsible for administering the Rivers and Harbors Act (RHA) of 1899, whose chief purpose was maintenance of navigable waterways. However, during the 1960s the Corps began using the RHA to address water pollution. Specifically, the agency employed section 10, which prohibits the creation of "obstructions" in navigable waters by the dumping of fill material, and section 13, which prohibits the dumping of refuse into navigable waters. These regulatory efforts helped lead to the passage in 1972 of the Federal Water Pollution Control Act Amendments, including section 404. This act, as amended, is known today simply as the Clean Water Act (CWA).

Today, enforcing CWA section 404 is one of the Corps's chief functions in the area of natural resources conservation. The Corps issues regulations to implement section 404, identifies areas to classify as wetlands, reviews applications for section 404 permits for proposed dredge-and-fill activities in wetlands or other "waters of the United States," denies permits found not to be in the public interest, and grants permits for other projects, often with conditions, such as for mitigating project impacts. Corps permit decisions are subject to review by the Environmental Protection Agency, which can veto any permit it decides "will have an unacceptable adverse effect on municipal water supplies, shellfish beds and fishery areas..., wildlife, or recreational areas."

The Corps manages millions of acres of federal land. Hundreds of Corps reservoirs nationwide, built for flood control, navigation, or water supply purposes, are also administered, along with the surrounding lands, for public uses, such as recreation and wildlife habitat conservation. According to the agency, it provides over 30 percent of the recreational opportunities on federal lands and is the biggest provider of water-based recreation. Corps reservoir projects fulfill a need for local recreational areas and facilities, especially in the East, Midwest, and South, where public lands are less abundant.

See also **Clean Water Act Section 404; Dredge and Fill; Environmental Protection Agency; Navigable Waters; Public Interest Review; Wetland.**

COUNTY SUPREMACY MOVEMENT   A self-described "populist" effort, emphasizing local sovereignty and personal property rights, and closely identified with the Sagebrush Rebellion. Loosely connected and based largely in the West, the County Supremacy Movement is rooted in the West's own brand of rebellious independence and fueled by anger and frustration at perceived federal interventions in daily life. The origins of the movement can be traced to acts such as those of a county commissioner in Nye County, Nevada, who bulldozed open a closed U.S. Forest Service (USFS) road to the cheers of armed supporters, driving a USFS official off the road and openly defying federal control of lands in the West. (The perpetrator's photograph subsequently appeared on the cover of *Time* magazine.) The action was ostensibly authorized by the Nye County Resolutions, a set of local ordinances asserting that the federal government does not own the public lands or traditional roads within the state of Nevada.

The National Federal Lands Conference, a Bountiful, Utah, group dedicated to the county movement, estimates that over 300 counties across the nation have asserted some degree of local sovereignty. Proponents of county supremacy assert local authority over public lands within their borders under the equal footing doctrine. The movement also has attempted to thwart federal control through "custom and culture" ordinances, mandating that federal land management decisions be made only in consultation with local officials and in accordance with local custom and culture and "wise use" ordinances. The Catron County, New Mexico, custom and culture ordinance, passed in 1991, has been marketed to counties nationally. Wise-use proponents have also employed procedural warfare, attempting to tie up federal officials in their own complex regulations.

The movement relies heavily on aggressive antigovernment rhetoric and direct confrontation, like the face-off in Nye County. In an incident in Arizona, Graham County supervisors used a bulldozer to clear a path across the then-dry Gila River. In Idaho, the Owyhee County sheriff revoked the local law enforcement authority of federal agents operating in his county. Throughout the West, incidents of antifederal violence, including the bombings of national forest campground facilities, a Nevada Forest Service official's home, and Bureau of Land Management and Forest Service offices, have been linked to the movement. In Elko County, Nevada, a grand jury was formed to investigate and prosecute federal land managers essentially for doing their jobs! A federal court held the procedure unconstitutional and quashed the first and only subpoena issued—to a Forest Service employee accused of no crime.

Critics charge that the County Supremacy Movement is simply a surrogate for consumptive users, like mining and logging companies and livestock grazers, who are out to divest the public of its lands. The U.S. government continues to assert federal supremacy over western public lands, and was successful in challenging the Nye County Resolutions in federal court in Nevada. In *United States v. Nye County* (1996), the court rejected the county's "equal footing" argument (as had another federal judge in Nevada in a case brought by a grazing permittee against the USFS), and it affirmed the federal government's ownership of, and authority to administer, the public lands in Nevada. The court did not rule on all issues in the case, however, and Nye County and the federal government subsequently negotiated an agreement to resolve the remaining issues. The agreement affirms federal authority but also recognizes the "concurrent jurisdiction" of state and local governments in such functions as "law enforcement and the protection of public health and safety in accordance with applicable federal law and regulations." This language essentially states existing law. The agreement also outlines procedures for settling disputes over the use of roads that transit public lands. A similar memorandum of understanding has been negotiated by the federal government and Catron County.

In addition to the decision in *Nye County,* the United States has won several affirmative civil or criminal suits in actions involving grazing violations, trespass, or illegal bulldozing. The government also has successfully defended at least half a dozen lawsuits brought by ranchers, miners, or counties challenging U.S. authority over the public lands. [Coppelman 1997]

See also *California Coastal Commission v. Granite Rock Co.* (1987); **Equal Footing Doctrine; Sagebrush Rebellion; Wise Use Movement.**

CRAIG, LARRY E.   Republican senator from Idaho. Craig sits on two important resource committees: Agriculture, Nutrition, and Forestry and Energy and Natural Resources. He also chairs the Republican Committee on Committees, which makes Republican committee assignments. Craig is an advocate for multiple-use and wise-use groups on issues ranging from grazing reform to salvage logging to Endangered Species Act reauthorization. In 1996 and 1997 he held several hearings on a draft "forest health" bill that not only addressed salvage logging issues but proposed to substantially rewrite many provisions of the National Forest Management Act. The draft bill aroused concerns among various groups, particularly environmentalists, and as of this writing had not been finalized or introduced.

See also **Senate Agriculture, Nutrition, and Forestry Committee; Senate Energy and Natural Resources Committee.**

CRITICAL HABITAT   Habitat that is formally designated, pursuant to section 4 of the Endangered Species Act of 1973 (ESA), as "critical" to a listed species' survival. The ESA defines critical habitat as (1) "specific areas within the geographical area occupied by the species, at the time it is listed," that contain "physical or biological features essential to the conservation of the species and which may require special management," and (2) "areas outside the geographical area occupied by the species," if the secretary of interior determines "that such areas are essential for the conservation of the species." One federal court described critical habitat as "the minimum amount of habitat needed to avoid short-term jeopardy or habitat in need of immediate intervention."

The statute directs the Secretary of Interior to designate critical habitat, "to the maximum extent prudent and determinable," concurrently with his decision to list any species of animal or plant as threatened or endangered. The secretary has delegated this responsibility to an Interior agency, the U.S. Fish and Wildlife Service (USFWS). When the USFWS proposes to designate habitat for a species, the secretary invites public comment. The final habitat designation is published as a federal regulation.

In reality, however, critical habitat is seldom designated at the time of the listing decision. Indeed, for many species critical habitat is *never* designated—even though one court has held that Interior can "properly defer" this responsibility only under "limited circumstances." As of 1991, critical habitat had *not* been designated for 546 of 651 listed species. In the well-known case of the northern spotted owl, the Interior secretary had to be sued twice—first, to force him to list the owl and, three years later, to designate critical habitat for this threatened bird. The law provides for interested citizens to petition the secretary both to list a species and to designate critical habitat (or revise such designations) for it.

The reasons for not designating habitat at the time of the listing, or not at all, may be several—notably, lack of sufficient information about a species' distribution and habitat needs, political considerations, and/or economic concerns. Although critical habitat designations, like listing decisions, are to be based on "the best scientific data available," the secretary is also instructed to consider "the economic impact, and any other relevant impact," of designating any area as critical habitat. Section 4 provides that the "secretary may exclude any area from critical habitat if he determines that the benefits of such exclusion outweigh the benefits" of including the area, "unless he determines, based on the best scientific and commercial data available, that the failure to designate such area as critical habitat will result in the extinction of the species." Thus, for example, the Interior secretary eventually designated nearly 7 million acres as spotted owl critical habitat, even though the scientific data supported designation of a considerably larger area. In other cases, critical habitat designations may cover as little as a few acres.

Federal courts have split on whether the decision to designate critical habitat is a major federal action subject to the environmental impact statement (EIS) requirement of the National Environmental Policy Act (NEPA). The Ninth Circuit held that it is not, while the Tenth Circuit more recently issued an opposite ruling. [Compare *Douglas County v. Babbitt* (1995) and *Catron County Board of County Commissioners v. U.S. Fish and Wildlife Service* (1996).] The Tenth Circuit also held that the Catron County commissioners, whose interest was in the potential *economic* impacts of habitat designation, had standing to challenge the agency's decision not to prepare an EIS. This ruling is consistent with a later U.S. Supreme Court ruling, *Bennett v. Spear* (1997).

See also *Bennett v. Spear* (1997); Endangered Species; Endangered Species Act of 1973; Habitat Conservation Plan; Northern Spotted Owl; Threatened Species; U.S. Fish and Wildlife Service.

CUMULATIVE IMPACT In general, the additive effect on the environment or some element of the environment of multiple stressors, disturbances, or agents, or of any individual stressor over time. A deer population may be impacted by the cumulative effects of a severe winter, overhunting, and a new highway that fragments its habitat. Alternatively, the same species might not be affected by one year of overhunting, but two or more years could take a toll.

The National Environmental Policy Act, as implemented by the Council on Environmental Quality's regulations, requires federal agencies to evaluate the cumulative impacts of their proposed actions. Consequently, all environmental assessments and environmental impact statements (EISs) contain discussions of the cumulative impacts of proposed projects. Agencies must consider the impacts of all existing and reasonably foreseeable developments and disturbances on lands under their control as well as on surrounding lands, whether public or private.

Cumulative impact assessment also plays a role in permitting decisions by the U.S. Army Corps of Engineers under Clean Water Act section 404. Before the Corps may issue a permit to dredge or fill a wetland, it must consider the cumulative impacts of the proposed project along with other existing and foreseeable impacts to water quality, wildlife habitat, etc.

The assessment of cumulative impacts becomes especially problematic in the case of staged developments (those that take place over a long period of time and/or a large area) or when the eventual extent of development, and hence the impacts thereof, may be uncertain. An illustrative example is the proposed natural gas development on lands managed by the Bureau of Land Management (BLM) in the Green River Basin of southwestern Wyoming and northwestern Colorado. The BLM proposes to permit, over a period of 15 to 20 years, exploration and development of up to 11,000 gas wells in the region. The agency proposes to analyze the project in parts, or segments, as the field is developed, but environmentalists claim this approach will underestimate the cumulative impacts—both spatially and temporally—of the project as a whole.

See also **Environmental Impact Statement; National Environmental Policy Act.**

DEFENDERS OF WILDLIFE (DOW) Focuses on wildlife and wildlife habitat issues, endangered species, and biodiversity conservation. DOW was founded in 1947 and has 118,000 members and supporters. One of the principal proponents of reintroducing wolves to the Greater Yellowstone Ecosystem, DOW established and maintains a fund for compensating ranchers who lose livestock to wolf predation. It publishes a magazine (*Defenders*), a newsletter, and various conservation education materials. In addition to its education efforts, DOW employs lobbying, litigation, and grassroots organizing to further its mission. One of its more important recent cases, *Lujan v. Defenders of Wildlife* (1992), was seen as a further setback for conservation interests attempting to establish standing to challenge federal agency actions.

See also **Biodiversity Conservation; Endangered Species;** *Lujan v. Defenders of Wildlife* **(1992); Wolf Reintroduction.**

DEFERENCE The respect accorded the decisions of administrative agencies by reviewing courts. Judicial deference is especially appropriate and typically given when the decision being reviewed has been made by an agency acting within the area of its special expertise. Courts are generally more deferential to an agency's factual determinations than to its legal interpretations. For instance, in a lawsuit challenging a U.S. Forest Service decision to harvest a certain amount of timber by clearcutting it, the court will look to see whether the agency followed proper procedures and has data to support its decision, but it is unlikely to second-guess the agency's interpretation of the data, i.e., its expert opinion regarding the amount of timber available or the appropriate harvest methods. Although some courts take a harder look than others, in general, judicial deference makes it difficult to prevail in lawsuits challenging the decisions of administrative agencies.

See also **Administrative Procedure Act;** *Chevron U.S.A., Inc. v. Natural Resources Defense Council* **(1984).**

DEPARTMENT OF AGRICULTURE   Federal cabinet-level department that houses the U.S. Forest Service, Natural Resources Conservation Service, Animal and Plant Health Inspection Service, and several other agencies with natural resources conservation, public land management, and/or farm services functions. The agency is directed by the secretary of agriculture, currently Dan Glickman. The secretary is named in many federal statutes as being responsible for administering department programs, although the authority is usually delegated to the heads and line officers of divisions or bureaus within the department. But for the efforts of Gifford Pinchot, first chief of the Forest Service in the early 1900s, the Forest Service probably would be located within the U.S. Department of the Interior rather than in Agriculture. Recommendations to combine the two departments, or at least their conservation functions, into one Department of Natural Resources have frequently been made and dismissed.

See also **Animal Damage Control; Department of the Interior; Natural Resources Conservation Service; U.S. Forest Service.**

DEPARTMENT OF THE INTERIOR   One of the original federal cabinet-level departments, created by an act of Congress in 1849. Interior houses nine divisions or bureaus with natural resources and/or public lands functions, notably the Bureau of Land Management (BLM), National Park Service (NPS), U.S. Fish and Wildlife Service (USFWS), Bureau of Reclamation, and National Marine Fisheries Service (NMFS). The department is directed by the secretary of the interior, a position currently held by Bruce Babbitt. The secretary is named in many federal statutes as being responsible for administering department programs, although the authority is usually delegated to the heads and line officers of divisions or bureaus within the department.

Interior manages more public land than any other department—500 million acres of federal lands (half of which are in Alaska), 10,000 miles of wild and scenic rivers, and 60 million acres of designated wilderness areas; it is also responsible for marine resources and the Outer Continental Shelf. Interior employs 75,000 full-time career civil servants and has an overall budget of about $7.25 billion. Its legal division, the Solicitor's Office, is run by John Leshy and has 260 lawyers in Washington, D.C., and 18 regional or field offices. This legal office is separate from the Interior Board of Land Appeals.

Over the years numerous proposals have been made to combine all or parts of Interior and the U.S. Department of Agriculture (USDA) into one Department of Natural Resources, but such plans have never progressed much beyond the drawing board. One of the most recent, put forward in 1997 by a conservative think tank, the Heritage Foundation, recommended combination of the BLM, USFWS, NPS, NMFS, and USDA's Forest Service into one Bureau of Natural Resources. The motivation for the plan is to balance the federal budget; to that end, most lands would be sold to private interests or transferred to the states. The Congressional Research Service (CRS) has examined many merger proposals and concluded that, after implementation costs, some cost savings might result, but numerous problems or disadvantages are likely, including disruption of current programs, impaired employee morale, and loss of competition (which actually may be enhancing the agencies' current effectiveness). The CRS further noted that a merger would be effective only if the agencies' statutory mandates were also changed—a decidedly unlikely and cumbersome undertaking.

See also **Bureau of Land Management; Bureau of Reclamation; Department of Agriculture; Interior Board of Land Appeals; National Park Service; U.S. Fish and Wildlife Service.**

DESERTIFICATION   Literally, the process by which land becomes more desertlike, or by which deserts become drier and less productive. Desertification is usually caused by a combination of factors, principally climate (drought) and grazing or cultivation. Misuse or overuse of arid and semiarid lands, especially in combination with climatic patterns, can result in erosion and soil loss, changes in vegetation, and alteration of the normal processes of nutrient and moisture cycling. The result of these changes is a land less productive of vegetation (particularly native species) and wildlife, more susceptible to erosion, and less capable of retaining moisture. According to a 1981 Council on Environmental Quality report, about 225 million acres, or 350,000 square miles, within the United States (chiefly in southern California, southern Nevada, Arizona, New Mexico, and western Texas) have experienced severe or very severe desertification; the area *threatened* with desertification is almost twice as large. Desertified areas extend from southern Canada well into Mexico.

Desertification can be traced in many instances to ill-advised federal land policies in the 1800s and early 1900s, which led to the plowing up of areas unsuited to cultivation, and to the ongoing practice of allowing livestock grazing (particularly yearlong) on arid and semiarid public lands not suitable for such use. Several laws could be used to address these problems—the Clean Water Act, Public Rangelands Improvement Act, Federal Land Policy and Management Act, and various state environmental and land-use statutes—but most have few teeth or are seldom enforced against the land uses to blame for the problems.) Moreover, many lands are in need of restoration, an expensive task that will require coordination among all landowners and managers—federal, state, and private.

See also **Federal Land Policy and Management Act; Public Rangelands Improvement Act; Range Reform.**

DINGELL-JOHNSON ACT (D-J ACT)   Common name of the Federal Aid in Sport Fisheries Act, passed in 1950. It and its counterpart, the Pittman-Robinson Act (P-R Act), are user-funded statutes designed to raise revenue to support wildlife conservation. The D-J Act imposes an excise tax on fishing equipment, thus indirectly taxing anglers. Revenues generated are apportioned among the states based on their area and the number of fishing license holders. Like the P-R Act, this statute is concerned with game and sport species, and is administered by the U.S. Fish and Wildlife Service.

In some circumstances, funds collected under the D-J and P-R acts may be merged to fund acquisition and development of aquatic habitats. Costs are shared in proportion to the expected benefits to fish and wildlife, respectively.

See also **Pittman-Robinson Act; U.S. Fish and Wildlife Service.**

DOMBECK, MICHAEL   Chief of the U.S. Forest Service (USFS), appointed by President Bill Clinton in 1997 to replace retiring chief and career USFS employee Jack Ward Thomas. Dombeck, a former USFS employee himself, was serving as acting director of the federal Bureau of Land Management (BLM) at the time of his appointment.

Press reports described Dombeck's first priority as chief as continuing the USFS "tradition of working closely with local communities to restore and maintain productive, healthy, and diverse ecological systems." During his first day on the job, Dombeck told USFS employees that timber harvesting was no longer to be the dominant use of national forests and that field officers would be held accountable for improvements in "streamside condition and health, water quality, watershed health, noxious weed management, and endangered species habitat management and protection." When he was acting director of BLM, a post he held for almost three years, Dombeck was noted for promoting a collaborative management style within the agency and for his leadership. Environmental groups generally favored his appointment, noting his balance and temperament as well as his training as a fishery biologist. Dombeck's relations with conservative western Republicans while at BLM, however, were often tense. That he was never nominated to the position of BLM director reflected the widely held view that he could not have survived the Senate confirmation process. (Appointment of the USFS chief is not subject to the advice and consent of the Senate, although a bill was introduced in the House in 1997 that would require Senate approval.)

Dombeck has a Ph.D. in fisheries biology. He served 12 years with the Forest Service, including as manager of the agency's fisheries program. In 1989 he moved from that post to a job with BLM as science adviser. He was appointed acting BLM director in early 1994.

See also **Bureau of Land Management.**

DOMENICI, PETE V.   Republican senator from New Mexico, who sits on the Senate Appropriations and Energy and Natural Resources committees. Domenici generally favors commodity development on public lands. He has been a staunch supporter of the western livestock industry, sponsoring major bills in recent years designed to reform public land grazing regulation.

See also **Range Reform; Senate Appropriations Committee; Senate Energy and Natural Resources Committee.**

DOMINANT USE   A variation of the federal multiple-use policy, in which one land or resource use, or a limited number of uses, is emphasized in a particular area. Dominant use is not a legal term and is nowhere found in statutes or regulations; however, a dominant-use approach was recommended by the Public Land Law Review Commission in 1970, and it is probably an acceptable application of the current broad and rather vague multiple-use principles in federal law, if not the prevailing land-use policy. An example of dominant use is the management of

productive timberlands principally for wood products, and only second-
arily for compatible uses, such as recreation and wildlife. Many groups—
environmentalists, Wise Use, and others—variously argue for something
like dominant-use management of certain public lands or, alternatively,
criticize the federal land management agencies for adhering to dominant-
use principles, rather than true multiple-use.

See also **Federal Land Policy and Management Act; Multiple Use;
Multiple-Use, Sustained-Yield Act of 1960; National Forest Management
Act of 1976.**

DREDGE AND FILL   Dredging a water body or wetland entails digging up and removing or repositioning sediment or other
bottom or bank material. Filling a water body or wetland entails raising
the bottom elevation with fill material, often dredged from the same water
body, so as to render the area dry. Draining a wetland and depositing solid
material into it to raise the level of the bottom is also considered a dredge-
and-fill activity. Because of the potential for damage to or destruction of
wetland and aquatic ecosystems, these activities are lawful only if permitted or exempted under Clean Water Act section 404, which regulates dredging and filling activities.

Dredging activities were originally regulated by the U.S. Army Corps of
Engineers (Corps) under the Rivers and Harbors Act (RHA) of 1899 to promote navigation. Since the passage of the Federal Water Pollution Control
Act Amendments of 1972, specifically section 404, the Corps has had primary regulatory authority over dredging and filling of "waters of the United
States" for purposes of maintaining water quality. The 1972 act, as amended,
is known today simply as the Clean Water Act (CWA).

Most dredge-and-fill activities require a 404 permit because they involve
the discharge of a "pollutant" from a "point source," and thus are regulated under the CWA unless specifically excepted. The act defines "pollutant" to include dredged spoil, rock, and sand—all classic fill materials—as
well as such things as sewage sludge, radioactive materials, heat, and industrial waste.

The definition of dredge-and-fill activities is a functional one. A discharge
is regulated as "filling" if: (1) a principal or primary purpose of the discharge is to replace a portion of the water with dry land or to raise the
bottom elevation; (2) the discharge results from activities, such as road construction, where the material to be discharged is generally identified with

construction-type activities; (3) a principal effect of the discharge is physical loss or physical modification of the water or wetland, including smothering of aquatic life or habitat; or (4) the discharge is of a type normally associated with sanitary landfill discharges.

Although it seems counterintuitive, if draining or dredging wetlands is accomplished without causing any discharge, it is exempted from 404 regulation. However, from 1993 until 1997 the Corps required a 404 permit for any excavation activity that resulted in "incidental fallback" of dredged material to water or a wetland. Known as the Tulloch rule, this requirement was recently rejected by a federal district court as exceeding the scope of the agency's authority under the CWA. [*See American Mining Congress v. U.S. Army Corps of Engineers* (1997).] The court reasoned that no dredging could be accomplished without some incidental fallback; hence, the Corps's rule essentially wrote out of the statute other permit prerequisites, including a "discharge." In June 1997, a federal appeals court stayed the ruling, pending an appeal by the federal government; a decision is expected in 1998. As a result, the Corps will continue to regulate incidental fallback, but will not pursue enforcement actions against excavation activities conducted during the first half of 1997.

See also **Clean Water Act Section 404; Wetland.**

DUCK STAMP   Common name for the fee and stamp required by the Migratory Bird Hunting Stamp Act of 1934, the first federal statute to establish a fund to be used exclusively for wildlife conservation. The act requires waterfowl hunters to purchase a duck stamp in addition to state licenses. The Duck Stamp Act is one of three complementary user-funded programs administered by the U.S. Fish and Wildlife Service; the other two—the Pittman-Robinson and Dingell-Johnson Acts—impose excise taxes on hunting and fishing equipment, the revenues from which are used for habitat conservation and management. The duck stamp fee has raised over $400 million, a significant portion of which has gone toward preserving 4 million acres of waterfowl habitat.

See also **Dingell-Johnson Act; Pittman-Robinson Act; U.S. Fish and Wildlife Service.**

EARTHJUSTICE LEGAL DEFENSE FUND
See **Sierra Club Legal Defense Fund, Inc.**

ECOSYSTEM MANAGEMENT
No consensus exists concerning the best definition of ecosystem management, but R. Edward Grumbine's definition incorporates the chief elements of most: "Ecosystem management integrates scientific knowledge of ecological relationships within a complex sociopolitical and value framework toward the goal of protecting native ecosystem integrity over the long term." [Grumbine 1994]

Growing Interest in Ecosystem Management

The notion of ecosystem management is becoming increasingly popular in the lexicon of managers, activists, and law scholars. Ecosystem-based approaches to management (EBAM) are being proposed and implemented by land management agencies, such as the federal Bureau of Land Management (BLM), U.S. Forest Service (USFS), and U.S. Fish and Wildlife Service; state forestry departments; owners of private timber holdings, such as Weyerhauser and Potlatch; large ranches, such as the Deseret Ranch in northeastern Utah and southwestern Wyoming; and conservation organizations, notably The Nature Conservancy.

Former Forest Service chief Dale Robertson issued a directive in June 1992 advocating ecosystem management on the national forests. The Forest Service's principles for achieving ecosystem management were set forth in a 1994 U.S. Department of Agriculture (USDA) publication, *Ethics and Course to the Future.* Ecosystem management principles have been applied to the northern spotted owl management situation in the Pacific Northwest and will be employed in the next round of forest plans. A 1997 appropriations bill passed by Congress, however, forbids the USFS from implementing "ecoregional planning exercises, such as the Interior

Columbia Basin Study, without prior Congressional approval." [*Public Lands News* 1997] The BLM has also embraced EBAM, and trains its employees in ecosystem management and related biodiversity conservation principles.

Ecosystem management is not limited to federal lands. Cooperative private initiatives for implementing ecosystem management are becoming more common, at least in forested ecosystems. The Plainfield Pilot Project is illustrative. A voluntary, incentive-based program, this project involves owners of ten acres or more of nonindustrial private forest (NIPF) lands within the 13,600-acre limits of this western Massachusetts town. Important features of the project include technical assistance from the Massachusetts Forest Stewardship Program (FSP) (a state-operated, USDA-sponsored program), leadership by a local conservation commission, university-sponsored natural resources and communication training for local conservation leaders, and the use of geographic information system (GIS) technology to compile and display landscape and other essential information.

With help from forestry consultants and funding from the FSP (up to 75 percent), landowners prepare a stewardship plan that combines a resource inventory and timber stand description of their land with the individual landowner's goals. The plan also describes the property's location within the watershed and land-use patterns in the vicinity of the property. The planning process is designed to induce the steward to consider resource concerns beyond his property boundaries. GIS information on forest types and age classes, wildlife and rare species habitats, hydrology, and property boundaries assists landowners in understanding where and how their parcels fit into the forest ecosystem. Landowners are also advised as to opportunities for cross-boundary cooperation, such as building recreational trails, undertaking stream enhancement projects, or collaborating on timber harvesting plans to maximize efficiency and minimize adverse impacts on wildlife and other values. The Plainfield Pilot Project is only now in the early implementation phase, but the prospects for obtaining broad participation and educating landowners appear promising.

Obstacles to Managing and Protecting Ecosystems

EBAM is most feasible on large tracts of land managed by one entity: large private ranches, timber company lands, or national parks or wildlife refuges. The more diverse the land ownership, the smaller or more fragmented the blocks of various habitat types, and the more developed or less "natural" the landscape, the more problematic EBAM becomes. An alarming trend detected in recent years is the increasing fragmentation of nonindustrial private forests. NIPF owners number approximately 10 million, 2 million more than in 1980. In addition, the turnover rate among NIPF owners is quite high; more than 40 percent have acquired their land since 1978. This has implications for management continuity.

Similar trends exist in nonforested areas. Subdivision—with its attendant building, fencing, and related development—fragments habitat, obstructs wildlife movements, and threatens ecosystems' stability. In addition, fragmentation can disrupt recreational access, interfere with commodity production, such as timber or livestock, and impact environmental (soil, water, and air) quality.

The Law of Ecosystem Management

The only federal law that could be considered to mandate ecosystem management is the Endangered Species Act of 1973, which requires protection of the ecosystems on which threatened or endangered species depend. Nevertheless, policies contained in several other federal laws, in particular the National Forest Management Act of 1976, Federal Land Policy and Management Act, Wilderness Act of 1964, and National Environmental Policy Act, are consistent with the practice and goals of ecosystem management.

Few if any state laws could be said to authorize ecosystem management, principally because land ownership patterns do not lend themselves to managing large tracts as units. Nevertheless, good stewardship practices on private forested lands are mandated by law or regulation in 11 states. Many observers advocate financial incentives, such as tax breaks or cost sharing, and technical assistance as more efficient ways of achieving forest management goals. At least five bills in the 104th Congress proposed changes to the federal income or estate tax systems designed to ease the tax burdens on timber-producing lands.

The Future of Ecosystem Management

A scientific report released in early 1997 concluded that the Earth's natural ecosystems generate on the order of $30 trillion in goods and services annually—or, as one of the scientist-authors put it, "they are priceless." These goods and services include such things as climate moderation and stabilization; maintenance of breathable air, potable water, arable soil, and genetic biological diversity; and myriad natural commodities, such as timber, fuels, game and fish, and agricultural products. The scientists noted that these assets continue to be disregarded or undervalued, often because many are not recognized in ordinary markets. Research like this, however, provides ammunition and incentives for continued cooperative efforts to define and manage whole ecosystems.

See also **Biodiversity Conservation; Bureau of Land Management; Endangered Species Act of 1973; Federal Land Policy and Management Act; Geographic Information System; National Forest Management Act of 1976; The Nature Conservancy; Partnerships; U.S. Fish and Wildlife Service; U.S. Forest Service; Watershed.**

ENDANGERED SPECIES   Those organisms most at risk of becoming extinct, designated and protected under the Endangered Species Act of 1973 (ESA).

The Law

The ESA defines an endangered species as "any species which is in danger of extinction throughout all or a significant portion of its range" (with the exception of certain insect pests). "Species" is defined to include "any subspecies of fish or wildlife or plants, and any distinct population segment of any species of vertebrate fish or wildlife which interbreeds when mature." "Fish or wildlife," in turn, means "any member of the animal kingdom," including vertebrates (mammals, fish, birds, amphibians, and reptiles), invertebrates (mollusks, crustaceans, arthropods), and "any part, product, egg, or offspring thereof, or the dead body or parts thereof." Section 7 of the ESA requires federal agencies to conserve endangered species and their critical habitats, and section 9 prohibits any person from taking or engaging in commerce in an endangered species.

The definition of species has been widely criticized as a matter of science or policy, or both. At least one prior interior secretary, Manuel Lujan, questioned why we need to protect *all* species of a particular kind of animal, such as squirrels. (Lujan was referring to the Mt. Graham red squirrel, Delmarva fox squirrel, etc.) Others claim that it is scientifically unnecessary, if not indefensible, to require protection of all "fringe populations" and genetic races of a species, such as isolated populations of wolves near the periphery of their range or individual runs of anadromous fish.

A National Marine Fisheries Service rule, which attempts to clarify the ESA definition of species, identifies an "evolutionarily significant unit" as the lowest taxonomic unit deserving of protection. To qualify, a population must be isolated reproductively from other populations of the species, and it must be significant in the evolution of the species. The U.S. Fish and Wildlife Service (USFWS) has established other criteria for identifying a "distinct population segment," including the population's geographic isolation, whether its ecosystem is threatened with destruction, and whether it is the only occurrence of that species or subspecies within the United States. The use of DNA fingerprinting has been suggested as a more efficient means of categorizing species, subspecies, and races than the traditional approach of identifying different characteristics of organisms and determining which represent significant evolutionary adaptations to local environments. Proponents argue that this would better ensure the protection of genetic diversity, an important component of biological diversity.

Endangered Species Statistics

As of 31 December 1995, 320 animals and 434 plants were listed as endangered. By comparison, The Nature Conservancy (TNC), in its 1997 annual Species Report Card, reported that as many as one-third of American species may be at risk. This includes 5,144 species of flowering plants, nearly 68 percent of all mussel species, 51 percent of crayfish, 40 percent of amphibians, 39 percent of freshwater fish, 16.5 percent of birds, and 15 percent of mammals. While 110 American species of plants and animals are known to be extinct, TNC reported that the actual figure is probably closer to 500. The report assesses the status of 20,500 species and is considered the most comprehensive appraisal of the status of native U.S. species. The USFWS admitted as much when it decided in 1996 to discontinue its practice of listing "Category 2" species.

See also **Biodiversity Conservation; Critical Habitat; Endangered Species Act of 1973; Listing; The Nature Conservancy; Take; Threatened Species; Wolf Reintroduction.**

ENDANGERED SPECIES ACT OF 1973 (ESA)   A federal statute designed to protect animals and plants that are threatened with extinction, variously termed "the pit bull" or "the crown jewel" of American environmental laws. The ESA's purposes are to "provide a means whereby the ecosystems upon which endangered species and threatened species depend may be conserved," to establish a "program for the conservation of such" species, and to take action to accomplish the goals of certain international agreements.

Key Provisions

The act contains four key requirements designed to achieve its purposes. First, the Secretary of the Interior is directed to list species in need of protection. Second, federal agencies must conserve the populations and habitats of listed species and may not take any action that would "jeopardize the continued existence" of any listed species. ("Conserve" is defined by the act essentially to mean the use of all methods that are necessary to improve the condition of threatened and endangered species so that they can be removed from the list.) Third, all federal agencies must consult with the U.S. Fish and Wildlife Service (USFWS) or, in the case of marine species, the National Marine Fisheries Service, on any of their activities that might adversely affect listed species. Finally, all persons are prohibited from taking endangered fish or wildlife.

The ESA also contains various other measures aimed at protecting threatened or endangered species (T&E species) and their habitats. For instance, the USFWS is required to designate critical habitat when it adds species to the list, and it may enter into agreements, called habitat conservation plans, with other agencies and private parties. The act also implements U.S. treaty obligations concerning T&E species by, among other things, restricting imports of protected species. The act establishes penalties for violations of the ESA and any regulations adopted by USFWS. Among its enforcement provisions is a section authorizing citizen suits. Citizens may sue to prevent any person from violating the ESA by taking a threatened or endangered species, for example. Citizens may also sue the Interior secretary to compel him to enforce the act's prohibitions, list a species as threatened or endangered, or designate critical habitat.

A potentially important but seldom-used provision of the ESA is section 7(e), added in 1978. It establishes a cabinet-level Endangered Species Committee, which is empowered to exempt, under certain circumstances, a federal agency action from complying with the act's "no jeopardy" requirement (see Section 7 Consultation). A 1982 amendment to section 10 of the ESA authorizes unintentional, incidental takings of listed species, if approved in advance by the USFWS.

Implementing the ESA

The ESA is administered by the Secretary of the Interior and, to a lesser extent, by the Secretary of Commerce. Listing decisions and responsibilities, assigned to the Interior secretary, have been delegated to the USFWS. The National Marine Fisheries Service, an agency within the Commerce Department, is responsible for conserving marine species and anadromous fish. USFWS shoulders many other responsibilities under the act as well, notably the preparation of biological opinions in the consultation process, development of habitat conservation plans and recovery plans, and enforcement of the ESA.

In 1990 the Interior Department estimated that recovering all threatened and endangered species then listed, and likely to be listed, would cost $4.6 billion. Admittedly no small sum, it is useful to compare this figure to the amount we spend on other things—for instance, in 1991, Americans spent ten times this amount on beer! More to the point, according to the U.S. Supreme Court in *Tennessee Valley Authority v. Hill* (1978) (*TVA*), the "plain intent of Congress in enacting [the ESA] was to halt and reverse the trend toward species extinction, *whatever the cost*" (emphasis added). The *TVA* Court also cited legislative history, showing that Congress believed the value of the "genetic heritage" of species was "incalculable." Despite this history, ESA appropriations have declined in recent years, and in 1995 Congress even imposed a moratorium on further listings of threatened or endangered species.

The ESA in the Courts

The most important recent judicial decision involving the ESA is the 1995 Supreme Court case *Babbitt v. Sweet Home Chapter of Communities for a Great Oregon*. In this case, the Court upheld the USFWS rule that defines "harm" as used in the ESA definition of "take." The rule states that harm includes "significant habitat modification or degradation where it actually kills or injures wildlife by significantly impairing essential behavioral patterns, including breeding, feeding or sheltering." The effect of the case is to confirm that even private landowners have obligations under the ESA not to injure listed species or damage their habitat.

Other important ESA cases include the litigation over the northern spotted owl in the Pacific Northwest and the red-cockaded woodpecker in the Southeast [*see Northern Spotted Owl v. Hodel* (1988), *Northern Spotted Owl v.*

Lujan (1991), and *Sierra Club v. Yeutter* (1991)]; *Lujan v. Defenders of Wildlife* (1992), a significant case concerning a plaintiff's standing to challenge an ESA regulation; and ongoing lawsuits in the Southwest that have resulted in injunctions against grazing and logging activities on certain national forests pending compliance with the ESA to protect the Mexican spotted owl [*see Silver v. Babbitt* (1995)].

ESA Reform

The ESA's statutory authorization for spending expired at the end of 1992. Reauthorization efforts over the next five years failed for a variety of reasons, including the radical reform attempts of western Republicans in the 104th Congress and environmental groups' fears that opening up the act to any reforms could jeopardize the statute as a whole. Two Republican senators, John Chafee (R-RI) and Dirk Kempthorne (R-ID), considered a moderate and a conservative, respectively, teamed up in 1997 to sponsor legislation to reauthorize the ESA. Chafee, who chairs the Senate Environment Committee, considers reauthorization a priority, and he intended to get a bill through the Senate in 1997. The Chafee-Kempthorne bill would maintain certain key features of the act, including the listing process and critical habitat designation, but would tighten recovery plan requirements, relax section 7 consultation provisions, and enhance the role of states. The bill includes provisions for a technical assistance program for landowners to advise them about habitat conservation planning and provide some financial aid. It also incorporates the Clinton administration's "no surprises policy," which environmentalists generally oppose. Kempthorne introduced a separate bill (S. 901), which set forth a package of financial incentives designed to encourage landowners to manage their lands for the benefit of threatened or endangered species. Believed to have nearly universal support, its incentives included allowing landowners who donate land for conservation purposes to deduct its full value, exclusive of ESA restrictions on its use or development; allowing the deferral of estate taxes on land subject to a conservation easement; and affording additional capital gains tax relief to persons who transfer land to qualified conservation organizations.

Also in early 1997, more than 20 environmental organizations released their consensus recommendations for ESA reauthorization and reform. They urged retention of the act's basic structure, but called for strict time limits on the listing process and developing recovery plans, better prelisting monitoring of species, and tax incentives for owners of private land providing habitat for T&E species. Congressman George Miller (D-CA) later introduced ESA legislation that reflected many of these recommendations and disapproved the no-surprises policy.

Few observers expected comprehensive reauthorization of the act in the 105th Congress, but consensus seemed to be growing on one point: Increased funding is desirable, both to enable improved species protection and to better accommodate private property owners' interests.

See also *Babbitt v. Sweet Home Chapter of Communities for a Great Oregon* (1995); *Bennett v. Spear* (1997); Department of the Interior; Endangered Species; Habitat Conservation Plan; Listing; Section 7 Consultation; Take; *Tennessee Valley Authority v. Hill* (1978); Threatened Species; U.S. Fish and Wildlife Service.

ENVIRONMENTAL DEFENSE FUND (EDF)   A nonprofit, tax-exempt national environmental organization founded in 1967, widely known and respected for its legal and economic policy work. *Outside* magazine recently ranked EDF number one for clout among national environmental organizations, defining "clout" as a measure of "how much influence the group...will wield on events of the coming year." EDF has more than 300,000 members, an annual budget of $25 million (about 80 percent of which funds program services), and a staff of 163, including more than 60 full-time scientists, economists, lawyers, and engineers. It operates seven offices, located in New York; Washington, D.C.; Boulder, CO; Oakland, CA; Austin, TX; Raleigh, NC; and Boston, MA.

EDF's conservation goals include protecting wildlife and wildlife habitats, conserving wetlands, controlling global warming, halting acid rain, and preventing the destruction of tropical rainforests. It lists among its recent successes two congressional acts that implemented EDF plans: in 1990 an acid rain reduction program, and in 1992 a water trading and funding program to benefit fish and wildlife in California's Central Valley. It also engineered an agreement between the federal government and the state of California to ensure adequate water flows in the San Francisco Bay and Delta, and was influential in the Environmental Protection Agency decision in 1990 to veto the controversial Two Forks Dam in Colorado. (Most observers consider Two Forks likely to be the last major dam proposal in the United States.) The organization works on a variety of western water issues, including nonpoint source pollution, water marketing, and protection of anadromous fish.

Although most EDF litigation concerns environmental pollution statutes and federal regulatory programs, the organization also has sued to: protect bottomland hardwood forest in Louisiana and forested wetlands in North Carolina's East Dismal Swamp, list sea turtles and several whales as endangered species, protect spawning Atlantic salmon, and halt construction of the Cross Florida Barge Canal. One of its most significant victories was attaining a nationwide ban in 1972 on the pesticide DDT, responsible for drastic declines in the populations of many birds, including bald eagles and peregrine falcons. Recently, EDF was one of several environmental organizations that advocated successfully for reintroduction of wolves to Yellowstone National Park and central Idaho, and it originated a plan, now in place, to protect endangered red-cockaded woodpeckers in privately owned longleaf pine forests in North Carolina.

EDF publishes a bimonthly newsletter (*EDF Letter*) and various reports, including *Ploughing New Ground*, an innovative plan for reducing nonpoint source pollution, which threatens wildlife and surface water quality in California; *Defending the Desert*, concerning the threats to public lands in the Southwest posed by mining, grazing, and off-road vehicles; and critiques of the writings of talk show host Rush Limbaugh and journalist Gregg Easterbrook, pointing out their inconsistencies with published, peer-reviewed scientific literature.

EDF also cooperates with the Advertising Council in a joint national recycling campaign.

ENVIRONMENTAL IMPACT STATEMENT (EIS) The "detailed statement" that the National Environmental Policy Act (NEPA) requires all federal agencies to prepare "on proposals for legislation and other major federal actions significantly affecting the quality of the human environment." The purpose of the EIS is to ensure informed decision making, not to dictate the ultimate agency decision on a proposed action. The requirements for EISs are set forth in regulations issued by the Council on Environmental Quality (CEQ); these rules are applicable to all federal agencies, but nearly all agencies also have their own tailored version of these NEPA-implementing regulations.

NEPA requires an EIS to address the environmental impact of the proposed action, any adverse effects that cannot be avoided if the proposal is carried out, alternatives to the proposal, the relation between short-term uses and long-term productivity of the environment, and any irreversible or irretrievable commitments of resources that would result if the project were implemented. CEQ rules have elaborated on these requirements so that nearly all EISs have standard parts: a discussion of the affected environment; an explanation of the purpose and need for the project; discussions of the proposed action and alternatives to it, including the environmental and socioeconomic impacts of each, how those impacts could be mitigated, and the impacts that cannot be avoided; and identification of the agency's preferred alternative. EISs must incorporate an interdisciplinary approach, and they must identify needed, but unavailable, information.

Under CEQ rules, agencies normally prepare a "mini-EIS," or environmental assessment, to determine whether an EIS will be necessary, that is, whether the proposed action is "major" and would "significantly affect" the environment. If those questions are answered yes, then an EIS must be prepared. If they're answered no, the agency issues a "finding of no significant impact," or FONSI, and may proceed with the proposed action. A FONSI may be challenged in court by someone who believes that an EIS should have been prepared. The plaintiff must also, of course, be able to demonstrate standing. If the agency writes an EIS, it first prepares a draft, which is made available for public comment and review by other agencies. The comments are reviewed by the acting agency, which then revises the draft EIS and issues a final EIS. Final EISs are submitted to the Environmental Protection Agency for review and may be challenged in court. An EIS may be found inadequate if it fails to consider certain environmental impacts or disregards relevant and readily available information. EISs have been the subject of literally tens of thousands of lawsuits since NEPA was enacted in 1969.

EISs have been criticized for being largely "boilerplate" discussions, expensive, and a nonproductive use of agencies' time. But they also serve the valuable purpose of forcing agencies to consider the ramifications of their actions, and in many cases have been the incentive for collecting useful environmental data. EISs have become a major planning tool for all federal agencies and an important source of information for the public.

See also **Mitigation; National Environmental Policy Act;** *Robertson v. Methow Valley Citizens Council* **(1989).**

ENVIRONMENTAL LAW INSTITUTE (ELI) A nonprofit public-interest organization. ELI advances environmental and conservation law and policy by informing educators, students, and professionals and by advocating reforms in law, management, and policy. Its principal vehicles for furthering these objectives are its publications—*The Environmental Law Reporter,* a looseleaf periodical service; *National Wetlands Newsletter;* and environmental "deskbooks" on topics such as wetlands law—and conferences and training courses. Its library is open to the public by appointment.

ENVIRONMENTAL PROTECTION AGENCY (EPA) An independent federal agency with wide responsibilities for protecting the environment, regulating industry, and encouraging innovative approaches to preventing pollution and using resources sustainably. In addition to its headquarters in Washington, D.C., the agency has ten regional offices. It is represented in litigation either by its own attorneys or by attorneys from the federal Department of Justice.

EPA's conservation programs (as distinguished from its environmental pollution control efforts) include protecting wetlands, promoting watershed- and ecosystem-based approaches to land and resource management, and encouraging recycling. The EPA Office of Water, for instance, includes a division on wetlands, oceans, and watersheds. EPA conservation activities are principally cooperative, educational, or research-oriented, although its regulatory authority under the Clean Water Act (CWA) is also relevant to its conservation programs.

EPA embarked on a "place-based ecosystem" approach to resource management and planning in the early 1990s. It established an Ecosystem Protection Task Force, and by 1995 it and its partners' ecosystem protection efforts covered the vast majority of the geographic area of the lower 48 states, plus small portions of Mexico along the Rio Grande River and the plains section of Canada. These projects range from large-scale, multistate initiatives to smaller regional or local efforts; all involve partnerships among EPA and state or local agencies and organizations and private individuals. These projects are as diverse as the lands and the problems they encompass: They may incorporate restoration efforts in wetlands, lakes, or waterfowl habitat; assessments of risk for pesticide exposure and wildlife habitat loss; evaluation of and response to invasions of exotic species; and, of course, pollution-control efforts. EPA may provide technical assistance or financial aid. The agency has also formed a "biodiversity research consortium," a cooperative effort to develop the information needed to assess and manage risks to biodiversity.

Although EPA's pollution-control programs are outside the scope of this dictionary, its responsibilities and efforts to coordinate state programs for controlling water pollution, particularly from nonpoint sources, are closely related to its ecosystem- and watershed-based programs. EPA is also developing a watershed approach to issuing discharge permits to point sources in its National Pollutant Discharge Elimination System, under CWA section 402. EPA recognizes that a watershed approach will be required to carry out the "total maximum daily load" (TMDL) assessments required by CWA section 303. EPA is responsible for setting TMDLs if the state fails to do so. As of late 1997, 26 legal actions against EPA relating to TMDLs were pending in 23 states. These actions, which include active lawsuits, notices of intent to sue, court orders, and consent decrees, are designed to force EPA to follow CWA requirements for setting and enforcing TMDLs.

In 1988, EPA initiated the Environmental Monitoring and Assessment Program (EMAP), whose broad goal is to identify emerging environmental problems before they become crises. The objectives of EMAP are to: (1) estimate the status and trends of ecological indicators and provide reports to the public and (2) monitor pollutant exposure and habitat condition, and identify relationships between human-caused environmental stresses and ecological conditions. EMAP includes several long-term regional monitoring efforts, including the Great Lakes, arid lands, agricultural lands, and estuaries.

See also **Biodiversity Conservation; Ecosystem Management; Watershed; Wetland.**

EQUAL FOOTING DOCTRINE   A doctrine developed by the courts that describes the status of new states admitted to the Union pursuant to article IV, section 3, clause 1 of the Constitution. The language was first employed in 1796 upon the admission of the third new state, Tennessee. Tennessee was declared to be "one of the United States of America," admitted "on an equal footing with the original States in all respects." Substantially similar language can be found in the admission act for every subsequently admitted state. As described by the U.S. Supreme Court in 1911, the doctrine provides basically that all states, regardless of when admitted to the Union, are "equal in power, dignity, and

authority, each competent to exert that residuum of sovereignty not delegated to the United States by the Constitution itself." [*Coyle v. Smith* (1911)]

As a result of certain language (since discredited) in an 1845 Supreme
Court opinion, the doctrine later acquired additional significance for some
western states and the proponents of the Sagebrush Rebellion and County
Supremacy Movement. In *Pollard's Lessee v. Hagan* (1845), the Supreme Court
indicated that Congress's power over federal public lands within the borders of newly admitted states would exist only until those lands could be
sold to retire the country's war debts or were organized into new states. At
such time, the Court said, "the municipal sovereignty of the new states
will be complete, ...and they, and the original states, will be upon an equal
footing, in all respects whatever." Relying on this language, county supremacy proponents and some states' rights activists argue that "equal
footing" means that the western, public land states were eventually intended to obtain title to the federal lands within their borders.

Pollard, however, has since been limited by the Supreme Court to its
narrow holding: Every state holds title to the beds and banks of navigable
waters within its borders. In *Arizona v. California* (1963), the Court declared
that *Pollard* did not limit the "broad powers of the United States to...regulate
government lands under Art. IV, § 3 [the Property Clause] of the Constitution." More recently, several lower courts have also rejected the *Pollard* version of the equal footing doctrine. For instance, *United States v. Nye County*
(1996) rejected the county's "equal footing" argument that the state of Nevada owned public lands in the state, and affirmed the federal government's
ownership of, and authority to administer, those lands. In *United States v.
Gardner* (1997) a federal appeals court rejected a U.S. Forest Service grazing permittee's argument that, because the state owned national forests in
Nevada, he was not required to pay grazing fees to the federal government. The court reaffirmed that the equal footing doctrine applies to lands
beneath navigable waters, not to federal public lands.

See also **County Supremacy Movement;** *Illinois Central Railroad Co. v.
Illinois* **(1892); Navigable Waters; Property Clause; Sagebrush Rebellion.**

EVEN-AGED MANAGEMENT   A term that refers to timber
harvesting techniques that result, after replanting and regeneration, in timber stands of essentially uniform age. The National Forest
Management Act of 1976 lists clear-cutting, seed tree cutting, and
shelterwood cutting as three such techniques, and establishes several pre-

requisites to their use in national forests. Even-aged management is controversial, especially when it involves the conversion of old-growth forest, because it reduces the structural and species diversity of the forest: A forest of many tree species, of different ages and heights, is replaced by a more homogeneous stand that will provide habitat for different, and probably fewer, wildlife species.

See also **Biodiversity Conservation; Clear-Cutting; National Forest Management Act of 1976; Old Growth.**

EXACTION   A requirement in a land-use or building permit, imposed by a city or county as a condition of the government's approval of the project or development. For instance, a city may require a developer to agree to build sidewalks or dedicate parkland in exchange for approving construction of a new subdivision. Exactions are useful land-use planning and regulatory devices, but they are sometimes challenged as unreasonable or even as an unconstitutional taking of private property.

An important recent U.S. Supreme Court decision established a new test for evaluating the propriety of exactions imposed by local governments as a condition for issuing land-use permits. *Dolan v. City of Tigard* (1994) involved a challenge by a landowner to two exactions imposed by an Oregon city as conditions of its approval of the major expansion of her hardware store and parking lot. Tigard required that the landowner dedicate a public easement to the city for construction of a bicycle path and a greenbelt along the creek across her property. The applicant challenged the requirements as an unconstitutional taking of her property.

The Court ruled (5-4) that a "nexus," or connection, existed between the city's concerns about increased traffic and flooding resulting from the development and its requirements for a bike path and greenway. However, the Court established a new test for measuring the *sufficiency* of that connection: Any condition imposed on the applicant must be "roughly proportional" to the expected impacts of the proposed development; if not, the exaction violates the Fifth Amendment. The new test does not require mathematical precision, but requires that the city make "an individualized determination" that the exactions are "related both in nature and extent to the impact." This test is essentially the same as the "reasonable relationship" test used by most state courts. The conditions in *Dolan* failed to meet this test because the city had not shown why the greenway needed to be *public* (dedicated to the city) nor to what extent the bike path could be expected to offset the expected increase in vehicular traffic.

See also **Land-Use Planning; Rehnquist, William H.; Taking.**

EXHAUSTION OF REMEDIES   A doctrine of administrative law related to ripeness. The doctrine requires a potential plaintiff to exhaust all avenues of administrative relief before seeking judicial review of an agency action. In other words, an agency action must be final, and the plaintiff must have exercised any administrative appeal opportunities before challenging the agency action in court. Appeal procedures vary by agency. Bureau of Land Management decisions may be appealed from the area manager or the district manager to the state director and then to the Interior Board of Land Appeals. Similarly, U.S. Forest Service decisions may be appealed from the district ranger or forest supervisor to the regional forester, chief of the Forest Service, and then to Department of Agriculture officials, such as an assistant secretary. The specific procedure also depends on the type of agency action or decision, such as adoption of a forest plan, issuance of a final environmental impact statement, or renewal of a grazing permit.

See also **Ripeness.**

FARM BILLS The generic name given to federal omnibus legislation relating to American agricultural programs and farmland conservation. The three most recent and significant bills were passed in 1985, 1990, and 1996. The most significant Farm Bill conservation programs are administered by the Natural Resources Conservation Service and the Farm Service Agency, both within the U.S. Department of Agriculture.

The 1985 and 1990 Farm Bills

Increasing concern over agriculture's contribution to soil erosion and the loss of wetlands led to passage in 1985 of the Federal Food Security Act (the 1985 Farm Bill). For the first time, eligibility for federal farm program benefits, such as commodity price supports and crop insurance, was linked to producers' willingness to protect wetlands and conserve soil on highly erodible croplands. The act created the Conservation Reserve Program and three compliance programs known as Swampbuster, Sodbuster, and conservation compliance. All except Swampbuster were aimed at reducing soil erosion. Conservation compliance provisions require farmers with highly erodible farmland to follow conservation plans to remain eligible for farm program benefits. Since 1985, more than 1.7 million conservation plans have been prepared for American farms. A 1995 review of 50,000 farm tracts encompassing 11.4 million acres revealed that plans had been fully implemented on 72 percent of the tracts; only 5.5 percent had no conservation plan in place. The Swampbuster provisions of the 1985 and 1990 Farm Bills have succeeded in reducing the annual rate of wetlands loss from 300,000 acres in the 1970s (half of which was due to agriculture) to less than 80,000 acres.

The 1990 Farm Bill continued and amended the 1985 conservation programs, adding a new focus: water quality (including groundwater) protection. The 1990 act also contained provisions concerning sustainable agriculture, gave priority to CRP enrollments in certain regions, and authorized a nationwide Forest Stewardship Program. This forestry program has been in effect since 1992; 866 parcels, encompassing nearly 80,000 acres, were participating by the end of 1995. Approval of a stewardship plan (a nonbinding, nonregulatory document) qualifies the landowner for cost sharing for habitat enhancement and soil erosion control projects, trail building, and other purposes.

The 1996 Farm Bill

The 1996 Farm Bill signaled several changes in American agricultural policy. It replaced the target-price deficiency program for grains and cotton with capped annual contract payments (no longer tied to market prices), which will expire in 2002; ended acreage reduction and planting requirements; and made significant changes to the conservation programs, notably converting most spending to entitlements financed with Commodity Credit Corporation funds. This makes the spending mandatory and removes it from the annual congressional appropriations process. Both the CRP and Wetland Reserve Program were reauthorized and converted to entitlements, Swampbuster was amended to increase program flexibility, and new conservation programs were set up for farmlands, floodplains, grazing lands, and wildlife habitat.

Under the 1996 act, the federal agricultural conservation program remains based chiefly on voluntary cooperation and technical and financial assistance from the government. Funding will increase by more than $2 billion over seven years. The act eliminated four federal cost-sharing programs and replaced them with one new cost-sharing program, the Environmental Quality Improvement Program (EQIP). Half of the $200 million authorized will be used to address livestock production-related problems. The act also contains new provisions that provide for greater producer flexibility, such as allowing violators up to one year to meet compliance requirements. The Department of Agriculture is now writing regulations to implement these and other new provisions in the law.

The 1996 act also broadened the scope of the cooperative forestry assistance program and established the Stewardship Incentive Program (SIP), a successor to the earlier Forestry Incentives Program. The SIP authorizes federal cost-sharing for improved forestry practices, fish and wildlife enhancement projects, and recreational access. The program stirred up controversy, however, and funding was cut significantly in 1996.

See also **Conservation Reserve Program; Natural Resources Conservation Service; Soil Erosion and Conservation; Swampbuster; Wetland.**

🏛 FEDERAL LAND POLICY AND MANAGEMENT ACT (FLPMA)
The Bureau of Land Management's (BLM) organic act, which was passed by Congress in 1976 and applies to approximately 270 million surface acres, plus 60 million acres of subsurface mineral interests, managed by the BLM. FLPMA (pronounced "flip-ma") established federal policy to retain BLM lands (also called, simply, public lands) except where disposal of particular parcels is in the national interest, and set forth planning and management guidelines for these lands. Prior to FLPMA, the BLM had no permanent authority or mandate to manage its lands and resources. FLPMA provides that public lands will be managed under principles of multiple use and sustained yield, and that the United States should receive fair market value for the use of public land resources. Multiple-use resources include fish and wildlife, recreation, timber, range, wilderness, minerals, watershed, and natural, scenic, scientific, and historical values.

The act directs the BLM to regulate the use and occupancy of the public lands through easements, permits, leases, rules, or otherwise, and to "prevent unnecessary and undue degradation of the lands." FLPMA also confers authority to regulate wildlife on the BLM and Forest Service, but no court has defined the scope of that authority.

FLPMA requires the BLM to prepare resource management plans, with input from the public, local governments, and other agencies. These plans, each of which is accompanied by an environmental impact statement and reviewed and updated every 15 years, describe generally how the planning area will be managed to provide the resources and services demanded by the public and commodity groups while protecting the lands. In preparing and revising plans, the BLM is to use an interdisciplinary approach, give priority to protecting "areas of critical environmental concern," incorporate resources inventory data (which the agency is directed to keep current), weigh short- and long-term benefits to the public, provide for compliance with environmental laws, and coordinate to the extent practical with state, local, and tribal land-use plans. Although FLPMA is known as the BLM's organic act, it contains numerous provisions applicable to all federal lands, or to both BLM lands and national forests. For instance, it sets forth criteria for exchanges of both BLM lands and those managed by the U.S. Forest Service (in the U.S. Department of Agriculture) and for withdrawing any public lands from operation of the public land laws. In addition, FLPMA's grazing and rights-of-way provisions apply to the Forest Service as well as to the BLM.

Although many of its provisions are general, FLPMA establishes specific requirements for mining claims, grazing permits, and rights-of-way for water-related facilities, pipelines, and transportation and utility facilities. The act calls for citizen advisory councils, requires the BLM to study and propose areas for wilderness designation, and established and provided for the management of the California Desert Conservation Area (more recently provided for by the California Desert Protection Act of 1994). The statute also provides for criminal penalties and civil enforcement of any regulations promulgated by the BLM under the act.

FLPMA repealed dozens of outdated public land laws, such as the homestead laws, but it left intact many others, including the Unlawful Inclosures Act of 1885 and the General Mining Law of 1872. Passage of FLPMA aggravated some westerners who believed that the BLM-managed public lands belonged to and/or could be better managed by the states, helping to trigger the Sagebrush Rebellion in the late 1970s. BLM's implementation of FLPMA remains a target of criticism by many groups, both environmental and commodity-oriented, and would be significantly affected if any of the many legislative proposals for rangeland reform or transfer of BLM land to the states were to succeed.

See also **Bureau of Land Management; County Supremacy Movement; Land Exchange; Organic Act of 1897; Resource Management Plan; R.S. 2477; Sagebrush Rebellion; Wildlife Management; Withdrawal.**

FISH AND WILDLIFE CONSERVATION ACT OF 1980

Nongame counterpart to the federal Pittman-Robinson Act and Dingell-Johnson Act. The Fish and Wildlife Conservation Act of 1980 was intended to fill a need for nongame program funding, which the sport- and game-oriented Pittman-Robinson and Dingell-Johnson acts did not meet. Unlike those programs, though, funding under the Fish and Wildlife Conservation Act depends on appropriations by Congress from the general fund and thus has been less certain. The act has promoted nongame planning, however, by reimbursing state fish and game agencies 75 percent of the costs of developing, and 90 percent of the costs of implementing, nongame conservation plans. In practice, projects can often be funded by any of the three programs.

See also **Dingell-Johnson Act; Pittman-Robinson Act.**

IIII FOREST PLAN Forest plans, or land and resource management plans (LRMPs), are planning documents required for each national forest by the National Forest Management Act of 1976 (NFMA). The NFMA requires coordination of the planning process with National Environmental Policy Act (NEPA) procedures; hence, the adoption of a forest plan is preceded by preparation of an environmental impact statement (EIS), including a discussion of alternatives for managing the forest. A draft EIS and draft forest plan are published simultaneously for public review and comment.

The EIS for each plan usually studies 8 to 15 management alternatives, one or a combination of which becomes the preferred alternative and the basis of the forest planning strategy. Among the alternatives typically evaluated are: (1) "no action" alternative, defined as maintaining the management status quo (the Council on Environmental Quality's NEPA-implementing regulations require that every EIS include this alternative); (2) one or more high-amenity alternatives, which provide for high levels of certain nonmarket amenities, such as wilderness, water quality, or wildlife habitat; (3) high-commodity alternatives, which seek to increase or maximize production of commodities such as timber and livestock forage; (4) a Resources Planning Act alternative, which translates forest-system-wide resource goals set at the national level into specific targets for the individual forest; and (5) a de facto "high budget" alternative, which hypothesizes a management scenario based on maximizing the forest's budget as advocated by forest consultant and economist Randal O'Toole.

The first set of NFMA plans was completed about 1989, and many national forest managers are now engaged in revising their plans. The act requires that plans be revised as necessary, but *at least* every 15 years. The U.S. Forest Service recently announced that the next generation of plans would be guided by ecosystem management principles. Nearly every one of the first-generation plans was appealed; the bases for challenging them often included claims under the Administrative Procedure Act and Endangered Species Act of 1973, as well as under NFMA and NEPA. Although few substantive challenges were successful, several of the court decisions interpreted the applicable NFMA provisions and clarified the procedures that the Forest Service must follow; these decisions will influence future planning efforts.

One of the most novel developments in forest planning is known as the Quincy Library Group plan. This proposed five-year pilot project is the result of collaboration among environmentalists, the timber industry, and local governments in northern California to develop a plan for the Plumas, Lassen, and a portion of the Tahoe National Forests that would be acceptable to all parties. The proposal sailed through the U.S. House of Representatives in July 1997 (by a 429-1 vote), after it was amended to ensure that all national forest activities would comply with NEPA and endangered species requirements and ensure protection of riparian areas. A similar bill was introduced in the Senate, but was apparently derailed when it lost the sponsorship of Senator Barbara Boxer (D-CA) and came under fire by environmentalists concerned about fire hazards and the potential for domination of the local planning group by commercial interests. The Quincy plan incorporates selective cutting to improve forest health and provide firebreaks. According to *Public Lands News*, the "effort is being closely watched as a prototype for a health policy for all the nation's forests."

See also **Deference; Ecosystem Management; Environmental Impact Statement; National Environmental Policy Act; National Forest Management Act of 1976; Resource Management Plan; U.S. Forest Service.**

FOREST SERVICE EMPLOYEES FOR ENVIRONMENTAL ETHICS (FSEEE)

A unique nonprofit organization founded in 1989 by government employees to promote accountability within the U.S. Forest Service (USFS). FSEEE's mission is to influence USFS management policies to be more sustainable and less extraction- or commodity-oriented, which it accomplishes by providing support to individual USFS employees, both upper management and field-level professionals, who advocate sustainability. FSEEE realizes that USFS field personnel, many of whom work in small towns or rural areas, can be susceptible to pressure from local citizens, including their own neighbors. Their participation in locally unpopular decisions, such as reducing timber sales or grazing permits, may result in reprimands, demotion or transfer, or even loss of job. The group cites a wide array of accomplishments, ranging from helping to stop a huge sale of timber in the Tongass National Forest by demonstrating that it violated the sustained-yield policy, to forcing the Forest Service to abandon a proposal to censor its internal e-mail network, to preparing a video for USFS managers describing the relationships among storms, logging practices, and landslides.

FSEEE publishes a newsletter, *Inner Voice*, which provides news about activities in forests around the country and changes in forest management practices and policies. It also produced a pamphlet, *Clarion Calling*, that instructs USFS employees regarding their individual rights, the requirements of national forest management laws, and how concerned employees can document forest mismanagement practices. In addition, FSEEE responds to individual employee questions about free speech protections, and it aids employees who allege retaliation or discrimination for their efforts to support environmental ethics. As the group puts it, FSEEE "provides an alternative for change when internal channels fail." Executive Director Andy Stahl served as chief natural resources and public lands adviser to Ohio Congressman John Seiberling, chair of the House Natural Resources Committee during the Reagan and Bush administrations.

See also **U.S. Forest Service.**

FRIENDS OF THE EARTH (FOE)   An international grassroots advocacy organization with an annual budget of more than $2.5 million and 52 affiliates worldwide. FOE merged with Environmental Policy Institute and the Oceanic Society in 1990. Its work includes fighting a wide range of environmental threats including global warming, loss of biological diversity, and ozone depletion. FOE advocates changes in tax and international lending policies to encourage sustainable resource use and development. It publishes a magazine, *Friends of the Earth News*.

FUND FOR ANIMALS   A national, nonprofit animal protection organization with 250,000 members. Established in 1967, the fund works to educate the public and lawmakers on animal welfare and wildlife conservation issues. The organization occasionally litigates (for instance, to halt bear-baiting practices on national forests), and its grassroots efforts include encouraging and participating in animal welfare ballot initiatives.

See also **Animal Rights Movement.**

GENERAL MINING LAW OF 1872 The basic law governing "hardrock" mining on federal public lands. The General Mining Law, which has been amended only slightly in 125 years, allows prospectors (individuals or mining companies) to go onto federal lands, without advance permission from the land manager, to explore for "valuable mineral deposits" and stake claims to and develop any minerals discovered. The lands must be open to mining, that is, not withdrawn from operation of the mining laws. The minerals subject to the law, known as "locatable" minerals, include precious metals such as gold and silver; other metals such as copper, uranium, and nickel; and minerals that have "distinct and special value," for example, chemical- or pharmaceutical-grade limestone. Certain minerals have been removed from the law's operation by other statutes, for example, oil and gas by the Mineral Leasing Act of 1920, and gravel and sand by the Common Varieties Act of 1947.

A valid mining claim under the 1872 law results when the miner makes a valuable discovery of minerals (measured by a marketability test) and properly locates and records his claim. At that point he acquires a legally recognized property interest: He has the right to occupy the surface for mining-related purposes and a vested ownership interest in the subsurface mineral deposit. Unless and until the land is patented, the United States retains ownership of the land surface; title to the mineral reverts to the federal government if the miner abandons his claims or otherwise forfeits his interest, such as by failing to comply with applicable law. The holder of a mining claim pays no fee to the federal government either to explore or develop a mine and extract the minerals. If he wishes to purchase the land itself, he can obtain a patent by complying with all application requirements and paying a small fee to the government ($2.50 per acre for placer claims, $5.00 per acre for lode claims). The owner of a mining claim can develop and sell the mineral himself, or he can sell his interest in the mineral to another person or company.

For more than a century the federal government took a laissez-faire approach to mining. The 1872 law was intended to encourage serious development of federal minerals, not to restrict miners' use of federal lands. The statute authorizes both local and federal regulation of mining on federal lands, but itself imposes few requirements on miners. The courts very early held that a miner could not use the surface of unpatented claims for purposes unrelated to mining, and Congress affirmed this rule in the Surface Resources Act of 1955. That statute also established that the federal government could manage the surface resources of mining claims and that the public (or permittees of the government) could use the surface of mining claims for other uses, such as recreation or grazing, so long as this use did not materially interfere with mining-related uses.

Government controls on mining were minimal prior to the 1980s. Historically, state and local laws specified how claims must be staked and recorded, and governed disputes among rival claimants to the same claims. The 1872 statute affords little protection to miners while they are exploring for minerals; thus, claim jumping and overfiling are common, and the rival parties can end up in court.

In 1976, with passage of the Federal Land Policy and Management Act (FLPMA), Congress recognized some of the problems resulting from 100 years of federal neglect of public land mining. [*See United States v. Locke* (1985).] FLPMA required all holders of mining claims to file a notice with the Bureau of Land Management (BLM) within three years, and annually thereafter to file a notice of intent to hold the claim and an affidavit that the assessment work required by the 1872 law had been performed. In 1993 the assessment work requirement was replaced with an annual filing fee. FLPMA also directs the Interior secretary (and, by delegation, the BLM) to manage the public lands so as "to prevent unnecessary or undue degradation of the lands." Subject only to these exceptions and certain provisions for mining in the California Desert Conservation Area and wilderness study areas, FLPMA proclaims that it does not "amend the Mining Law of 1872 or impair the rights of any locators or claims under that Act."

The BLM is responsible for administering the mining laws, including maintaining records of claims, determining the validity of claims, and regulating mining activities on BLM lands. Where mining occurs on national forests, however, it is subject to further regulation by the U.S. Forest Service (USFS). Between 1974 and 1980, both the USFS and BLM issued surface management regulations designed to regulate the environmental impacts of mining activities. USFS rules were issued under the 1897 Organic Act, which authorizes the agency to regulate the occupancy and use of national forests. The regulations require, among other things, approved plans of operation for all mines and compliance with all applicable state environmental requirements in order to "minimize adverse environmental impacts" on national forest resources. The rules were challenged in court and upheld. BLM regulations, authorized by the FLPMA, were issued in 1980. Although similar to the USFS rules, they except small operations (those that disturb less than five acres per year) from the operating plan requirement, and they do not require reclamation bonds for all operations. Moreover, the BLM regulations do not require impacts to surface resources to be minimized, but presumably incorporate the FLPMA mandate that "unnecessary or undue degradation of the lands" be prevented.

Mining on public lands today may be subject to substantially more regulation than in the past, but mining policy still largely reflects nineteenth-century attitudes. Because the law does not afford the BLM the discretion or flexibility to plan for hardrock mineral development (as the agency plans for leasable minerals), and because the law acts as a drain on the U.S. Treasury, it is a prime target of legislative and administrative reform efforts. So far, these efforts have borne little fruit, but they continue to sprout and grow.

See also **Leasing; Location; Mining Law Reform; Patent; Patent Moratorium; Royalty;** *United States v. Locke* **(1985); Withdrawal.**

GENETIC DIVERSITY   One of three elements of biological diversity; the others are species and community diversity, and structural diversity. Congress appeared to recognize the value of the genetic diversity of organisms and habitats when it passed the Endangered Species Act of 1973 (ESA). One House committee report on a bill substantially similar to the law ultimately enacted contained this statement: "The value of this genetic heritage is, quite literally, incalculable." The U.S. Supreme Court quoted this language in *Tennessee Valley Authority v. Hill* (1978), its first important opinion applying the Endangered Species Act. Moreover, the ESA itself defines "species" to include "any subspecies of fish or wildlife or plants, and any distinct population segment of any species of vertebrate fish or wildlife." Distinct populations would be expected to exhibit genetic differences; thus, this definition reflects an appreciation of the value of preserving genetic variability within species.

Despite these somewhat oblique references in the law to this important scientific or conservation-biology principle, the law actually does little to advance a goal of conserving genetic diversity. First, the ESA applies only to species that have been listed or proposed for listing as threatened or endangered species. Although it indirectly provides protection for other species that share a listed species' habitat, especially the habitat designated as critical to the listed species' survival, the act makes no provision for conserving the genetic diversity of that habitat or its inhabitants. Furthermore, even though other federal laws have been interpreted as affording some protection to biodiversity, none is specific as to genetic diversity.

See also **Biodiversity Conservation; Critical Habitat; Endangered Species; Endangered Species Act of 1973;** *Tennessee Valley Authority v. Hill* **(1978).**

GEOGRAPHIC INFORMATION SYSTEM (GIS)   Computer technology for compiling and digitizing spatial information, such as aerial photographs or other visual depictions, and displaying it in one or more layers (computerized base maps and overlays) so that it can be analyzed and used. Sometimes called computer mapping, GIS technology actually does much more. It can display a variety of information, including habitat area boundaries, wildlife use or occurrence, vegetation type, soils data, hydrology, elevation, property ownership (e.g., by federal agency, private party, or state), land status (e.g., subject to conservation easement), surface water distribution, mineral interests, and zoning schemes.

An ongoing, nationwide application of GIS technology is the "Gap Program," whose goal is to compile information concerning species and habitat distributions using existing data available from current and historical sources to facilitate identification of common, rare, and at-risk species and communities. Combining these data with information about land status—specifically protection requirements, such as conservation easements or federal conservation requirements—allows land managers to identify areas where protection is needed and to analyze other management problems. Gaps in the data can be identified, suggesting information needs. Gap Programs have been undertaken in all 50 states. A project of the former National Biological Service, the programs are now being administered and continued by The Nature Conservancy, state fish and game agencies, universities, and cooperative efforts of these and other groups.

GEOTHERMAL RESOURCES   Defined by federal statute to include "all products of geothermal processes," including heat, steam, and other gases; hot water; hot brines; and any byproducts, such as minerals (subject to certain conditions) associated with these substances.

Geothermal resources on federal lands, or on private lands where the mineral estate has been reserved by the federal government, are treated as minerals and are subject to leasing under the Geothermal Steam Act of 1970. Geothermal resources are not widely distributed, but developable deposits are found in California, Idaho, Nevada, and northwestern Wyoming-southwestern Montana. In recent years controversy has simmered over the development of geothermal steam on private land owned by the Church Universal Triumphant just outside Yellowstone National Park. Park officials and environmentalists are concerned that tapping geothermal deposits in this area may disrupt or otherwise affect geothermal phenomena, such as geysers and hot springs, inside the park. The landowners claim the right to make use of the steam to heat greenhouses and for other domestic purposes. Congress has attempted several times to legislate a solution, so far unsuccessfully. The 1970 act was amended in 1988, however, to require that all leases contain conditions "necessary to protect significant thermal features" within parks whenever the Interior secretary has "scientific evidence" that geothermal development is "likely to adversely affect" such features. [30 U.S.C. § 1026]

See also **Leasing.**

GORE, ALBERT, JR.   Vice president of the United States under President Bill Clinton. Gore represented Tennessee in the U.S. House of Representatives from 1977 to 1985, and in the U.S. Senate from 1985 to 1992, until he left that office to become a candidate for vice president. He was a Democratic candidate for president in 1988. Before entering politics, Gore worked as a journalist for seven years and operated a small home-building business. He has a degree in government from Harvard University, and attended both divinity school and law school.

Gore is the author of *Earth in the Balance: Ecology and the Human Spirit* (Houghton Mifflin 1992), a science and policy analysis of the global ecological crisis. Long considered an environmental advocate, Gore has written that his "earliest lessons on environmental protection were about the prevention of soil erosion on our family farm." He currently owns a small farm in Tennessee. In Congress he focused on environmental issues, including Superfund legislation, global warming and the greenhouse effect, and international environmental cooperation. He has argued that environmental protection is "becoming a matter of national security." In 1992 he chaired the U.S. Senate delegation to the Earth Summit in Rio de Janeiro,

Brazil. As vice president he oversaw the Clinton administration's "Reinventing Government" initiative, which resulted in hundreds of efficiency measures, personnel reductions in numerous agencies including the federal land management agencies, and new programs.

The League of Conservation Voters, which awarded Gore a grade of 73 percent for his seven years (1985 to 1992) in the Senate, calls him "the most committed environmentalist ever to hold the office of vice president." In that position Gore has focused on climate change and international environmental issues, and has participated in several of the Clinton administration's conservation initiatives, including wetlands policy and the Northwest Forest Summit.

Gore was widely considered the front-runner for the Democratic nomination for president in 2000, at least until he was implicated in 1997 in allegedly improper political contributions to President Clinton's 1992 re-election campaign.

The vice president's duties include presiding over the U.S. Senate when it is in session, and voting in the case of a tie. Of course, he is also next in line to serve as president if the elected president dies or becomes incapacitated.

See also **Clinton, William Jefferson.**

GRAND STAIRCASE-ESCALANTE NATIONAL MONUMENT

Designated by proclamation by President Bill Clinton in 1996, pursuant to his power under the Antiquities Act of 1906. The national monument encompasses 1.7 million acres in southeastern Utah, including the Kaiparowits Plateau, and is situated between Bryce Canyon and Capitol Reef National Parks.

The designation has been a source of intense controversy, condemned from the outset by local and state political leaders as a classic example of federal "arrogance" and the "mother of all land grabs." Many observers viewed the move as politically motivated. Clinton was seen as having little to lose in Utah (he placed third there in the 1992 presidential election), but a tremendous amount of political capital to gain among national environmental groups and other advocates of protecting Utah's "red rock" wilderness. Indeed, many environmentalists praised the designation as the crowning achievement of Clinton's administration; according to the Southern Utah Wilderness Alliance, the action placed Clinton "among the greatest conservationists in history."

Much of the opposition to monument designation stems from fears that it will prevent mineral development of the area. The region is known to contain tremendous coal reserves, and significant petroleum deposits are also believed to exist. A Dutch mining company, Andalex, holds a coal lease to what is thought to be one of the largest coal reserves in the world; it planned to build a major mine on the Kaiparowits Plateau. Monument designation did not rescind that lease, but it will preclude mine development, which would require major road and power-line construction and result in tremendous increases in traffic. Similarly, the area contains valid existing rights relating to oil and gas. In late 1997 the federal government issued a permit to Conoco to drill an exploratory well on a lease it holds within the monument. Even before the permit was issued, The Wilderness Society had listed the new monument among the ten most endangered wild lands, identifying Conoco's exploratory drilling for oil as the chief threat.

Another objection relates to the 200,000 acres of state school lands, estimated to be worth as much as $1 billion, located within the boundaries of the monument. Utah officials are concerned that their inability to freely develop these lands or their resources will deprive the state of substantial funds for public education. Numerous proposals have been made to exchange these lands for federal lands or resources elsewhere. And in mid-1997 two lawsuits were filed, by the Utah Association of Counties and the School and Institutional Trust Lands Administration, challenging the monument designation.

Finally, some environmental groups express reservations about the monument because they fear it will undercut efforts to provide wilderness protection to many of the remaining qualified acres in Utah (nearly 5.3 million), and that 350,000 acres of monument lands will receive less protection than if they were designated as wilderness.

Designation of the monument incited a flurry of proposed legislation in Congress. Bills ranged from a proposal by Congressman Bennett (R-UT) to require the area to be managed according to principles of multiple use and sustained yield, to measures that would amend the Antiquities Act. These latter bills took various forms. Some deprived the president of his unilateral power to designate national monuments and/or required public notice and comment prior to new designations, while others limited the size of monuments established under the act. A bill introduced by Senator Orrin Hatch (R-UT), for instance, would require action by Congress and consultation with the governor of the affected state to designate a monument larger than 5,000 acres.

See also **Antiquities Act of 1906; Clinton, William Jefferson; Southern Utah Wilderness Alliance.**

GREATER YELLOWSTONE COALITION (GYC) Formed in 1983 in response to development pressures in the Greater Yellowstone Ecosystem and a desire to preserve the region's unique natural attributes: wildlife populations and habitat, scenic values, geothermal resources, and wilderness. GYC's mission is to "preserve and protect the Greater Yellowstone Ecosystem and the unique quality of life it sustains." The nonprofit organization now has more than 7,000 individual members and more than 127 member organizations (sportsmen's groups, conservation organizations, etc.).

GYC helped pioneer the concept of ecosystem management and works for its implementation in the Greater Yellowstone area. GYC's publication *Sustaining Greater Yellowstone: A Blueprint for the Future* responds to the diverse land ownership patterns and management policies (four federal agencies, state, and private) in the region by proposing designation of the Greater Yellowstone as the first National Sustainable Ecosystem, and setting forth recommendations for preserving and managing the region as an entire ecosystem.

GYC has been active in legislative efforts to designate wilderness areas and wild and scenic rivers and to protect the geothermal features of the ecosystem from disruption by drilling and development activities in the region; monitoring and responding to federal agency plans for grazing, logging, oil and gas exploration, and endangered species management; advocating reintroduction of gray wolves to the ecosystem; and political negotiations that led to a proposed land exchange between the federal government and a Canadian corporation, Noranda Minerals, to avoid development of the proposed New World Mine immediately northeast of Yellowstone National Park.

GYC publishes a quarterly journal, *Greater Yellowstone Report*, and hosts an annual conference, workshops, and field trips. Its staff includes several professionals in its Bozeman office and field representatives in Idaho Falls, Idaho, and Cody and Dubois, Wyoming. The organization is governed by a 23-member board of directors, 17 of whom live in or adjacent to the ecosystem. A 16-member science council serves the organization in an advisory capacity.

See also **Ecosystem Management; Greater Yellowstone Ecosystem; New World Mine; Wolf Reintroduction.**

GREATER YELLOWSTONE ECOSYSTEM   An area of nearly 18 million acres (28,000 square miles) in southwestern Montana, northwestern Wyoming, and southeastern Idaho. The Greater Yellowstone is often touted as the largest, still relatively intact temperate zone ecosystem in the world. At its core, the ecosystem contains the world's oldest national park, Yellowstone, established by an act of Congress in 1872. Yellowstone Park is surrounded or adjoined by Grand Teton National Park, seven national forests, three national wildlife refuges, several wilderness areas, and other federal lands, as well as state and private lands—all within the ecosystem boundaries. It is a region of superlatives: It contains the world's largest petrified forest, North America's largest high-elevation lake, the world's highest concentration of geothermal features, and the largest herd of (relatively) free-roaming bison. Although in jeopardy, its biodiversity, or species richness, rivals that of any ecosystem on the continent. Only two vertebrate species—the gray wolf and black-footed ferret—are known to have been lost from the region. The wolf was reintroduced in 1995 and appears to be thriving.

The Greater Yellowstone Ecosystem has been the subject of numerous books, law review and other articles, and proposed legislation. A private organization, the Greater Yellowstone Coalition, was established for the express purpose of protecting and preserving the ecosystem; its publication *Greater Yellowstone: A Blueprint for the Future* proposes designation and management of the area as the nation's first National Sustainable Ecosystem.

The continued cohesion of the ecosystem is jeopardized by its diverse ownership pattern and management systems, by a variety of resource development activities and land uses, and simply by increasing human use. These threats include clear-cut logging, especially in the Targhee National Forest in Idaho; oil and gas exploration and development; development of geothermal resources; invasion of exotic species; the proposed New World Mine just north of Yellowstone National Park; land subdivisions, especially around Bozeman, Montana; and escalating recreational visitation.

The region's economy has become increasingly service industry-oriented. By 1987, 62 percent of all jobs were in the service industry sector, which includes retail businesses, insurance, real estate, government, and recreation. Yet pressures still exist to allow development or extraction of the region's natural resource commodities: timber, minerals, and livestock forage.

See also **Biodiversity Conservation; Ecosystem Management; Greater Yellowstone Coalition; New World Mine; Wolf Reintroduction.**

GREENPEACE International nonprofit environmental organization, which evolved from the "Don't Make a Wave Committee," organized in 1971 to protest the testing of nuclear weapons on Amchitka Island. By 1996, Greenpeace claimed more than 5 million members worldwide. It works on issues ranging from nuclear disarmament, "safe energy," and global warming, to protection of the world's forests, oceans, and fish stocks, to the preservation of Antarctica as a world park. The organization is nonpartisan and apolitical, but lobbies extensively. It is perhaps best known for the nonviolent acts of civil disobedience and obstruction by individual members—for instance, the efforts of its flagship, the *MV Greenpeace,* to prevent the operations of Norwegian whalers and the harvest of baby fur seals and protest the harvest of old-growth forests in several countries. It relies heavily on volunteer activists.

In August 1997, the Greenpeace board of directors announced that it was closing all regional offices, laying off 300 employees, and limiting its issue work to climate change and logging. The organization's voting members (172 staff members and volunteers) challenged the board, calling for a vote on these actions. At press time, the imbroglio had not been resolved.

Habitat Conservation Plan (HCP)

Habitat Conservation Plan (HCP) A plan for conserving and managing an area of habitat on which one or more threatened or endangered species depend, authorized by the Endangered Species Act of 1973 (ESA), as amended in 1982, and often taking the form of an agreement entered into by private landowners, local government entities, the U.S. Fish and Wildlife Service (USFWS), and occasionally other federal agencies. An HCP allows a permittee to proceed with development or land-use activities under the plan, despite the incidental taking of protected species, in exchange for "adherence to long-term conservation commitments." That is, by taking steps to mitigate the effects of his or her activities and otherwise conserve the species' habitat, the developer is insured against prosecution or civil penalties imposed under the ESA for actions that incidentally harm a threatened or endangered species. Between 1983 and 1992, only 14 HCPs were approved. By October 1995, the number had increased to 112, and USFWS expected that about 350 would be in place or under development by the end of 1997. HCPs were the subject of a major national conference in early 1997.

The popularity of HCPs got a boost largely due to the Clinton administration and former USFWS director Mollie Beattie's efforts. Beattie encouraged greater use of long-term habitat conservation planning under the ESA as a means of conserving whole ecosystems, including both listed and unprotected species, and avoiding future listings. For it to work, she said, state and local officials and landowners would have to "come to the table" with USFWS officials and "agree on long-term conservation." She called this approach to management "anticipatory and aggressive." The Clinton administration also developed a simplified approach to HCPs for small projects with limited impacts.

In early 1997, the largest forest-lands HCP ever approved was finalized in Washington. The plan, which involves the Washington State Department of Natural Resources and four timber companies, encompasses 2.135 million acres, including 1.6 million acres of state-managed forests, and has a time span of 70 years. The area contains habitat for the northern spotted owl and several species of salmon and trout. The plan provides for harvesting a set amount of timber (650 million board feet) despite any future changes in federal ESA regulations, in exchange for managing the covered lands as an integrated ecosystem.

No Surprises

The Washington HCP illustrates that achieving insurance against the uncertainty of future regulation is a strong motivation for private parties' participation in HCPs. In 1994 the USFWS and National Marine Fisheries Service issued the so-called "No Surprises Policy," whose purpose is to assure "non-federal landowners participating in Habitat Conservation Planning (HCP) that no additional land restrictions or financial compensation will be required from an HCP permittee for species adequately covered by a properly functioning HCP in light of unforeseen or extraordinary circumstances." The agencies explained the policy as an attempt to reconcile two competing considerations: developers' need for certainty and the possibility of changed circumstances, necessitating the need to reconsider the mitigation measures in an HCP agreement. (According to the policy, certainty is the major benefit of HCPs.) In late 1996, several environmental groups sued to block implementation of the policy, which had not been properly promulgated under the Administrative Procedure Act. Subsequently, the administration agreed to publish it as a proposed rule.

Essentially, the policy provides that USFWS may seek additional mitigation, *other than* land or financial compensation, from HCP permittees, but only in "extraordinary circumstances." Moreover, any changes to the terms of an HCP must be limited "to the maximum extent possible." The policy further declares that the primary obligation to take additional mitigation measures will rest not with permittees, but with others, presumably the USFWS itself, other governmental entities, or subsequent developers.

"Extraordinary circumstances" is not defined, but the USFWS is required to use the best scientific and commercial data available in order to demonstrate that they exist. The policy lists several factors the agency must consider in making this determination, such as "the ecological significance of that portion of the range affected by an HCP" and "whether failure to adopt additional conservation measures would appreciably reduce the likelihood of survival and recovery of the affected species in the wild."

Publication of a final rule is expected in 1998, but may be delayed pending the outcome of congressional ESA reform efforts. A 1997 bill introduced by Senators Chafee and Kempthorne to reform the ESA would incorporate the "no surprises policy" into federal law.

See also **Biodiversity Conservation; Ecosystem Management; Endangered Species Act of 1973; Incidental Taking.**

HOFFMAN HOMES, INC. V. ENVIRONMENTAL PROTECTION AGENCY (1993) This important case considered the scope of the U.S. Army Corps of Engineers' (Corps) regulatory jurisdiction under Clean Water Act section 404 (CWA). The issue was whether the developer, Hoffman Homes, had violated the CWA by filling a one-acre seasonal pond without a section 404 permit. The Corps characterized the pond as a wetland, and maintained that it was within the regulatory definition of "waters of the United States," and thus subject to permitting. The pond had no direct connection with either groundwater or any other surface water; it merely collected rain and snowmelt. Hoffman Homes admitted that the pond was a wetland but denied that it was subject to regulation.

For purposes of regulation, the Corps and the Environmental Protection Agency define "waters of the United States" as including "all other waters such as intrastate lakes, ...wetlands, ...or natural ponds, the use, degradation or destruction of which could affect interstate or foreign commerce." [40 C.F.R. § 230.3(s)(3); 33 C.F.R. § 328.3(a)(3)] Also included are "wetlands adjacent to waters (other than waters that are themselves wetlands) identified in [the other paragraphs of the definition]." The term "adjacent" is defined to mean "bordering, contiguous, or neighboring." [33 C.F.R. § 328.3(c)] An administrative law judge initially determined that the pond was isolated, i.e., not "adjacent," and thus not subject to the permit requirement.

The Seventh Circuit Court of Appeals, however, focused on the phrase "*could* affect interstate...commerce" in the regulatory definition of "waters of the United States." It determined that the Corps *could have* regulated the fill if there had been evidence of a *potential*, minimal connection with interstate commerce. Evidence of use by migratory birds, such as waterfowl, could have satisfied this test, the court said, but the government had offered no evidence that the pond was, in fact, so used. Government testimony that the pond provided suitable waterfowl habitat was "merely speculation," the court ruled, and hence insufficient.

Hoffman Homes implicitly rejects the notion that isolated wetlands are necessarily exempt from section 404 regulation [the issue the U.S. Supreme Court had found unnecessary to reach in *United States v. Riverside Bayview Homes* (1985)]. As long as potential connections with interstate commerce are sufficient to trigger federal Commerce Clause authority, the Corps's regulatory jurisdiction is engaged.

See also **Clean Water Act Section 404; Commerce Clause; Corps of Engineers; Navigable Waters;** *United States v. Riverside Bayview Homes, Inc.* **(1985); Wetland.**

HOUSE AGRICULTURE COMMITTEE A 49-member committee that considers measures relating to all aspects of protecting and regulating agricultural production, agricultural research, and soil conservation. Other conservation-related activities include protection of wildlife in national forests and regulation of acquired forest lands. One subcommittee is devoted to resource conservation, research, and forestry.

When Rep. Bob Smith (R-OR) became committee chair in 1997, he lamented the generally poor state of federal forests and announced that "forestry—the health of the forests and our communities—will be a principal focus" for the committee in the 105th Congress. He proposed a strategy for restoring forest ecosystems based on a "demonstration program" of "ecosystem health pilot projects" in one or two national forests in each affected state. These projects would involve "credible science, citizen involvement from diverse interests..., management at a landscape or watershed level, and flexibility for federal land managers at the ground level."

See also **House Appropriations Committee; Senate Agriculture, Nutrition, and Forestry Committee; Senate Appropriations Committee; Senate Energy and Natural Resources Committee; Senate Environment Committee.**

HOUSE APPROPRIATIONS COMMITTEE A 58-member congressional committee responsible for all appropriations of revenue to support the workings of government, as well as the rescission of appropriations already made. Its conservation-related subcommittees include Agriculture, Energy and Water Development, and Interior. Robert L. Livingston (R-LA) serves as chair.

Conservation bills that would not survive the legislative process on their own are often attached to appropriations bills to ensure their consideration. Recent examples include public land grazing reforms and salvage logging measures.

See also **House Agriculture Committee; House Resources Committee; Senate Agriculture, Nutrition, and Forestry Committee; Senate Appropriations Committee; Senate Energy and Natural Resources Committee; Senate Environment Committee.**

HOUSE RESOURCES COMMITTEE A 49-member congressional committee currently chaired by Alaska Republican Don Young, who deleted the word "Natural" before "Resources" in the committee's name when he took office in 1995. The Resources Committee considers all measures relating to public lands and natural resources, including forests, parks, rivers, water and mineral development, reclamation, grazing, and wilderness, and various other matters pertaining to Indian tribes, energy development, preservation of archaeological resources, etc. Western Republicans currently dominate the committee membership, and they are generally considered much more conservative than the full House on environmental and natural resource issues. Thus, the committee can act as a roadblock to full consideration of moderate legislation.

The three-member Alaska delegation controls three of the most important congressional committees for purposes of natural resource policy: House Resources (Don Young), Senate Energy (Frank Murkowski), and Senate Appropriations (Ted Stevens).

See also **House Agriculture Committee; House Appropriations Committee; Senate Agriculture, Nutrition, and Forestry Committee; Senate Appropriations Committee; Senate Energy and Natural Resources Committee; Senate Environment Committee.**

HUGHES V. OKLAHOMA **(1979)** A U.S. Supreme Court decision that overruled a portion of *Geer v. Connecticut* (1896), decided by the Court nearly a century earlier. *Geer* held that a state could forbid the export of wild game taken within its borders without violating the "dormant" Commerce Clause of the U.S. Constitution. *Geer*'s reasoning rested in part on the premise that states "owned" wildlife within their borders and held it in trust for their citizens. In *Hughes*, the U.S. Supreme

Court ruled that states neither possess nor control wildlife. According to the Court, the notion that states owned wildlife was a "nineteenth-century legal fiction" that had diminished "to the point of virtual extinction."

The *Hughes* Court struck down an Oklahoma statute that prohibited the transportation of minnows taken within the state for sale outside the state, ruling that it violated the dormant Commerce Clause of the U.S. Constitution. (The Commerce Clause authorizes Congress to regulate interstate commerce. The dormant Commerce Clause doctrine generally prohibits states from enacting laws that would burden interstate commerce, even if Congress hasn't passed legislation in the particular field.) However, the *Hughes* Court reassured states that they retain ample authority, consistent with constitutional limits, to conserve and protect their wildlife.

As if to confirm this assurance, the Court, in *Maine v. Taylor* (1986) upheld a Maine statute that prohibited importing into the state live bait fish (which competed with Maine's own bait fish industry) because of concerns that parasites in the imported fish might threaten native Maine fish. The Court held that a state law that has discriminatory effects on interstate commerce may nevertheless be valid if no less discriminatory means of protecting a legitimate state interest exists. The Maine statute was such a law.

In addition to the Commerce Clause, the Privileges and Immunities Clause and the Equal Protection Clause of the Constitution also limit states' ability to discriminate against nonresidents whose livelihood involves harvesting wildlife. However, to date no court has held that the Constitution prohibits states from imposing different requirements on nonresident and resident hunters and fishermen.

See also *Baldwin v. Fish and Game Commission of Montana* (1978); *Clajon Production Corporation v. Petera* (1995); **Commerce Clause; Hunting.**

HUNTING   The taking of wild animals for sport or subsistence by a hand-held weapon, such as a firearm or bow and arrow. Hunting is regulated for the most part by states, although the federal government regulates (usually pursuant to its Commerce Clause or Property Clause authority) the taking of certain species, such as migratory birds, threatened or endangered species, and wild horses. Federal regulations may also apply in certain areas; for instance, hunting is prohibited in most national parks, and may be subject to special requirements in national wildlife refuges.

According to the most recent annual survey conducted by the Census Bureau for the U.S. Fish and Wildlife Service, the number of hunters and anglers in the United States has remained relatively constant since 1991. Approximately 14.1 million people, ages 16 and older, hunted in 1991; the comparable figure for 1996 was 14 million (7 percent of the population). The number of anglers decreased over the same period from 35.6 to 35.2 million (18 percent of the population). Although the proportion of the population participating in these sports is declining, spending by hunters and anglers, along with spending by bird-watchers, photographers, and other wildlife enthusiasts, has increased dramatically—to $96.9 billion in 1996. This is an increase of more than 59 percent in five years and comprises 1.3 percent of the nation's gross domestic product. By comparison, 31 percent of the adult U.S. population participates in nonconsumptive wildlife-related recreation.

"Bear baiting" is an especially controversial form of hunting. Hunters use rotten meat, fish, or some other smelly attractant to entice bears to the "bait station." Hunters with bows and arrows generally just wait nearby; rifle hunters typically visit the area frequently after placing the bait, hoping to catch a bear at the station or at least pick up its tracks. Animal rights activists and others who claim the sport gives hunters an unfair advantage have called for a ban on the practice. Some states have outlawed bear baiting: Colorado voters banned it by initiative. Voters in Idaho, however, rejected such a ban in 1996.

The threat of a lawsuit caused the U.S. Forest Service to ban bear baiting on Wyoming national forests in 1993 until the agency could formulate a uniform policy regarding the sport. The next year, without having issued the promised policy, the Forest Service announced that it would nevertheless allow bear baiting during that season. The Fund for Animals promptly sued. The Forest Service subsequently issued a formal policy, which in essence allows baiting where it is allowed by the state and prohibits it where it is prohibited by the state. However, the federal agency may, under certain prescribed circumstances, restrict or prohibit baiting on a site-specific basis even where it would be allowed by state law.

Trapping of fur-bearers is another controversial form of hunting, made so largely by the efforts of animal rights groups. The economic revenues generated by trapping have dwindled in recent years, except perhaps in localized areas. Louisiana, for instance, still has a healthy fur industry. Some states have banned trapping altogether; in most states where it is allowed, it is strictly regulated, although enforcement is sometimes lax.

Confrontations in recent years between hunters and animal rights activists have become more common. Activists' tactics include causing a disturbance in the vicinity of hunters so as to scare away wildlife, as well as more traditional public relations techniques. Some states have enacted statutes that protect hunters lawfully engaged in their sport and provide a cause of action against persons who interfere with lawful hunting activities.

See also **Animal Rights Movement;** *California Coastal Commission v. Granite Rock Co.* **(1987); Dingell-Johnson Act; Fund for Animals; Pittman-Robinson Act; State Ballot Initiatives; Wildlife Management.**

ILLINOIS CENTRAL RAILROAD CO. V. ILLINOIS
(1892) A U.S. Supreme Court decision, generally credited as the Court's principal pronouncement on the public trust doctrine. The Court ruled that the Illinois state legislature could not transfer title to the Chicago waterfront (along the shore of Lake Michigan) and part of the submerged lands in the Chicago harbor because those lands, which the state had acquired at statehood, were held in trust for the benefit of Illinois citizens. The trust could not be "relinquished" or "abdicated" by transferring title to the Illinois Central Railroad. The trust applies to the beds and banks of all navigable waters, that is, the shores of and lands beneath those waters deemed navigable at the time of statehood. In an earlier opinion, *Pollard's Lessee v. Hagan* (1845), the U.S. Supreme Court had determined that states held title to these lands, but did not describe the nature of that title.

The Court held that a state might permissibly sell or dispose of parcels of these submerged lands or convey a temporary interest in them if such conveyances were in the public interest, but the state could never transfer "the whole property"; rather, it must retain the lands and manage them for the benefit of the public. In a later case, the U.S. Supreme Court held that the United States may reserve or transfer title to submerged lands prior to statehood, thus preventing the new state from obtaining title, but only if it expresses its intent clearly. [*See Utah Division of State Lands v. United States* (1987).]

Determination of which waters were navigable at the time of statehood, and hence which lands are held in trust by the states, can become an issue in modern times under several circumstances, for instance, in determining title to minerals in submerged lands or establishing management responsibilities on rivers within national parks or other federal lands. The issue has special significance in Alaska, which encompasses vast federal land holdings as well as significant amounts of state- and Native-owned lands, and abundant water. In *Alaska v. United States* (1997), the Court applied the strict test established in *Utah Division of State Lands* and concluded that the United States had expressly reserved title to submerged lands in the

National Petroleum Reserve and what is now the Arctic National Wildlife Refuge in Alaska. Thus, Alaska did not acquire title to these lands at statehood, and the United States had authority to offer these lands for mineral leasing.

The *Illinois Central* Court distinguished the nature of the state's title to lands beneath navigable waters "from that which the State holds in lands intended for sale [and] from the title which the United States holds in the public lands which are open to preemption and sale." Nevertheless, an analogous "public trust doctrine" has been applied by some courts and legal commentators to other lands and resources, such as national parks, wilderness areas, water, and endangered species.

See also **Equal Footing Doctrine;** *National Audubon Society v. Superior Court of Alpine County* **(1983); Navigable Waters; Public Trust Doctrine.**

INCIDENTAL TAKING   A "taking" (i.e., killing or harming) of an endangered species that otherwise would be unlawful, but which is authorized in advance by permit pursuant to section 10 of the Endangered Species Act of 1973 (ESA). The Secretary of the Interior may permit such a taking if it is "incidental to, and not the purpose of, the carrying out of an otherwise lawful activity." Incidental take permits may be issued in conjunction with a biological opinion rendered by the U.S. Fish and Wildlife Service at the conclusion of an ESA section 7 consultation. An applicant for an incidental take permit must submit, and obtain approval of, a habitat conservation plan (HCP). The HCP must document the likely effect on the species, describe the measures that will be taken to mitigate the impacts and the alternatives considered, and demonstrate that funding for the plan exists. Only 21 incidental taking permits had been issued as of early 1994. The Clinton administration greatly expanded the use of HCPs and, concomitantly, issued many more incidental take permits.

See also **Endangered Species; Endangered Species Act of 1973; Habitat Conservation Plan; Section 7 Consultation; Take.**

INHOLDING   A tract of privately owned land surrounded by federal land, usually land managed by the U.S. Forest Service, Bureau of Land Management (BLM), or National Park Service. Approximately 17 percent of the land within national forest boundaries and 40 percent of the land within BLM district boundaries are private or state land. Inholdings give rise to important land management concerns.

In the West, inholdings resulted largely from federal land disposition policies in the 1800s and early 1900s. Homesteaders often settled on lands along streams or around springs in the arid and semiarid West, and the surrounding upland areas often remained public. In the East, where most national forests are "acquired lands" (once-private lands reacquired by the federal government), about half the land within the boundaries of the 51 national forests is privately owned.

Inholders number nearly 1.4 million, and their rights are of increasing importance in the private property movement; membership is growing in advocacy groups, such as the National Inholders Association. Not all inholders oppose federal ownership of the surrounding lands; indeed, many inholders value the seclusion and buffering from development that federal lands can afford. Others, however, see federal lands as a source of limitations on how they can use their private property.

Inholding management problems usually relate to access—most often private access through public land to the private inholding, but sometimes public access across the private inholding to surrounding public lands. Other problems include the impacts of private land development on public lands and resources, and the potential for fire.

The 450,000 acres of wilderness inholdings, often stemming from old patented mining claims, are particularly problematic. The Wilderness Act of 1964 made special provisions for access to inholdings within designated wilderness areas, as have individual wilderness bills enacted since. The federal government is prohibited from exercising any right of condemnation on lands within the wilderness. Wilderness inholdings can be acquired only through willing sales or land exchanges. As a result, some inholders have engaged in development incompatible with preservation of the surrounding wilderness, and the Forest Service can do little to prevent or remove them. Still other inholders simply use the threat of incompatible development to demand exorbitant exchange value for their lands.

Inholding access provisions also can be found in the Alaska National Interest Lands Conservation Act (which has been held applicable to all national forests, not just lands in Alaska) and the Federal Land Policy and Management Act.

Federal agencies, especially the U.S. Forest Service, are interested in acquiring inholdings but often lack both the funds and administrative flexibility to do so. Third-party groups, such as the Wilderness Land Trust, founded in 1991, work to acquire wilderness inholdings for inclusion into surrounding public lands. The Forest Service reimburses the trust when funds are made available, often through the federal Land and Water Conservation Fund. Buying out inholdings was a major emphasis of early Land and Water Conservation Fund spending, but in recent years Congress has not fully authorized spending.

See also **Land and Water Conservation Fund; Land Exchange.**

INSTREAM FLOW In water law, a right to use, or the use of, water for *instream* purposes, i.e., channel maintenance, fisheries, wildlife habitat, recreation, and aesthetics. Obtaining an instream-flow right in several western states, where water is allocated according to the prior appropriation doctrine, was disallowed for many years. Most states' water law required that water be diverted from the stream and put to one of several designated "beneficial uses" (irrigation, domestic purposes, mining, etc.) in order to qualify for a water right. Instream flows do not entail diversion and were not identified as a beneficial use in most states. The effect in areas where streams were fully, if not overly, appropriated was that watercourses could literally be dried up at certain times of the year, with devastating effects on fish and wildlife that depended on aquatic and riparian habitat.

In the past 10 to 20 years, most western states have amended their water law, either by statute or judicially, to require that water appropriations serve the public interest and provide for the maintenance of minimum stream flows at least in certain waters. The mechanisms vary, but usually only a state agency (such as the state fish and game agency) is allowed to hold an instream flow right. Because the prior appropriation doctrine is based on the principle "first in time, first in right," instream flow rights are junior to all previously established rights. In dry years, they may be no more than "paper rights," if more senior water users are entitled to take all the water in a stream. Thus, some states have devised mechanisms for allocating water from more senior right-holders in order to serve the purposes of maintaining minimum stream flows where needed.

Water pollution control law may provide another means of maintaining instream flows. When a state establishes water quality requirements for streams and lakes, it must also designate the desired uses of those waters, such as cold-water fishery or contact recreation. Those uses then become enforceable under the scheme set up in the federal Clean Water Act (CWA) as part of the state's water quality standards. In 1994, the U.S. Supreme Court upheld the state of Washington's requirement that a proposed hydroelectric facility maintain a minimum stream flow in a river designated as a salmon fishery as a condition of obtaining a federal permit that it needed to operate. [*See PUD No. 1 of Jefferson County v. Washington Department of Ecology* (1994).] The requirement was imposed as a condition of obtaining state certification, under CWA section 401, that the facility would comply with all applicable state water quality requirements. The Court had no trouble in finding that a minimum flow must be maintained to sustain the river's designated use as a salmon fishery. CWA section 401 applies only to activities or facilities that require a federal permit, but in such cases it can provide states with an important additional means of protecting stream flows.

See also **Prior Appropriation;** *PUD No. 1 of Jefferson County v. Washington Department of Ecology* **(1994).**

IIIII **INTERGENERATIONAL EQUITY**   A term used, especially in international law, to refer to the moral if not legal obligation owed by members of the current generation to conserve resources and protect the environment so that future generations are not disadvantaged. Proponents of intergenerational equity believe that the present generation of humans stands in a trust relationship with past and future generations: Members of the present generation both hold the Earth in trust for future generations and enjoy beneficiary status, entitled to use and benefit from the Earth's resources. If the current generation maximizes its own welfare at the expense of future generations, it violates its intergenerational obligations. Thus, the sustainable use of natural resources becomes an intergenerational problem.

Intergenerational equity is based on several principles. First, the current generation should preserve biological diversity and the health of the Earth's ecosystems. Depleting resources, particularly genetic diversity, denies options to future generations. Second, long-term, irreversible environmental degradation should be avoided, especially since the values of future generations cannot be readily predicted; some resources not considered valuable today may in time acquire value. Third, if environmental degradation in one sector of the environment is unavoidable, it should be compensated for by improvements in other sectors. Finally, where problems, such as pollution or invasion of exotic species, already exist, the costs of rehabilitating the environment should not be deferred to future generations. However, *inter*generational equity should not be achieved at the expense of *intra*generational fairness. That is, today's poor should not be denied access to natural resources if they have no viable economic alternatives.

Support for a policy of intergenerational equity exists at international, national, and state levels. The Stockholm Declaration of the UN Conference on the Human Environment, drafted in 1972, acknowledges a "solemn responsibility" to protect the environment for future generations. The constitutions of a number of foreign nations, including Guyana, Namibia, and Vanuatu, recognize the environmental rights of future generations. In a landmark 1994 ruling, the supreme court of the Philippines recognized the right of a group of schoolchildren to sue to stop logging of old-growth rainforests on behalf of their generation and succeeding ones.

In this country, proponents of intergenerational equity find support in the preamble of the U.S. Constitution, which identifies as a national goal "secur[ing] the blessings of Liberty for ourselves and our Posterity." The National Environmental Policy Act, section 101(b), provides that it is "the continuing responsibility of the Federal Government to use all practicable means...to the end that the Nation may—fulfill the responsibilities of each generation as trustee of the environment for succeeding generations." Other federal statutes, such as the Wilderness Act of 1964 and Federal Land Policy and Management Act, also make it federal policy to manage the lands so as to meet the needs of future generations. Similarly, the constitutions of Hawaii, Illinois, Montana, and Pennsylvania recognize an obligation to preserve the environment for future generations.

Implementing or enforcing such a policy is difficult at best. One problem is that U.S. courts have not recognized standing to raise intergenerational environmental claims. Proponents of intergenerational equity argue that standing should not be an obstacle. They point out that representatives of charitable trusts may sue on behalf of unborn beneficiaries and that courts appoint guardians for unborn heirs and unborn fetuses. Intergenerational standing for environmental claims, they assert, would be just another step in protecting the interests of future generations. Thus, a public trust concept is probably the best approach to the task of ensuring that future generations' needs will be met.

See also **Genetic Diversity; Public Trust Doctrine; Standing; Sustainable Development.**

INTERIOR BOARD OF LAND APPEALS (IBLA)

Adjudicative body in the Department of the Interior that decides appeals from agency decisions concerning the use and management of public lands. The IBLA reviews decisions by the Bureau of Land Management, Minerals Management Service, Office of Surface Mining, and Bureau of Indian Affairs, and renders final decisions under the Surface Mining Control and Reclamation Act of 1977. Decisions by the IBLA are in turn reviewable in federal district court.

See also **Bureau of Land Management; Department of the Interior.**

KLEPPE V. NEW MEXICO (1976)

One of the strongest statements by the U.S. Supreme Court of Congress's power over the public lands under the Property Clause of the U.S. Constitution. The case grew out of a rather mundane set of circumstances. Cattle belonging to a New Mexico rancher were being "molested" and kept from scarce water and forage by wild burros on federal lands managed by the Bureau of Land Management (BLM). The rancher sought the aid of the New Mexico Livestock Board, which rounded up and removed several of the burros pursuant to its (state) estray law authority. BLM objected that this action violated the federal Wild, Free-Roaming Horses and Burros Act (WFRHBA), which forbids anyone (except BLM or the U.S. Forest Service, subject to conditions specified in the act) from killing, capturing, or harassing these animals on federal lands. The state of New Mexico responded by suing to have the federal statute declared unconstitutional. As Professors Coggins and Glicksman have written, "From such small circumstantial acorns grow the oaks of constitutional principle."

Giving short shrift to New Mexico's arguments, the Court unanimously rejected its contentions that wild horses and burros are the property of the state in which they are found and that the Property Clause authorizes the federal government to protect its *lands*, but not the wildlife living there. Although the Court did not decide who, if anyone, owned the animals, it did note that "it is far from clear that...Congress cannot assert a property interest in [them] superior to that of the State."

The Court found ample authority for the WFRHBA in the Constitution's Property Clause (article IV, section 3, clause 2), which provides: "The Congress shall have Power to dispose of and make all needful Rules and Regulations respecting the Territories or other property belonging to the United States." The act and its legislative history established that free-roaming horses and burros are "an integral part of the natural system of the public lands" and that "their management was necessary 'for achievement of an ecological balance.'" The Court declared: "[W]e have repeatedly observed that '[t]he power over the public land thus entrusted to Congress is without limitations.'" Furthermore, "The 'complete power' that Congress has over public lands necessarily includes the power to regulate and protect the wildlife living there." The Court concluded that the WFRHBA was clearly a "'needful' regulation 'respecting' the public lands" authorized by the Property Clause and thus a valid exercise of congressional authority.

The Court acknowledged the states' "unquestionably...broad trustee and police powers over wild animals" as well as their authority, in most circumstances, to enforce their civil and criminal authority on public lands. "But where those state laws conflict with [federal] legislation passed pursuant to the Property Clause, the law is clear: the state laws must recede." Accordingly, the Court held that the New Mexico estray law was preempted, and invalid, to the extent that it conflicted with the federal statute.

Significance of *Kleppe*

Kleppe v. New Mexico should have erased any doubt either that the United States owns the public lands or that Congress may regulate their uses and resources as it sees fit. In fact, in the same year that *Kleppe* was decided, Congress passed the Federal Land Policy and Management Act, which established the national policy to retain in federal ownership the public lands managed by the Bureau of Land Management. Nevertheless, states' rights advocates and so-called Wise Use proponents, county supremacists, and Sagebrush Rebels persist in their arguments that these lands rightfully belong to the states or should be transferred to the states or into private ownership. The courts continue to reject claims that the federal government does not own the public lands; for example, in 1996, the United States won a challenge to the Nye County Resolutions in federal court in Nevada. [*United States v. Nye County*] The government also has successfully defended at least half a dozen lawsuits brought by ranchers, miners, or counties challenging U.S. authority over the public lands. Faring poorly in the courts, the "rebels" increasingly are taking their cases to their congressional representatives, state and county legislative bodies, and the media. Even violence has become a more common tactic.

See also **County Supremacy Movement;** *Hughes v. Oklahoma* **(1979); Hunting; Preemption; Property Clause; Sagebrush Rebellion; Wild, Free-Roaming Horses and Burros Act; Wildlife Management; Wise Use Movement.**

🏛 KNUTSON-VANDENBERG (K-V) FUND Fund estab-

lished by an act of Congress in 1930, intended to finance reforestation of old fields and lands acquired by the U.S. Forest Service (USFS) during the Depression. The fund became increasingly controversial after the National Forest Management Act of 1976 allowed use of the monies for any "improvements" in the timber sale area, and the USFS began to conduct larger, more expensive timber cuts to increase the funds available to it. Since 1983 about half of K-V monies have been used for reforestation; 25 to 45 percent of monies have been spent on other resources and activities.

The Forest Service can put in a K-V fund whatever amount of timber sale money it estimates is needed to "clean up" the sale area, replant it, cover agency overhead costs, and finance related improvements or mitigation. The agency may keep nearly 100 percent of timber receipts for these purposes. This results in deficits to the U.S. Treasury, since 25 percent of timber sale receipts must, by other law, be paid to local counties.

National forest managers find K-V monies highly desirable as they are in addition to appropriations from Congress and thus significantly supplement agency operating funds. The problem with the law is that it encourages below-cost and destructive logging practices. The more costly it will be to rehabilitate and reforest a sale area, the more money the Forest Service can retain to cover those expenses *and* use for other purposes. Some ludicrous examples of K-V fund uses have been documented. For instance, the Gallatin National Forest sold timber and used the receipts to close existing forest roads to enhance grizzly bear habitat—even though logging would require the building of roads in other grizzly habitat! The Bighorn National Forest planned to use timber sale receipts to fund an inventory of prehistoric cultural resources, but the timber sale destroyed some of the artifacts.

The K-V fund is criticized because it encourages both more logging and more destructive logging practices, such as clear-cutting, and it discourages the use of selective cutting, which is normally followed by natural regeneration. Several legislative solutions have been proposed, including eliminating the fund, restricting spending to the fund's original purposes (reforestation and timber stand improvement), limiting the amount of money that can be placed in the fund, or requiring timber contractors to reforest logged areas. Recent Congresses have considered a few of these proposals, but no action has been taken.

See also **Below-Cost Timber Sales; Clear-Cutting; National Forest Management Act of 1976.**

LACEY ACT Prohibits the interstate transportation of "any wild animals or birds" (later amended to include fish) taken in violation of state, federal, or tribal law, as well as the import or export of wildlife contrary to law. Passed in 1900, this federal statute is a relatively straightforward exercise of the federal government's power under the Commerce Clause. For instance, if a hunter kills more than the state's bag limit of pheasants and then crosses a state line in taking his birds home, he would commit a federal crime. The Lacey Act also prohibits the importation of certain listed exotic species, known as the "black list," determined to be pests or otherwise undesirable. It provides both civil and criminal penalties for violations. Civil penalties are based on the market value of the plant or animal taken or possessed; criminal penalties include both fines and imprisonment.

In 1988, after federal courts split over whether the statute applied to hunting guides and outfitters who provided hunts in which game laws are violated, Congress amended the Lacey Act to expressly include such conduct. The act now provides that both offering and purchasing guiding or outfitting services for the illegal taking of wildlife are punishable. This amendment made the act a more effective tool for combating the commercialization of wildlife.

Although there have been relatively few published cases and no decisions by the U.S. Supreme Court, federal courts have uniformly upheld the Lacey Act, including against Commerce Clause challenges based on the recent U.S. Supreme Court decision in *United States v. Lopez* (1995). In another recent case, a federal appeals court held that the Lacey Act does apply to captive-bred wildlife, but that exporting wildlife for breeding purposes is not the kind of harm that the statute seeks to avoid. [*United States v. Bernal* (1996)]

See also **Commerce Clause**.

🏛 Land and Water Conservation Fund (LWCF)

Fund established by section 2 of the federal Land and Water Conservation (LWC) Act of 1964, since amended, to provide for the acquisition of natural resource lands and to finance outdoor recreation projects by federal, state, and local governments. The fund is financed by certain federal revenues (up to $900 million annually), including portions of receipts from oil and gas leasing on the Outer Continental Shelf (OCS), federal taxes on motorboat fuel, sales of surplus lands, and entrance fees at certain recreation areas. Some funds are available to states on a 50 percent matching basis; to be eligible, states must have an approved State Comprehensive Outdoor Recreation Plan, and the project must be consistent with the plan. Since its inception, expenditures of $8 billion of fund monies, including more than $3.2 billion in matching grants to states, have protected thousands of acres of parklands, recreation areas, and wildlife habitat, including national wildlife refuges; the major federal land management agencies have all been fund beneficiaries. State grants alone have contributed to the purchase of 8,551 tracts totaling 2.3 million acres, and helped build tens of thousands of parks, swimming pools, and other facilities.

Two important original purposes behind the fund included acquiring inholdings within national parks, forests, and refuges, and establishing significant recreation areas easily accessible to major cities. The former purpose secured the support of some western conservatives who otherwise would have been inclined to oppose the fund for adding to federal land holdings.

Environmental law professor and scholar William H. Rodgers selected the LWC Act as first in his list of the U.S. laws that "have contributed most to the protection of the natural world." He describes the fund as "changing the face of urban and rural America." Explaining that "recreational opportunities for the poor and underprivileged were a prominent theme" of the LWC Act when it was passed, he traces today's environmental justice movement to the vision of this legislation. Rodgers gives Stewart L. Udall, Interior secretary under Presidents Johnson and Carter, significant credit for passage of the LWC Act.

Congressional support for the LWC has been waning in recent years, however. Even though annual expenditures of $900 million were authorized by Congress (in 1976), and OCS yearly revenues have been $2.7 *billion*, annual congressional *appropriations* to the fund have averaged only about $250 million in recent years, and most of that has been used to purchase federal conservation lands. The appropriation dropped to $138 million in 1996, its lowest level ever. Appropriations for state projects, which in 1979 exceeded $369 million, have all but ceased.

The fund's decline began with the Reagan administration, but even under President Clinton it has languished. In 1994, the House Natural Resources Committee declared that "the early vision of the LWCF has been lost" and recommended that the fund be merged with the smaller Urban Parks and Recreation Recovery Program. The committee cited growing urban populations, loss of open space and scenic views to development, and a shortage of urban recreational opportunities as justifying an overhaul of the two programs and a new emphasis on providing urban conservation and recreation lands across the country, but especially in the East. Other arguments against the use of fund money for land acquisition include the future costs to the government for maintaining those lands and the need to balance the federal budget. Indeed, since the 1980s, monies that should have gone into the fund have been diverted, used to cut the deficit or underwrite other government programs.

A coalition of conservation groups annually publishes a wish list of projects that the groups would like to see funded by the LWCF. There is some indication that LWCF appropriations may increase. In 1997, Senator Frank Murkowski (R-AK), conservative chair of the Senate Energy Committee, expressed his intent to try to renew funding for state LWCF projects. Nevertheless, Murkowski (and others, including the House Appropriations Committee) opposed a provision in the 1997 budget proposal by the Clinton administration (and approved by a Senate subcommittee) that would have authorized additional LWCF funding to acquire the Headwaters Grove of redwoods in California and the New World Mine site just north of Yellowstone National Park. Murkowski called the deal a "land grab" and a distortion of the purposes of the LWCF program, and said the money would be better spent on state-identified needs.

See also **Inholding; Murkowski, Frank H.; New World Mine; Udall, Stewart.**

LAND EXCHANGE   Land transactions authorized by numerous federal statutes, notably the Federal Land Policy and Management Act, for a variety of land-management and conservation-related purposes. Exchanges are negotiated by the executive department, and provide an important means of obtaining desired tracts in an era when congressional appropriations for such purposes are limited or nonexistent. The government uses exchanges to prevent development on lands with high natural values, to eliminate private inholdings within federal reserves, and to block up dispersed holdings, such as in the "checkerboard" areas along major railroad routes in the West. Exchanges can be controversial for a variety of reasons, including perceptions about the relative values of the lands, that the federal government's land holdings are being expanded improperly, or that congressional authority over land acquisition is being undermined or overridden.

A recent transaction among the Bureau of Land Management, U.S. Forest Service, three timber companies, and 37 private landowners involved a trade of 9,000 acres of private lands for 8,200 acres of federal holdings. The purpose of the exchange was to protect 24 miles of critical spawning habitat of the endangered Snake River chinook salmon in northeastern Oregon. A Montana exchange between the government and a lumber company involved a swap of a few parcels of federal land near the Big Sky ski resort for 55,000 acres of forested land. An apparently similar trade between the government and a lumber company in Washington fell through, however, after an appraisal revealed that the public would be getting only 1,800 acres of forested land while giving away 3,000 acres. Several land exchanges have brought together the Bureau of Land Management and ranchers or other landowners in the West. An ongoing exchange effort seeks to make accessible to the public a block of 55,000 acres of land adjacent to a popular Wyoming reservoir. The private participant, a rancher, would obtain BLM lands that could be used in his sheep operation. One of the most widely publicized proposed land exchanges (not yet finalized) involves the New World Mine just north of Yellowstone National Park.

See also **Checkerboard; Federal Land Policy and Management Act; Inholding; Land and Water Conservation Fund.**

LAND TRUST Government organizations or private, non-profit corporations, associations, or trusts whose goals are to preserve the ecological, aesthetic, or historic attributes of land. Land trusts preserve open space and wildlife habitat, keep lands agricultural, and provide income and estate tax relief. The means used to achieve these goals include taking title to land (often only temporarily), holding conservation easements, and managing property. In these ways, trusts offer an alternative, or a transitional phase, to government ownership. Land trusts are a major manifestation of the so-called "partnership movement" that exploded in the 1980s—cooperative efforts between the public and private sectors to acquire or otherwise protect publicly significant lands. In 1994, land trusts in the United States numbered 1,095, up 23 percent from 1990. The methods employed by land trusts seem limited only by the creativity of the parties involved in a transaction and, of course, by state and federal property and tax laws. In fact, many transactions are designed to take advantage of provisions in the federal tax code, such as "bargain sales," which qualify the seller to claim a charitable contribution equal to the difference between the appraised value and the selling price.

Land trusts are as varied as land itself. They have helped protect urban lands bordering wildlife sanctuaries and parks in a historic residential neighborhood, both in New York City; maintained inner-city community gardens in Boston, Philadelphia, and elsewhere; helped acquire undeveloped, recreational lands adjacent to Huntsville, Alabama; preserved some open space in rapidly growing Tucson; prevented the sale and destruction of a historic building in downtown Tampa; and assisted the National Park Service in numerous ways, including acquiring a parcel adjacent to a national battlefield in Virginia, selling transferable development rights to prevent development within a national recreation area in California, negotiating donations of land and easements on lands surrounding Acadia National Park, and assisting with management and maintenance of the Appalachian Trail.

Land trusts have been especially popular and useful in the East (the oldest is the Trustees of Reservations, which operates in New England), but the size of the areas protected is often larger in the West. In the western states, outside of California, 107 land trusts protect 918,842 acres, or 23 percent of all lands protected by trusts in the United States. Of those 107 land trusts, 33 are involved in protecting ranch lands. According to Jean Hocker, president of the Land Trust Alliance, the use of land trusts to protect ranch land has been hindered by family lawyers' unfamiliarity with these legal tools and a widespread skepticism among western ranchers toward what they view as protectionist organizations and infringements on private property rights. These aspects are changing, however.

See also **Conservation Easement; Land Trust Alliance.**

LAND TRUST ALLIANCE (LTA) A nonprofit, tax-exempt national umbrella organization of land trusts. The Land Trust Alliance was created *by* land trusts *for* land trusts in 1982. It provides a variety of informational and educational services and advice for its members—several hundred land trusts, conservation organizations, and individuals—and others, via its newsletter (*LTA Landscapes*), a quarterly journal (*Exchange*), and a variety of books and other publications. It also hosts an annual national conference, the only such conference devoted to land trusts, and works for tax laws and other public policies that promote the conservation of land and encourage land trust operations. In addition to its headquarters office, LTA maintains regional offices in New York and the Pacific Northwest.

LTA's *Guidebook to Standards and Practices* provides standardized guidance concerning land trust operations and conservation practices, professionalism, and ethics.

See also **Conservation Easement; Land Trust.**

LAND-USE PLANNING Literally, the process by which the government or agency with jurisdiction over land use in a given area plans for the present and future uses of that area, rather than simply reacting to problems or land-use disputes as they arise. Cities, counties or boroughs, states or provinces, and federal land management agencies all conduct land-use planning for lands they control. Zoning, on the other hand, is the process whereby governments *actually control* the use of land— usually by enacting all or some parts of a land-use plan and providing tools for enforcing it. In most jurisdictions, the plan itself is not enforceable, but zoning or other ordinances that implement the plan can be enforced.

Land-use planning for private lands ordinarily involves determining the kinds of land uses desired (e.g., residential, agricultural, industrial), the relative proportions and locations of the land area allotted to each, densities of development, timing of growth and other growth controls, and the expected needs for services and infrastructure (schools, roads, police services, etc.). Planning is governed by state or local law. It may be optional, but most states now mandate the preparation of some sort of land-use plan. Oregon, California, Florida, and Hawaii are considered leaders among the states in land-use planning. California, for instance, requires every planning agency to prepare a Comprehensive Land Use Plan, the components of which are prescribed in detail by state statute. Each plan must include both a text and a diagram or map, outlining planning policies, objectives, and proposals. Specific elements that must be addressed include: land uses (types, locations, etc.), transportation, housing, conservation and development of all natural resources, open space, noise, and safety (fire, geologic hazards, etc.).

On federal lands, land-use planning is governed by the respective agency's statutory mandate. The Bureau of Land Management operates under the Federal Land Policy and Management Act, and the U.S. Forest Service under the National Forest Management Act of 1976. Under these laws, land-use plans are more like zoning; actions taken by the agencies are required to be "in accordance with" or "consistent with" the plans. Thus, the plans establish enforceable requirements.

See also **Forest Plan; Resource Management Plan; Zoning.**

LANDSCAPE This familiar word has taken on new significance in recent years in the contexts of conservation biology and ecosystem management. Most landscapes are mosaics, encompassing more than one community or habitat type; the interrelationships, both biotic and abiotic, between these communities help make the whole landscape a functioning system. For instance, think of a scenic landscape that you might photograph—it could include a valley surrounded by mountains, with a stream and its associated riparian area in the valley bottom. Or it might be a meadow ringed by forest, or a desert scene comprised of a valley floor, shrub-covered foothills, and rocky outcrops or bluffs. Each of these landscapes is probably at least a mile wide, and its component parts (the meadow and forest, in the second example) fit together like the pieces in a puzzle. The component communities share various ecological processes: moisture, nutrient, and energy cycling; wildlife movements; and erosion and soil formation.

Ecosystem management plans are generally targeted at the landscape or regional level, even though an "ecosystem" can be defined as narrowly as a wetland or even one decaying log. Similarly, most conservation biologists believe that biodiversity conservation efforts should proceed at a landscape or larger scale (referred to as "beta" or "gamma" diversity). Landscape-level attention helps ensure protection of a wider array of species—those with narrow habitat requirements and home ranges; those that inhabit the edges between the pieces of the landscape mosaic; and those that require, and move across, whole landscapes and even between landscapes.

Although no federal law and few if any state laws yet recognize the significance of scale in conservation efforts, many scientists, environmentalists, and conservation groups do. Thus, the issue surfaces in comments on federal agencies' land management plans and environmental impact statements, occasionally in litigation, and commonly in efforts by groups like The Nature Conservancy and Trust for Public Lands to protect land for conservation purposes.

See also **Biodiversity Conservation; Ecosystem Management.**

LEAGUE OF CONSERVATION VOTERS (LCV) Founded in 1970 by the environmental organization Friends of the Earth, the LCV calls itself the political arm of the environmental movement. The league is the only environmental organization dedicated to the use of political power to achieve its environmental and conservation agenda; it strives to elect environmentally concerned political candidates and defeat those who are not. In 1994, its political action committee made donations of more than $750,000 to congressional candidates (95 percent of recipients were Democrats).

One of the LCV's best-known and most effective tactics (in use for 27 years) is its National Environmental Scorecard, in which it publishes the voting record of every member of Congress on key environmental votes selected by experts from 27 environmental groups. In 1996, the league's "Dirty Dozen Campaign" helped defeat 7 of 12 congressional candidates on its "dirty dozen" list, including the only congressional incumbent defeated. LCV members receive the league's quarterly newsletter and campaign updates.

See also **104th Congress.**

LEASING The means by which certain minerals, or minerals on certain lands, are made available for development. On federal public lands, fuel and fertilizer minerals (coal, oil, natural gas, geothermal resources, phosphate, sodium, etc.) are leased, while hardrock (metallic) minerals (copper, gold, silver, etc.) are subject to location, and common varieties (sand, gravel, etc.) are sold. An apparent exception to this scheme is uranium; although it is probably better classified as a fuel mineral, it is subject to location, not leasing. On acquired federal lands (those purchased by the government from private owners), all minerals are leased. Minerals subject to disposition under state laws (those on state or private lands) are also generally leased.

Leasing requires that the would-be developer of the mineral acquire from the owner of the mineral a right to search for and extract it. The compensation required for the lease varies according to the mineral and the ownership status of the lands involved (i.e., these two factors determine what law applies). Most leases are issued on a competitive basis; federal law still contains limited provisions for noncompetitive leasing, such as lotteries. Leases are issued subject to conditions, including limits on the duration of the lease and requirements for environmental protection, reclamation, avoidance of waste, and diligent development. The landowner or management agency can plan for development of the minerals and control the timing and location of development. Contrast these features with the hardrock mining situation on federal lands under the General Mining Law of 1872.

Some of the relevant federal laws are the Mineral Leasing Act of 1920, the Federal Onshore Oil and Gas Leasing Reform Act of 1987, and the Geothermal Steam Act of 1970. Federal laws relating to mineral development are found in Title 30 of the U.S. Code. The Bureau of Land Management supervises mineral leasing on 270 million acres of public lands and on another 300 million acres of mineral estate underlying lands where the surface is owned by other entities.

Mineral leasing on federal lands is subject to analysis under the National Environmental Policy Act as well as to the surface management regulations of the respective federal agency. Mineral leasing raises issues concerning environmental impacts and reclamation, the sufficiency of revenues to the government, the timing of development (or conservation versus development), and conflicts with other uses on multiple-use lands.

A 1997 decision by the U.S. Forest Service and BLM not to allow oil and gas leasing on more than 300,000 acres of national forest lands is being appealed by the oil and gas industry. The case raises questions concerning the agencies' authority to disallow leasing without complying with formal withdrawal procedures prescribed by the Federal Land Policy and Management Act.

See also **Cumulative Impact; Location; Mining Law Reform; Royalty.**

LEOPOLD, ALDO   Author of *A Sand County Almanac*, considered a natural history literary classic and the bible of conservationists. *A Sand County Almanac and Sketches Here and There* was published in 1949, after Leopold's death. Aldo Leopold is known as the father of wildlife biology and originator of "the land ethic." He earned a forestry degree from the Yale School of Forestry in 1909 and was employed by the U.S. Forest Service (USFS) from 1909 to 1928. Leopold is known for his work and writings concerning wildlife management, soil erosion control (particularly in the Southwest), and recreation planning. He wrote the classic text *Game Management* in 1933, and served as chair of the first university department of wildlife management, created for him at the University of Wisconsin in 1939. In his first year in the position, he created and taught a course called Wildlife Ecology, open to both wildlife and liberal arts students.

While employed by the USFS, Leopold was largely responsible for administrative designation of the nation's first wilderness area, the Gila wilderness in New Mexico, in 1924. In 1935, he cofounded The Wilderness Society; in 1936, he helped establish a professional organization of wildlife scientists, which was renamed the Wildlife Society in 1937; this organization remains the principal professional organization of wildlife biologists. These accomplishments contributed to his reputation as the father of both wildlife management and the national forest wilderness system. Although he died in 1948, his writings gained popularity during, and were at the forefront of, the environmental movement in the 1960s, and have enduring relevance today for conservation biology and ecosystem management. *A Sand County Almanac*, in particular, has inspired substantial legal scholarship and both public and private land management philosophies. When former U.S. Fish and Wildlife Service director Mollie Beattie was sworn in, along with the Bible she held a copy of *A Sand County Almanac*.

LET-BURN POLICY   A policy adopted with respect to some federal lands in the 1970s for dealing with wildfires, that is, lightning-caused fires. After 80 years of attempting to suppress all fires on public lands, particularly national forests, federal land management agencies decided that natural fires should be allowed to burn in some areas if they did not pose a threat to human life or property. Lands subject to the policy included some national parks, wilderness areas, and roadless areas of national forests. The plan was prompted in large part by the belated realization that certain communities and ecosystems had evolved with fire, and that decades of suppressing fires and altering the natural fire pattern were dramatically altering vegetation and wildlife habitats in some of those areas.

However, the let-burn policy was hampered by the legacy of long-term fire suppression that preceded it as well as by the practice of public-lands livestock grazing, which removes the "fine fuels" (grasses and other low-growing plants) that in the past had sustained frequent, low-intensity fires. The buildup of larger, woody fuels that occurred under the former policy makes fires today burn bigger and hotter—by as much as several hundred degrees—when they do occur. Fires allowed to burn now cause significantly more ecological damage than fires occurring under natural (pre-settlement) conditions. A much greater percentage of the vegetation, including the tree canopy, burns; soils can actually be sterilized and nutrients vaporized as a result of the intense heat. The consequences are drastic for wildlife, and for fish as well. Furthermore, fires can quickly get out of control, especially if the weather changes unexpectedly. This is exactly what happened in the infamous Yellowstone fires of 1988, when 700,000 acres in the Greater Yellowstone Ecosystem burned after National Park Service and U.S. Forest Service officials were unable to control prescribed burns and lightning-caused fires that they initially decided to "let burn."

Aftermath of Policy and New Directions

In a 1997 speech, Interior Secretary Bruce Babbitt described how fires in southern Idaho had burned 3,000 acres a year prior to 1986, but 63,000 acres per year more recently, and noted some of the disastrous consequences of Idaho forest fires, including the loss of a bull trout population and postfire floods and mudslides. According to Babbitt, "We don't have a 'fire problem' in the West. We have a fuels problem." As an example, he cited Idaho forests that once supported 20-25 ponderosa pines per acre; they now contain 155 pines *and* 300 Douglas firs per acre. He proposed more extensive and intensive use of prescribed fires and "pre-treatment" to address the fuels problem, and noted the need for much greater interagency cooperation in setting and implementing fire policy.

One agency solution to the problem of fuel buildup has been salvage logging, but this generally involves clear-cutting—removal of all trees, dead or alive—a practice that environmentalists oppose. Another solution is prescribed burns—controlled burning designed to reduce fuel loads. The Forest Service began prescribed burning in the 1970s, but these burns occasionally escape control, as they did in Yellowstone in 1988, and the public often opposes the practice. After the agency essentially halted its prescribed burn program in 1990, it and the National Park Service were criticized by the Government Accounting Office for not having well-developed plans for preventing fires. In the meantime, federal agencies spend increasing amounts of money on fire suppression—up from $100 million to $1 billion annually today, according to Secretary Babbitt.

A draft Federal Wildland Fire Management Policy and Program Review was published in the Federal Register in 1995. This interagency report, a cooperative effort of the U.S. Forest Service and the Interior Department, was the culmination of a review of federal fire policy undertaken after the deadly fire season of 1994. The report noted that "wildfire has historically been a major force in the evolution of our wildlands, and it must be allowed to continue to play its natural role wherever possible." The report recommended 13 new or revised fire management policies. Comments were invited on the draft report, but no final report or recommendations had been published as of this writing.

Some states are getting more involved in fire management. Colorado, under the leadership of Governor Roy Romer, sponsors an annual strategy-development conference that brings together concerned federal and state agencies. Agencies in Colorado and other states are also making greater use of geographic information system and satellite imagery technologies in their fire management efforts.

See also **Clear-Cutting; Salvage Logging; Soil Erosion and Conservation.**

LINKAGE AREA A conservation biology term for an area that connects two preserves or habitat areas. Linkage areas themselves may not be of sufficient size or adequate in other respects to provide sustainable habitat, but by linking areas together they may create usable habitat, or they may serve as corridors between areas, enabling species dispersal and genetic exchange. Conservation biologists urge landowners and public land managers to manage and use lands so as to create and protect linkage areas. A variety of techniques are available: conservation easements, special designations, land exchanges, acquisition of private lands by public agencies or land trusts, dedication of greenways, etc.

See also **Biodiversity Conservation; Genetic Diversity; Landscape.**

LISTING The process by which plants or animals, domestic or foreign, are added to the list of species protected by the federal Endangered Species Act of 1973 (ESA).

LISTING   147

The Listing Process

Section 4 of the ESA directs the secretary of the interior and the secretary of commerce to consider several factors in determining whether a species is endangered or threatened. Section 4 lists the following factors as contributing to species' decline: actual or threatened modification of habitat, overuse of species for commercial or other purposes, disease, predation, inadequacy of existing regulatory protections, and other "natural or manmade factors affecting [a species'] continued existence." Listing decisions are to be made "solely on the basis of the best scientific and commercial data available." The secretary is obliged to conduct a periodic review of the lists to determine whether any species should be removed from the list, upgraded from endangered to threatened, or downgraded from threatened to endangered. These "delisting" and status change decisions must also be based on the best scientific data.

The statute further directs the secretary to designate, concurrently with the listing decision, any habitat then considered to be critical habitat for the newly listed species. Like listing decisions, designations of critical habitat are to be based on "the best scientific data available;" in addition, these decisions must also "tak[e] into consideration the economic impact, and any other relevant impact," of designating any area as critical habitat. The Interior secretary has delegated listing and critical habitat designation responsibilities to the U.S. Fish and Wildlife Service (USFWS), an Interior agency. (The National Marine Fisheries Service, within the Department of Commerce, is responsible for listing and habitat designations for marine species and anadromous fish.) Species lists are published in the Federal Register, as are proposals for additions or changes to the list.

Citizen Input to Listing Decisions

The ESA's citizen suit provision authorizes any person to sue the secretary to compel him to list a species as threatened or endangered or to designate critical habitat. In the well-known case of the northern spotted owl, the Interior secretary had to be sued to force him, first, to list the owl, and three years later, to designate critical habitat for this threatened bird. Section 4 also provides for "interested persons" to petition the secretary, according to informal rule-making procedures set out in the Administrative Procedure Act, to list or delist any species. If the petition contains "substantial scientific or commercial information," the secretary is required to undertake a prompt review of the species' status and to publish his findings in the Federal Register.

The secretary's decision to list a species may also be challenged. In 1994, a federal district court ruled that the decision to list the California gnatcatcher as threatened was arbitrary and capricious because the USFWS had failed to make the results of certain scientific studies available to the public during the notice and comment period prior to listing. The data were in dispute because one scientist had reached inconsistent conclusions regarding the existing range of the coastal bird. Although the agency is not usually required to make available to the public the raw data on which it relies for listing decisions, the court held that these facts obligated the USFWS to make the reports public.

History and Status of the ESA List

As of October 1993, 627 U.S. animal species (including 56 mammals, 74 birds, 15 insects, and 5 arachnids) and 324 plant species were listed as endangered; 187 species were listed as threatened. By late 1996 the federal list included a total of 1,520 species, 965 of which occur within the United States and its territories. Of these, 627 were covered by recovery plans (which are not binding on agencies or private landowners).

Until the USFWS eliminated the practice in late 1996, its so-called Category 2 list contained the names of 3,540 species (1,840 vertebrate and invertebrate taxa and 1,700 plants) that were possibly deserving of listing but for which available data were insufficient. The USFWS gave as one reason for discontinuing the Category 2 list the fact that other agencies and organizations maintained similar lists. The Nature Conservancy, for example, maintains a list of more than 5,000 domestic species that may deserve threatened or endangered status.

The USFWS has identified 114 Category 1 species for which listing is "warranted but precluded"; that is, listing is warranted as a matter of science, but inadequate funding or higher priorities prevent the agency from listing them. (This category has been called a "black hole," where species in need of protection may languish for years.) But survival is not assured even for species that make the official list. Only a very few listed species have been "recovered," and 18 endangered species have become extinct. Twice as many protected species are declining as are recovering; the condition of 238 is stable or improving.

The USFWS averaged 35–40 listings per year until 1990. Then, in a settlement of a lawsuit brought against it, the agency agreed to a quota of 100

LISTING   149

listings per year. Nevertheless, its progress ground to a halt in 1995 as a result of moratoria enacted by the 104th Congress. Subsequently, a federal appeals court ruled that the USFWS was still obligated to list species for which it has sufficient information, although it conceded that funding posed problems for the agency. In 1997, the USFWS and the Fund for Animals entered into an agreement that calls for the USFWS, by the end of 1998, to "resolve the conservation status" of 85 candidate species, that is, either to list these species or publish a determination that listing is not warranted. The agreement is contingent on the availability of sufficient funds.

Only 11 species have been delisted due to their recovery; seven have been delisted due to better information about their status. According to one study, the status of 41 percent of listed species has stabilized or improved since listing, but seven species have become extinct while on the list.

Implications of the Listing Decision

The decision to list a species as threatened or endangered has become an increasingly charged political issue. Private property owners, developers, and other commercial land users often oppose new listings out of fear— whether unfounded or real—that listing will have consequences for their use of lands occupied by the species. A listing petition received in 1994 by the USFWS reflected the emotionalism and rhetoric that characterize the debate. Submitted by a man from Roswell, New Mexico, the (only partly facetious) petition asked the USFWS to list as an endangered species the "American *Homo sapien agriculturist*" and the "Western Red-necked American *Homo sapien agriculturist.*" The petition detailed the decline of these "species" and the loss of their "custom and culture." The service denied the petition, on the ground that the animals did not meet the definition of "species" under the ESA.

Several courts have held that the decision to list a species as threatened or endangered is not a major federal action subject to the environmental impact statement (EIS) requirement of the National Environmental Policy Act (NEPA). For instance, the federal Sixth Circuit Court of Appeals in *Pacific Legal Foundation v. Andrus* (1981) held that, because the Interior secretary is limited to considering scientific data when listing species, he does not have the discretion to consider other criteria, such as socioeconomic factors and alternatives, that NEPA requires to be considered in an EIS. In addition, the court held, the act of listing species "furthers the purpose of NEPA."

See also **Anadromous Fish; Critical Habitat; Endangered Species; Endangered Species Act of 1973; Northern Spotted Owl;** *Tennessee Valley Authority v. Hill* **(1978); Threatened Species.**

LOCATION The system by which hardrock (generally metallic) minerals (copper, nickel, gold, silver, uranium, etc.) are made available for development on federal public lands. These minerals are also called locatable minerals. The location system—basically a "first in time, first in right" scheme—was developed by miners themselves in the 1840s and 1850s and first ratified by Congress in 1866. The General Mining Law of 1872, which incorporated the provisions of the 1866 statute, sets forth the law applicable to hardrock mining on public lands, including the requirements for location. The 1872 law also authorizes states and "mining districts" to regulate location and other aspects of mineral exploration and development. Many states have prescribed requirements for marking and recording mining claims, performing assessment work, and other matters.

The principal distinguishing feature of the location system is known as the right of self-initiation. This means that prospectors or mining companies seeking hardrock minerals have the right to go onto any public lands that are open to mining and look for minerals without obtaining prior authorization from the federal government and without paying a fee. On lands managed by the Bureau of Land Management (BLM), actual mining activity can even be conducted without prior approval if it will disturb less than five acres per year; these small operators need only notify the agency of their activity. Larger operations on BLM lands, however, and all mining operations on national forest lands must obtain approval of an operating plan. Even so, self-initiation is preserved by regulations allowing mining to proceed while the agency reviews the proposed plan, as long as environmental damage is minimized in the meantime.

The location system enables a miner to obtain both a possessory interest in the land surface—while "diligently searching" for minerals and actually occupying the surface of his claims—as well as a property interest in the mineral itself. The U.S. Supreme Court called the unpatented mining claim a "unique form of property." [*See United States v. Locke* (1985)] The first miner who (1) properly locates a claim (meeting all federal and state requirements for marking it, recording the claim, etc.), and (2) makes a "valuable" discovery of a hardrock mineral (the deposit must be "marketable") obtains the equivalent of a fee simple ownership interest in the mineral deposit. To put it simply, he owns the mineral. Unless the miner applies for and receives a patent to the land, however, the government continues to hold title to the surface of the land, subject to the miner's right to occupy the surface in order to develop the mineral deposit.

The effects of the location system in practice are best understood when contrasted with the leasing system that applies to most other minerals on federal and state lands. The federal government cannot plan for hardrock mineral development as it can for development of oil, gas, or coal, because it is up to miners to decide where and when and how diligently to mine. The government can, however, withdraw lands, that is, identify lands as off-limits to mining. The government also has no discretion to choose among miners. As explained above, the first miner who meets the location and discovery requirements owns the mineral deposit within the bounds of his claim(s), and has the right to extract the mineral. The government earns no return on the mineral; unlike leasable minerals, locatable minerals are "free for the taking." These drawbacks of the location system—at least from a government or public-interest perspective—explain in large part why conservationists and many politicians have been pushing so long for mining law reform. A further reason is the provision in the law for obtaining a patent to the land for a ridiculously low fee.

See also **General Mining Law of 1872; Leasing; Mining Law Reform; Patent;** *United States v. Locke* **(1985); Withdrawal.**

LUCAS V. SOUTH CAROLINA COASTAL COUNCIL (1992)

A significant Supreme Court takings decision, authored by Justice Antonin Scalia. *Lucas* is known for the "categorical" rule it established: a government regulation that limits the use of land and thus "deprives land of all economically beneficial use" amounts to a taking of private property, *unless* the "proscribed use interests were not part of the [landowner's] title to begin with."

The Case

In 1988, the state of South Carolina enacted the Beachfront Management Act, which prohibited construction of habitable structures within specified zones subject to natural erosion along the state's coastline. Lucas had bought two lots before this law was passed, intending to build single-family homes on them. All the surrounding landowners had already built homes on their lots prior to passage of the law, but the entire area was now located in an "erosion zone." Unable to proceed with construction, Lucas sued the state, claiming that the law "took" his property. The trial court agreed, and awarded compensation of $1.2 million.

The South Carolina Supreme Court reversed the lower court, however, ruling that the case fell within the "nuisance" or "noxious use" exception to takings—that is, that private property rights are subject to the state's power to abate nuisances. The 1988 statute contained the legislature's findings that new construction in coastal areas subject to erosion causes serious harm. Lucas did not challenge this finding, and the state supreme court construed this as a tacit admission by Lucas that the proposed use of his property would be harmful. Thus, prohibition of this "noxious use" did not entitle Lucas to any compensation even though the statute prevented any economically viable use of his property.

On appeal, the U.S. Supreme Court reversed the South Carolina Supreme Court's decision. Justice Scalia, writing for the Court, explained that the "nuisance exception" to takings—that is, that private property rights are subject to the state's power to abate nuisances—encompasses only those restrictions that inhere in the landowner's title. Thus, if the government prohibits some use or activity that has not traditionally been deemed a nuisance under the state's common law of nuisance, and the prohibition destroys the economic value of private property interests that predate the regulatory prohibition, the government must pay for the property "taken."

The Supreme Court remanded the case to the South Carolina court to determine whether construction of a beachfront house would be considered a common-law nuisance in South Carolina. The state court decided that it would not, and ordered compensation. The state eventually paid Lucas $1.2 million for his property.

Commentary

Lucas has been both praised and criticized. Some legal scholars—as well as two dissenting justices in the case—argue that *Lucas* essentially "freezes common law," making it difficult if not impossible for states to revise legal principles to conform with modern, scientific knowledge concerning environmental harms. Others have called the "all economically beneficial use" test arbitrary; they ask, does "all" mean 100 percent? Why not 99, or 95, or some other number? Furthermore, how does one make that determination? If Lucas could sell his lot to an adjoining landowner who simply wanted to secure more open space around his existing house, wouldn't that indicate that Lucas's land retained *some* "economically beneficial use?" Some scholars praise *Lucas* for establishing a desirable limit on states' exercise of their police power and giving landowners greater assurance that their property won't be subjected to excessive regulation without compensation. Other observers counter that the same result could have been achieved under existing takings law without establishing a new, confusing "categorical" test.

One of the more interesting and insightful criticisms of *Lucas* was offered by law professor Eric Freyfogle (1996). He wrote that South Carolina lost the case because not enough of the Supreme Court justices "were able to understand the ecosystem disruptions that come from building on ecologically sensitive lands." He quoted a Wisconsin Supreme Court decision regarding the alteration of a wetland: "An owner of land has no absolute and unlimited right to change the essential and natural character of his land so as to use it for a purpose for which it was unsuited in its natural state." [*Just v. Marinette County* (1972)] The *Just* court's reasoning, Freyfogle suggests, supplies "the attitude needed to bring land degradation to a halt, or at least to remove constitutional protection from abusive land uses." Freyfogle concluded that without better ecological education, "ownership norms will remain in a pre-ecological age." Ironically, most of the homes surrounding Lucas's property, including the house between his two lots, had been damaged by Hurricane Hugo in 1989, the year after the Beachfront Management Act was passed.

See also **Scalia, Antonin; Takings; Wetland.**

LUJAN V. DEFENDERS OF WILDLIFE **(1992)** A U.S. Supreme Court opinion that further tightened the standing requirements that must be met by environmental plaintiffs. In *Lujan v. Defenders of Wildlife,* the Court considered a challenge to a Department of the Interior regulation that limited federal agencies' duty to consult with the U.S. Fish and Wildlife Service before taking action that affected threatened or endangered species outside the United States. The Court conceded that the Defenders of Wildlife (DOW) members' desire to be able to observe the threatened animals was a recognizable interest for purposes of standing. Nevertheless, the Court held that DOW had not established standing to challenge the rule because its members' intent to return to the subject countries, "without any concrete plans for doing so," was insufficient to establish the requisite "imminent injury." (Even the existence of a civil war in one of the countries—Sri Lanka—did not justify the plaintiffs' inability to specify when they might return to the country.) Three justices dissented, criticizing the majority for its "slash-and-burn expedition through the law of environmental standing."

See also *Lujan v. National Wildlife Federation* (1990); Ripeness; Scalia, Antonin; Section 7 Consultation; Standing.

Lujan v. National Wildlife Federation (1990)

A significant environmental standing decision. The U.S. Supreme Court held, in this 1990 case, that to survive the defendant's motion for summary judgment based on the plaintiff's lack of standing, a plaintiff must allege facts showing specifically how it would be harmed by the government action that its lawsuit challenges. The National Wildlife Federation (NWF) challenged the Bureau of Land Management's (BLM) land withdrawal review program, a comprehensive evaluation of whether to maintain existing classifications of land and restrictions on mining and oil and gas leasing on millions of acres of public lands in 11 western states. NWF alleged that the agency's conduct of the program violated several statutes. In support of its claims, NWF submitted affidavits of two members, who stated that their recreational use of lands "in the vicinity of" some of the withdrawn lands would be adversely affected by reclassifying those lands and opening them to mining and oil and gas leasing activities. In particular, they stated that these extractive activities threatened the "aesthetic beauty and wildlife habitat potential" of the lands.

The Court held that alleging use of "unspecified portions of an immense tract of territory," only some of which might be impacted by the withdrawal review program, did not satisfy the requirement that a plaintiff set forth "specific facts" showing that it would be "adversely affected or aggrieved" by the government action. Thus, the Court ruled that NWF had failed to establish that it had standing to contest the program; accordingly, BLM was entitled to summary judgment.

The Court's decision was criticized as tightening unnecessarily the requirements for environmental plaintiffs to establish standing; indeed, four of nine justices on the Court dissented from the decision. However, in the view of many legal scholars and commentators, the case merely imposed more stringent pleading requirements on environmental plaintiffs. That is, to demonstrate standing, plaintiffs must simply include more specific facts in their complaints and affidavits. In fact, plaintiffs in numerous cases filed since *Lujan v. National Wildlife Federation* have survived standing challenges on summary judgment motions.

Lujan v. National Wildlife Federation's greater significance for environmental litigation may stem from the Court's dicta concerning whether the BLM's land withdrawal review program was a "final agency action" appropriate for review by a court. ("Dicta" refers to statements within a court's opinion that are not crucial to its actual disposition of the case.) The federal Administrative Procedure Act (APA) provides for judicial review only of final agency actions. The Supreme Court stated that agency actions, or regulations, are not ordinarily considered "'ripe' for judicial review under the APA until the scope of a controversy has been reduced to more manageable proportions, and its factual components fleshed out, by some concrete action applying the regulation to the claimant's situation in a fashion that harms or threatens to harm him." The Court noted that the BLM land withdrawal review program encompassed at least "1,250 or so individual classification terminations and withdrawal revocations," and stated that "flaws in the entire program...cannot be laid before the courts for wholesale correction under the APA, simply because one of [the individual actions] that is ripe for review adversely affects one of [NWF's] members." This reasoning suggests that an environmental plaintiff who objected to the BLM's program would have to challenge each and every individual classification decision. The resulting burden on plaintiffs—and the court system—would be substantial.

See also *Lujan v. Defenders of Wildlife* **(1992); National Wildlife Federation; Ripeness; Standing.**

⛬ MARINE MAMMAL PROTECTION ACT (MMPA)

Passed in 1972 and significantly amended in 1994, this statute asserts federal authority over the conservation of all marine mammals (dolphins, whales, walruses, etc.) in U.S. waters. Subject to limited exceptions, such as the incidental taking of porpoises and dolphins by tuna fishermen, the MMPA established a moratorium on the killing or capturing of, and all commerce in, marine mammals. The statute thus preempted all state laws applicable to the taking of these animals. The law is administered by the secretaries of Commerce and Interior and the Marine Mammal Commission. Its purposes are to conserve marine mammals by maintaining (or recovering) their populations at optimum levels and to protect essential habitats.

The 1994 amendments added three new sections applicable to commercial fishing. These require the preparation of marine mammal stock assessments for all species in U.S. waters, plans for reducing the take of marine mammals whose stocks are depleted or are below optimum levels because of interactions with commercial fishing operations, and studies of interactions between pinnipeds (e.g., seals, walruses) and commercial fisheries. The amendments prohibit the intentional killing of marine mammals while fishing and establish a goal of achieving zero incidental mortality within seven years. They also provide new, express authority for protecting marine mammal habitats, direct the Commerce Department's National Marine Fisheries Service (NMFS) to assess the health of marine ecosystems, and provide for cooperative agreements between Alaska Native organizations and NMFS or the U.S. Fish and Wildlife Service.

The secretary of commerce is responsible for enforcing the MMPA and regulations issued thereunder and for issuing "incidental take" permits to commercial fishermen. (These are different from the incidental take permits authorized by the Endangered Species Act of 1973.) All commercial fishing vessels that operate in waters where interactions with marine mammals are considered occasional or frequent must be registered with the NMFS and must comply with a "take reduction plan." All mortalities and serious injuries of marine mammals must be reported within 48 hours of returning from a fishing trip, and fishing vessels may be asked to carry an agency observer.

See also **Endangered Species Act of 1973; Hunting; Preemption.**

MIGRATORY BIRD TREATY ACT OF 1918 (MBTA)

One of the earliest federal efforts to conserve and regulate wildlife. The MBTA was the first federal law to directly preempt state control over wildlife, although it expressly preserved the rights of states to enact laws providing *additional* protection to migratory species. It was challenged as unconstitutional in *Missouri v. Holland* (1920), but upheld as a valid exercise of Congress's treaty power under the Constitution. Most conservation-related statutes since then have been defended, and upheld, as exercises of Congress's power under the Constitution's Commerce Clause or Property Clause.

The MBTA sets up a federal system for managing migratory birds, supervised by the Department of the Interior. Under the statute, the U.S. Fish and Wildlife Service (by delegation from the secretary of the Interior) sets hunting seasons, bag limits, and permissible methods for taking migratory birds, chiefly waterfowl. Violation of regulations issued under the statute is a criminal offense, punishable by fine. In 1929, passage of the Migratory Bird Conservation Act supplemented the federal government's ability to promote conservation of migratory birds by authorizing the acquisition of their habitat, marking the beginning of the national wildlife refuge system.

In recent years the MBTA's prohibition against taking migratory birds, except as permitted by federal regulation, has been applied by some courts in prosecutions of landowners for causing the deaths of migratory birds due to negligent spraying of pesticides or, in the case of a mining company, operation of cyanide pits. Other courts, however, have held that the statute is too vague to be enforceable against negligent conduct. In 1985 the secretary of the Interior announced that continued operation of the Kesterson National Wildlife Refuge in California—where birds were dying due to selenium in waters feeding the refuge that drained out of a federal-state water project—violated the MBTA. However, two federal appeals courts recently held that the MBTA does *not* apply to federal government activities. In *Sierra Club v. Martin* (1997), the plaintiffs claimed that logging and road building proposed by the U.S. Forest Service would harm migratory neotropical birds in Georgia national forests. The Eleventh Circuit Court of

Appeals ruled that the MBTA is a criminal statute and does not authorize a court to enjoin federal land management activities. The Eighth Circuit reached a similar result in *Newton County Wildlife Association v. U.S. Forest Service* (1997).

See also **National Wildlife Refuge System; Preemption; Selenium; U.S. Fish and Wildlife Service.**

MILLER, GEORGE   Democratic congressman representing California's Seventh District since 1975 and chair of the House Interior and Insular Affairs Committee (now the House Resources Committee) from 1991-1994. Miller, an attorney, lost the Resources chairmanship upon the Republicans' ascent to power in the 104th Congress, but he remains the ranking minority member of the committee. In 1995 he was elected vice-chair of the House Democratic Policy Committee.

Miller has been a stalwart supporter of conservation of public lands and natural resources and an untiring opponent of "corporate welfare" programs, such as federal water and hydropower policies and the General Mining Law of 1872, which provide "outdated and expensive federal subsidies" to industry. Miller's legislative accomplishments include reform of California water law, timber reform, and passage of the California Desert Protection Act of 1994, the 1990 Oil Pollution Act, and the 1992 Energy Policy Act; he authored significant portions of the latter two laws. Miller led the congressional investigation into the *Exxon Valdez* oil spill in Alaska in 1989, and he managed the House bill that led to passage of the Tongass Timber Reform Act of 1990. More recently, he has introduced or cosponsored bills that would require the federal government to obtain the fair-market value of public land resources sold or leased (including timber, minerals, forage for livestock grazing, national park concessions, and ski area permits), make conservation of natural resources the primary goal of the national wildlife refuge system, reauthorize and reform the Endangered Species Act of 1973 (ESA), and reform the 1872 Mining Law. He also supports reform of federal grazing laws.

Widely supported by environmentalists, Miller's ESA measure would, among other things, require the designation of "survival habitat" using biological factors only (while retaining the consideration of economics in critical habitat designations) and require land users who might damage habitat to post bonds of up to $1 million. His mining law reform bill provides for a 5 percent net smelter return royalty and a reclamation fee on all hardrock minerals, and would eliminate the depletion allowance (tax credit) provided to mine operators by federal tax law.

See also **House Resources Committee; Mining Law Reform.**

MINE RECLAMATION Rehabilitation of mined areas to prevent or reduce erosion, blend topography with that of the surrounding area, and reestablish vegetative cover. Where possible, reclamation efforts attempt to create habitat for wildlife species that formerly occupied the site. The success of reclamation depends on many factors, including climate; topography; the availability of moisture, topsoil, and seed sources; and the extent to which the site can be protected from disturbances while reclamation efforts are in progress. Reclamation can be especially difficult in arid areas, at high elevations, and in steep terrain.

Reclamation is governed by federal and state law. Reclamation of coal-mined areas is regulated by the Surface Mining Control and Reclamation Act of 1977; hardrock mines on federal lands come under the surface management regulations of the respective agency, chiefly the Bureau of Land Management (BLM) and the U.S. Forest Service (USFS). The BLM is in the process of revising its rules, which have been criticized for being less stringent than the Forest Service's requirements. The USFS requires all mine operators to post a bond to ensure that reclamation costs will be covered; BLM's current rules exempt some small operations from bonding. Reclamation of mining activity is also subject to state laws and regulations; state requirements for conducting and reclaiming mining activity vary considerably.

A number of old mining sites are being reclaimed, or "remediated," under the federal Comprehensive Environmental, Response, Compensation, and Liability Act (CERCLA, or Superfund). Many of these sites have been included on the National Priority List of hazardous-substance–contaminated sites posing substantial risk of harm to the environment. Mining activity can result in "acid mine drainage" and can introduce toxic quantities of heavy metals into water supplies and soils. Reclamations of Superfund sites are known as removal or remedial actions. The extent of contamination is assessed, hazardous substances are either removed or contained on site, water quality is restored where necessary, health studies of people living in the vicinity of the site may be conducted, and any other actions necessary to protect human health and the environment, including long-term monitoring, are carried out. Superfund cleanups are funded by the responsible parties, if they can be found and if they are solvent. Potentially responsible parties include the current owner of the site, the person who owned or operated it at the time hazardous substances were deposited, and anyone who "arranged" for hazardous substances to be deposited. Money from the federal Superfund created by CERCLA may also be available for cleanup. One of the most well known Superfund mine sites is the entire city of Butte, Montana; the river running through town was rendered essentially lifeless by copper mining, and mine tailings are spread along the river and scattered throughout the area.

See also *California Coastal Commission v. Granite Rock Co.* (1987); **Mineral Policy Center; Mining Law Reform; Surface Mining Control and Reclamation Act of 1977.**

MINERAL POLICY CENTER   A small, nonprofit, national environmental organization whose missions are to reform the 1872 Mining Law and protect the environment from damage caused by mining and onshore oil development activities. The Mineral Policy Center was organized in 1988 and is funded by private donations and foundation grants. It has acquired a reputation for being well informed on a wide range of mining issues: mining engineering, pollution, waste remediation, and economics, as well as mining law and policy. It conducts research on these issues and uses the information acquired to inform the public, provide technical and organizational assistance to local groups around the country, lobby Congress on mining law reform and the application of other environmental statutes to the mining industry, and work for improved state regulation of mining practices.

The Mineral Policy Center was cofounded by Stewart Udall, former secretary of the Interior, and Philip Hocker, former treasurer of the Sierra Club; Hocker served as its executive director until 1998. The Mineral Policy Center has field offices in Bozeman, Montana, and Durango, Colorado. It publishes a journal, *Clementine*, and has produced a variety of information packets and videos about mining issues.

See also **Mining Law Reform; Udall, Stewart.**

MINING LAW REFORM   A perennial federal legislative issue for the past ten years, and a goal—as yet unrealized—of environmentalists for even longer. By now, nearly all interested parties— politicians, the minerals industry, other public land users, environmentalists, and local governments, as well as four out of five Americans, even in the West—agree that the federal law governing hardrock mining on federal lands needs to be revised. The devil continues to be in the details.

Brief History and Operation of 1872 Law

The need for reform stems from the age and obsolescence of the General Mining Law of 1872. This statute, which has been amended only slightly in 125 years, allows prospectors, either individuals or companies, to go onto federal lands to explore for "valuable mineral deposits" and stake claims to and develop any minerals discovered. The minerals subject to the law, known as locatable minerals, include precious and other metals, such as gold, silver, copper, and uranium, and minerals with "distinct and special value," for example, chemical- or pharmaceutical-grade limestone. Under the 1872 law, the holder of a valid claim has the right to occupy the land for mining-related purposes and has a vested ownership interest in the mineral deposit. The claimant pays no fee to the federal government to mine, nor any tax or royalty on the minerals produced. He can develop and sell the mineral, or convey his interest in the deposit to someone else. If the miner wants to purchase the land, he applies to the government for a patent and pays a meager $2.50 or $5.00 per acre. This latter feature of the act— that it literally gives away federal resources—goes a long way toward explaining why both conservationists and many politicians (especially fiscal conservatives) have been pushing so long for mining law reform.

The 1872 law authorizes both local and federal regulation of mining on federal lands, but regulation was minimal prior to the 1980s. For the most part, state and local laws regulate how claims must be staked and recorded, and also govern disputes among rival claimants. The 1872 statute itself affords little protection to miners while they are exploring for minerals; claim jumping and overfiling are common, and the rival parties often end up in court. The federal government has generally taken a laissez faire approach to mining. The 1872 law was intended to encourage serious development of federal minerals, not to restrict miners' use of federal lands.

Between 1974 and 1980, both the U.S. Forest Service (USFS) and the Bureau of Land Management (BLM) issued surface management regulations designed to regulate the environmental impacts of mining activities. USFS rules were issued under the 1897 Organic Act, which authorizes the agency to regulate the "occupancy and use" of national forests. The regulations require, among other things, approved plans of operation for all mines and compliance with all applicable state environmental requirements. Their purpose is to "minimize adverse environmental impacts" on national forest resources. The USFS rules were challenged in court and upheld. BLM regulations, authorized by the Federal Land Policy and Management Act (FLPMA), were issued in 1980. Although similar to the USFS rules, they exempt small operations (those that disturb less than five acres per year) from the operating plan requirement, and they do not require reclamation bonds for all operations. Moreover, the BLM regulations do not require that impacts to surface resources be minimized, but rather incorporate FLPMA's mandate that "unnecessary or undue degradation of the lands" be prevented.

In recent years, the magnitude of mine reclamation needs has become more apparent. Because historically nothing prevented mine owners and operators from simply walking away from played-out deposits or from a mine they could no longer afford to keep open, as many as 557,000 abandoned mine sites now dot the public lands. They pose a variety of environmental, health, and safety hazards: acid mine drainage, leaching of toxic metals into groundwaters and pollution of more than 12,000 miles of rivers, subsidence of the land surface, treacherous mine openings and pits, erosion of tailings piles and mined slopes, etc. Fifty-nine mines have become Superfund sites, included on the National Priority List of areas where the occurrence of hazardous substances poses special environmental risks. These sites, listed pursuant to the Comprehensive Environmental Response, Compensation, and Liability Act, will be the object of federally funded cleanup efforts. Cleanup of the bankrupt Summitville mine in Colorado, for instance, has cost the federal Environmental Protection Agency $100 million.

Legislative Reform Proposals

Several key features of the General Mining Law are the target of reform efforts: the federal government's limited ability to regulate where and how mining activities take place, so as to protect environmental values and other public land uses; the uncertainty of miners' interests during the exploration phase; the provisions for patenting the surface of mining claims; and the lack of any provision for either revenues to the federal treasury from mineral extraction or reclamation of abandoned or exhausted mines. Most reform bills have proposed changes in all these areas. Some propose eliminating the patent option; others would retain it, but require the payment of fair market value. Most reform measures provide for payment of a royalty on minerals extracted, but the royalty rate and assessment method (e.g., on gross production, net profits, etc.) have been vigorously debated. (For comparison, the federal royalty on oil, gas, and coal is 12.4 percent of gross income. Gold royalties on private land mines range from 5 to 18 percent.) Various approaches to protecting miners' interests during exploration have been proposed. One sensible suggestion would require the land management agency to issue a permit.

In 1997, Senators Frank Murkowski (R-AK), Larry Craig (R-ID), and Harry Reid (D-NV) introduced their mining reform bill, S. 1102. (A Murkowski-Craig bill had fared poorly in the 104th Congress.) The bill would establish a royalty of 5 percent of net proceeds (reflecting deductions from gross proceeds for such things as mining, transportation, and processing costs), but would exempt small mines (those making less than $50,000 per year) from the royalty; allow patents but require payment of fair market value; require annual assessment fees (again exempting small operators); adopt FLPMA's standard of no "unnecessary or undue degradation" as the criterion for environmental protection and reclamation; and establish an abandoned mine fund. The National Mining Association called the bill a "reasonable approach" to mining reform. Senator Dale Bumpers (D-AR), a longtime advocate of mining law reform and author of several prior reform measures, and Congressman George Miller (D-CA) also introduced legislation in 1997; these bills enjoyed the general support of environmentalists and the influential Mineral Policy Center. (Bumpers had earlier announced that he would not seek reelection to another term, and environmentalists were concerned that the loss of his leadership might handicap their efforts to achieve satisfactory reforms.) These bills proposed a 5 percent net smelter royalty (down from Bumpers's earlier proposal of 8 percent of gross), extended the annual assessment fees on mines, imposed a reclamation fee on all hardrock minerals produced on federal lands, and ended the depletion allowance available to mines under current tax law. Bumpers also introduced separate legislation imposing a reclamation fee on all lands patented under the 1872 law.

Although mining law reform is said to be a priority of several powerful members of Congress, including House Resources Committee chair Don Young (R-AK), most observers agreed that legislative reform was no more likely to succeed in the 105th Congress than in prior legislatures.

Administrative Reform Efforts

Frustrated by Congress's inability to reform the antiquated 1872 law, Interior Secretary Babbitt announced in early 1997 that his department would amend the BLM mining rules (known as the "3809 regulations," for their location in Title 43 of the Code of Federal Regulations). Babbitt proposed to complete the rule-making process, which would include forming a task force, holding several field hearings, and preparing an environmental impact statement (required by the National Environmental Policy Act) by March 1999. The agency planned to redefine FLPMA's "unnecessary or undue degradation" criterion, establish mine performance standards (taking into account best available mining technology and practices), and consider reclamation standards for small mines (less than five acres).

Officials in certain western states and some members of Congress reacted sharply to the BLM announcement. Utah, Nevada, and Colorado notified BLM that states have "primacy" over environmental regulation of mining operations, and warned the agency that they would oppose any federal effort to usurp or duplicate state authority. Senator Reid introduced an amendment to the Interior spending bill that requires consensus of the 12 western governors before Interior could implement new regulations. Senator Bumpers criticized the amendment, calling it "veto bait," and said that the governors' ability to participate in the rule-making process is assured by FLPMA. In 1997 Congress passed an appropriations bill that delayed proposal of BLM's 3809 rules by six months and required consultation with (but not consensus among) the governors of public land states.

Dissension also has marked implementation of a new Interior regulation requiring bonding for all mining operations. The rule eliminates the exemption for small mines, while preserving it for existing mines if they do not expand their operations. The rule requires that bond amounts be either the full cost of reclamation or $1,000 to $2,000 per acre (depending on size), whichever is greater. Environmentalists, however, decried the rule as "window dressing" and the rates as "ludicrously low." The Mineral Policy Center noted that the rule leaves bonding levels up to the states, which in the past have set bonds too low. Under the rules, the BLM has the option of requiring a federal bond in addition to a state bond for operators with a history of noncompliance. A mining group in Alaska sued Interior, objecting that the bonding rule had not been promulgated properly, and the House Resources Committee ordered the U.S. Marshal to subpoena Interior documents, which Interior Solicitor John Leshy claims are privileged and is withholding based on his concern that the committee would release them to the plaintiff in the lawsuit.

See also *California Coastal Commission v. Granite Rock Co.* (1987); **General Mining Law of 1872; Leasing; Location; Patent; Patent Moratorium; Royalty; Withdrawal.**

MITIGATION   Prevention or alleviation of the effects of human activities on the environment. Mitigation of environmental impacts is mandated by the National Environmental Policy Act (NEPA), Clean Water Act section 404, and the Swampbuster provisions of the Food Security Act. The definition of mitigation found in the NEPA regulations has been expressly adopted by the Environmental Protection Agency (EPA) and the U.S. Army Corps of Engineers (Corps) in setting guidelines for mitigating impacts resulting from activities authorized by section 404 dredge-and-fill permits. Mitigation under Swampbuster is mandated for the same broad policy reasons: to minimize or rectify environmental impacts of human activities. However, the three statutes approach mitigation in dissimilar ways.

NEPA

NEPA regulations define mitigation as avoiding the environmental impact of an action, minimizing impacts by limiting the magnitude of the action, rectifying the impact by repairing the affected environment, reducing or eliminating the impact over time, or compensating for the impact by replacing or providing substitutes for it. NEPA is a procedural statute governing federal decision making regarding major federal actions. Although the required environmental impact statements (EIS) must discuss mitigation, the statute itself does not require the agency to take—or avoid—any particular on-the-ground action, including mitigation, with respect to a proposed project. [*See Robertson v. Methow Valley Citizens Council* (1989).] An agency need not prepare an EIS if it determines that a proposal is not a "major federal action" or would not significantly affect the environment. If the agency relies on mitigation in making the latter determination, thereby avoiding the procedural requirement to prepare an EIS, it likely will be required to implement and enforce the relied-on mitigation measures. [*See, e.g., Cabinet Mountains Wilderness v. Peterson* (1982).] The Council on Environmental Quality recently reported that agencies are increasingly proposing ways to mitigate the adverse effects of a proposed project in order to avoid preparing an EIS. The ironic result is that projects with the potentially greatest impacts, described in detail in a comprehensive EIS, may be constructed in disregard of the need for mitigating their environmental impacts, unless other relevant federal and state environmental regulations require corrective measures.

Clean Water Act Section 404

In contrast to the procedural requirements of NEPA, the Clean Water Act and Swampbuster contain substantive standards for mitigating environmental impacts. In addition, the past two presidential administrations have supported a goal of "no net loss" of wetlands under both these statutes. Mitigation is an important tool for achieving this goal, but the processes differ slightly under the two statutes.

Under CWA section 404, a mitigation plan is a required part of every Corps-issued dredge-and-fill permit. Pursuant to an agreement between the Corps and EPA, applicants must mitigate adverse environmental impacts according to the following sequence: The applicant should first attempt to avoid adverse impacts. (If the activity is not water-dependent, the rules assume that a practicable alternative to dredging and filling exists.) If impacts cannot be avoided, they must be minimized. Where minimum impacts are still unacceptable, the applicant may mitigate the impact on-site, perhaps through wetlands enhancement or restoration of the site. If the first two routes are not available, however, an applicant may propose to mitigate adverse wetland impacts by undertaking compensatory measures off-site. Typically, off-site mitigation is limited to the same watershed.

The goal of mitigation under section 404 is to compensate for lost wetland values and functions, *not* merely to replace lost wetlands acre for acre. For instance, if an applicant undertakes to create a wetland off-site, on land that has been cropped, the likelihood of successfully in restoring native vegetation, soil chemistry, and hydrology to sustain a wetland community is low. Thus, the Corps might require the applicant to restore or create two acres of "new" wetland for every acre lost as a result of his dredge-and-fill operation. In fact, the Corps reports that in recent years, 1.15 acres of wetlands have been mitigated for every acre filled. In 1997, a federal judge in Colorado approved a settlement between the EPA and a ski developer who had illegally filled an alpine wetland to build a golf course. The settlement requires the developer to pay $1.1 million in civil penalties and fund a three-year, $2.7 million restoration project on 17 acres of converted wetland.

A recent study in Ohio of compensatory wetland mitigation projects performed in connection with 404 permits shows a net gain in wetland acreage and no loss in vegetative species diversity, but notes reductions in wetland functions and the percentage of native plant species.

Swampbuster

Unlike CWA section 404, Swampbuster is an incentive program, not a regulatory program. Failure to obtain a 404 permit or comply with its mitigation terms may lead to civil or criminal penalties. By contrast, Swampbuster's mitigation requirements are voluntary. A farmer who acts without the permission or assistance of the Natural Resources Conservation Service (NRCS) to convert a wetland to cropland, and who does not mitigate the adverse environmental impact of his actions, will merely lose his eligibility for farm program benefits. Granted, farm program benefits can mean the difference between success and failure for many in agriculture, but the choice to comply with Swampbuster wetland mitigation—and, indeed, with Swampbuster in general—is the landowner's.

For those who opt to participate in Swampbuster, the NRCS may grant permission to convert a wetland to farmland on the condition that the farmer mitigate the loss of the wetland through restoration of another wetland, typically in the same watershed, to "equivalent wetland values and functions." As originally enacted, Swampbuster provides that if a wetland has been "frequently cropped" (that is, if NRCS determines that historically the land has been cropped more often than not), a farmer may convert the wetland, provided that he mitigates the loss by restoring a previously converted wetland. Amendments in 1996 expanded both the lands on which the NRCS will consider conversion requests and the lands eligible for mitigation. Conversions are allowed on wetlands dried by drought; wetlands on which conversion began prior to 1985, but where wetland conditions were reestablished due to lack of maintenance of the drainage works; wetlands restored through voluntary actions; and in several other circumstances. Mitigation may be undertaken for all wetlands, frequently cropped or not. Mitigation may be satisfied by restoration, enhancement, or creation of new wetlands.

Congress's intent in expanding (in 1996) the actions and lands to which mitigation could apply was to afford NRCS greater flexibility in implementing the statute. The statute's original, narrower language might have been easier for NRCS to implement lawfully, however. Mitigating wetlands loss by means of restoring lands *other* than prior converted cropland is likely to be very difficult. The statute still calls for mitigation to "replace full wetlands functions and values." As applied, this means that NRCS, in cooperation with the U.S. Fish and Wildlife Service, undertakes a biological assessment of the wetland to be converted and determines whether the proposed mitigation lands will be an adequate ecological replacement for those to be converted. Wetlands with soils that are not sufficiently hydric or that lack remnant hydrophilic plant communities may be very difficult to restore. It thus may be necessary for NRCS to require a restoration ratio higher than 1:1 to ensure that the act's mitigation goal is achieved. Moreover, wetland creation and enhancement are expensive and difficult operations. For these reasons, Congress's desire to provide flexibility may result instead in continued NRCS supervision of those persons required to conduct mitigation and, potentially, in litigation.

NRCS has been slow to implement Swampbuster's mitigation provisions by rule-making, and those rules that the agency has proposed appear to be broader than the statutory language. The possibility of eventual legal challenges thus cannot be overlooked.

According to the Competitive Enterprise Institute, a Washington, D.C., think tank, wetlands are now being restored and enhanced at a rate that exceeds their destruction. The group criticized the section 404 mitigation program as burdensome, claiming that incentive-based programs, such as the Wetlands Reserve Program and Partners for Wildlife, are more cost-effective.

See also **Clean Water Act Section 404; Mitigation Banking; National Environmental Policy Act; Swampbuster.**

MITIGATION BANKING   A strategy for mitigating losses of or damage to wetlands, governed by informal guidance issued by the Environmental Protection Agency (EPA) and U.S. Army Corps of Engineers (Corps) in 1995. [*See* 60 Federal Register 12,286 (6 March 1995).] The Clinton administration's wetlands policy has embraced mitigation banking, and recent Senate and House bills to reauthorize and amend the Clean Water Act contain mitigation banking provisions. The 1996 Farm Bill also approved a pilot mitigation banking effort for the Swampbuster program. Many public or private banks have been established; about 20 states have or are developing mitigation banking policies.

Mitigation banking involves the creation, enhancement, or restoration of wetlands in advance of damaging or destroying other wetlands pursuant to a Clean Water Act section 404 permit or subject to provisions of the federal Swampbuster program. The banked wetlands account can be debited later to provide the mitigation required by a section 404 permit, or the banked wetlands can be sold to other section 404 permit applicants.

Wetlands mitigation banking has environmental, financial, and regulatory advantages. Creating or restoring wetlands in advance of actual wetland losses helps achieve the federal "no net loss" policy and serves to avoid even temporary wetland shortages. When implemented appropriately, it can create larger and better-functioning wetland systems than might individual, uncoordinated efforts to mitigate losses due to numerous individual 404 permits. The economies of scale that may apply, and the enhanced regulatory certainty (because of the relative ease of providing the necessary mitigation on which permit issuance may hinge) are likely to appeal to developers. Disadvantages or shortcomings include overconcentration of wetlands in one or a few areas to the detriment of other areas that lack wetlands; the practical difficulties in creating functioning, self-sustaining wetlands; and the scientific uncertainty in assessing and hence compensating for lost wetland values.

One legal scholar praises the potential of wetland mitigation banking for "improving the overall biodiversity of the wetlands ecosystems of the nation." Probably few conservation biologists would share his optimism, however, given the scientific uncertainty over whether we can create wetlands that will function ecologically and sustainably like natural wetlands.

See also **Clean Water Act Section 404; Corps of Engineers; Environmental Protection Agency; Swampbuster; Wetland.**

MOUNTAIN STATES LEGAL FOUNDATION (MSLF)

A nonprofit, public interest legal center that describes itself as "dedicated to individual liberty, the right to own property, limited government, and the free enterprise system." MSLF provides legal representation to clients with natural resource (usually commodity) interests in the federal public lands. Its caseload centers around Rocky Mountain and Intermountain regional issues; a similar organization, the Pacific States Legal Foundation, works primarily on issues in the far West. MSLF might be considered the Republican or right-wing counterpart to environmental law firms, such as the former Sierra Club Legal Defense Fund. MSLF currently represents clients who oppose the National Park Service's closure to climbing of Devil's Tower in Devil's Tower National Monument by all but "land-based religious practitioners," i.e., Indians for whom the tower has religious significance. The organization also has filed suit, challenging presidential designation of the Grand Staircase-Escalante National Monument. One of its contentions is that the monument exceeds the president's Antiquities Act authority because it is larger than necessary.

Former Interior Secretary James Watt served as a lawyer on MSLF's staff before assuming his duties in Washington in the Reagan Administration. Ironically, he was sued several times in his capacity as Interior secretary by his former employer.

MULTIPLE USE   Term used to refer to the broad management philosophy pertaining to federal public lands and national forests (usually used in combination with the term "sustained yield"), as well as to one or more of the multiple uses for which those lands are managed. "Multiple use" is defined in the Multiple-Use, Sustained-Yield Act (MUSYA), which is applicable to national forests managed by the U.S. Forest Service, and in the Federal Land Policy and Management Act (FLPMA), applicable to lands managed by the Bureau of Land Management (BLM).

The definitions of multiple use in these two statutes are substantially alike; indeed, Congress indicated in FLPMA that both "multiple use" and "sustained yield" have traditional, accepted meanings. MUSYA lists the following multiple uses for national forests: "outdoor recreation, range, timber, watershed, and wildlife and fish purposes," and further states that management of portions of the forests as wilderness areas is consistent with multiple use. FLPMA's list is more open-ended; it refers to "renewable and nonrenewable resources, including, but not limited to, recreation, range, timber, mineral, watershed, wildlife and fish, and natural scenic, scientific and historical values." It should be noted that mineral development also occurs on national forests, even though mining is not one of MUSYA's multiple uses. This no doubt reflects the fact that the BLM manages the mineral estate on all federal lands, including national forests.

Both statutes define "multiple use" in terms of "making the most judicious use of the land for some or all of these resources or related services over areas large enough to provide sufficient latitude for periodic adjustments in use to conform to changing needs and conditions," and utilizing the lands "in the combination that will best meet the [present and future] needs of the American people." Each clarifies that multiple use does "not necessarily" mean "the combination of uses that will give the greatest dollar [or economic] return or the greatest unit output," and both call for use and management of the land "without impairment of the productivity of the land."

This language, and that of the counterpart term "sustained yield," has been widely debated by legal scholars and the popular press. However, few courts have construed these terms, and they have found "little law to apply." The bulk of opinion seems to be that the law is fuzzy and provides little guidance to the agencies. Professor George Coggins (Coggins 1981) agrees that multiple-use statutes, including MUSYA, are "not very good law"; they "represent congressional buck passing" to the management agencies. Nevertheless, he argues that the statutory provisions do have some teeth if the agencies and courts are willing to apply them. He refers to the "series of 'shalls' and 'shall nots' that ought to be binding" (for instance, "due consideration *shall* be given"), and the strong language used to define both "multiple use" and "sustained yield," e.g., significant expressions such as "without impairment of the productivity of the land," references to "best meeting" the present and future needs of the American people, and the language "achievement and maintenance *in perpetuity* of a high-level" output of renewable resources (emphasis added).

In the Wise Use and County Supremacy movements, "multiple use" has taken on a new connotation, one that emphasizes the commodities produced on public lands (timber, minerals, livestock forage), and minimizes the noncommercial or nonmarket amenities, such as scenery, wilderness, and wildlife habitat.

See also **Coggins, George Cameron; Federal Land Policy and Management Act; Multiple-Use, Sustained-Yield Act of 1960; Sustained Yield; Wise Use Movement.**

MULTIPLE-USE, SUSTAINED-YIELD ACT OF 1960 (MUSYA)

A federal statute that sets forth the general principles for managing the national forests. The act lists alphabetically these multiple uses: "outdoor recreation, range, timber, watershed, and wildlife and fish purposes." It declares that national forests shall be administered for these purposes, which are "supplemental to" the purposes for which national forests were established under the Organic Act of 1897 (i.e., "to improve and protect the forest, or...securing favorable conditions of water flows, and to furnish a continuous supply of timber").

The statute provides that, in administering the national forests, "due consideration shall be given to the relative values of the various resources in particular areas," and it defines "multiple use" and "sustained yield." Instead of including wilderness among the itemized multiple uses, Congress declared that the "establishment and maintenance of areas of wilderness are consistent with the purposes" of the MUSYA. In the National Forest Management Act of 1976, Congress reaffirmed the applicability of the MUSYA to planning and management of the national forests and expressly included wilderness among the "products and services" of the national forests that are to be managed according to multiple-use, sustained-yield principles.

Nearly half the statute consists of definitions. The definition of "multiple use" calls for "making the most judicious use of the land for some or all of these resources or related services over areas large enough to provide sufficient latitude for periodic adjustments in use to conform to changing needs and conditions." It further directs that forests be "utilized in the combination that will best meet the needs of the American people," although "not necessarily the combination of uses that will give the greatest dollar return or the greatest unit output." "Sustained yield" means the "achievement and maintenance *in perpetuity* of a high-level annual or periodic output of the various renewable resources" (emphasis added). Both definitions call for use and management of the land "without impairment of the productivity of the land."

The MUSYA has been criticized as vague and providing little guidance to the U.S. Forest Service in managing the forests. Extremely little case law interprets or applies the statute. One court construed the act's "due consideration" requirement (quoted above) to mean simply that the Forest Service must give "some consideration" to all resources. On appeal, in an unpublished opinion that has no precedential value, the appellate court accepted this interpretation but added that it believed the agency must "informedly and rationally" take "into balance" the relative values of resources when deciding the uses of the forest.

See also **Multiple Use; National Forest Management Act of 1976;** *United States v. New Mexico* **(1978).**

MURKOWSKI, FRANK H. Conservative Republican senator from Alaska and chair of the Senate Energy and Natural Resources Committee. Consistently prodevelopment and sympathetic to commodity uses of public lands, Murkowski has long advocated opening the Arctic National Wildlife Refuge to oil and gas drilling and continued logging of the Tongass National Forest. He and Representative Don Young (R-AK), chair of the House Resources Committee, were the targets of a 1997 Wilderness Society petition drive aimed at removing them as chairs of their respective committees and replacing them with less conservative Republicans.

In a move that surprised many, especially environmental groups, Murkowski announced in early 1997 that he would hold a series of workshops to assess the status of outdoor recreation opportunities in the United States. He said that it had been a mistake for Congress and the Clinton administration to halt budget appropriations (beginning in FY 1996) from the Land and Water Conservation Fund for state projects, and he indicated that he would seek to renew such funding. Perhaps as recognition for these efforts, in 1997 Murkowski received the American Recreation Coalition's "Sheldon Coleman Great Outdoors Award," given to "an outstanding American leader whose personal efforts have enhanced our nation's outdoor legacy and the ability of Americans to enjoy this recreational legacy."

See also **Arctic National Wildlife Refuge; Land and Water Conservation Fund; Senate Energy and Natural Resources Committee; Tongass National Forest.**

NATIONAL **A**UDUBON **S**OCIETY A national membership environmental organization perhaps best known for its
namesake, naturalist and painter John James Audubon, and for its award-
winning magazine, *Audubon*. Audubon was founded in 1905 and claims
600,000 members, whose dues support the nonprofit group's wildlife protection, energy conservation, and other environmental programs. It also
owns and operates numerous nature preserves around the country and
nature centers in California, Connecticut, New Mexico, Ohio, and Wisconsin. The organization has chapters throughout the United States and Latin
America, and offices in New York, Washington, D.C., and nine field locations. It engages in lobbying, policy research, science, and education efforts, and occasionally in litigation. Some of its chief issues include
migratory bird conservation, endangered species protection, and conservation of wetlands, including the Everglades.

*N*ATIONAL *A*UDUBON *S*OCIETY *v*. *S*UPERIOR *C*OURT
*O*F *A*LPINE *C*OUNTY **(1983)** Commonly known as the
Mono Lake decision, this California Supreme Court case is considered the
leading case on the application of the public trust doctrine to appropriations and use of water under state law. Exercising water rights it had obtained 40 years earlier, the city of Los Angeles diverted water from four
tributaries of Mono Lake. The diversions significantly lowered the lake
level, adversely impacting wildlife. In order to resolve the dispute, the court
believed that it was required to "integrate" two "competing systems of
thought": the public trust doctrine and the prior appropriation doctrine.
The court held that the "human and environmental uses of Mono Lake—
uses protected by the public trust doctrine—deserve to be taken into account," and that the appropriative water rights system did not render the
state "powerless to protect" those uses. In other words, rights to divert
water obtained under state law could be limited as necessary to protect
other uses of water embraced within the concept of the public trust.

Since *Mono Lake* was decided, other courts have also relied on the public trust doctrine to limit diversions of water, and the California court later held that even federal water projects are subject to the public trust limitation. After 25 years of litigation, two lawsuits brought by Inyo County ultimately resulted in orders that Los Angeles restore the ecosystem of the lower Owens River.

See also **Instream Flow; Prior Appropriation; Public Trust Doctrine.**

NATIONAL BIOLOGICAL SERVICE (NBS) A federal agency established administratively by Interior Secretary Bruce Babbitt in 1993 by consolidating the biological research, inventory and monitoring, and information transfer programs of seven Interior Department bureaus, notably U.S. Fish and Wildlife Service, National Park Service, and Bureau of Land Management. The agency became operational in late 1993 with an appropriation in the fiscal year 1994 budget bill—basically a reassignment of the scientific personnel and the related budget appropriations of the original agencies. This equated to 1,850 employees, four "ecoregional" offices, 13 research centers, and more than 60 cooperative wildlife and fisheries research units and 100 field stations.

The chief functions of the NBS are to collect and assemble existing biological data from sources such as universities, state heritage programs, and state wildlife agencies, and to make that data available to policy makers and managers in the other divisions of Interior. Babbitt believed that separating the science and policy-making functions of Interior would enhance the department's credibility and insulate it from charges that it was manipulating science for political purposes. Policy makers in Congress would be better able to sort out the science from the agency's management choices, and override those choices if necessary.

The new agency immediately attracted attention and criticism—from within Interior ranks and on Capitol Hill. Originally called the National Biological *Survey* (and modeled after the U.S. Geological Survey), the agency's name was changed in early 1995. Many in Congress and the public at large apparently believed that NBS researchers would be overrunning the countryside, including private property, surveying everything and, it was feared, finding new species to list under the Endangered Species Act of 1973. According to Secretary Babbitt, the word "service" in the new name was meant to reflect the true mission of the agency—to be a science service organization for other Interior bureaus.

However, the NBS never received congressional authorization as an independent agency. Indeed, Congress repeatedly threatened to strip it of all funding, which not only left NBS in limbo but jeopardized the science funding of other Interior agencies. Recently, the bureau was renamed and relocated to the U.S. Geological Survey-Division of Biological Resources.

NATIONAL ENVIRONMENTAL POLICY ACT (NEPA)

Outlines broad policy goals for the nation and establishes procedural requirements applicable to every federal agency. It is the one common thread in all public land and public natural resources decision making. Passage of NEPA in 1969 heralded a new age of concern for the environment in this country.

The Statutory Scheme

NEPA has three parts: (1) a set of broad, rather vague environmental goals for the country; (2) an "action-forcing" mechanism, the chief element of which is the environmental impact statement (EIS) requirement; and (3) a section creating the Council on Environmental Quality (CEQ). The goals section of the act has largely been ignored by courts, but legal scholars seem to be turning to it increasingly. For instance, NEPA recognizes "the profound impact of man's activity on the interrelationships of all components of the natural environment" and "the critical importance of restoring and maintaining environmental quality." The statute then declares it to be federal policy to "use all practicable means...to create and maintain conditions under which man and nature can exist in productive harmony," and to "preserve important...natural aspects of our natural heritage, and maintain, wherever possible, an environment which supports diversity and variety of individual choice." This language has been cited by scholars in support of a federal agency duty to promote biodiversity conservation.

The most important section of NEPA, and the one with far-reaching consequences for the workings of the federal government and for environmental law, is section 102. It requires that all federal agencies "utilize a systematic, interdisciplinary approach" in their planning and decision making, and that they prepare a "detailed statement" concerning the environmental impacts of, and alternatives to, "every recommendation or report on proposals for legislation and other major federal actions significantly affecting the quality of the human environment." This detailed statement is the EIS.

As noted, the third section of the statute establishes the CEQ. Located within the office of the president, this agency promptly issued guidelines for implementing NEPA, including preparing EISs. The U.S. Supreme Court has ruled that these guidelines are binding on all federal agencies. Most agencies, however, have also issued their own rules for incorporating NEPA procedures into their operations.

NEPA in the Courts

NEPA has spawned considerable litigation—hundreds of thousands of cases—since its enactment. Most cases deal with one of two basic questions: Should an agency have prepared an EIS on a proposed action or, if an EIS was prepared, was the analysis adequate? Most public land litigation involves NEPA issues, whether the case is brought by an environmental group or by public land users, such as a grazing permittee or timber contractor. This is true even of cases arising under one of the land management statutes, the Endangered Species Act of 1973, or agency regulations.

The U.S. Supreme Court has consistently held that NEPA imposes only procedural requirements on federal agencies. That is, agencies must "take a hard look at" the consequences of their proposed actions, and at alternatives and other means of mitigating the adverse impacts of those actions, but NEPA does not require any substantive outcome. Simply, NEPA does not dictate what agencies may or must do. Nevertheless, Congress certainly contemplated that, if agencies were fully informed in advance as to the environmental consequences of their proposed actions, the overall quality of decision making would likely be improved. As the Supreme Court said in *Robertson v. Methow Valley Citizens Council* (1989), "these procedures are almost certain to affect the agency's substantive decision." Indeed, NEPA has had substantive effects on natural resources and public land law, notably in the regulation of grazing, hardrock mining, timber harvesting, and oil and gas exploration and development.

Criticisms of NEPA Implementation

The CEQ recently reported that many federal agencies produce the documents called for by NEPA, yet ignore the law's intent. That is, agencies ignore NEPA in developing their overall policies, while examining "in microscopic detail" the environmental impacts of individual projects in their environmental assessments and EISs. The council bemoaned the "millions of dollars, years of time, and tons of paper that have been spent on [NEPA] documents that have little effect on decision-making." A better approach, according to CEQ, would be to monitor the actual impacts of projects during and after construction to ensure the effectiveness of mitigation measures and enable better predictions about the probable impacts of future proposals.

One legal scholar recently argued that NEPA's EIS requirement should apply to agency decisions that alter federal tax policies.

See also **Environmental Impact Statement; Federal Land Policy and Management Act; Mitigation; National Forest Management Act of 1976; Robertson v. Methow Valley Citizens Council (1989).**

NATIONAL FOREST MANAGEMENT ACT OF 1976 (NFMA)

One of the major statutes governing the U.S. Forest Service's administration of the national forests; the others are the Organic Act of 1897, the Multiple-Use, Sustained-Yield Act of 1960, and the Resources Planning Act of 1974, which the NFMA amended. The NFMA has been called a "new organic act for the Forest Service." It and the Bureau of Land Management's organic act, the Federal Land Policy and Management Act, also passed in 1976, are comparable in many respects.

The bulk of the NFMA's provisions are procedural, relating to the land and resource management plans, or forest plans, that the agency is required to prepare for each forest. However, the statute also contains numerous substantive provisions, relating particularly to harvesting timber from national forests. The statute reaffirms that forests are to be managed according to multiple-use and sustained-yield principles, and it recognizes the Forest Service's role in encouraging owners of private and state forest lands to manage their lands under the same principles. The act also requires the agency to keep a current inventory of forests and forest resources.

The forest planning provisions of the NFMA direct that the Forest Service develop and periodically revise individual plans for all national forests. Planning must involve the public, be interdisciplinary, incorporate National Environmental Policy Act (NEPA) procedures, and reflect multiple-use, sustained-yield principles. After a plan is prepared for a forest, management (including other resource activity plans and permits) "shall be consistent with" the forest plan.

NFMA directed the secretary of agriculture to promulgate regulations guiding the development of forest plans, and it lists a number of specific requirements that the rules must include, the most specific of which pertain to timber harvesting. The act requires the agency to determine which lands are physically and economically suitable for logging; requires the maintenance of "diversity of plant and animal species," including the "diversity of tree species similar to that existing in the region"; specifies when clear-cutting and other even-aged management techniques may be used; and requires regeneration of timber stands within five years. The physical and economic suitability requirements, although brief, are invoked by environmental groups in opposing below-cost timber sales.

National forest management today is beset by a number of issues, including protection and logging of old-growth forests, clear-cutting, below-cost timber sales, salvage logging, fire suppression policy, ecosystem management, biodiversity conservation, and the traditional competition between preservation and pro-use interests. In 1997, Senator Larry Craig (R-ID) held a number of field hearings and released a draft "discussion bill" dealing nominally with "forest health" but also proposing substantial revisions to the NFMA. As of August 1997, no bill had been formally introduced.

The NFMA and the Forest Service are the subjects of a comprehensive new review by public land scholar Charles F. Wilkinson. [Wilkinson 1997]

See also **Below-Cost Timber Sales; Clear-Cutting; Even-Aged Management; Federal Land Policy and Management Act; Forest Plan; Old Growth; Organic Act; Salvage Logging; U.S. Forest Service.**

NATIONAL MINING ASSOCIATION (NMA) Formerly the American Mining Congress, its members include producers of coal and other minerals and metals. The NMA lobbies on behalf of its members and monitors federal agency activities relating to regulation of mining and mine safety, availability of public lands for mining activities, and mine-related research. It funds research and issues reports concerning the economic contributions of the mining industry. NMA is one of the industrial groups that helped fund the emerging Wise Use Movement.

See also **Mining Law Reform; Wise Use Movement.**

NATIONAL PARK SERVICE (NPS) Established in 1916 with passage of the National Park Service Organic Act. The NPS is an agency within the U.S. Department of the Interior with management responsibility for a diverse and far-flung national system consisting of 376 units and about 80 million acres, two-thirds of which are in Alaska. System units include national parks, monuments, recreation areas, seashores, and trails. There is no typical park system unit; areas managed by the NPS range from Ellis Island, the Washington Monument, and the Gettysburg battlefield to Yellowstone and Yosemite National Parks and Death Valley National Monument. In 1993 the NPS registered 273 million recreational visits. The agency protects natural and cultural resources while promoting outdoor recreation, environmental education, and historic preservation. National parks can be established only by an act of Congress, although occasionally a national monument designated by a president (pursuant to his Antiquities Act power) is later made a park by Congress.

In 1997, for the first time in history, the NPS director nominee was subject to confirmation proceedings in the Senate. The requirement for Senate confirmation, along with a proviso that the appointee have substantial land management experience, was added by Representative James Hansen (R-UT) and enacted as part of the Omnibus Parks Bill passed in 1996. The change was supported by the National Parks and Conservation Association, which believes that Senate hearings will allow greater public input to the choice of director and the direction of the agency.

Funding for the parks is of increasing concern. Many parks do not have sufficient money to keep up with basic maintenance, much less improve or add new facilities. The agency labors under a maintenance and operations backlog of $5 billion and has an $8 billion acquisitions wish list. In the face of threats that some parks might have to close, Representative Hansen introduced a bill in Congress in 1996 to relinquish all but the "crown jewels" of the park system to states or private interests. The bill was roundly defeated on the House floor. More legitimate remedies include reforming concessions policy, increasing visitor fees, and encouraging corporate sponsorship. In addition, the Park Service and several conservation groups favor efforts to enhance the fund-raising abilities of the National Park Foundation, the quasi-private partner of the NPS established by Congress. Some environmentalists opposed a bill in the 104th Congress that would have allowed the foundation to accept corporate advertising and solicit corporate donations, claiming that it would commercialize the parks.

Another pressing park issue is overcrowding. Grand Canyon National Park, for instance, currently attracts 5 million visitors annually and expects that number to increase to 7 million in the near future. The park has only 2,300 parking spaces, yet experiences 6,000 cars on a typical summer day. Consequently, the park proposed and is seeking public input on a mass transit plan that would replace park visitors' vehicles with a light rail system or a fleet of buses. A bus system is already in place in Denali National Park in Alaska. Overcrowding results in excess pressure on park infrastructure (roads, visitor centers, campgrounds, water and sanitary facilities, etc.), which compounds the funding shortages.

Parks are also threatened by so-called external threats from activities on nonpark lands—air pollution that affects scenic vistas, tourist overflights, logging on surrounding multiple-use lands, tourist facilities crowding park borders, and development on inholdings. [*See* Public Trust Doctrine.] Unfortunately, the Park Service's own policies contribute to internal threats or at least give rise to controversies regarding those policies, such as the ecological consequences of its let-burn policy and alleged wildlife overpopulations, the bison-brucellosis crisis in Yellowstone, wolf reintroduction, and the permissibility of motorized vehicles in several park units. Even the Park Service's mandates—to preserve park resources while providing for their continued use and enjoyment—are apparently conflicting and often pose a dilemma for the agency.

See also **Antiquities Act of 1906; Biosphere Reserve; Land and Water Conservation Fund; National Park Service Organic Act of 1916.**

NATIONAL PARK SERVICE ORGANIC ACT OF 1916

The federal statute that created the National Park Service and sets forth its mission. Section 1 of the statute establishes that the fundamental purpose of national parks and monuments is "to conserve the scenery and the natural and historic objects and the wild life therein and to provide for the enjoyment of the same in such manner and by such means as will leave them unimpaired for the enjoyment of future generations." Section 2 requires that "promotion and regulation" of park system units "shall be consistent with" the purpose set forth in section 1 and that all activities shall be administered "in light of the high public value and integrity" of the park system.

The act authorizes the secretary of the interior to provide for emergency services and law enforcement, erect communication and fire protection facilities, acquire rights-of-way, provide for the cutting of timber where necessary to control insects, and issue regulations deemed necessary to provide for use and management of the parks. General management plans are required for each park system unit; the act makes only very general provisions concerning the plans' contents. The act further provides for administration of individual units of the park system in accordance with the terms of any statute relating specifically to it.

A separate section of the act charges the Secretary of Commerce with promoting tourist travel in the United States.

See also **Antiquities Act of 1906; National Park Service.**

NATIONAL PARKS AND CONSERVATION ASSOCIATION (NPCA)

Founded in 1919 to watchdog the National Park Service (NPS) and work to preserve the nation's park system. NPCA has 450,000 members and supporters and eight regional field offices throughout the country. Its activities, which include grassroots organizing, education, lobbying, and agency monitoring, focus on ensuring adequate funding for the NPS, improving park planning and management, and protecting both the health of the entire park system and specific park resources. It publishes *National Parks*, a magazine.

See also **National Park Service.**

NATIONAL TRAILS SYSTEM ACT OF 1968

The purposes of the Trails Act are to "provide for the ever-increasing outdoor recreation needs" of the American people and "to promote the preservation of, public access to, travel within, and enjoyment and appreciation of the open-air, outdoor areas and historic resources of the Nation." The act established priorities for trail designation, with preference going to trails near urban areas. Trails with scenic or historic value are given secondary priority.

The initial components of the trails system established by the 1968 act were the Pacific Crest and Appalachian trails. Many other trails have since been designated or identified for study for possible inclusion in the system. The act set standards for including additional trails, and two categories of trails are defined: recreation and scenic/historic. The secretaries of the Agriculture and Interior Departments may designate recreation trails, but only Congress can establish national scenic or historic trails. This scheme resembles the one established by Congress in the National Wild and Scenic Rivers Act (also passed in 1968).

The Trails Act provides for advisory councils, and calls for the preparation of comprehensive plans for both trail systems. Plans are to be prepared by the secretary having responsibility for the lands involved, in consultation with the relevant advisory council. Trails can be established on private land with the landowner's consent. The act contains rather extensive provisions for acquiring lands and obtaining rights-of-way, minimizing adverse effects of trail designation on adjacent landowners, determining permissible activities and facilities on and along trails, etc. The use of motorized vehicles on trails by the general public is prohibited, subject to limited exceptions. In general, trail uses may include bicycling, cross-country skiing, hiking and backpacking, horseback riding, and snowmobiling.

The act further provides that landowners who contribute land or interests in land, such as conservation easements, for inclusion in the trail system to "qualified organizations" (under specified provisions of federal law) can qualify for tax deductions.

See also **Conservation Easement.**

NATIONAL WILDLIFE FEDERATION (NWF) The nonprofit, tax-exempt NWF calls itself the nation's largest conservation group, claiming more than 5.3 million members and supporters, including members of its affiliate organizations in all 50 states. Founded in 1936 by editorial cartoonist J. N. "Ding" Darling, it is also one of the oldest conservation groups. It has a staff of approximately 600, including lawyers, economists, and various scientists and environmental specialists, in its headquarters and ten "natural resource center" field offices around the country. NWF's numerous publications include the magazines *National Wildlife, International Wildlife, Ranger Rick,* and *Your Big Backyard* (the latter two for children); an affiliate newspaper; *EnviroAction* newsletter; an annual *Conservation Directory* (listing federal and state agencies, congressional members and committees, national and regional commissions, and international, national, regional, state, and local organizations); and a variety of environmental education materials.

NWF has been a major player in natural resource litigation. The staff of each of its natural resource centers includes one or more lawyers, who bring citizen suits and other cases on behalf of NWF members and/or in collaboration with other environmental and public interest groups. Among the best known is *Lujan v. National Wildlife Federation* (1990), an important U.S. Supreme Court environmental standing decision. The organization has been involved in numerous challenges to the federal coal leasing program, forest plans, and public land grazing decisions. NWF also has an active administrative appeals agenda. For instance, it challenged the Bureau of Land Management over its livestock grazing practices in the Comb Wash allotment of southeastern Utah. After considering extensive expert testimony and other evidence, the Interior Board of Land Appeals (IBLA) ruled that overgrazing was responsible for the general degradation of canyon riparian areas, including adverse effects on recreation use, wildlife habitat, archaeological resources, and aesthetics.

Issues of principal interest to its natural resource centers include protection and sustainable use of the Northern Forest in the Northeast and ancient forests in the Pacific Northwest; protection of nationally significant wetlands, such as those in the Everglades, the north-central prairies, and Alaska; rangeland reform; wolf reintroduction in Yellowstone; and endangered species protection.

NATIONAL WILDLIFE REFUGE SYSTEM A complex of federal lands designated in 1966 in conjunction with passage of the first Endangered Species Act, and managed principally for wildlife conservation purposes. The refuge system is managed by the U.S. Fish and Wildlife Service (USFWS) within the Department of the Interior. The earliest refuges were established by President Theodore Roosevelt in the first decade of the twentieth century. Since then, refuges have been created by both presidents and the Congress; they have been reserved from multiple-use (or public domain) lands or acquired with funds from such sources as the sale of duck stamps. Refuges range in size from a few to more than a million acres, as in the Arctic National Wildlife Refuge. The system includes 511 refuges and 51 coordination areas, comprising 91 million acres nationwide.

Until 1997, management of the refuge system was guided by several statutes, including the Migratory Bird Conservation Act of 1929 as amended, the Refuge Recreation Act of 1962, and the National Wildlife Refuge System Administration Act of 1966, and a 1996 executive order, E.O. 12,996. The 1966 act authorizd the Secretary of the Interior to permit, by regulation, the use of any refuge "for any purpose, including but not limited to hunting, fishing, recreation and accommodations, and access whenever he determines that such uses are compatible with the major purposes for which such areas were established." The compatibility of certain uses, such as hunting and grazing, has been the basis of some controversy and litigation since the mid-1970s. Courts have consistently rejected challenges to hunting on refuges, but restrictions on the use of motorized watercraft have been upheld.

The compatible-uses issue arises in part because the 1966 act was not an organic act mandate for managing the refuges comparable to the organic acts that guide administration of national parks by the National Park Service, national forests by the U.S. Forest Service, or public lands by the Bureau of Land Management. [*See* National Park Service Organic Act of 1916, Organic Act of 1897, and Federal Land Policy and Management Act.] That is, it did not define a mission or overarching purpose for the refuge system, nor did it specify how compatibility determinations should be made. Passage of an organic act for the refuge system was attempted unsuccessfully several times in Congress. A bill in the 104th Congress, H.R. 511, would have given recreational "uses" of refuges the status of "purposes." It had wide support from sportsmen's groups, but was firmly opposed by the Clinton administration and environmentalists.

Organic act legislation finally passed in late 1997. The bill, H.R. 1420, was sponsored by Representative Don Young (R-AK). It received unanimous support from House Resources Committee members and the endorsement of the administration, including Interior Secretary Bruce Babbitt. Environmental groups were less enthusiastic, but agreed that it was an improvement over H.R. 511. Many of its provisions are patterned on those of E.O. 12,996, including the system's mission statement, designation of priority public uses, and a requirement that the biological integrity and diversity of refuges be maintained. The bill provided that the USFWS shall "administer a national network of lands and waters for the conservation, management, and where appropriate, restoration of the fish, wildlife and plant resources and their habitats...for the benefit of present and future generations."

H.R. 1420 declares that compatible, wildlife-dependent recreation is "a legitimate and appropriate general public use of the system," and identifies certain forms of recreation—including hunting, fishing, and wildlife photography—as meriting priority over others. The bill defines "compatible use" as one that "will not materially interfere with or detract from the fulfillment of the mission of the system or the purposes of a refuge." The bill also provides for preparation of refuge management plans and increased public participation in planning and management.

The House passed the bill almost unanimously in June 1997. In September the Senate passed the House bill, but only after amending it to clarify that commodity uses (e.g., oil and gas development or grazing) can continue in refuges so long as they are compatible with the refuge's purposes. Public Law 105-57, known as the National Wildlife Refuge System Improvement Act of 1997, was enacted in October.

See also **Arctic National Wildlife Refuge; Organic Act; U.S. Fish and Wildlife Service.**

NATIONWIDE PERMIT
See CLEAN WATER ACT SECTION 404.

NATURAL RESOURCE DAMAGES

Damages authorized by the Comprehensive Environmental Response, Compensation, and Liability Act (CERCLA) or the Clean Water Act (CWA) for injury to natural resources resulting from an oil spill or release of hazardous substances. Natural resources damages are available to compensate a state, the federal government, or an Indian tribe for the costs of assessing injury to natural resources under its jurisdiction, and the costs of restoring or replacing those resources. Resources may include fish and wildlife, vegetation, coastlines, and water quality. To recover, the government or tribe must sue the potentially responsible party or parties, usually the owner and/or operator of the facility or vessel from which the spill occurred. The litigation is likely to be very complex and involve many scientific experts because of the difficulty of proving the extent of the harm (what resources are actually damaged or destroyed) and how or whether the damaged resources can be rehabilitated or replaced. The best-known natural resource damages case involved the *Exxon Valdez* oil tanker, which ran aground in Alaskan waters in 1989. Negotiations in that case led to a series of scientific studies of the marine and coastal environments to determine the extent of the harm and to formulate plans for restoring or replacing damaged resources, such as marine mammals, sea birds, coastlines, aquatic vegetation, and fish and shellfish.

Regulations governing the assessment of natural resource damages have been issued by the National Oceanic and Atmospheric Administration (within the Department of Commerce) and the U.S. Fish and Wildlife Service (within the Department of the Interior). These rules have been controversial; early versions were successfully challenged in court and subsequently rewritten. The current regulations authorize the use of contingent valuation methods to assign monetary values to resources for which there is no market (for instance, certain mollusks or sea grasses) or whose value for aesthetic enjoyment exceeds any commodity value they might have (e.g., the value to tourists of seeing a sea otter versus the market value of an otter's pelt).

Natural resource damage claims are a separate component of complex CERCLA or CWA cases. The government will also sue the potentially responsible parties to clean up a spill or a contaminated site, and private parties may sue under other laws for damages they have incurred as a result of the spill.

See also **Contingent Valuation.**

NATURAL RESOURCES CONSERVATION SERVICE (NRCS)   The NRCS is the new incarnation of the Soil Conservation Service (SCS), a federal agency established by Congress in 1935 in response to the Depression and the Dust Bowl "to provide permanently for the control and prevention of soil erosion and thereby to preserve natural resources." The U.S. Department of Agriculture (USDA) Reorganization Act of 1994 changed the agency's name to better reflect its broad mission, and mandated revisions in the agency's organization designed to better achieve that mission.

Unlike the U.S. Forest Service (USFS) and Bureau of Land Management, NRCS is not a land or resource management agency, nor is it a regulatory agency like the Environmental Protection Agency (EPA) or U.S. Army Corps of Engineers (Corps). Instead, the NRCS/SCS was established to provide information and technical assistance to ranchers and farmers on private lands (approximately 1.5 billion acres, or 70 percent of the land area of the United States). Initially, it was proposed that the SCS be organized around watershed-based conservation districts, and that those districts be authorized to promulgate and enforce regulations concerning land-use practices, but this scheme was rejected in favor of the largely county-by-county, technical assistance approach still in place. NRCS/SCS programs since 1935 have been largely voluntary.

The agency offers information and technical assistance to landowners, local governments, and organizations on a variety of topics, including: managing water and preventing upland flooding, handling of animal wastes, enhancing crop production, managing riparian areas, strip-cropping, establishing windbreaks, preparing land unit conservation plans, and implementing best management practices to prevent soil erosion and protect water quality. Every five years NRCS conducts the National Resource Inventory to determine the conditions of land, soil, water, and related resources on nonfederal lands. It is currently preparing its third appraisal of these resources pursuant to the Resource Conservation Act of 1977 (RCA). The RCA appraisal is a planning tool designed to guide USDA conservation policies and programs, similar to the ten-year strategic plans prepared by the USFS (another USDA agency) under the Resources Planning Act (RPA).

In order to provide these diverse services, NRCS employs soil conservationists, fish and wildlife biologists, hydrologists, sociologists, landscape architects, foresters, range specialists, cartographers, ecologists, and other professionals. The agency is in the process of reducing staffs in its national headquarters and state offices while expanding the ranks of its field offices. In addition, it has established offices in six agriculturally/ecologically defined regions, somewhat analogous to the USFS's regional offices.

NRCS is moving steadily toward an ecosystem- or watershed-based approach to farm planning. The NRCS Science and Technology Consortium brings together NRCS specialists and experts from academia to discuss such topics as grazing lands technology, wetland and watershed sciences, resources inventory and analysis, and soil quality. To support its research and technology transfer efforts, NRCS increasingly relies on modern techniques, such as geospatial mapping, digitized soils information, and geographic information system (GIS) technology. It also consults with other agencies to assess whether they are collecting comparable resource data and to determine whether cooperative data collection efforts are possible.

NRCS programs include the (1) Wetlands Reserve Program, which involves obtaining easements to restore degraded wetlands; (2) Water Bank Program, whose aim is to protect wetlands and adjacent areas used by waterfowl, particularly in the Mississippi flyway; (3) Small Watershed Program (including an information database), designed to facilitate locally directed watershed-based projects to prevent soil erosion and flooding and enhance water quality; and (4) Forestry Incentives Program, which entails cooperative efforts between NRCS and state and private foresters to promote sound forest management practices on private lands. Through the National Agroforestry Center, founded in 1995, NRCS and the USFS cooperate to advise private landowners of the benefits of such techniques as using windbreaks or riparian forest buffers, and combining trees or shrubs with other crops and/or livestock in their operations. NRCS and the USFS, along with the EPA, Corps, and appropriate state agencies, are also cooperating at the state level on technical committees to set local priorities and establish approaches for handling resource issues.

See also **Conservation Reserve Program; Ecosystem Management; Swampbuster; Watershed; Wetland.**

NATURAL RESOURCES DEFENSE COUNCIL (NRDC)

NRDC is a nonprofit, tax-exempt environmental organization with more than 175,000 members and offices in Washington, D.C., San Francisco, and Los Angeles, as well as New York. Founded in 1970, it litigates, lobbies, educates, and conducts research in the cause of conserving natural resources and protecting human health and the environment. The organization reported total contributions and revenues of $25.8 million in fiscal year 1995. Total expenses were $23 million, 77 percent of which was spent on program services such as legal programs, scientific support, public education, and legislative action. In its mission statement, NRDC advocates environmental restoration and protection of endangered species, sustainability and the welfare of future generations of humans, and the right of all people to have a say in decisions that affect their environment. Among its principal resource conservation accomplishments, it cites the protection of coasts and public lands and energy conservation. Current efforts include promoting sustainable management of timber and global fish stocks and conserving biodiversity. NRDC employs 80 lawyers, scientists, and environmental specialists.

NRDC was a leader among the environmental groups that fought efforts of the 104th Congress to roll back federal environmental protections. During 1995 it wrote op-ed pieces in major newspapers and several reports exposing those efforts. One of those reports, *Selling Our Heritage*, documented congressional proposals to sell, lease, or give away federal public lands to states and private individuals. Another, *Save Our Summers*, described proposals to gut coastal protection laws. NRDC fought the so-called "Dirty Water Bill," which would have drastically reduced protection of wetlands; resisted measures that subsidized logging of the Tongass National Forest and authorized oil and gas drilling in the Arctic National Wildlife Refuge (ANWR); and opposed a bill that would have exempted a dam in the Pacific Northwest from complying with laws to protect salmon. In addition to its reports and the usual lobbying strategies, NRDC participated in the Environmental Bill of Rights signature campaign and a

"Twenty-one Chainsaw Salute" outside the White House to protest the salvage rider in the Supplemental FY 95 Appropriations and Rescissions Act.

NRDC has long been an active, effective advocate for environmental and conservation causes. One law professor points out that "the leading law school environmental treatise [contains] fifty-five cases named 'NRDC.'" A *U.S. News & World Report* story in 1995 suggested that NRDC lawyers "know more about environmental law than the government does." Jim Baca recently wrote that when he was director of the Bureau of Land Management and could not get information "quickly from the bureaucracy," he would call NRDC, on whom he could rely for "accurate and well researched" information "within hours."

Significant NRDC litigation includes the landmark 1974 suit *Natural Resources Defense Council v. Morton*, which forced the Bureau of Land Management to begin writing environmental impact statements on its public land grazing program. More recent cases include suits against the state of California to ensure continued implementation of the state Endangered Species Act and to add the California gnatcatcher, a songbird, to the list of endangered species; settlements between the federal government and major oil companies that canceled offshore drilling leases in Bristol Bay, Alaska, and the Florida Keys; and litigation to compel the Department of the Interior to make public an updated agency assessment of the oil and gas potential of ANWR. The organization also worked with the Cree Tribe to halt construction of the James Bay Hydroelectric Project in northwestern Quebec. According to NRDC, development of the facility would have disrupted the largest remaining de facto wilderness in eastern North America.

THE NATURE CONSERVANCY (TNC)   The Nature Conservancy was incorporated in 1951 as an outgrowth of the Ecologists Union, a professional association of scientists who sought to convert their expertise into action to protect nature. Today it is the largest private, nonprofit owner of nature preserves in the world, operating in all 50 states and internationally.

The TNC Personality

Although nonprofit and tax-exempt, TNC is the wealthiest environmental organization. It is funded by individual and corporate donations, foundation grants, membership dues (from its 828,000 members), and its real estate dealings. Its professional employees include corporate and real estate lawyers, business experts, ecologists, and other scientists. TNC's president, John C. Sawhill, formerly served as deputy secretary of the Department of Energy (1979–1980), head of the Federal Energy Administration (1973–1975), and associate director of the Office of Management and Budget (1973–1974). He has also been president of New York University, Chairman of U.S. Synthetic Fuels Corporation, and a director of several corporations.

One reporter wrote that TNC "uses only gentle persuasion and hard cash to accomplish its goals." [Fitzgerald 1992] Another article referred to TNC as "the Donald Trump of environmental organizations—Mother Nature's real estate broker." [Wolkomir & Wolkomir 1989]. TNC itself describes its methods as "market-based" and "nonconfrontational," saying, "our thing is to let money do our talking." Unlike most national environmental organizations, TNC does little lobbying and no litigating. Perhaps not surprisingly, the conservancy's nonactivist tactics and coziness with big business have attracted criticism from some environmental groups. Corporations, however (also not surprisingly), generally praise the organization, whose practical approach to business they understand and respect. In fact, TNC lists among its admirers 1,500 corporate associates such as Louis-Dreyfuss Corporation, Homestake Mining, Chemical Bank, FMC Corporation, Crest Foods, Honeywell, and Harcourt Brace; other corporate donors include Burlington-Northern, Unisys, Sears, Procter & Gamble, Liz Claiborne, Gulf Oil, and Chevron.

TNC's Conservation Work

In the United States, TNC owns and manages more than 1,500 nature sanctuaries and has secured the protection of more than 9.3 million acres. It has also helped protect 44 million acres in Latin America, the Caribbean, and the Pacific. TNC is preeminent among organizations dedicated to protecting biological diversity. In addition to buying and managing land, TNC purchases ecologically significant parcels for subsequent sale to other conservation buyers, including governments; purchases conservation easements on ecologically significant lands; enters into land management agreements with other entities (the first of these was with the Bureau of Land Management in 1961); and accepts donations of land or interests in land from owners desiring to protect it from development.

A monumental TNC endeavor is its Natural Heritage Inventory Programs, begun in 1974 and now established in all states—along with their counterpart Conservation Data Centers in several foreign countries—to collect and maintain inventory data and protection status information on species and habitats. TNC then focuses its conservation efforts on those areas that support species most urgently in need of protection. TNC's Biological and Conservation Data System, a computer database that allows users to contribute and share inventory and conservation information, merited a Smithsonian Institution award in 1994.

One of TNC's most significant land purchases, and by far its largest, is the 502-square-mile (397,000-acre) Gray Ranch in southeastern New Mexico, acquired for $18 million in 1987. The ranch is significant not only for its size, but because it is home to species from several ecosystems, including the Chihuahuan and Sonoran deserts, the Rocky Mountains, and Mexico's Sierra Madres. Some biologists believe that the ranch may support more species of mammals than any other refuge in the United States. The conservancy sold the ranch in 1993 to the Animas Foundation, a private organization formed to protect rangeland and the ranching lifestyle. A team of scientists representing both TNC and the Animas Foundation monitor annually the ecological condition of 125 established sampling sites. Plans for the ranch include using livestock grazing and fire as ecosystem management tools.

Along the eastern border of the country is another, smaller example of TNC's conservation efforts: Rhode Island's Block Island. The island is a crucial haven for wildlife, insect, and plant species, and is a vital stopover point for birds migrating along the Atlantic Coast. Over the past 20-plus years, more than 1,200 acres of the 6,500-acre island have been protected from development. Several groups and many individuals have been players in the process, but the conservancy's donations, negotiated land exchanges, easement acquisitions, and outright purchases have been key.

In 1991, TNC embarked on its "Last Great Places: An Alliance for People and the Environment" campaign to save large ecosystems. TNC received the first President's Environment and Conservation Challenge Award for this multinational, cooperative program. Block Island is one of these "Last Great Places," and the only such site identified to date in the Northeast.

TNC supports land protection strategies that incorporate partnerships among it and other conservation organizations, individual landowners, and government agencies. For instance, the conservancy is a player in several partnerships aimed at promoting both agricultural and environmental interests, including rice growers and migratory waterfowl in California, beet farmers and sharp-tailed grouse and other wildlife in Idaho, and farmers and other landowners and aquatic species in watersheds in Indiana,

Ohio, and Virginia. It participates in similar programs with ranchers in several states, including Arizona, Wyoming, Colorado, Nebraska, Utah, and Kansas. One innovative example involved the UX Ranch in Ruby Valley, Nevada, an area with important wetland, upland, resident, and migratory wildlife habitat values. To help the family owners of the ranch avoid foreclosure, TNC essentially offered a five-year interest-free loan in exchange for a conservation easement allowing traditional ranching but precluding subdivision and other development uses. The owners were later able to repurchase the property, which they continue to manage for cattle ranching and conservation purposes.

Similarly, TNC works in partnership with utilities, mining companies, oil and gas interests, and timber companies. The purposes of these arrangements may be to conserve surface resources, such as rare plant or animal species or ecologically significant communities, or to protect hydrological resources, such as desert springs or other important water supplies, while allowing concurrent development or redirecting development to less vulnerable sites. The methods employed in such partnerships are myriad: conservation easements, joint management arrangements, two- and three-way land exchanges, initiation of best management practices, etc. In still other cases, the objective of the partnership may be to promote conservation-related research.

Two of TNC's highest profile conservation undertakings are a cooperative plan to protect habitat of the endangered fringed-toe lizard in Coachella Valley, California, while allowing real estate development to continue in the rapidly growing area, and a complex plan involving multiple preserves to protect several rare species and water supplies threatened by burgeoning development around Austin, Texas. In both cases, TNC officials helped develop proposals and served as mediators for the negotiations among the many and diverse parties. Development and conservation interests were served, lands were protected voluntarily (without the need for government condemnation proceedings), and litigation has thus far been avoided.

TNC publishes a bimonthly magazine, *Nature Conservancy*.

See also **Biodiversity Conservation; Conservation Easement; Habitat Conservation Plan; Land Trust.**

NAVIGABLE WATERS A term with different meanings, depending on the context. For purposes of federal regulatory power, "navigable waters" referred historically to those rivers, lakes, and coastal waters that were navigable in fact or capable of being made navigable and used in commerce. The Commerce Clause of the Constitution is the source of Congress's power to regulate these waters. However, the modern Clean Water Act, beginning with the 1972 amendments, defines "navigable waters" simply as "waters of the United States." This term has been interpreted very broadly in regulations issued by both the Environmental Protection Agency and the U.S. Army Corps of Engineers; "waters of the United States" includes *virtually all* bodies of water, even seasonal and some man-made waters, as well as wetlands. In *United States v. Riverside Bayview Homes, Inc.* (1985), the U.S. Supreme Court upheld the agencies' definition. Pollution control laws are also an exercise of Congress's Commerce Clause power; a few lower courts have held that in Clean Water Act section 404, Congress legislated to the full extent of its Commerce Clause authority.

"Navigable waters" has an entirely different, and much narrower, meaning for purposes of determining who owns the lands along and underneath bodies of water. As a matter of federal law, title to the beds and banks of navigable waters passed to states upon their admission to the Union. For this purpose, a body of water was navigable if it was usable by customary modes of travel, in its natural and ordinary condition, at the time of statehood. "Natural" and "ordinary" mean without artificial improvement, such as by dredging or impoundment.

To complicate the matter even further, some *states* may define "navigable water" more liberally for purposes of (1) establishing state ownership of the beds and banks of *other* waters, not only those navigable by the federal test at the time of statehood; or (2) providing for and regulating public use of waters, such as for fishing or recreational boating, even if the waters and lands below them are privately owned. In these cases, the meaning of "navigable waters" is a question of state law.

See also **Equal Footing Doctrine;** *Hoffman Homes, Inc. v. Environmental Protection Agency* **(1993);** *Illinois Central Railroad Co. v. Illinois* **(1892);** **Public Trust Doctrine;** *United States v. Riverside Bayview Homes, Inc.* **(1985); Wetland.**

NEW WORLD MINE   A proposed gold mine just 2.5 miles northeast of Yellowstone National Park in southeastern Montana. The New World Mine has an estimated value of $500-800 million and could produce 1,200 to 1,800 tons of gold-, silver-, and copper-bearing ore per day for up to 20 years. The mine has been the object of impassioned controversy and the subject of negotiations among its owners, the federal government, environmental groups, and state and local leaders over how to protect the national park (our nation's first) and other natural resources from the environmental threats posed by mine development, while accommodating the significant private property interests at stake. It is generally agreed that the mine would destroy wetlands and irreparably damage the alpine environment, and could pollute streams in and near Yellowstone Park. In fact, because of the "catastrophic" damage posed by the New World Mine to the Clarks Fork of the Yellowstone River, the Clarks Fork has been at the top of American Rivers's list of the country's most endangered rivers for the past three years. (The Clarks Fork is a designated "wild" river in the national wild and scenic river system.)

In 1995 President Clinton imposed a two-year moratorium on mining New World's claims on federal land. Then in 1996 the President, mine operator Crown Butte Mines, Inc. (a subsidiary of Noranda Minerals), and the Greater Yellowstone Coalition entered into an agreement known as the New World Mine Agreement, which called for an end to mine construction. In early 1997 the Clinton administration offered Crown Butte $65 million in federal assets (minerals and timber) elsewhere in exchange for an agreement to stop mine development and to set aside more than $20 million to fund reclamation of the area, which has been damaged by 120 years of mining activities. Concerned members of Congress and certain environmental groups argued that any deal must be fair to the public and not sacrifice other valuable natural resources just to save the Yellowstone area. Congressional leaders were also leery of the precedent the exchange could set. In late 1997 Congress appropriated $77 million (from the Land and Water Conservation Fund) for acquisition of the mine site (which will be managed by the U.S. Forest Service) and for related purposes. President Clinton exercised his line-item veto authority to eliminate one provision of the act—the transfer of $10 million worth of federal minerals to the state of Montana designed to compensate it for lost revenues from the New World Mine. There was debate in Congress over whether the transfer provision was subject to the president's line-item veto authority, and at press time Montana was considering a legal challenge.

The Forest Service had begun preparing a draft environmental impact statement on the mine. But preparation was delayed while exchange negotiations were underway, and presumably abandoned after Congress authorized acquiring the lands.

See also **General Mining Law; Greater Yellowstone Coalition; Land Exchange; Mining Law Reform**.

NONRESIDENT LICENSE   A state hunting or fishing license issued to a person who resides in another state. States employ a variety of license allocation systems, but often use residency as a basis for decisions about license price and availability. When the species of game or fish being pursued is relatively abundant, the only difference between resident and nonresident licenses may be the required fee, with nonresidents often paying substantially more for the right to hunt or fish. The U.S. Supreme Court has ruled that such seemingly discriminatory treatment of nonresidents is constitutional; hunting and fishing are merely recreational sports, not fundamental rights. [*Baldwin v. Fish and Game Commission of Montana* (1978)]

When the number of hunting or fishing licenses must be manipulated to achieve conservation or revenue goals, license allocation schemes become more elaborate, and state residency often plays a determinative role. The extreme positions are represented by Colorado, which does not distinguish between resident and nonresident big-game hunters, and Arizona, which allocates all of its big-game licenses to residents, with up to 10 percent of these licenses going to nonresidents only if residents don't apply for them.

In between the extremes, many states opt for license systems that allocate a fixed number or percentage of the available licenses to nonresidents. States employ various methods for distributing nonresident licenses. Some, such as Wyoming, employ a random drawing wherein all nonresident applicants have an equal chance to draw a limited-quota nonresident license. Alternatively, a state may opt for a preference-point system, in which an applicant acquires a preference point for every year in which he or she applies unsuccessfully for a license; the accumulation of points increases the probability of drawing a license in any subsequent year.

Many western states link some or all of the available nonresident licenses to the nonresident hunter's use of the services of resident guides and outfitters. Such "set-aside license" systems allocate a fixed number or a certain percentage of the available nonresident licenses to hunters who have entered or agree to enter into an agreement with a state-licensed outfitter or guide.

More than ever, states are looking at market-driven license systems as a means of increasing revenues. In Oregon, a small number of big-game licenses are available each year through an auction sale, with no preference given to residents over nonresidents. Theoretically, the price of the license is established by market factors, such as demand for the opportunity to hunt a particular species.

See also *Baldwin v. Fish and Game Commission of Montana* (1978); *Clajon Production Corporation v. Petera* (1995); **Commerce Clause.**

NORTHERN SPOTTED OWL   A federally listed threatened species inhabiting old-growth and mature forests of the Pacific Northwest. This owl has been the center of controversy concerning the logging of old growth on public lands, which contain virtually all of its remaining habitat. Despite almost unanimous scientific opinion that the owl was jeopardized by the loss and fragmentation of old-growth forests (only 1,500 pairs were located in a 1989 survey), the U.S. Fish and Wildlife Service (USFWS) had declined to protect it under the Endangered Species Act of 1973 (ESA). The bird was listed as threatened only after several environmental organizations sued the agency in 1988. The USFWS was again sued in 1991 to compel it to designate critical habitat for the species, as required by the ESA. In 1992 the USFWS designated 190 tracts totaling nearly 7 million acres as critical habitat; these were mostly national forests and lands managed by the Bureau of Land Management (BLM).

Concern for the owl, and protests by environmentalists against federal agency logging practices, led to the formation of the Interagency Scientific Committee (or Thomas Committee, after its chair, Jack Ward Thomas). In 1990 this group made a number of recommendations for protecting owl habitat, which critics claimed would result in the loss of 12,000 to 50,000 jobs in the Northwest timber industry. Environmentalists began to sue the agencies, asking the courts to enjoin timber sales that jeopardized the owl's survival. Congress got into the fray in 1990 by passing the Northwest Timber Compromise. This statute prescribed logging practices for 13 national forests and BLM districts in Oregon and Washington, and specified that management according to those guidelines would be "sufficient" to meet the statutory requirements (ESA, National Environmental Policy Act, National Forest Management Act of 1976) that were the subject of the pending lawsuits. Relying on the 1990 statute's sufficiency language, the federal agencies subsequently sought to have the lawsuits dismissed, but the Ninth Circuit ruled that the 1990 law violated constitutional separation of powers principles; that is, Congress had interfered with the proper functioning of the courts by directing a certain outcome in ongoing litigation. The U.S.

Supreme Court reversed, holding that the Northwest Timber Compromise merely established different standards applicable to the logging at issue in the pending cases, which was within Congress's power to do, and that it did not direct the courts to reach any particular result. [*See Robertson v. Seattle Audubon Society* (1992).]

On another front, the Endangered Species Committee, or "God Squad," was asked to exempt 44 proposed BLM timber sales from ESA requirements. It exempted 13 of the sales, but imposed numerous conditions. Environmentalists sued, and the BLM eventually dropped the exempted sales. Meanwhile, proposed sales were being enjoined for violations of other laws, such as requirements applicable to BLM's land-use plans. All these circumstances heightened the tension in Northwest logging communities and led to the Northwest Forest Summit, convened by the Clinton Administration in 1993. The result of this collaborative effort was the Northwest Forest Management Plan, the first cooperative ecosystem management plan. The agencies' selected alternative, known as Option 9, provided for harvesting 1.2 billion board feet (bbf) of timber, compared to harvests of 5.6 bbf in the 1980s. Job losses are expected to continue in the timber industry, but most sources now agree that these will result from modernization and changes in the industry itself, not from environmental restrictions.

Recent court decisions by the Ninth Circuit suggest that a similar controversy is brewing in the Southwest over the Mexican spotted owl. [*See*, e.g., *Silver v. Babbitt* (1995).] This subspecies was listed as threatened in 1993, and in 1995 critical habitat totaling 6.4 million acres was designated in Arizona, Colorado, Utah, and New Mexico. As a result of litigation brought by the Southwest Center for Biological Diversity and others, about 65 percent of logging activities on 11 national forests in the Southwest were halted because the forest plans failed to provide adequately for protection of the owl and other species. The USFS subsequently amended the plans, but indicated that it did not intend to apply the new requirements to timber sales retroactively. Environmentalists again sued, and won. The Ninth Circuit ruled that no activities may be conducted in these forests unless they are consistent with the new plans, a ruling expected to have significant ramifications for livestock grazing as well as logging. The USFS has also been sued for failing to consult with the USFWS concerning the Mexican spotted owl as required by ESA section 7.

See also **Critical Habitat; Endangered Species Act of 1973; Listing; Section 7 Consultation; Thomas, Jack Ward; Threatened Species.**

NUISANCE　Essentially, a use of land by one person that unreasonably interferes with another person's use or enjoyment of his or her land. Nuisance is a common-law claim. A person claiming to be harmed by a neighbor's land use can seek an injunction and damages from a court. The court will analyze the facts and balance the interests and harms involved. If the harm that the defendant would incur if ordered to stop the activity outweighs the harm to the plaintiff of allowing the activity to continue, the court will not enjoin the activity but may order the defendant to pay damages to the plaintiff.

The common law recognizes both private and public nuisances; essentially, a public nuisance is one that affects a large number of persons or an entire community. A "nuisance per se" is an activity that has been expressly identified as a nuisance by a state legislature. Nuisances per se may be prohibited altogether, or may be impermissible in certain locations.

Many environmental laws are based on, or incorporate, the nuisance concept or another common-law claim, trespass. For instance, polluting a river or draining a wetland can be considered a nuisance; clear-cutting a slope and thereby causing a mudslide onto your neighbor's property might be a nuisance or a trespass. Some environmental statutes expressly replace these common-law remedies, but most simply supplement the remedies that would otherwise be available to address environmental wrongs. For this reason, litigation often involves claims raised under a modern environmental statute (state or federal) as well as a state's common law.

See also **Common Law.**

◫ OFFICE OF SURFACE MINING RECLAMATION AND ENFORCEMENT

See SURFACE MINING CONTROL AND RECLAMATION ACT OF 1977.

◫ OLD GROWTH

This term is used to describe mature forests, but it has no precise, universally accepted definition. Congress has adopted various temporary definitions of old growth, using minimum size, age, and density standards, to facilitate management of mature forests and restrict the amount of acreage designated old growth. Generally, trees over 200 years old are considered old growth. Most old-growth stands in the Pacific Northwest's Douglas-fir region developed over 250–750 years. Trees between 400 and 500 years old are common in the Cascade Range, and trees of 1,000 years of age are not unusual. Eastern old-growth forests consist of red oaks, sugar maples, and other hardwoods over 400 years old.

Scientists view old-growth forests as complex ecosystems of uneven ages, unaltered by human management actions. They emphasize the ecological diversity, structure, and function of the forest rather than the age, size, or density of various tree species. The U.S. Forest Service defines old growth as a forest displaying a considerable degree of decadence, with snags, dead trees, and decaying logs, and containing multiple canopy layers, including young saplings and larger trees that are at least 200 years old.

The dense, multistoried canopy of old growth provides thermal cover for forest wildlife, protecting inhabitants from temperature extremes. Broken treetops and cavities in the large old trees provide habitat for birds that do not build nests, such as the northern spotted owl. Snags and decaying matter on the forest floor create habitat for many smaller species, and the dense cover protects prey from predators.

Logging has fragmented and drastically reduced the extent of old-growth forests in many regions, thus posing a risk to many species that depend on this habitat type and limiting the area available for forage, nesting, and dispersal. It has been estimated that less than 5 percent of all old growth in the United States remains.

See also **Biodiversity Conservation; National Forest Management Act of 1976; Northern Spotted Owl; Tongass National Forest.**

104TH CONGRESS The 1995-1996 Congress, a product largely of the November 1994 election, gave the Republican party control of both the Senate and the House of Representatives for the first time in more than 40 years. The Congress was characterized initially by strong antiregulatory sentiments and a partisan campaign to pass into law the Republicans' so-called Contract with America. Although the word *environment* appeared nowhere in the contract, the document nevertheless contained several proposals that would have undermined existing conservation and environmental laws, such as its unfunded mandates and private property takings proposals and a regulatory moratorium. The contract was quickly dubbed by environmentalists and others the Contract *on* America. The League of Conservation Voters reported that the average member of the 104th Congress voted against the environment more than half the time; 44 of its members earned zero ratings from the league. The Wilderness Society called the 104th Congress "the worst Congress ever" for the environment and published a report by that title.

With a majority on their side and led by overly zealous freshmen, House Republicans passed all the planks in their agenda within the first 100 days of the first session, including a Clean Water Act bill that would have drastically curtailed wetland protections. Bills were introduced in both chambers that would have turned Bureau of Land Management lands over to the states, reduced regulation of and given more power to public land livestock grazers, transferred title of national forest ski areas to ski corporations, opened the Arctic National Wildlife Refuge to oil and gas drilling, and mandated salvage logging on national forests and exempted salvage sales from environmental laws.

The 104th's chief antienvironmental victory was passage of the salvage logging rider, which was attached to a rescissions bill that canceled some 1995 appropriations. (Nonappropriation riders are often tacked onto appropriations bills. Attachment to budget bills, which must be passed to keep the government running, sometimes provides the only means for assuring that such measures would ever be considered by Congress.) The nominal purpose of these salvage sales was to harvest diseased, dead, or dying timber, but the language of the rider actually allowed the harvest of healthy, green trees. The rider also exempted salvage sales from compliance with federal laws that would ordinarily govern timber harvest. The Clinton administration subsequently abandoned its support of these sales and in February 1996 called for repeal of the rider, or at least of its application to Pacific Northwest old-growth forests. The rider expired by its own terms on 31 December 1996.

Several factors combined to slow the momentum of the 104th Congress: The Senate was far more cautious in its approach to deregulating, many House Republicans themselves began to get cold feet as national polls continued to warn that a substantial majority (often two-thirds or more) of Americans favored maintaining if not strengthening our environmental laws, and budget battles between President Clinton and the Congress caused three government shutdowns in late 1995 and early 1996. Media portrayals of tourists shut out of national parks and monuments as a result of the shutdowns were partly responsible for a reversal in the tide of public opinion—against the extreme positions of the Republican Congress and in favor of President Clinton's tough stance. Moreover, by that time, the 1996 election campaign season had begun, and most political commentators were predicting that, preoccupied by the budget and the elections, the Congress was likely to do little more damage (or good, for that matter) in its second session.

The damage could have been substantial—all major environmental laws except the Clean Air Act were up for reauthorization in 1995. As it turned out, most antienvironmental victories were short-lived and limited to one house of Congress or vetoed by the president. The House initially slashed the budgets of most environmental and resource agencies. Especially hard hit was the Environmental Protection Agency (EPA), but the 1996 appropriations bill that ultimately passed actually increased EPA's funding. The Senate declined to follow the House's lead in curtailing wetlands protections under the CWA or passing a takings bill that would have compensated private property owners for regulation that reduced the value of their property by a specified amount. Both the Senate and the House Resources Committees passed bills that would have relaxed environmental regulation of public land grazing while increasing grazing fees gradually, but the president's veto threats prevented the measure from reaching the Senate floor. Most environmental laws due for reauthorization—including the CWA and Endangered Species Act of 1973 (ESA)—escaped rewriting, and none was significantly weakened. Of those overdue for reauthorization, the CWA and/or ESA are most likely to be taken up by the 105th Congress, although commentators disagree on this point. However, the 104th Congress did enact two moratoria on further listings of species under the ESA.

Conversely, the 104th Congress scored some environmental victories. It reauthorized the Safe Drinking Water Act, Coastal Zone Management Act, and the Farm Bill, and it passed a narrowly tailored amendment to the Resource Conservation and Recovery Act. It also enacted an Omnibus Parks Bill, designating or protecting locally popular parks in several parts of the country (e.g., the Presidio in San Francisco and Sterling Forest in New York), and added several new rivers to the national wild and scenic rivers system.

Fiscal year 1997 environmental budget cuts were less deep, and a few agencies actually saw increases. Moreover, the House leadership discouraged members from their practice of the year before of attaching unrelated riders to appropriations bills. House Speaker Newt Gingrich (R-GA), a leading proponent of the contract in its early days, was later credited for encouraging moderation among his colleagues during the second session and for moving to the legislative back burner such controversial issues as ESA reauthorization.

See also **Clinton, William Jefferson; League of Conservation Voters; Salvage Logging.**

ORGANIC ACT A general term for legislation that contains an administrative agency's overall mandate and delegates it the authority to act. Examples discussed in this book are the National Park Service Organic Act of 1916, the Organic Act of 1897 (Forest Service), and the Federal Land Policy and Management Act of 1976 (Bureau of Land Management).

ORGANIC ACT OF 1897 Federal legislation that prescribed the purposes for which forest reserves (now national forests) could be designated, and specified the authority of the managing agency (then, the Department of the Interior; since 1905, the U.S. Forest Service within the Department of Agriculture). Portions of this 1897 legislation were amended or repealed by the National Forest Management Act of 1976, which is sometimes referred to as the Forest Service's new organic act. Important provisions still in effect are the sections specifying the purposes of national forests, conferring authority to sell timber, and authorizing the agency to "make such rules and regulations...as will insure the objects of" the national forests and to "regulate their occupancy and use and to preserve the forests thereon from destruction."

See also **National Forest Management Act of 1976;** *United States v. New Mexico* **(1978).**

PARTNERSHIPS A collaborative approach to promoting conservation objectives. Partnerships may involve multiple private parties or various combinations of private and governmental interests, such as landowners, nonprofit organizations, business or industrial interests, and regulators. Partnerships are undertaken to protect land from development for its own values or to buffer other lands, such as parks or wildlife sanctuaries, to solve pollution problems, or to manage renewable resources. The partners contribute according to their means and interests: A landowner may make her land open to other users, such as recreationists, or assist in the management of a resource, such as timber. Governments and foundations may provide funding or technical expertise. Nonprofit organizations may negotiate the arrangement and provide legal advice.

The Nature Conservancy (TNC) probably has more experience than any other organization or agency in using partnerships to achieve conservation goals. In 1991 it launched its "Last Great Places" campaign to protect about 75 entire ecosystems or bioreserves. Each of these preservation efforts depends on the cooperation of landowners, both public and private, and local governments and developers. TNC's program, like the efforts of other groups, such as the Trust for Public Lands and American Farmland Trust, reflects the growing interest in watershed or ecosystem management, sustainable development, and landscape-level efforts to protect biological diversity.

Partnerships are also employed by federal agencies to conduct habitat management and restoration projects. The Bureau of Land Management (BLM), for instance, is working with private landowners and environmental groups in the Rio Puerco drainage in New Mexico, a watershed highly degraded by erosion resulting from grazing and cultivation. Efforts to restore damaged riparian areas include reseeding, fencing, and adjusting grazing practices. The U.S. Fish and Wildlife Service (USFWS) preserves wildlife and wetlands habitat through partnerships with private landowners under the North American Wetland Conservation Fund and North American Waterfowl Management Plan. With the help of nonprofits, the

USFWS and National Park Service (NPS) together acquired 273 tracts of land between 1985 and 1991, at a savings to the government of more than $32 million. A partnership program sponsored by the U.S. Forest Service (USFS) and BLM —"Bring Back the Natives"—involves private and public landowners in joint efforts to restore damaged watersheds and reestablish native fish populations.

A Senate committee recently expressed support for Wetlands Reserve Program (WRP) partnership efforts, which the committee viewed as expanding the government's ability to promote conservation by leveraging funds and enhancing wildlife values. As a result of such partnerships, many WRP easements and agreements are now funded by nonfederal dollars, and in 1997 Congress exempted these acres from the statutory acreage limitations.

Similarly, state partnerships include programs to preserve open space, ensure a supply of affordable housing, and promote sustainable timber harvests. Common sources of state funding are excise or mineral severance taxes, revenue bonds, direct appropriations, and lottery proceeds. States often offer matching grants to nonprofits. Between 1983 and 1993, 13 states adopted programs for funding conservation efforts that encourage partnerships with private groups. Public funding supplemented by nonprofit organization labor and expertise can significantly reduce the costs of land protection. States can also be instrumental in providing technical expertise or tax incentives. Local governments may make the zoning changes necessary to enable a project to proceed or to ensure that the land to be protected will not be developed. The Massachusetts Wetlands Restoration and Banking Program, part of the Partnership to Restore Massachusetts Wetlands, is an alliance of businesses, individuals, agencies, and nonprofit organizations.

See also **Land Trust; Mitigation Banking; The Nature Conservancy; Watershed.**

PATENT A document issued by the Department of the Interior that conveys title to federal lands described in it. Ordinarily, the title conveyed by a patent is in all respects equivalent to the title (called fee simple title) that a person obtains when he purchases real property from another person. An exception applies to mining patents issued in wilderness areas, where patents convey title only to the mineral (subsurface) estate.

Patents were issued for lands acquired under the homesteading laws of the 1800s and early 1900s. Patents are still issued for mining claims, *if* the claim holder applies for a patent and meets the requirements for patenting—basically, proof of a valuable mineral discovery, compliance with all location and recording requirements, and satisfaction of the patent application and documentation requirements. (Mining usually proceeds on federal lands, however, without the benefit of patent.) Lode claim patents are available for $5.00 per acre; placer claim patents cost $2.50 per acre. Environmental groups, fiscal conservatives, and Interior Secretary Bruce Babbitt, among others, decry the ability of mining companies to obtain title to federal land at such ridiculously low prices. This feature of the General Mining Law of 1872 is a major impetus for federal mining law reform efforts.

In 1993, Interior Secretary Bruce Babbitt, an outspoken critic of patents and the 1872 Mining Law generally, revoked the existing delegations of authority in the patenting process and directed that henceforth patents would be issued only with secretarial approval. This change increased the processing time from about three years in 1992 to five years. Babbitt's order was challenged by a Nevada mining company but upheld by a federal court.

See also **General Mining Law of 1872; Location; Mining Law Reform; Patent Moratorium.**

PATENT MORATORIUM   A temporary, congressionally imposed prohibition on issuing patents for mining claims on federal public lands. Unable to agree on needed reforms to the General Mining Law of 1872 despite perennial attempts to amend the statute, Congress has instead included in appropriations bills provisions forbidding the issuance of patents for a specified period, usually one year. In late 1997, Congress imposed the fourth consecutive one-year moratorium on patenting claims.

See also **General Mining Law of 1872; Location; Mining Law Reform; Patent.**

PITTMAN-ROBINSON ACT (P-R ACT)   President Franklin Roosevel signed the Federal Aid in Wildlife Restoration Act (the Pittman-Robinson Act, commonly referred to as the P-R Act) in 1937. Like the 1934 Duck Stamp program, the act was one of three user-funded statutes designed to raise revenue to support wildlife conservation. The P-R Act imposes an excise tax on manufacturers and importers of arms and ammunition. The 1950 Federal Aid in Fish Restoration Act (the Dingell-Johnson Act, known as the D-J Act) imposes a similar tax on fishing equipment. Both laws thus indirectly tax hunters and anglers.

Administered by the U.S. Fish and Wildlife Service, the P-R Act provides funds for state wildlife conservation programs. Much of the revenue collected, which increased from $1 million in 1939 to $120 million in 1985, is apportioned among the states for approved wildlife restoration or management projects or, following a 1970 amendment of the act, for comprehensive wildlife resource management plans. Although not statutorily required, funding is restricted by regulation to programs for game birds and animals. Monies are distributed twice a year to eligible states, based on a complex formula that takes into account both the state's land area and the number of licensed hunters. An eligible state must enact wildlife conservation laws and prohibit the use of hunting license fees for purposes other than administration of its fish and game agency. Over $1.5 billion has been distributed to the states under the act, enabling states to acquire 4 million acres of wildlife habitat, manage an additional 40 million acres for wildlife purposes, and improve the science and technology of wildlife management.

The P-R Act, D-J Act, and Fish and Wildlife Conservation Act of 1980 (known as the Nongame Act) overlap significantly, and projects often can be financed using any of the three funds. Together, these federal programs fund the bulk of state fish and wildlife research and management activities.

In late 1996 a federal court held for the first time that environmentalists and sportsmen may sue a state to force it to use Pittman-Robinson funds only for authorized purposes. [*Sportsmen's Wildlife Defense Fund v. U.S. Department of the Interior* (1996)] The plaintiff challenged Colorado's use of state lands near Rifle, which had been purchased with P-R funds, for a prison rather than for wildlife purposes.

See also **Citizen Suit; Dingell-Johnson Act; Duck Stamp; Fish and Wildlife Conservation Act of 1980.**

POLICE POWER   The fundamental, sovereign authority every state possesses to legislate for the welfare of its citizens. Police power is broad and not well defined; it is often said to encompass any "conceivable public purpose." State and municipal governments can regulate safety, welfare, and the environment. The police power is the source of authority for all environmental and land-use regulations.

By contrast, the federal government is a government of "enumerated powers." It has only those powers expressly conferred by the Constitution; the states retain "all other powers," expressly confirmed by the Tenth Amendment. The federal government has expanded dramatically its regulatory program over the past 60 years or so, relying largely on authority conferred by the General Welfare, Commerce, and "Necessary and Proper" Clauses of the Constitution. Federal powers are still considered interstitial, however. Only states possess a full complement of police powers—to regulate traffic, business, zoning, building codes, domestic relations, health and safety, property taxes, etc.

See also **Taking; Zoning.**

PREEMPTION   A doctrine of federal-state relations, rooted in the Supremacy Clause of the U.S. Constitution, which provides that federal law prevails in the event of a conflict with a state law. Congress may express its intent in legislation to preempt state law, although it has done so in relatively few areas (regulation of nuclear facility siting, immigration, and Indian affairs are examples). More often, a court must determine whether Congress has "occupied" the particular regulatory field to such an extent that no room is left for states to regulate, *or* that a particular state law actually conflicts with or frustrates the purposes of a federal statute or valid federal regulation.

Courts rarely find that state regulation has been preempted. Indeed, in the environmental arena, most federal statutes expressly provide that states have primary responsibility for pollution control. States also are chiefly responsible for regulating land use and providing for conservation of natural resources on private and state lands. On public lands, the presumption is that state law applies, unless the land is a federal enclave.

See also *California Coastal Commission v. Granite Rock Co.* **(1987);** *Kleppe v. New Mexico* **(1976); Police Power.**

PRIOR APPROPRIATION DOCTRINE   The principal method of allocating water rights in western states. The prior appropriation doctrine evolved largely because of the relative scarcity of water in the West and the inappropriateness of the English common-law riparian doctrine, which recognizes adjoining landowners' rights in a water course. (The rule of "reasonable use," followed in eastern states, derives from the riparian doctrine.) Several western states adopted by case law the "California doctrine," which recognizes both appropriative and riparian rights, but nearly all western states except California have adopted the prior appropriation system by statute. Eight western states (Colorado, Arizona, Idaho, New Mexico, Montana, Nevada, Utah, and Wyoming) follow the "Colorado doctrine," which recognizes only appropriative rights.

As the West was settled, the need for water, such as for mining or watering livestock, where it didn't exist led to the practice of diverting water from streams and moving it by ditch or flume to the place where it was needed—even to another watershed. Rights to water were established based on the principle "first in time, first in right." The one who diverted the water first and put it to a recognized "beneficial use" established the best, most senior right to the water. This right is a vested property interest. Other, "junior" appropriators could claim rights to any water still remaining in the stream or left over after use by a senior, upstream appropriator. Seniority, or the priority of water rights, was established chronologically. The federal government is subject to state water law, but it may also establish title to water via the federal reserved water rights doctrine. Federal reserved rights are recognized by states; their priority date is the date of the applicable reservation.

At some point, available water can become totally appropriated. In dry years, water rights on some streams are only "paper rights": There is no water to satisfy them. This explains the old saying in the West that "whiskey is for drinking; water is for fighting over." Or, as Coggins, Wilkinson, and Leshy (1993) put it: "Taking water out of priority is roughly equivalent to an act of war."

Most states initially required that water be diverted from the stream and put to one of several designated beneficial uses (irrigation, domestic use, mining, etc.) in order to qualify for a water right. Diversion was not only necessary for most of these uses of water, it also put other would-be appropriators on notice that the water was being used. The specification of beneficial uses helped ensure that water would not be squandered on unproductive or nonessential uses. The result of this system, however, was the complete dewatering of some streams at certain times of the year or in very dry years, with devastating effects on fish and wildlife. Consequently, in recent years most western states have amended their water law, either by statute or judicially, to require that water appropriations serve the public interest, and to allow or require the maintenance of minimum stream flows at least in certain streams.

All appropriation-doctrine states provide for some system of administering water rights and regulating the use of water. Most states employ a permit system, supervised by an administrative agency; Colorado has a court-administered system. Every state has rules regulating such things as the waste of water, storage, transfer of rights between uses or from one watershed to another, and abandoning or forfeiting a water right after an extended period of nonuse.

As the population of the West increases, so do demands on scarce water supplies. Irrigation for agricultural uses consumes 80 to 90 percent or more of water used in the western states. Major conservation issues for the future will revolve around the appropriateness of such uses in desert and near-desert environments (which characterize most of the West), the cost of agricultural water (which is now subsidized by the government and much cheaper than municipal or industrial water), conversion of agricultural water rights to "higher" purposes (chiefly municipal) by water marketing or other means, and the "mining" (depletion) of groundwater. Even though groundwater and surface waters are often connected hydrologically, most states have a separate system for regulating groundwater; its use is regulated under five different doctrines. Many people are concerned that groundwater allocation systems do not provide adequately either for the sustainable use of groundwater or for protection of its quality.

See also **Instream Flow;** *National Audubon Society v. Superior Court of Alpine County* **(1983); Reserved Rights Doctrine.**

PRIVATIZATION   A term describing proposals to convert federal lands or natural resources to private ownership. Public lands or resources might be privatized by transferring them first to the states, assuming that the states would then make all or most of them available for lease or sale; making them directly available for purchase or lease, either to the highest bidder or by giving preference to current users such as livestock grazers or timber companies; or allowing "entry" by means similar to the homestead laws of the 1800s and early 1900s.

The history of the western public lands is marked by recurrent efforts and schemes to dispose of the lands—dating to the era of homesteading and railroad grants. In the 1930s, President Herbert Hoover proposed to cede much of the public domain to the states. In 1970 the Public Land Law Review Commission proposed that Congress make available for sale those lands that lacked significant public values and were chiefly valuable for commodity development.

Congress disregarded this advice, however, in the Federal Land Policy and Management Act of 1976 (FLPMA). FLPMA declared that it is federal policy to retain lands in federal ownership unless disposal of a particular parcel would serve the national interest. Passage of FLPMA fueled the Sagebrush Rebellion in the late 1970s and early 1980s. Sagebrush Rebels advocated direct takeover of federal lands by the states, based in part on the theory that the states should have obtained title to the lands at statehood. The term "privatization" may have first been used to describe the proposal of one very prominent Sagebrush Rebel—President Ronald Reagan—to sell public lands in order to reduce the federal deficit. One of the most recent proposals was embodied in a bill introduced in 1995 by Wyoming Congressman Craig Thomas (R) that would have allowed states to take title to lands now managed by the Bureau of Land Management.

None of these schemes has attracted anything more than mild interest; many have encountered vehement opposition, especially from conservationists and recreationists concerned that important public values would be lost if the lands left federal control. Few states, and fewer public land commodity interests, have expressed serious interest in acquiring federal lands. States are concerned about the management costs and potential liability; commodity users fear the tax consequences and lost subsidies. One of the most recent proposals to shift management of federal lands to the states, offered by Senator Larry Craig (R-ID), would have allowed states to seek title to the lands after ten years. The draft bill attracted little support, and only among the livestock industry and a few states, such as Wyoming. Environmentalists and the mining industry opposed it.

See also **Checkerboard; County Supremacy Movement; Sagebrush Rebellion; Subsidy; Wise Use Movement.**

PROPERTY CLAUSE　Article IV, section 3, clause 2 of the U.S. Constitution. The clause provides: "The Congress shall have Power to dispose of and make all needful Rules and Regulations respecting the Territories or other property belonging to the United States." This power has been described by the U.S. Supreme Court as "plenary," "without limitations," and "complete." [*See, e.g., Kleppe v. New Mexico* (1976).] Although Congress also has significant authority under the Commerce Clause and the treaty power of the Constitution to regulate use of public lands and natural resources, the Property Clause is the chief source of federal power over the public lands. It provides the authority for an incredibly wide range of federal legislation—the Wild, Free-Roaming Horses and Burros Act, Federal Land Policy and Management Act, National Forest Management Act of 1976, General Mining Law of 1872, and Wilderness Act of 1964, among others. However, the Property Clause does not prevent states from exercising their police power jurisdiction on federal lands.

See also **Commerce Clause; Equal Footing Doctrine;** *Kleppe v. New Mexico* **(1976); Police Power; Preemption.**

PUBLIC DOMAIN   A nontechnical term used variously to describe the United States's original land holdings, obtained from foreign governments by treaty or purchase, or unreserved federal lands existing as of 1934, when the Taylor Grazing Act was passed, which were generally considered available for disposal under federal land laws. The term has also been used to refer to lands managed by the federal Bureau of Land Management (BLM) since that agency assumed responsibility in 1946 for all unreserved public lands, including those subject to the Taylor Grazing Act. The term "public domain" is thus generally interpreted to exclude national forests managed by the U.S. Forest Service, national parks administered by the National Park Service, and lands managed by other federal agencies.

The original public domain encompassed 1.8 billion acres, from the Appalachian Mountains to the Pacific Ocean. Two-thirds of that area was transferred to states, homesteaders and other private citizens, and railroads. Millions of acres were reserved as parks, forests, and for other public purposes. The remaining public domain managed by BLM consists of 270 million acres, plus an additional 300 million acres of subsurface mineral estate.

See also **Bureau of Land Management; Public Lands; Reservation.**

PUBLIC INTEREST REVIEW   A portion of the regulatory process by which the U.S. Army Corps of Engineers (Corps) reviews applications for Clean Water Act (CWA) section 404 permits. The Corps may deny a permit if it finds that granting it would not be in the public interest. The agency evaluates the cumulative impacts of the proposed activity on the public interest. This determination involves balancing the reasonably expected benefits and reasonably foreseeable detriments attributable to the proposal. The Corps considers all relevant factors, including "conservation, economics, aesthetics, general environmental concerns, wetlands, historic properties, fish and wildlife values, flood hazards, floodplain values, land use, navigation, shore erosion..., [and] recreation."

The public interest review regulation references and incorporates the so-called "404(b) guidelines," regulations issued by the Environmental Protection Agency pursuant to CWA section 404(b). A permit application must be denied if the proposed activity would not comply with these guidelines.

See also **Clean Water Act Section 404; Cumulative Impact.**

PUBLIC LANDS This term's meaning depends on the context. Unless a more specific scope is intended, "public lands" usually refers to federally owned lands that are open to public use. This broad category of lands includes lands managed by the U.S. Forest Service, Bureau of Land Management (BLM), National Park Service, U.S. Fish and Wildlife Service, U.S. Army Corps of Engineers, and Bureau of Reclamation, and even some areas managed by the Department of Defense. However, the Federal Land Policy and Management Act of 1976 (FLPMA) defines "public lands" as "any land and interest in land owned by the United States...and administered by the Secretary of the Interior through the Bureau of Land Management"; lands on the Outer Continental Shelf or held for the benefit of Indians or Alaska Natives are excluded. (The reference to "interest in land" encompasses millions of acres of mineral estate owned by the federal government and managed by the BLM.) FLPMA's definition also applies under the Alaska National Interest Lands Conservation Act. Although both statutes contain provisions applicable to lands managed by the U.S. Forest Service (national forests and national grasslands), those lands are treated separately from public lands.

Lands owned by states or local governments may be available for some public uses, but are not usually included with the term "public lands."

PUBLIC RANGELANDS IMPROVEMENT ACT (PRIA)
In this 1978 statute, Congress reported that "vast segments of the public rangelands" remained in unsatisfactory condition; that is, they were "producing less than their potential for livestock, wildlife habitat, recreation, forage, and water and soil conservation benefits." The statute reaffirmed "a national policy and commitment" to manage these lands "so that they become as productive as feasible for all rangeland values in accordance with management objectives and the land use planning process established by [the Federal Land Policy and Management Act]." The un-

satisfactory range conditions cited in PRIA include soil erosion, desertification, and land underproductivity, which in turn impact the quality (including siltation and salinity) and quantity of scarce water supplies, threaten fish and wildlife habitat, affect the aesthetic and recreational values of the lands, and may even "lead to unpredictable and undesirable long-term local and regional climatic and economic changes." The statute defines "range condition" broadly, in terms of its soil quality, forage values, wildlife habitat, watershed and plant communities, and overall productivity. "Native vegetation" is defined as endemic species or communities that "would normally be identified with a healthy and productive range condition occurring as a result of the natural vegetative process of the area."

PRIA relies heavily on range improvements, particularly structural improvements, such as water developments, fencing, and seeding, to accomplish its objective. It authorized for this purpose federal appropriations, in addition to the portion of grazing fee receipts already used for range rehabilitation and improvements. Although the statute recognizes as attributes of "range condition" several values other than livestock forage, range improvement funding since 1980 has drastically favored livestock: as much as 96.5 percent of the money spent in the field has been for projects to benefit livestock.

Even though implementation of PRIA has been biased in favor of livestock, section 4(b) recognizes that grazing might need to be "discontinued (either temporarily or permanently) on certain lands." The act also provides that "*the goal*" of range management is to improve the condition of public rangelands so they become as "productive as feasible" for all rangeland values (emphasis added). According to Professor George Coggins, this section of PRIA is "the most important provision in all the range management statutes." He calls it "the first nonambiguous policy statement in rangeland legislation."

Although PRIA neither imposes new obligations on the land management agencies nor grants them additional authority, it does reflect a broader congressional view of the value of public rangelands.

See also **Desertification; Federal Land Policy and Management Act; Range Reform; Taylor Grazing Act.**

PUBLIC TRUST DOCTRINE   In general, a trust relationship involves some thing or property (the body, or "corpus," of the trust) that is held in trust by a trustee, who has a fiduciary duty to manage and preserve the trust for the benefit of the beneficiary, who is considered the "equitable" owner of the trust. The public trust doctrine is a common-law doctrine that traces to ancient English and Roman law. In its original, most narrow form in this country, the doctrine applied to the beds and banks of all navigable waters, that is, those waters deemed navigable in fact at the time of statehood. [*See Illinois Central Railroad Co. v. Illinois* (1892).] These are the lands to which all states received title at statehood under the equal footing doctrine. The *Illinois Central* Court ruled that the state (as trustee) holds these lands (the trust corpus) for the benefit of all its citizens (the beneficiaries of the trust). The state may not "relinquish" or "abdicate" the trust by transferring title to the lands to any other party if this would interfere with the public interests in the lands, for example, wharfage, commerce, navigation, or fishing. The trust has also been held to protect environmental and recreational interests in navigable waters and the lands below and bordering them.

The *Illinois Central* Court distinguished the nature of the state's title to these submerged lands from its title, or the title of the federal government, to other lands that are intended or available for sale. (In 1892 essentially all federal lands except forest preserves and Yellowstone National Park were available for disposal.) Nevertheless, the public trust doctrine has been expanded significantly in the past 30 years by some courts and legal commentators to encompass other lands and resources, such as national parks, wilderness areas, water, and endangered species. The doctrine is seen by some legal scholars and environmental advocates as a potential limit on the discretion of land management agencies; they believe it should impose on these agencies a higher standard of care in managing public lands and resources. Not all legal experts believe that a public trust applies to the federal public lands, however. Whether state school lands are held subject to a public trust is also an issue of increasing importance and controversy.

See **Equal Footing Doctrine;** *Illinois Central Railroad Co. v. Illinois* **(1892);** *National Audubon Society v. Superior Court of Alpine County* **(1983); Navigable Waters; Public Lands; Sax, Joseph L.; State School Lands.**

PUD No. 1 of Jefferson County v. Washington Department of Ecology **(1994)**   An important U.S. Supreme Court decision, interpreting section 401 of the federal Clean Water Act (CWA), in which the Court upheld a state's right to impose on a federal hydroelectric facility an instream flow condition designed to protect the fishery in the river. The project proposed to divert water from the

Dosewallips River, run it through an electric generating facility, and return the water to the river about a mile downstream. Under CWA section 401, all states have authority to review any federally permitted facility or activity that may result in a discharge to state waters to determine compliance with state and federal water quality requirements. The state may "certify" the project, certify it with conditions, or deny certification if it decides that the facility would violate water quality requirements. After reviewing the Dosewallips project, the state of Washington determined that, unless a minimum stream flow were maintained through the bypass reach (the stretch of river between the diversion and return points), the project would be incompatible with the river's designated use as a salmon fishery. Accordingly, its certification included a condition that the permittee maintain a specified minimum flow.

The Supreme Court approved the flow condition. It held that the facility met the two requirements: It required a federal permit, and it involved at least two kinds of discharges to water. Accordingly, the state was authorized under section 401 to review the facility for compliance with Washington water quality standards. The Court further ruled that the designated uses of a river or stream are part of a state's water quality standards and, as such, can be implemented by means of a condition in a 401 certification. Finally, declaring any distinction between quality and quantity of water "artificial," the Court upheld the minimum flow requirement as an appropriate condition to protect the river's designated use as a salmon fishery.

PUD No. 1's significance for conservation law is twofold. First, it is a strong statement of the states' power under the Clean Water Act to require all federally permitted facilities or activities to meet state water quality standards. The limits of this power have not been tested, but *PUD No. 1* supports an argument that the authority is quite broad and should extend to *any* federally permitted activity that may affect water quality—dams, irrigation projects, grazing and logging on public lands, right-of-way grants for pipelines or roads that cross streams, and any water-related developments, such as marinas or bridges. States should be able to impose on such projects any conditions designed to ensure that they do not negatively affect a stream's quality or its ability to support designated uses, such as fisheries, recreation, or public water supply. Second, the Court's dismissal of the quality/quantity distinction may have ramifications, especially in the West, for state law concerning the allocation of water. Litigation aimed at deciding these issues can be anticipated.

See also **Anadromous Fish; Instream Flow.**

RANGE REFORM A shorthand expression for the efforts of President Bill Clinton and Interior Secretary Bruce Babbitt to revise management of public land grazing under the Federal Land Policy and Management Act. Issues include grazing fees, ownership of range improvements, water rights, rangeland health standards, protection and restoration of riparian areas (streamside areas and wetland habitats that are grazed preferentially, and often damaged, by livestock), and water quality.

Background and Need for Reform

Approximately 270 million acres of land managed by the Bureau of Land Management (BLM) or U.S. Forest Service are grazed by domestic livestock, but these lands provide less than 10 percent of all livestock forage and produce only 2 to 3 percent of the beef in the nation. Furthermore, federal grazing privileges are held by only about 23,000 permittees; some of these permittees are family ranches, but many are large companies or wealthy individuals for whom ranching is a hobby or a tax write-off. Despite their minuscule numbers, public land graziers have traditionally been championed in Congress by western Republicans, and, at least until recent years, members of Congress generally deferred to western congressmen on western public land issues, particularly grazing, which is restricted to the 11 western states.

Public land ranching has long been controversial, the issues too polarized to be taken up by Congress in individual reform bills and thus most often addressed via appropriations riders or administratively. In 1994, BLM director Jim Baca resigned under pressure brought chiefly by western livestock interests. A filibuster by westerners prevented Senate passage of a conference committee grazing reform bill in 1994. Then in 1995, the Senate approved—and President Clinton vowed to veto—a grazing bill sponsored by Pete Domenici (R-NM) that would have radically rewritten federal grazing law to favor public land ranchers. Forest Service chief Jack Ward Thomas called this bill the "worst public land management legislation to surface

221

in Congress in recent times." The 105th Congress considered grazing legislation, but some observers speculated that it would postpone acting pending the outcome of the *Public Lands Council* appeal (discussed below).

Federal grazing fees have been a bone of contention for nearly 100 years. In 1996 the grazing fee for federal lands was reduced to the minimum allowed by current law, $1.35 per animal unit month (AUM, an amount of forage defined as that needed to feed one cow and calf, one horse, or five sheep or goats for a month). Fees charged to graze comparable private or state land are consistently higher, often sixfold or even more. The federal fee fails to cover even the cost of administering the public land grazing program; according to the Congressional Research Service, the BLM grazing program alone may cost the U.S. Treasury as much as $200 million annually. Environmentalists and many politicians decry this federal subsidy, which benefits a small group of ranchers, disadvantages operators who lack federal grazing privileges, and, critics claim, encourages degradation of public lands. The stockmen and their advocates in Congress counter that the fees for grazing federal and nonfederal lands cannot be compared because the lessors of private (and sometimes state) grazing lands often provide fencing, livestock supervision, or other services or facilities in exchange for the fee, while permittees on federal public lands are responsible for all those expenses.

Interior's New Rules Are Challenged

Following completion of its "Rangeland Reform '94" environmental impact statement, the Interior Department issued new livestock grazing regulations in 1995. To help implement the new rules, 24 Resource Advisory Councils (RACs) in 14 western states were formed to replace district grazing advisory boards. The RACs' purpose is to advise federal land managers; members consist of grazing permittees, local officials, recreationists, environmentalists, tribal representatives, and the public at large. In Wyoming a dispute between Interior Secretary Babbitt and Governor Jim Geringer over RAC appointments led to Geringer's assertion of state control over the council. The panel consequently lost its federal authorization. Wyoming's RAC differs from all others in that it is chaired by the governor and the initial appointments were probationary, with only one-year terms. RAC appointments are made by the Interior secretary, who must consider nominations by the governor and the public.

The 1995 regulations were challenged in *Public Lands Council v. Babbitt* (1996). The court ruled that portions of the regulations violated the Taylor

Grazing Act, holding that the Interior Department may not (1) eliminate grazing preference, (2) assume title to range improvements financed by a permittee, (3) issue "conservation use" permits to conservation groups, or (4) issue grazing permits to persons not in the livestock business. On the other hand, the court upheld other portions of the rules, including provisions for new rangeland health standards, environmental documentation requirements, and sharing water developments.

The *Public Lands Council* decision, which has been appealed by the federal government, is questionable on several counts. The opinion's fundamental flaw is its repeated use of the term "right" to graze. This contradicts Congress's choice of the term "privilege" in the Taylor Act and the act's clear pronouncement that a grazing permit "shall not create any right, title, interest, or estate in or to the lands." Congress reaffirmed this provision of the law when it passed FLPMA in 1976. The case also cannot be squared with the interpretations of the Taylor Grazing Act by several higher courts, including the U.S. Supreme Court. The district court cited no case law to support its view that "preference" can be equated with an "adjudicated right" to graze public lands, nor did the court cite FLPMA in discussing "preference," even though FLPMA expressly recognizes the secretary's authority to cancel, suspend, or modify grazing permits, and to dispose of grazing lands or devote them to another public purpose. Some observers speculated that Congress might postpone further action on grazing legislation until resolution of the *Public Lands Council* appeal.

Another recent court decision ruled that issuance of federal grazing permits is subject to the federal Clean Water Act (CWA). Specifically, the court held that CWA section 401 authorizes states to review proposed grazing permits for compliance with all state water quality requirements and to veto permits if grazing activities would not meet those requirements. [*Oregon Natural Desert Association v. Thomas* (1996)] Livestock grazing has been identified as a chief, if not the principal, cause of nonpoint source water pollution in Western states.

See also **Federal Land Management and Policy Act; Taylor Grazing Act.**

RECYCLING The recovery of materials from waste for reuse. More than 40 states have established recycling goals for products, such as paper, plastics, and glass, and more than 100 million Americans are now served by curbside recycling programs. The key to the success of recycling programs, however, is providing an end-use for recyclables. States are increasing demand for recyclables through tax incentives and innovative procurement policies. All 50 states have "buy recycled" policies for products such as office paper, concrete, antifreeze, latex paint, and tires. Similarly, in 1993, President Clinton issued an executive order to federal agencies to increase use of recycled materials.

Private investment also can increase demand for recyclables. The aluminum industry set up a recovery structure for cans; the average aluminum can now contains 50 percent recycled aluminum. The paper, glass, and plastics industries are also developing recycling programs to stabilize the recycled-materials market, and to increase both the demand for and the quality of products containing recycled materials.

REHNQUIST, WILLIAM H. U.S. Supreme Court justice since 1972, nominated by President Richard Nixon; chief justice since 1986, nominated by President Ronald Reagan. Rehnquist received a B.A. degree from Stanford University, M.A. degrees from Stanford and Harvard Universities, and a law degree (LL.B.) from Stanford. He was engaged in the private practice of law in Phoenix from 1953-1969. Rehnquist is a conservative, a Republican, and fascinated by western history and geography. He has written several important Supreme Court decisions in cases involving land and resource issues as well as Indian tribes.

In *Leo Sheep Co. v. United States* (1979), Rehnquist's opinion for the Court ruled that, in areas of the West where the federal government had granted alternating sections of land (so-called "checkerboard" areas) to railroads in the mid-1800s, the government had not reserved an easement that would now allow recreational users of public lands access across the adjoining private sections. The Court was clearly concerned with not upsetting settled expectations regarding property rights. If the government wanted to build a road across these private lands for that purpose, the Court said, it must pay the property owners. In *United States v. New Mexico* (1978), Rehnquist's majority opinion held that national forests are reserved for only two primary purposes: water yield and timber. Thus, any federal reserved water rights on national forests are limited to the amount needed to support these purposes. *United States v. Fuller* (1973) was a condemnation case. Writing for the Court, Rehnquist stated that the United States did not owe compensation to a rancher for that portion of the value of his private land attributable to its use in conjunction with federal lands, for which the rancher held a *revocable* federal grazing permit.

Justices Rehnquist and Scalia are credited with a new approach to takings law taken by the Supreme Court in recent years, heralded by Justice Scalia's opinion in *Lucas v. South Carolina Coastal Council* (1992). In 1994, Rehnquist wrote the majority opinion in *Dolan v. City of Tigard*, a 5-4 decision in an important private land-use case. The case established a new test for evaluating the propriety of "exactions" imposed by local governments as a condition for issuing land-use permits: any condition imposed on a permit applicant must be "roughly proportional" to the expected impacts of its proposed development; if not, the exaction violates the Fifth Amendment.

Justice Rehnquist has also written opinions concerning water rights. *Kansas v. Colorado* (1995) resolved several disputes between the two states as to rights and responsibilities under the Arkansas River Compact. In *United States v. Idaho* (1993), Rehnquist wrote for a unanimous Court that the United States was not obligated by the McCarran Amendment to pay state filing fees in order to participate in an adjudication of rights to waters of the Snake River system in Idaho.

Two other recent Rehnquist opinions with potential significance for a broad array of substantive law areas are *United States v. Lopez* (1995) and *Seminole Tribe v. Florida* (1996). Both of these were split decisions (5-4). *Lopez* was a rare instance of a federal court overruling a federal statute as having insufficient connections with interstate commerce to come within Congress's broad Commerce Clause authority. *Seminole Tribe* held that the federal Indian Gaming Regulatory Act (IGRA) violated states' sovereign immunity under the Eleventh Amendment by authorizing tribes to sue states in federal court to enforce the states' IGRA duty to negotiate gaming compacts with tribes.

See also **Checkerboard; Exaction; Scalia, Antonin; Takings;** *United States v. Fuller* **(1973);** *United States v. New Mexico* **(1978).**

RELEASE An issue relating to the future management of areas proposed, but passed over by Congress, for designation as wilderness areas. Wilderness areas can be established only by Congress, but the respective federal land management agencies are responsible for inventorying and studying their lands and recommending which meet the statutory qualifications for wilderness areas. When wilderness legislation excludes certain qualified areas, the bill usually includes language "releasing" those areas from consideration or treatment as wilderness in future management plans and agency decision making. The nature of that release has fractionalized public lands interest groups and stalled passage of numerous wilderness bills. Commodity interests, particularly mining and timber companies, favor "hard release" language, which makes the area fully available for multiple uses and basically forbids future reconsideration of the area for wilderness status. Conservation groups, on the other hand, oppose *any* release language. They believe that areas with wilderness potential should continue to be treated as wilderness in the agencies' planning and management activities so long as they remain roadless.

In the mid-1980s, "soft release" language was developed as a compromise approach. It provides that areas not designated as wilderness in that bill will be released from future wilderness consideration until the agency next revises its management plan. Another option employed by Congress is to designate the lands for "further planning." This directs the land management agency *not* to release the lands to nonwilderness uses, essentially ensuring that their wilderness qualities will be maintained until the lands are once again reviewed for wilderness designation. All wilderness legislation thus has consequences for the remaining roadless areas not designated as wilderness.

No statewide wilderness bill has ever contained hard release language, but the current Utah wilderness bills backed by the Utah congressional delegation include such language, requiring the immediate release for development of 4 million roadless acres and precluding those acres from being designated wilderness in the future.

See also **Roadless Area; Southern Utah Wilderness Alliance; Wilderness; Wilderness Act of 1964.**

RESERVATION A term with several meanings in public land law. The first, and probably most familiar, is a reservation of land for an Indian tribe. "Reservation" refers to the fact that the land has been reserved, or set aside, for particular purposes. At the same time, other uses are limited or prohibited. To illustrate, the original national forests were created by reserving them from the public domain. (Some later, particularly eastern, forest lands are "acquired" lands, and hence are not technically reservations.) These first forest preserves were set aside to protect the forests and watersheds, and were no longer available for disposal under the homesteading laws. Wilderness areas and national parks are also reservations, also set aside for particular purposes and withdrawn from other, incompatible uses. Wilderness areas were not reserved from the public domain, however. Indeed, the first wilderness areas were reserved from the national forests, themselves reservations. Uses of wilderness areas are subject to additional restrictions, and their purposes are more limited than those of national forests.

Reservations of land also have implication for water rights. The courts have held that when Congress creates a reservation of land it may implicitly reserve enough water to fulfill the purposes of the reservation—whether Indian reservation, national park, wilderness area, or whatever. This can have significant implications for water rights under the prior-appropriation doctrine followed in most of the West.

Both Congress and the president (executive branch) can reserve lands, although certain reservations (e.g., national parks and wilderness areas) can be made only by Congress, and Congress can undo or override any executive reservation. Reservation status does not always mean that the land's uses are more limited than those of nonreserved lands. The best example is lands managed by the Bureau of Land Management (BLM). BLM lands were never reserved in the sense that national forests were. Instead, they are, in large part, the leftover public domain lands—those not transferred to states, railroads, or homesteaders or reserved for national forests. Nevertheless, the management of most BLM lands and national forest lands is for multiple uses and is very similar.

"Reservation" has a second important meaning in this area of the law. When Congress makes a grant of federal land to a private party or state, it may reserve some interest in the land, that is, retain it for the federal government. The most common reservations in federal land grants have been of minerals. Homestead patents issued under the Stockraising Homestead Act of 1916 conveyed the surface but reserved the minerals. Most land grants to railroads and states excluded mineral lands or reserved the minerals from the lands transferred. This practice led to the phenomenon known as "split-estates," where one party owns the "surface estate" and another, the subsurface "mineral estate." Where split-estates exist, the conflicting interests of the two owners (e.g., ranching or residential use and coal development) can pose vexing land management problems.

"Reservation" has a third, though less important connotation, which is of relevance only to some federal enclaves (e.g., lands purchased or otherwise acquired from a state by the federal government under its Enclave Clause authority in the Constitution). In this context, "reservation" refers to any authority over the area that the state reserves for itself when it transfers jurisdiction to the federal government.

See also **Reserved Rights Doctrine; Withdrawal.**

RESERVED RIGHTS DOCTRINE A federal legal doctrine holding that a reservation of federal land (for instance, a national forest or national park) also implicitly reserves that amount of unappropriated, appurtenant water necessary to meet the purposes of the reservation.

Origin and Development of the Doctrine

The doctrine originated around the turn of the century. The U.S. Supreme Court held in *Winters v. United States* (1908) that creation by Congress of an Indian reservation implicitly reserved sufficient water to fulfill the purposes of the reservation. The date of the water right is the date of the reservation of land. The Supreme Court subsequently extended the doctrine to any reservation of federal land, not just those for Indian tribes, where water is necessary to fulfill the purposes of the reservation. [*Arizona v. California* (1963)] Thus, the Supreme Court has held that reserved water rights attach to national monuments, national forests, national recreation areas, and wildlife refuges.

A 1979 opinion by the solicitor of the Department of the Interior examined the purposes of various federal reservations and described the kinds of water uses that the doctrine encompasses for each category of reservation. The solicitor concluded that the doctrine applies not only to those reservations ruled on by the Supreme Court but also to national parks, wild and scenic rivers, and wilderness areas. The purposes for which water has been reserved depend on the kind of reservation and the language of the statute or executive order establishing the reservation; such purposes include administrative and agency personnel uses at all areas, protection of fish and wildlife habitat in wildlife refuges and wilderness areas, and the maintenance of specific features, such as geysers or waterfalls, in certain national parks or monuments. The solicitor concluded that the doctrine does not apply to Bureau of Land Management lands generally, since the vast majority of these lands have not been reserved from the public domain for specific purposes. An exception, however, applies to a 1926 executive order that reserved public lands around springs and waterholes for public watering purposes.

Incorporation of Reserved Rights in the Prior Appropriation System

Congress and the federal courts have long recognized the right of Western states to regulate the allocation of water within their borders, even water arising or used on public lands. The federal reserved rights doctrine, however, superimposes federal water rights on western state systems designed around the prior appropriation concept. Prior appropriation is based on a "first in time, first in right" principle. The priority date of a federal reserved water right is the date of the reservation of land (e.g., creation of an Indian reservation, establishment of a forest reserve, or designation of a wilderness area), not the date when the water right was first claimed or the water actually put to use. Under the prior appropriation system, the federal reserved right is senior to any later appropriations of water recognized by the respective state, and junior to any earlier appropriations. This is so even though the federal water right may not have been asserted until many years after the land was reserved. In the *Winters* case, for instance, the reservation was created in 1888, ten years before construction of the irrigation project for which the water right was claimed. In other cases, an even greater period of time may elapse. The result is that exercise of a federal reserved right may "trump" a state water right with a junior priority date, even though the holder of the state water right had used his appropriated water for years before the federal government asserted its claim. Federal reserved water rights typically are immune from state law diversion and beneficial-use requirements, and federal reserved rights cannot be lost by nonuse.

Congress passed the McCarran Amendment in 1952 to allow a state to join the United States in any general adjudication of water rights to a river or stream. These judicial (or administrative) proceedings result in comprehensive determinations of the rights (including priority dates, amounts, and types of use) to water within a basin. The federal government is currently participating in a massive undertaking by the state of Idaho to determine rights to the Snake River system in southern Idaho.

Judicial Review of Reserved Rights

Because they are potentially disruptive of settled expectations respecting rights to scarce water supplies in the West, federal reserved water rights are controversial. Although the U.S. Supreme Court has taken a restrictive view of the scope of these rights [*see United States v. New Mexico* (1978)], traditional water users, especially irrigators, are concerned about the impacts on water availability if the federal government were to claim rights to water to fulfill purposes of reservations predating the priority dates of their state water rights. All national forests in the West were reserved from the public domain around the turn of the century; some national monument and wildlife refuge reservations date to the early 1900s. Even wilderness areas, many of which were designated in 1964, may be entitled to water rights that, if asserted, could impact existing water users. However, the location of most wilderness areas at higher elevations, upstream from most water users, indicates that downstream users would be affected little if at all by use of the water to fulfill wilderness purposes, such as maintaining stream flows to support fish and wildlife needs.

The question of reserved water rights for wilderness areas has not been finally resolved. Although at least one federal court held that the Wilderness Act of 1964 implicitly reserves water sufficient to fulfill the purposes of the lands designated under the act, its opinion was ultimately vacated on appeal. [*Sierra Club v. Yeutter* (1990)] The plaintiff, the Sierra Club, sued the U.S. Forest Service to compel it to assert reserved water rights for wilderness areas in Colorado national forests. Relying on *Lujan v. National Wildlife Federation* (1990), the appellate court held that the case was not ripe for adjudication because the plaintiff had not alleged or demonstrated any imminent harm to the wilderness areas.

Because federal agencies have been reluctant to assert reserved rights for wilderness areas and other federal reservations, water rights have been an issue with nearly every wilderness bill before Congress in recent years. In the acts establishing several new wilderness reservations (for example, a Washington state wilderness bill in 1988), Congress has expressly reserved water, subject to valid existing rights, to meet the needs of the wilderness area. Even these express reservations, however, leave open the questions of the precise purposes for which water is reserved and the amount of water needed. The National Wild and Scenic Rivers Act of 1968 also contains an express, though ambiguous, reservation of water, but fails to identify the specific purposes or the amounts of water reserved. Another issue yet to be resolved by the courts is whether the reserved water rights doctrine applies only to surface water or to groundwater as well.

See also *Lujan v. National Wildlife Federation* (1990); **Prior Appropriation; Reservation;** *United States v. New Mexico* (1978).

RESOURCE MANAGEMENT PLAN (RMP)

An RMP is a land-use plan prepared by the Bureau of Land Management (BLM) as required by the Federal Land Policy and Management Act (FLPMA). The RMP is the BLM counterpart to the U.S. Forest Service's forest plan, or land and resource management plan; in fact, BLM's planning regulations were patterned on those of the Forest Service. The bureau prepares an RMP for each resource area, the smallest management area, or division, within BLM. Plans must be interdisciplinary, be based on inventory data, reflect the principles of multiple use and sustained yield, and meet several other requirements set forth in FLPMA. The statute provides for public involvement in planning, and for coordination of BLM plans with the planning activities of other federal agencies and state and local governments in the vicinity.

The planning process begins with issues "scoping," which helps identify the land-use issues that should be addressed in the RMP—issues such as which lands should be designated areas of critical environmental concern, open to off-road vehicle use, or available for mineral leasing or timber harvesting; how environmental requirements for air and water quality will be met; and which lands will be studied for wilderness suitability or managed to protect their wilderness qualities. The agency considers public comments received during this stage, and incorporates them in its formulation of alternatives that will be addressed in a draft plan. An environmental impact statement is prepared simultaneously with the RMP, and both documents are released for public review and comment before the agency issues a final plan and decision.

See also **Environmental Impact Statement; Federal Land Policy and Management Act; Forest Plan.**

RIGHT-TO-FARM LAWS

Laws designed to allow farmers and ranchers to raise their crops and livestock without fear of lawsuits if land-use patterns change around them. Adopted by virtually every state and many localities, right-to-farm laws protect farmers from nuisance lawsuits when they follow generally accepted agricultural practices. Although varying in their details, these laws share the goal of encouraging farmers to continue devoting their land to agricultural purposes.

The 1981 *National Agricultural Lands Study* revealed that American farmland was being converted to nonagricultural uses at the alarming rate of more than 3 million acres per year. Roughly 70 percent was being converted to urban or transportation uses; more than 40 percent of the homes built during the 1970s were constructed on rural land. The impact on the nation's agricultural capacity was exacerbated by suburbs expanding into fertile river valleys or coastal plains from cities founded along major land and water transportation routes. Over a third of the converted agricultural land, a million acres, was deemed prime farmland with the best physical and chemical characteristics for producing food, feed, forage, fiber, and oil-seed crops.

To assure agriculturalists that they would not be pushed off the land by changes in their rural neighborhoods, right-to-farm laws modify the law of nuisance, often reversing a traditional preference for development over less-intensive agricultural uses. Historically, any activity that unreasonably interfered with another person's right to use and enjoy his property was deemed a nuisance. A typical nuisance lawsuit involves a balancing process: The social values of the conflicting land uses are weighed against one another. The court considers such factors as the degree of interference, the practicability of avoiding the conflict, and the appropriateness of the uses in that locality.

However, where the statute clearly spells out the legislature's intent to preserve and conserve agricultural land for the public good, the court no longer has to balance conflicting land uses on a case-by-case basis. In most statutes, the preference is restricted to preexisting agricultural use, often for a set period of time. If agricultural use was reasonable for the area when it was initiated, the farmer or rancher has a defense to any nuisance actions resulting from subsequent changes in land use around him, even if those changes effectively alter the predominant use of the area. The farmer thus acquires a "right to farm," a legal right to continue his traditional agricultural operations.

See also **Nuisance.**

RIPENESS　A doctrine of administrative law related to the constitutional requirement that courts may be called on to resolve only "cases or controversies," not to issue advisory opinions. Under the federal Administrative Procedure Act (APA), only final agency actions are subject to judicial review. The Supreme Court has stated that agency actions or regulations are not ordinarily considered "'ripe' for judicial review under the APA until the scope of a controversy has been reduced to more manageable proportions, and its factual components fleshed out, by some concrete action applying the regulation to the claimant's situation in a fashion that harms or threatens to harm him." The existence of an actual controversy helps assure that the issues are framed in a way that aids a court's understanding of their implications, and the requirement that the agency has taken some final action assures a court that it will not subsequently "change its mind," thus altering or mooting the dispute.

See also **Administrative Procedure Act; Exhaustion of Remedies;** *Lujan v. National Wildlife Federation* **(1990).**

ROADLESS AREA   Usually used to describe an area of public land that potentially qualifies for designation as a wilderness area because it is sufficiently large (generally at least 5,000 acres) and lacks developed or maintained roads. The Wilderness Act of 1964 uses the term *roadless* but does not define *road*. As a result, each of the land management agencies has adopted its own definition of *road;* these generally exclude travel ways that are not improved. The term *roadless* also is used in a general sense by environmental groups to refer to any roadless area of public land, which they consider a resource worth preserving. Public lands have become increasingly roaded since the surge in popularity of the automobile after World War II. The U.S. Forest Service, for instance, maintains a road system on national forests consisting of more than 380,000 miles, eight times the length of the federal interstate highway system. Roads are often an issue in timber harvesting proposals; proposed logging in roadless areas may be opposed chiefly, if not solely, because it would entail building new roads. Environmental groups and others oppose additional road building because of the increased potential for erosion, the fragmenting effect roads have on wildlife habitat, and the impacts of roads on opportunities for primitive or dispersed forms of recreation. The protection and management of nonwilderness roadless areas are nearly always issues addressed in federal land management agencies' land-use plans.

See also **Biodiversity Conservation; Federal Land Policy and Management Act; Release; Wilderness Act of 1964.**

ROBERTSON V. METHOW VALLEY CITIZENS COUNCIL (1989)

An important U.S. Supreme Court opinion interpreting the National Environmental Policy Act (NEPA). The Court was asked to decide two issues: (1) whether NEPA requires a federal agency to develop a plan to mitigate the environmental harm that will result from implementing a proposed action, and (2) whether the environmental impact statement (EIS) prepared for the proposed action must include a "worst case analysis" of potential environmental harm where relevant data are unavailable or too expensive to obtain. The plaintiff conservation groups challenged the EIS prepared by the U.S. Forest Service for a proposed four-season resort and ski area in Washington. The EIS predicted that the development would have significant adverse effects on air quality and wildlife, including the potential loss of as much as half of the local deer population. The plaintiffs claimed that the Forest Service's discussion of measures that *could be used* to mitigate the development's impacts was inadequate, and that the agency failed to include a "worst-case analysis" of the impacts on deer. The federal appeals court had ruled for the plaintiffs on both issues.

The Supreme Court agreed that a "detailed discussion of possible mitigation measures" is an "important ingredient" of an EIS. Such a discussion is implicitly required, the Court held, by NEPA's mandate that the EIS address "any adverse environmental effects which cannot be avoided." Furthermore, the Council on Environmental Quality's (CEQ) guidelines expressly require a discussion of mitigation (which the rules define as avoiding, minimizing, rectifying, reducing, or compensating for impacts). However, the Court ruled, NEPA does not require the agency to actually implement mitigation measures. That would be inconsistent with the position the Court has always held—that NEPA imposes only procedural requirements on federal agencies; it does not dictate substantive outcomes. Agencies must "take a hard look at" the consequences of their proposed actions, but NEPA does not direct them to take—or avoid—any particular on-the-ground action. As the *Methow Valley* Court put it, "NEPA merely prohibits uninformed—rather than unwise—agency action." Still, the requirement to discuss mitigation is not a mere paperwork exercise. According to the Court, NEPA "procedures are almost certain to affect the agency's substantive decision."

The Court also decided the second issue against the plaintiffs, ruling that the Forest Service was not required to conduct a worst-case analysis. The CEQ rules had been amended to delete this requirement, and neither NEPA itself nor case law interpreting it imposed such a burden on agencies. The Court seemed to agree with the CEQ that "overemphasizing highly speculative harms" serves no useful purpose. The duty imposed by the new CEQ rule is based on science rather than speculation. It provides that the agency simply evaluate the "consequences of a remote, but potentially severe impact," relying on "existing credible scientific evidence." The Court found the rule change "well-considered" and "entitled to substantial deference." Accordingly, it rejected the plaintiffs' claim, and approved the Forest Service's EIS.

Methow Valley was a significant statement by the Court on the importance of considering mitigation. Ironically, however, the CEQ recently criticized federal agencies for going through the motions of satisfying NEPA procedures but producing documents that "have little effect on decision-making." A better approach, according to the council, would be to monitor the actual impacts of projects during and after construction to ensure the effectiveness of mitigation measures and enable better predictions about the probable impacts of future proposals. Unless CEQ believes there is some reason to predict impacts more accurately just so they can be ignored when agencies make decisions (which seems unlikely), this advice suggests that NEPA *does* impose a substantive duty to mitigate impacts.

See also **Environmental Impact Statement; Mitigation; National Environmental Policy Act.**

ROCKY MOUNTAIN ELK FOUNDATION (RMEF)

A rapidly growing nonprofit, tax-exempt organization formed in 1984 to "ensure the future of elk, other wildlife and their habitat." RMEF membership increased by more than 30 percent in 1995. The organization claims more than 100,000 members, many of whom are hunters, in 50 states and 27 countries; it has more than 425 chapters in 49 states and four Canadian provinces. RMEF's quarterly magazine, *Bugle,* has a readership of 350,000, and the group also publishes a newsletter.

RMEF does not lobby or litigate, but it occasionally serves as mediator or facilitator in resource conflicts. Its principal strategies involve acquiring (by donation or purchase) land and conservation easements, facilitating land exchanges, and cooperating (by lease agreements and other means) in habitat management projects. When it subsequently sells lands to state or federal agencies, it attempts to ensure, via a "statement of intent for future management" and by retaining the first option to repurchase, that the property will be managed for wildlife habitat purposes.

RMEF focuses its habitat protection efforts predominantly in the West, but it has also assisted with habitat projects in several eastern and central states with elk populations. It has helped conserve more than 1.8 million acres of wildlife habitat, either by purchasing interests in the land or by conducting habitat enhancement projects. These efforts have involved more than 1,300 separate projects in 41 states and five provinces, and have earned the organization several awards. RMEF frequently works with timber companies and ranchers to alter logging and grazing practices so as to benefit wildlife, particularly elk. It also published a brochure informing landowners about conservation easements—the mechanics of selling or donating easements and their tax advantages.

RMEF depends largely on its members' volunteer labor; their annual big-game banquet fund-raisers in communities across the country are well known. Volunteerism helps the organization devote more than 80 percent of revenues to accomplishing its mission. RMEF habitat enhancement projects often involve prescribed burns, water developments, and research. These projects are usually cooperative efforts with either the Bureau of Land Management or the U.S. Forest Service; projects are generally selected and designed with the input of these agencies and state wildlife managers. RMEF also works with several other conservation organizations, such as The Nature Conservancy and the Foundation for North American Wild Sheep, on habitat and land conservation efforts.

See also **Conservation Easement.**

ROYALTY A payment, either monetary or "in kind," made to the owner of minerals for the right to extract or produce them. The federal government receives royalty payments for all leasable minerals. States charge royalties on minerals produced from state lands. The amount of the royalty depends on the mineral and on other factors, such as the extraction method or production rate. The minimum federal royalty for surface-mined coal is 12.5 percent (the rate for underground coal may be less). Onshore oil and gas royalties range from 12.5 to 25 percent; geothermal resources, 10 to 15 percent. Applicable law may require other payments, in addition to royalties, such as a one-time "bonus payment" included with the bid for the lease, and rental payments to occupy the land covered by the lease.

See also **Leasing; Location; Mining Law Reform.**

R.S. 2477   Revised Statute 2477, part of a mining law passed by Congress in 1866, provided: "The right of way for the construction of highways over the public lands, not reserved for public uses, is hereby granted." The statute was repealed by the Federal Land Policy and Management Act (FLPMA) in 1976, but "valid existing rights" were preserved. That is, any rights-of-way perfected under the old law as of the date FLPMA passed (21 October 1976) could remain in effect. The scope of the right (the basic type of road and the kinds of uses it supports) may not be expanded, however, without complying with FLPMA's or other applicable requirements for rights-of-way. [*See, e.g., Sierra Club v. Hodel* (1988).] This 130-year-old law has led to heated controversy in the West over whether two-track dirt trails, four-wheel-drive routes, or even dry creekbeds, identified by private persons or local governments as "roads," are entitled to R.S. 2477 rights-of-way. Most claims are to lands managed by the Bureau of Land Management (BLM) because national forests were "reserved" around the turn of the century. Under the statute, a road would have to have been in existence before the date the forest was reserved to qualify for a right-of-way. In Utah alone, more than 6,000 R.S. 2477 rights-of-way are claimed, including 56 miles of claims within an unroaded area of Canyonlands National Park.

The existence of R.S. 2477 rights-of-way has evolved into a states' or counties' rights issue, especially in Nevada, Utah, Montana, and Alaska. Wilderness supporters and many environmentalists oppose recognition of rights for many of these claimed routes because they are located in otherwise roadless areas and these groups fear that allowing rights-of-way would lead to development or uses that would impact natural values of the backcountry. Counties and commodity interests see R.S. 2477 as a means of ensuring continued access for development purposes and even for avoiding wilderness designation of certain BLM lands. Unauthorized construction or maintenance has taken place on some of these claimed "roads," including trails in wilderness study areas. The federal government sued three Utah counties in late 1996 after they used road graders and other heavy equipment on "roads" for which R.S. 2477 claims had been filed. (One county, San Juan, apparently had conducted maintenance on 500 to 600 miles of "roads.") The Southern Utah Wilderness Alliance, which is attempting to catalog and inventory all R.S. 2477 claims in southern Utah, contends that the sole purpose of such claims (and of the unlawful grading) is to prevent wilderness designation.

The Clinton administration (particularly Interior Secretary Babbitt) and the Republican-dominated Congress have clashed over this matter repeatedly since 1995. A key issue is who should bear the burden of demonstrating the existence of an R.S. 2477 right-of-way. Many Republicans believe that the federal government should be required to prove that a claim is not valid. One bill would have required the Interior Department to litigate and disprove all claims in court. Alaska Senator Ted Stevens attempted to attach to an emergency 1997 flood-control bill a rider that would have prevented the federal government from denying a right-of-way to any primitive "road" across public land, including footpaths, dogsled trails, and ice roads. Secretary Babbitt is adamant that claimants should have to prove their claims, and in 1994, Interior proposed rules that would have required claimants to show that construction had occurred on a claimed right-of-way. Western Republicans reacted by including a provision in a 1997 appropriations bill (which became law) requiring that any rules proposed by the Interior Department must be approved by Congress before they could be promulgated. This provision has been interpreted as a substantive limit on Interior's authority, not limited to fiscal year 1997.

In late 1997, Babbitt sent to Congress proposed legislation that would require R.S. 2477 claimants to provide both evidence of construction activities on claimed roads and evidence that the road is a "highway," that is, that it has received routine government maintenance and use by the public. The bill's chances for introduction seemed slim. Meanwhile, litigation over several contested R.S. 2477 claims is ongoing.

See also **County Supremacy Movement; Roadless Area; Southern Utah Wilderness Alliance.**

SAGEBRUSH REBELLION "Revolt" by certain western state governments and private interests in the late 1970s and early 1980s. The Sagebrush Rebellion was fueled by passage of the Federal Land Policy and Management Act (FLPMA), whose first provision announced the federal policy to retain public lands managed by the Bureau of Land Management (BLM) in federal ownership. Sagebrush Rebels advocated state takeover of federal lands. Some believed that the BLM-managed public lands actually belonged to the states, based in part on the theory that the states should have obtained title to the lands at statehood. Others contended that these lands could be better managed by states and should be transferred to them.

The movement was led by public land grazing interests, particularly in Nevada. In 1979 the Nevada state legislature passed a bill, signed by the governor, that purported to "return" 49 million acres of federal lands within Nevada to state ownership and control. Ronald Reagan, during his campaign for president in 1980, declared: "Count me in as a sagebrush rebel!" Other states and public land commodity interests joined the campaign. Utah, for instance, proposed that western states unite in litigation based on the equal footing doctrine and *Pollard's Lessee v. Hagan* (1845). Reagan's Interior secretary, James Watt, attempted to advance the rebellion's aims with many of his land-management policies. He became the target of a Sierra Club-sponsored petition to impeach him, and ultimately resigned.

Many westerners and some western states distanced themselves from the rebellion. Environmental and recreation interests generally favored continued federal control of the public lands, and many commodity interests and some states opposed state takeover for economic reasons: they were concerned about the costs to states of assuming management responsibility for these lands, as well as the loss of federal benefits. The rebellion eventually fizzled out, having accomplished none of its political or legal objectives. The current Wise Use and County Supremacy movements can be viewed as reincarnations of the Sagebrush Rebellion.

See also **County Supremacy Movement; Equal Footing Doctrine; Privatization; Wise Use Movement.**

SALINIZATION The process by which topsoils or surface waters become more saline (higher in salt concentration), principally as a result of irrigation. Many surface waters and soils in the West normally have high levels of salts. Irrigation dissolves some of them, thus increasing the concentration of salts in the irrigation water. Salts also are concentrated at the soil surface. The process can lead to soils that are unusable for agriculture or will no longer grow certain crops, and water that is unusable for nearly any purpose without prior, expensive treatment (desalinization).

The same processes can also lead to toxic concentrations of metals or trace elements in irrigation waters and eventually in surface soils and vegetation. The classic example is Kesterson National Wildlife Refuge in California, where selenium from upstream agricultural area soils has been deposited in highly toxic amounts. Kesterson is the termination point for irrigation water draining out of part of the Central Valley Reclamation Project, a major federal-state water project. Selenium leached from the soils in the project area is carried downstream to the refuge, where it causes mortalities, deformities (with rates as high as 42 percent), and reproductive failure in many species of birds. Selenium is a problem in several other areas of the West as well, especially where selenium-rich soils and irrigation occur at the same location.

Salinization problems can be traced in large part to federal laws and policies. Federal reclamation projects have made more water available for agricultural use at cheap, subsidized rates. Not surprisingly, irrigated agriculture is the single largest user of water in the West. The current federal Clean Water Act exempts irrigation return flows from permitting requirements; they are considered nonpoint source pollution and escape federal regulation. Irrigated agriculture is the largest remaining (and unregulated) source of water pollution in the United States. In the past few years, most bills to reauthorize and reform the Clean Water Act have included provisions attempting to deal with the problems posed by nonpoint source pollution.

One of the best solutions to salinization is less irrigation, or using less water to irrigate crops. Several projects have been undertaken by federal agencies in cooperation with states and landowners to reduce salt loadings in irrigation return flows and, consequently, in the rivers and streams to which they return. The largest and most well known are in the Colorado River Basin. In 1996, Congress incorporated the Colorado Basin Salinity Control Program (and three other Farm Bill cost-sharing erosion-control programs) into the new Environmental Quality Improvement Program. The Colorado River is also the focus of a major Environmental Protection Agency (EPA) watershed/ecosystem protection project. Reducing salt levels by reducing irrigation water usage poses a separate problem, however— the loss of irrigation-induced wetlands and riparian habitats. The EPA recognizes this problem and requires mitigation of wetland losses for all Bureau of Reclamation salinity control projects.

See also **Watershed.**

SALVAGE LOGGING   Logging practices aimed at harvesting timber that is dead, dying, or damaged by fire, wind, insects, or disease before it deteriorates and loses its value for lumber or other wood products, and reducing the fire hazard that such timber poses. The term can be traced to the National Forest Management Act of 1976 (NFMA), which authorizes a special fund "in situations involving the salvage of insect-infested, dead, damaged, or down timber, and to remove associated trees for stand improvement," and which exempts "salvage sales" from certain requirements applicable to the harvesting of other timber.

Salvage logging on public lands has become increasingly sought-after— and contentious—as other forms of timber harvesting have been curtailed in response to environmental concerns about endangered species, erosion, and old-growth protection. Beginning in 1996 it also became a "forest health" issue. The purported benefits of salvage sales include increasing supplies of wood for the wood products industry, clearing sites to prepare them for reforestation, and reducing fire hazard by removing large-diameter fuels. The costs encompass adverse effects on aesthetics, water quality and stream flows, wildlife and fish populations, and other forest uses, such as recreation. Salvage logging may actually increase short-term fire hazards by adding to ground-level fuels. Moreover, the ecological consequences of removing dead and dying trees are not well understood; these trees may be crucial to forest health through nutrient cycling and maintenance of important microorganisms.

Salvage logging took a tortured course through the 104th Congress. President Clinton vetoed the first salvage logging bill passed by that Congress, but in late July 1995, Clinton signed Public Law 104-19, a rescissions bill that canceled some 1995 appropriations and to which was attached a rider providing for salvage logging in national forests. The program it authorized became known as the emergency salvage program. The Clinton administration later claimed that the intent and effects of the rider had been mischaracterized, and in February 1996 called for its repeal. Environmentalists vehemently opposed the program, arguing that it allowed the harvesting of healthy timber that posed no fire danger. They decried its provisions suspending appeals and limiting lawsuits (by deeming such sales to satisfy the requirements of environmental laws), and they claimed that it allowed the harvest of timber in roadless areas. They further objected to its provisions for freeing up "section 318" timber sales from logging restrictions stemming from the spotted owl litigation. (Section 318 refers to a provision of the 1990 Department of the Interior appropriations bill.) A federal appeals court affirmed that the rider applied to timber sales on both national forest and Bureau of Land Management lands occurring even after the period covered by the 1990 appropriations bill.

According to a 1997 Government Accounting Office (GAO) report, the U.S. Forest Service offered for sale 4.6 billion board feet (bbf) of timber under the emergency salvage program, or 1.2 bbf more than it would have offered without the rider. Although this volume exceeded the agency's target for the program, it was considerably less than it could have been, had the Secretary of Agriculture not placed restrictions on classifying sales as salvage sales. These restrictions were implemented largely in response to the environmental groups' charges described above. GAO reviewed 14 sales, however, and concluded that they met the rider's definition of a salvage sale.

The salvage rider expired by its own terms on 31 December 1996. Nevertheless, the issue is likely to recur, probably not as stand-alone legislation but in the context of debates on the use of salvage logging to address forest health issues. A 1997 bill circulated for comment by Senator Larry Craig (R-ID), which proposed broad reforms to the NFMA, may pave the way for future salvage logging debates. President Clinton's FY 1998 budget plan proposed to cap funds received from salvage logging at about half the levels of 1996 and 1997, and further proposed to funnel any receipts over $100 million into a new Forest Ecosystem Restoration and Maintenance Fund. Such a fund would require congressional approval.

See also **Below-Cost Timber Sales; Let-Burn Policy; Old Growth; 104th Congress.**

SAX, JOSEPH L. Attorney and legal scholar. Professor Sax currently serves as counselor to the Interior solicitor, a position to which he was appointed in 1994. Sax's varied legal experiences include the private practice of law; professor of law at the University of Colorado-Boulder and University of Michigan-Ann Arbor; visiting professor at University of California School of Law-Berkeley, University of Paris, and Stanford Law School; government positions, both employment and advisory; and service on director boards, including the Environmental Law Institute's. He earned an A.B. degree from Harvard University and a law degree (J.D.) from the University of Chicago.

Professor Sax has written widely about natural resource and public land law issues, including water rights, national park preservation, and endangered species protection. His 1970 article on the public trust doctrine is considered one of the most influential, and largely responsible for the surge in the doctrine's popularity and use in the 1970s. His major water law publications include *Waters and Water Rights* (1967); *Water Law, Planning, and Policy* (1968); and *Legal Control of Water Resources* (1991).

As counselor to the Interior solicitor, Sax is intimately involved in the Clinton administration's efforts to reform implementation of the Endangered Species Act, particularly through the use of habitat conservation plans. Sax is the author of dozens of law review articles and other publications. Two of his better known books are *Defending the Environment* (1971) and *Mountains without Handrails: Reflections on the National Parks* (1980).

See also **Habitat Conservation Plan; Public Trust Doctrine.**

SCALIA, ANTONIN U.S. Supreme Court justice, nominated by President Ronald Reagan first to the U.S. Court of Appeals for the District of Columbia Circuit in 1982, and then to the Supreme Court in 1986. Scalia was educated at Georgetown University and the University of Fribourg (Switzerland); he earned a law degree (LL.B.) from Harvard University. His prior employment included the private practice of law in Ohio from 1961–1967, and service as Professor of Law at the University of Virginia from 1967–1974 and visiting law professor at several other universities.

Known as a conservative and an intellectual, Scalia has authored several Supreme Court decisions with far-reaching significance for natural resources conservation, land-use, and environmental law. *Lucas v. South Carolina Coastal Council* (1992) established a new "categorical" test to be used in analyzing takings claims in land-use regulation cases. *Lujan v. National Wildlife Federation* (1990) and *Lujan v. Defenders of Wildlife* (1992) resulted in more stringent tests for satisfying standing requirements in environmental cases. *Bennett v. Spear* (1997) confirmed that parties other than those with environmental interests can establish standing to bring citizen suits under the Endangered Species Act. Scalia has also dissented in important land-use and environmental cases, indicating that his thinking on these issues is out of the majority mainstream. [*See*, e.g., *California Coastal Commission v. Granite Rock Co.* (1987) and *Babbitt v. Sweet Home Chapter of Communities for a Great Oregon* (1995).]

Scalia disfavors the extension of standing to those without property interests, especially environmental groups, and his two *Lujan* decisions set up what are now considered the major hurdles that environmental plaintiffs must surmount to challenge government agency action. His views about standing are related to his philosophies concerning the value of land and land ownership. Scalia has been called the "most important exponent of the land ethic of opportunity." [Bosselman 1994] His land ethic is based on anthropocentrism, tradition, and opportunity: Wherever possible, land-use regulation should maximize an owner's opportunity to use and profit from his land. Indeed, in *Lucas*, Scalia stated: "For what is land but the profits thereof?" (quoting the nineteenth-century English lawyer Edward Coke). In Scalia's view, regulation of land use is acceptable if it serves a valid public purpose, affects all landowners similarly, and provides advantages to those persons in exchange for any limits on use of their land. His emphasis on the economic or commodity value of land to its owner necessarily deemphasizes land's public and ecological values. Scalia's philosophy is at odds with that of many conservation biologists, and his approach to land regulation will be difficult to reconcile with some conservation strategies, such as the regulation challenged and struck down in *Lucas*.

Scalia is known for his opposition to judicial reliance on legislative history, such as committee reports and official statements during debates on congressional bills. He argues that judges should restrict themselves to the plain text of statutes to ascertain and enforce Congress's intent. He criticizes judicial activism, remarking that it "is simply not compatible with democratic theory that laws mean whatever they ought to mean and that unelected judges decide what that is." But other legal scholars counter that Scalia's "textualist" approach actually leads to greater judicial activism by allowing judges to ignore legislative history as evidence of congressional intent and come to their own conclusions about what statutory language "means."

In *City of Chicago v. Environmental Defense Fund* (1994), Justice Scalia interpreted a significant provision of the Resource Conservation and Recovery Act. His legal writings outside the courtroom include articles about standing, the responsibilities of regulatory agencies under environmental laws, and review of federal administrative agency actions in public lands cases.

See also *Bennett v. Spear* **(1997);** *Lucas v. South Carolina Coastal Council* **(1992);** *Lujan v. Defenders of Wildlife* **(1992);** *Lujan v. National Wildlife Federation* **(1990); Standing; Taking.**

SECOND GROWTH A silvicultural term describing the regrowth of trees that occurs on a site after it has been logged. Second growth usually refers to a timber stand generated by even-aged management, such as clear-cutting. There is increasing concern that forest managers do not know how (and may be unable) to re-create, in a second-growth forest, conditions that existed in the original forest, for example, soil and nutrient conditions. This may have serious ecological consequences, as well as reduce the wood-product productivity of timber stands.

See also **Biodiversity Conservation; Clear-Cutting; Even-Aged Management.**

SECTION 7 CONSULTATION A mandatory process required by section 7 of the Endangered Species Act of 1973 (ESA), whose purpose is to ensure that federal agencies meet their duty to "insure that any action authorized, funded, or carried out" by them "is not likely to jeopardize" the continued existence of any listed threatened or endangered species or result in the "destruction or adverse modification" of its designated critical habitat. If a proposed action may have such a result, section 7 requires that the "action agency" first take steps to consult with the U.S. Fish and Wildlife Service (USFWS) to determine whether and how impacts can be avoided. The section spells out when such a consultation must occur and the procedures for conducting it.

The Process

The consultation process, which often takes place simultaneously with the environmental study required by the National Environmental Policy Act, consists of three steps: First, the action agency (for instance, the U.S.

Forest Service planning a timber sale, or the U.S. Army Corps of Engineers proposing to issue a dredge-and-fill permit) must inquire of the USFWS whether any listed species (threatened or endangered) "may be present" in the area of the proposed project. If the USFWS answers yes, the action agency must next prepare a "biological assessment," which evaluates whether the listed species "is likely to be affected" by the proposed action. Finally, if the assessment determines that it is, the agency then consults formally with the USFWS, which prepares a "biological opinion" concerning the probable effects of the proposed action. If the USFWS renders a so-called "jeopardy opinion"—that is, a decision that the proposed project would jeopardize the species or destroy or adversely modify its critical habitat—the action may not proceed unless the USFWS suggests an alternative that would avoid the prohibited, adverse consequences. Even if the USFWS determines that "no jeopardy" would occur, it still may require the action agency to take steps to mitigate the project's impacts.

The USFWS has extended the section 7 consultation process by regulation to species that have been *proposed* for listing as threatened or endangered. The process parallels the one described above, with a "conference" instead of consultation. It culminates in advisory recommendations by the USFWS, which may ripen into a biological opinion if the species is ultimately listed.

Implementing the Section 7 Process

Section 7 has been called the "pit bull" of environmental statutes, and noted environmental law professor William H. Rodgers rated it fourth in his list of U.S. laws that have "contributed most to the protection of the natural world" over the past 25 years. Despite its reputation, however, the statute is more flexible and its impacts less onerous than widely believed. First of all, section 7's no-jeopardy obligation applies only to federal agencies. It affects private individuals only to the extent that they need federal permission to conduct an activity (for instance, a dredge-and-fill permit to fill a wetland). Otherwise, section 7 does not constrain the use of private property. Individuals are subject, though, to the provisions of ESA sections 9 and 10.

Second, the USFWS has adopted "informal consultation" procedures, which are frequently invoked. In fact, during the period 1989 to 1995, the USFWS conducted almost 100,000 section 7 consultations, nearly 95,000 of which were informal—done quickly, often by telephone, and resulting in no project delay or modifications. The 2,719 formal consultations during the same period produced 2,367 no-jeopardy opinions; thus, those projects proceeded as planned. More than half of the 352 jeopardy opinions resulted from only two sets of proposals: timber sales in the Pacific Northwest and the Environmental Protection Agency's (EPA) pesticide registration program. Only 54 projects were terminated as a result of jeopardy opinions rendered in the consultation process, and many of these involved permits for building marinas in manatee habitat in Florida. Most jeopardy opinions resulted in relatively small operational changes designed to avoid the harm, such as boat speed limits in manatee waters or prohibitions on dredging during bald eagle nesting periods.

The "God Squad"

Still another feature of section 7 serves as a potential check on its tendency to constrain development. If the USFWS issues a jeopardy opinion, the action agency, project proponent, or governor of the state where the action would occur may appeal the decision to the Endangered Species Committee. This cabinet-level committee, established by section 7(e), is comprised of the secretaries of Agriculture, Army, and Interior; the chairman of the Council of Economic Advisors; the administrators of the EPA and National Oceanic and Atmospheric Administration; and a representative, appointed by the president, of each affected state. The committee is empowered to exempt the action agency from compliance with the no-jeopardy requirement of section 7 if it finds that: (1) no "reasonable and prudent alternatives" to the proposed action exist; (2) the "benefits of such action clearly outweigh the benefits of alternative courses of action consistent with conserving the species, and such action is in the public interest;" (3) the "action is of regional or national significance;" and (4) neither the action agency nor the project proponent has made any "irreversible or irretrievable commitment of resources" that has foreclosed any reasonable alternatives. The committee has become known as the "God Squad," reflecting its power to make "life or death" decisions about the continued existence of listed species. Its powers have seldom been invoked, however, and in only a very few cases has the committee granted even a partial exemption.

See also *Babbitt v. Sweet Home Chapter of Communities for a Great Oregon* (1995); **Biological Opinion; Critical Habitat; Endangered Species Act of 1973; Take;** *Tennessee Valley Authority v. Hill* (1978); **U.S. Fish and Wildlife Service.**

🏛 **SELENIUM**   A trace mineral found in some soils. Selenium is required by humans and other organisms, but only in extremely small amounts; at higher doses, it is highly toxic. Selenium can be concentrated in soils and surface waters by irrigation practices. This mineral has been responsible for mortalities, deformities, and reproductive failure in many species of birds in areas of the West where irrigated agriculture and selenium-rich soils occur together (e.g., the Kesterson National Wildlife Refuge in California and the Kendrick water project near Casper, Wyoming).

Other land uses, such as grazing, lead to the invasion of certain plant species that convert selenium in the soil to a form available to mammals. In some areas of the West, hunters have been advised not to consume the livers of antelope they kill, because selenium is relatively abundant in area soils and some vegetation, and mammalian livers concentrate minerals in the animal's bloodstream.

See also **Salinization.**

🏛 **SENATE AGRICULTURE, NUTRITION, AND FORESTRY COMMITTEE**   This Senate committee's 18 members consider measures relating generally to agriculture, forestry, and soil conservation. Larry E. Craig (R-ID), sponsor of a 1997 bill proposing major changes to the National Forest Management Act of 1976, chairs the subcommittee on forestry, conservation, and rural revitalization.

See also **House Agriculture Committee; House Appropriations Committee; Senate Appropriations Committee; Senate Energy and Natural Resources Committee; Senate Environment Committee.**

🏛 **SENATE APPROPRIATIONS COMMITTEE**   This committee is responsible for all proposed legislation that involves appropriation of revenue for government programs. Conservation bills that would not survive the legislative process on their own, such as public land grazing reforms or salvage logging measures, are often attached to appropriations bills to help ensure their consideration. This practice is easily abused; for instance, in 1997 a rider that would have resurrected the 1866 statute known as R.S. 2477 and repealed in 1976 was attached to an appropriations bill aimed at providing flood relief.

The 28-member committee has three subcommittees whose chief responsibility is for conservation matters: Agriculture, Interior, and Energy and

Water Development. The chair was assumed in 1997 by Ted Stevens (R-AK), which means that the three-member Alaska congressional delegation controls three of the most important committees for purposes of natural resource policy: Senate Appropriations, Senate Energy (Frank Murkowski), and House Resources (Don Young). Political observers suggested that the use of riders to obtain consideration of natural resource measures would increase because of the Alaska delegation's control of these committees, particularly Appropriations.

See also **House Agriculture Committee; House Appropriations Committee; Senate Agriculture, Nutrition, and Forestry Committee; Senate Energy and Natural Resources Committee; Senate Environment Committee.**

SENATE ENERGY AND NATURAL RESOURCES COMMITTEE

COMMITTEE Chaired by Alaska Senator Frank Murkowski, this 20-member committee is concerned with a wide range of public lands and resources issues: grazing, parks, mining, recreation, wilderness, energy (including hydroelectric power) development and conservation, irrigation and reclamation, and mineral development. A majority of its members are westerners. The three-member Alaska congressional delegation controls three of the most important committees for purposes of natural resource policy: Senate Energy, Senate Appropriations (Ted Stevens), and House Resources (Don Young).

See also **House Agriculture Committee; House Appropriations Committee; Senate Appropriations Committee; Senate Agriculture, Nutrition, and Forestry Committee; Senate Environment Committee.**

SENATE ENVIRONMENT COMMITTEE

Also known as the Committee on Environment and Public Works, this 18-member committee is chaired by John H. Chafee (R-RI). Its conservation-related duties pertain to oceans, fish and wildlife, water resources, recycling, flood control, wetlands, and Outer Continental Shelf lands. The committee also prepares reports on environmental protection and resource use and conservation.

See also **House Agriculture Committee; House Appropriations Committee; Senate Appropriations Committee; Senate Agriculture, Nutrition, and Forestry Committee; Senate Energy and Natural Resources Committee.**

SHEA, PATRICK The fifteenth director of the Bureau of Land Management (BLM), nominated by President Clinton and confirmed by the Senate in August 1997. Shea replaced Acting Director Sylvia Baca, who had replaced Acting Director Michael Dombeck. Shea was the first permanent, confirmed director of the agency since February 1994, when Jim Baca (no relation to Sylvia Baca) was forced to resign after conflicts with westerners, particularly grazing interests. Shea is a Utah lawyer, businessman, and adjunct professor of political science at Brigham Young University. In 1992 he was a candidate for governor of Utah. Considered a moderate on public lands issues, Shea's chief natural resources experience has come from representing clients, such as ranchers, and serving on the Utah board of trustees for The Nature Conservancy.

Shea's nomination was viewed by many as a peace offering from President Clinton to the state of Utah, and particularly the Utah congressional delegation. Clinton was excoriated for ignoring Utahans in designating the Grand Staircase-Escalante National Monument in 1996. The Clinton administration probably also hoped that Shea could help facilitate some compromise among the Utah delegation, others in Congress, and the environmental community over wilderness designations in southeastern Utah. The Utah delegation uniformly supported Shea's nomination, but Shea was opposed by the Public Lands Foundation, a group of retired BLM personnel, which claims he does not meet the experience qualifications specified by the Federal Land Policy and Management Act, that the BLM director "shall have a broad background and substantial experience in public land and natural resource management." They pointed out that Shea had never managed an agency or a large company dealing with natural resources. The three prior BLM directors had served as a western state lands commissioner (Jim Baca), a House Interior Committee staff member (Cy Jamison), and a rancher and state legislator (Bob Burford).

See also **Bureau of Land Management; Dombeck, Michael.**

SIERRA CLUB The Sierra Club describes itself as the "world's oldest and largest nonprofit grassroots environmental organization." It was founded by conservationist John Muir in California in 1892 and currently boasts 65 chapters, 396 local groups, and 550,000 members. Its stated purposes are to "explore, enjoy and protect the wild places of the Earth; to practice and promote the responsible use of the Earth's ecosystems and resources; ...and to use all lawful means to carry out these objectives." The means employed by the group include grassroots activism, lobbying, litigation, and education. It is nearly unique among national environmental groups in that it does not have federal 501(c)(3) (tax-free) status. The Sierra Club actively supports or opposes political candidates according to their environmental views. It publishes *Sierra* magazine, *The Planet* newsletter, and a wide variety of books (photography, children's, travel, trail guides, etc.) and calendars.

Among its most important contributions to the conservation movement, the Sierra Club cites the creation of the National Park Service in 1916 and subsequent protection of several national parks and monuments, such as the Grand Canyon, Admiralty Island, Mount Rainier, and the California Desert; passage of several environmental statutes, including the Endangered Species Act; and reintroduction of wolves to Yellowstone National Park and central Idaho. It works for the election of proenvironment political candidates and lobbies strenuously for environmental legislation and appropriations for land management agencies and against cutbacks in environmental protections. Sierra Club members and local groups played a major role in preventing passage of private property takings laws in 27 states in 1995.

The Sierra Club helped lead the campaign that resulted in obtaining 1.2 million signatures on an Environmental Bill of Rights petition delivered to Congress in 1995, and, along with other major national environmental organizations, it fought efforts of Republicans in the 104th Congress to open the Arctic National Wildlife Refuge to oil and gas drilling, transfer federal public lands to the states, and reduce wetland protections. Some of its current conservation programs include legislative efforts to ensure permanent protection of old-growth forests, better protection of wetlands, and reauthorization of the Endangered Species Act, and litigation to force federal agencies to conserve biological diversity.

The Sierra Club has adopted official policies on a wide array of resource and environmental issues, ranging from agriculture to Antarctica to feral animals to wilderness management. In 1996, it adopted the controversial policy of opposing all commercial logging on federal public lands. The group provides copies of these policy statements, as well as brochures on a variety of environmental issues and education topics, such as global warming, wetlands, wild and scenic rivers, and the federal land management agencies, free of charge to the public.

Approximately 65 percent of Sierra Club revenues are spent on programs (excluding member services).

SIERRA CLUB LEGAL DEFENSE FUND, INC. (SCLDF)

An independent, nonprofit, public-interest law firm established in 1971. Because it has often been confused with the Sierra Club, with which it is not affiliated, SCLDF changed its name in 1997 to EarthJustice Legal Defense Fund. The Sierra Club has been a plaintiff in most SCLDF cases, but the firm brings lawsuits on behalf of a wide variety of other clients, including national, state, and local conservation and environmental organizations and citizen groups. SCLDF/EarthJustice also participates in administrative proceedings and negotiates settlement agreements. Today SCLDF employs about 100 persons, including more than 30 attorneys, working out of offices in San Francisco (headquarters), Denver, Washington, D.C., Juneau, Seattle, New Orleans, Honolulu, Tallahassee, and Bozeman, Montana. Its litigation docket for 1994 reported approximately 150 cases in progress; conservation-related issues included wildlife and habitat, forest planning, coasts and wetlands, public water rights and access, and wilderness.

SCLDF has been highly influential in the development of conservation law in the past 25 years. Its president, Victor Sher, was chief litigator and strategist in the northern spotted owl cases, including the case that forced the U.S. Fish and Wildlife Service to list the owl as a threatened species. (When Interior Secretary Bruce Babbitt arrived at the Pacific Northwest forest policy summit, organized by the Clinton administration early in its first term, he reportedly sat down next to Sher and said, "So you're the one responsible for all this.") According to Sher, SCLDF "is the only organization on a national scale whose mission is still focused clearly on using the courts to make environmental change."

SCLDF's current litigation strategy is to focus on ecosystems in need of protection. Some of its earlier, well-known battles include the Redwood Park cases (important "external threats" and public trust doctrine cases, undertaken to protect California's Redwood National Park from impacts of logging outside the park); the Utah Burr Trail case (undertaken to protect wilderness study areas and to establish the limits of road rights-of-way obtained under the nineteenth-century statute R.S. 2477); endangered species litigation, involving the red-cockaded woodpecker and U.S. Forest Service logging practices in the Southeast, and the federal recovery plan for grizzly bears in the Rocky Mountains; and wilderness reserved water rights litigation, involving national forest wilderness areas in Colorado.

See also **Sierra Club.**

SOIL EROSION AND CONSERVATION   A natural process, which occurs at generally slow rates, varying with the location. Usually, though, the term refers to *unnatural* rates of soil loss caused by human activities and land uses. In this sense, erosion occurs whenever the rate of soil loss from a site exceeds the rate (extremely slow) at which new soil is being formed. Soil erosion can be induced by anything that removes vegetative cover, disturbs the soil surface, or decreases the infiltration of moisture and increases runoff: agriculture (cultivation and grazing), land-clearing and construction activities, off-road vehicle use, logging, mining, paving, etc. Both water and wind can erode soils. In the past 50 years, an area the size of India and China combined has suffered moderate to severe soil erosion due to human activities. The Mississippi River dumps millions of tons of topsoil annually into the Gulf of Mexico.

The term "soil erosion" also encompasses the deterioration of soil qualities, such as texture, moisture retention capacity, and nutrient content. Soil erosion not only reduces the productivity of land, it can reduce the capacities of reservoirs (as they fill up with silt), smother fish spawning areas and estuaries, promote and exacerbate flooding, and alter stream courses.

Soil conservation refers to human activities designed to prevent or reduce erosion, or to enhance soil quality or new soil formation. Soil conservation practices are diverse, including a variety of simple cultivation techniques, such as contour plowing, crop rotation, green tillage, and fallowing; "high-tech" practices, such as the use of lasers to level fields and reduce runoff; and avoidance of certain activities, for example, cultivating thin soils or steep slopes and removing streambank vegetation. Soil conservation measures incorporated into farm plans or in nonpoint source pollution control programs under the federal Clean Water Act are referred to as best management practices, or BMPs.

Government programs to address soil erosion date to the Dust Bowl era of the 1930s. The Soil Conservation Service, renamed the Natural Resources Conservation Service (NRCS) in 1994, was established to provide technical and financial assistance to farmers. A variety of state and federal programs—regulatory, assistance, and cooperation—exist today. Soil conservation is but one goal of many of these programs. They may also target wetland protection, wildlife habitat enhancement, water quality, and/or water conservation as well; some of the principal programs are described elsewhere in this book. According to the NRCS, American farmers reduced cropland erosion from more than 3 billion tons in 1982 to 2.13 billion tons in 1992.

See also **Conservation Reserve Program; Desertification; Farm Bills; Natural Resources Conservation Service.**

SOUTHEAST ALASKA CONSERVATION COUNCIL (SEACC)

Nonprofit, tax-exempt organization, a coalition of 15 groups representing 12 local communities in southeast Alaska. SEACC was founded in 1969 to protect the region's forests, fish, and wildlife and the traditional ways of life dependent on those resources. Its members include environmentalists, subsistence and sport hunters and fishers, and workers in local mills and factories. SEACC litigates, lobbies Congress and the Alaska legislature, and does grassroots organizing to mobilize individual citizens to become involved in resource conservation issues.

Despite its small membership and minimal staff, SEACC has played a lead role in monitoring and reforming management of the Tongass National Forest. SEACC executive director Bart Koehler (also a cofounder of the environmental group Earth First!) won the National Wildlife Federation's Conservationist of the Year Award in 1991 for leading conservationists' efforts to pass a Tongass Reform Bill through Congress. SEACC remains involved in Tongass planning and management activities by participating in the U.S. Forest Service's (USFS) revision of the Tongass Land Management Plan. It has proposed a "Transition Alternative" for managing the Tongass that would ensure sustainable logging of the forest and provide for a "planned restructuring of the Tongass dependent timber industry...to an integrated, higher value-added [industry]." Meanwhile, SEACC continues to monitor proposed timber sales, and it watchdogs congressional proposals to increase logging levels and relax export restrictions on Tongass timber. SEACC has a staff attorney, but is represented by the Sierra Club Legal Defense Fund in lawsuits appealing water-quality violations by pulp mills and other polluters, USFS timber sales, and other agency actions.

SEACC's newsletter, *Ravencall*, informs members about developments in Congress and the federal agencies that affect Southeast Alaska, member group activities, and regional resource economics and environmental issues, such as pollution of the waters around Ketchikan by Ketchikan Pulp Company, hardrock mining proposals that would impact Juneau and Admiralty Island, and timber marketing plans.

See also **Tongass National Forest.**

⭳ SOUTHERN UTAH WILDERNESS ALLIANCE (SUWA)

A nonprofit, tax-exempt conservation organization founded in 1983 and dedicated to preserving and protecting southern Utah's canyon country, with 21,000 members and offices in Salt Lake City, Moab, and St. George, Utah, and in Washington, D.C. SUWA publishes a quarterly newsletter and frequent bulletins on resource issues. Its chief focus is passage of a Utah wilderness bill and interim protection of roadless areas from various development threats, including roads, coal mining, oil and gas exploration and development, salvage logging, and unrestricted off-road vehicle (ORV) use. Utah's canyon country, SUWA proclaims, "contains some of the largest remaining blocks of unroaded land in the lower 48."

SUWA was a founding member of the Utah Wilderness Coalition (UWC), an umbrella organization of 120 local, regional, and national groups that favors preserving as wilderness 5.7 million of the 22 million acres managed by the Bureau of Land Management in Utah; this amounts to 10 percent of Utah's land area. UWC claims that 93 percent of nearly 25,000 respondents in a 1994 poll by *USA Weekend* favored the 5.7-million-acre citizens' wilderness proposal. By the end of 1997, the coalition had obtained 127 cosponsors on a House bill, referred to as America's Redrock Wilderness Act, which would designate these 5.7 million acres as wilderness. Also in 1997, a companion bill was introduced for the first time in the Senate.

SUWA has been largely responsible for making Utah wilderness a national issue and preventing passage in Congress of a 1.9-million-acre wilderness bill backed by the Utah delegation. The Utah delegation's bills also provided for unprecedented levels of nonwilderness activities and developments, including ORV use and communication sites, and contained "hard release" language that would have immediately opened 4 million roadless acres to development and forbidden the future designation of any of those areas as wilderness. A *Washington Post* editorial about the Utah delegation's bill declared: "This is legislation that would do more to weaken the wilderness system than to extend it. It shouldn't pass."

SUWA justifies the size of its proposal, which exceeds the area identified by the BLM itself as suitable for wilderness by 2.5 million acres, on the basis of on-the-ground surveys (which it is now updating) by its members and others. The group also points out that the BLM has been widely criticized for its wilderness inventory—by, among others, BLM employees themselves, the Interior Board of Land Appeals, and Salt Lake City's *Deseret News*. In fact, in 1996, Secretary of the Interior Bruce Babbitt ordered a reinventory of roadless lands in Utah, which is now nearly complete. This new inventory was appealed by the state of Utah, Utah counties, and other parties in October 1996; SUWA and other UWC members joined the suit as *amici curiae* (friends of the court) to support the reinventory effort.

In addition to its lobbying and grassroots organizing activities, SUWA monitors the federal agencies' land planning and management activities, and occasionally litigates to stop actions it considers damaging to the public lands and to their wilderness potential. For instance, it has sued several Utah counties that have been illegally blading new roads or "maintaining" trails in BLM-designated wilderness study areas, and it appealed state authorizations for coal mining in what is now the Grand Staircase-Escalante National Monument. Other resource issues of interest to SUWA include salvage logging, R.S. 2477 rights-of-way, public land grazing, mining and oil and gas development, and protection of archaeological sites.

See also **Grand Staircase-Escalante National Monument; R.S. 2477; Wilderness Act of 1964.**

STANDING A procedural hurdle that plaintiffs must overcome in order to maintain a lawsuit. Plaintiffs must demonstrate that they are the appropriate persons to bring the suit, that is, that they have been or will be harmed by the agency action or other conduct of which they complain. The requirement in federal courts stems from a provision of the U.S. Constitution that gives courts jurisdiction over "cases or controversies." If a plaintiff will not be adversely affected by the challenged conduct, presumably no real controversy exists between the parties, nor any "case" for the court to decide. Most states impose similar requirements.

Standing has been an important issue in environmental cases, although at least since 1972 it has been well established that a plaintiff need not allege an economic injury to demonstrate standing; an environmental or aesthetic injury will suffice. Organizations may sue on behalf of their members, but they must allege an actual or imminent injury to one or more of their individual members. Thus, a conservation organization concerned about the impacts of some agency action on the scenic beauty or recreational values of an area must allege that its members use the area and would suffer if such impacts occurred.

Two recent Supreme Court decisions, *Lujan v. National Wildlife Federation* (1990) and *Lujan v. Defenders of Wildlife* (1992), tightened federal standing requirements for environmental plaintiffs. The first case established that a plaintiff must set forth "specific facts" showing that it would be "adversely affected or aggrieved" by the government action. The second held that the mere intent of the organization's members to return to the areas potentially affected by the challenged agency rule, "without any concrete plans for doing so," was insufficient to establish the requisite "imminent injury."

The latest standing case to arise in an environmental context was *Bennett v. Spear* (1997). Two lower courts had ruled that the plaintiffs (farmers and ranchers) did not have standing because their economic interests were not within the "zone of interests" protected by the Endangered Species Act of 1973 (ESA). (The zone of interests test for standing has been applied by the Supreme Court and other courts in numerous cases where a plaintiff challenged that an agency had violated a particular statute.) In *Bennett*, the Supreme Court reversed, holding that the zone of interests test is inapplicable because the ESA's citizen suit provision authorizes "any person" to sue. Thus, the Court ruled, no basis exists for restricting the right to sue under the ESA to those who claim environmental harm. Even plaintiffs, such as those in *Bennett*, who claim economic harm and seek to *prevent* application of the ESA's environmental protections, are entitled to sue.

Patricia Wald, former chief judge on the U.S. Court of Appeals for the District of Columbia, has criticized the recent judicial trend in environmental standing as "madness." She argues that, when real disputes exist, the courts should not get bogged down in minutiae, citing as an example *Humane Society v. Babbitt* (1995). What we need, she says, are "more realistic notions of which affected persons or communities have the right to protest environmental violations." Until then, she warns, "Gotcha is still the name of the standing game."

See also **Administrative Procedure Act;** *Bennett v. Spear* **(1997);** **Citizen Suit;** *Lujan v. National Wildlife Federation* **(1990);** *Lujan v. Defenders of Wildlife* **(1992).**

STATE BALLOT INITIATIVES

An increasingly common tool for amending or supplementing state conservation law. Citizen initiatives are authorized by a state's constitution. Procedures and requirements vary, but in general, a petition is prepared setting forth the text of a proposed law or statutory amendment, and copies of the petition are circulated for signature. A minimum number of signatures (either a specified number or a certain percentage) of registered voters is required to get the proposed law, or "initiative," on the ballot, usually at the next general election. Some intermediate step, such as consideration by the legislature, may be required by state law. Initiatives can then be approved or rejected like any other question on the ballot.

In recent years, wildlife and conservation law have been popular topics for ballot initiatives. Successful initiatives in 1996 included a sales tax to benefit the Arkansas Game Protection Fund; an Alaska law prohibiting hunting wolverine, lynx, wolf, or fox on the same day the hunter has been airborne in a plane; a constitutional amendment in Colorado prohibiting the taking of wildlife by leghold traps, snares, or poisons; two measures in Florida designed to protect the Everglades; mandates from Iowa and West Virginia voters to dedicate hunting, trapping, and fishing license fees to the state fish and game department (Iowa) or for the exclusive purposes of fish and wildlife programs (West Virginia); a Massachusetts constitutional amendment prohibiting trapping of nearly all fur-bearing animals; an Oregon law reversing the prohibition on hunting mountain lions and bears; and bans on black bear baiting and the use of dogs to hunt bears or wildcats in Washington.

A smaller number of initiatives were rejected in 1996. Voters in Idaho and Michigan rejected bans on baiting and on hunting bears with dogs. Michigan voters also defeated a measure that would have given its Natural Resources Commission exclusive authority to regulate hunting. A proposed tax on sugar grown in the Everglades was defeated.

See also **Fund for Animals; Hunting.**

STATE SCHOOL LANDS Lands received at statehood by all states admitted to the Union since 1802 as part of their statehood compact with the federal government. In exchange for receiving one or more sections of land (a section is one square mile, or 640 acres) per township (a township consists of 36 sections) to be used to support schools, states renounced any claim to, or authority to tax, the remaining unoccupied federal lands within their borders. The U.S. Supreme Court has referred to these enabling acts or agreements as "solemn compacts." Utah, New Mexico, and Arizona each received four sections per township—sections 2, 16, 32, and 36. All other states admitted in 1850 or after were granted sections 16 and 32; states admitted before 1850 received section 16.

Most midwestern and southern states sold their lands. Many used the proceeds to create permanent funds for the benefit of public schools. Often, though, there was no market for western lands. Furthermore, the land selection process continued in some western states through the 1980s or even later, a result of slow progress in completing the prerequisite land surveys and the unavailability of many of the predesignated sections (due to homestead patents, mining claims, inclusion in national forests or other federal reserves, etc.). As a result, most western states still own the bulk of their original "school lands," and as land values rise, the debate over their proper use and disposition is escalating.

Nature of States' Title in School Lands

Many western states' constitutions require that these lands or the revenues generated from them be maximized and/or that they be held in trust by the state for the benefit of schools. Trust language can be found in the constitutions of Washington, Idaho, Montana, Utah, Nebraska, and Oklahoma. The only *enabling act* that contains such trust language, however, is the New Mexico-Arizona Enabling Act of 1910, which also contains specific requirements for obtaining fair market value from the sale or lease of school lands. (Trust language in Alaska's granting statute was later repealed.)

The U.S. Supreme Court interpreted Arizona's trust responsibilities in *Lassen v. Arizona Highway Department* (1967), holding that the state could not use its trust assets for any purposes other than the exclusive benefit of public schools and that the United States has a continuing interest in the proper management of the trust. In a later case the Supreme Court held that the state could not subsidize one industry (mining on school lands) with the revenues going to schools. [*Asarco, Inc. v. Kadish* (1989)] On the other hand, in a subsequent statute, Congress may override a state's compact with the federal government to obtain the maximum benefit for schools from its lands. [*See Case v. Bowles* (1946); *Board of Natural Resources v. Brown* (1993).]

The courts in many other western and plains states began to apply *Lassen*'s strict requirements, even though (unlike Arizona) their state enabling acts do not contain a trust duty. Such decisions have been rendered in Oklahoma, Montana, Alaska, Nebraska, and Washington. One federal court relied on *Lassen* in holding that Nebraska could not grant the United States a right-of-way over state lands to benefit a reclamation project because it violated the state's trust responsibility with respect to schools. *Lassen* has come to stand for limits on what states can and cannot do with their school lands: They cannot waste those lands or their resources, but must manage them prudently; they may not subsidize businesses unrelated to education. Some specific applications include requirements that grazing levels on school lands be sustainable, leases be awarded by competitive bidding, and leases allow conversion to more lucrative future uses.

Current Controversies over Use and Management of State Lands

Because the state's trust responsibilities for schools may conflict with other state interests or policies, the use and management of western school lands have become the subject of increasing contention and uncertainty. In particular, tension exists between developing and preserving these lands. [*See, e.g., National Parks and Conservation Association v. Board of State Lands* (1993).*] Many western school sections are used solely or predominantly for grazing, and the only revenues generated are grazing lease fees, which may amount to a few thousand dollars per year per lease area. In some areas the lands hold tremendously greater value for development. For instance, state lands on Emerald Mountain near Steamboat Springs, Colorado, generate $27,000 annually from grazing and hunting lease fees. However, the estimated value of the lands for development purposes— residential and resort uses in connection with the nearby Mount Werner ski area—is $6–7 million. The Colorado state land board has sold some land for development near McCoy, 30 miles from another ski development—Vail.

The Emerald Mountain controversy is representative of situations throughout Colorado and other states. Interested parties may include the state land board, governor's office, area residents and environmentalists intent on maintaining open space, county commissioners wanting to retain control over county growth and development, and the current lessees or other users of the lands.

Colorado voters approved an initiative in 1996 (Amendment 16 to the Colorado constitution) that requires the state land board to preserve 300,000 acres of state school lands in their natural condition, for the benefit and enjoyment of future generations, and makes other provisions for managing state lands. The initiative, drafted by Governor Roy Romer, was challenged in federal court on the ground that it violates the Supremacy Clause of the U.S. Constitution; that is, it violates federal law (the Colorado statehood act), which requires that these lands be used to benefit schools. The trial judge upheld the initiative, ruling that a trust responsibility exists, but that Amendment 16 does not violate it. [*See Branson School District v. Romer*

(1997).] At least one legal scholar (Hager 1997) suggests that the decision is flawed, arguing that only state lands in Arizona and New Mexico are subject to a *federally* enforceable trust.

Meanwhile, other states are simply debating how their lands should be managed and whether they may be sold. Wyoming has imposed temporary moratoria on state land sales while attempting to assess the legal ramifications of, and devise criteria for, disposal of these lands. The failure of the Wyoming legislature in 1996 to extend the moratorium left the future of state lands in considerable doubt. In Idaho, an environmental group has been trying to obtain grazing leases on overgrazed state lands, with the intent to rest them from grazing. Although the group is consistently the high, if not the *only*, bidder for these leases, the state legislature and Board of Land Commissioners have blocked the group from getting any lease— leading one scholar to suggest that the state is not acting in the best interests of the beneficiary, Idaho's schools (Fairfax 1996).

See also **Public Trust Doctrine.**

STEVENS, TED   Republican senator from Alaska and chair of the powerful Senate Appropriations Committee. A political conservative on public lands and natural resources issues, Stevens has been said to favor use of the appropriations process to pass measures that would not survive the legislative process as stand-alone measures, such as takings bills that failed in the 104th Congress. These measures can be attached as "riders" to money bills; they are not subject to the president's line-item veto authority.

SUBDIVISION   The legal process by which a tract of land is divided into two or more (in some states, three or more) parcels. The term is also used to refer to the subdivided property itself—particularly new residential housing developments. Subdivision is governed by state law; requirements vary considerably from state to state. Subdivision raises numerous concerns from the governmental, or public, perspective, including growth control issues, such as sprawl, traffic flow and congestion, infrastructure adequacy, and compatibility of land uses. Property owners may share these concerns, but often are also concerned about property values and neighborhood aesthetics or making an economic return on their property. Depending on how "subdivision" is defined, other issues may arise, such as whether leases (as in a mobile home park) or nonresidential subdivisions are regulated; whether divisions of property in an estate, either by will or intestate, are subdivisions; and whether condominium projects are covered.

Subdividing usually requires government approval, either city or county, and compliance with applicable ordinances. Local subdivision regulations are usually authorized by state statute, which may impose minimum requirements for subdividing land. Requirements may include minimum lot size, soil and other engineering surveys, assurances concerning the availability of water and sanitary facilities, provisions for other utilities and roads, and recording. Subdivisions may also be subject to density limitations in applicable zoning regulations. Most jurisdictions require approval of a sketch and/or "plat" (map or diagram) of the proposed subdivision.

A common question relating to subdivision concerns "vested rights": At what stage in the permitting or approval process does an applicant to subdivide property acquire the right to proceed with the development? Most jurisdictions require approval of the subdivision, including site-specific plans; acquisition of a building permit; *and* some construction or expenditures made in reliance on the building permit. Before a subdivider's rights vest, the local government may amend the applicable requirements, or even deprive the developer of the right to proceed, without incurring any obligation to compensate him.

See also **Taking; Zoning.**

SUBSIDY An economic benefit or protection provided by government, usually to an industry or other sector of the economy. Subsidies may take the form of price supports, tax breaks, or disposal of natural resources at below-market prices.

While states can and do subsidize business or industries, most subsidies—and the most controversial ones—come from the federal government. Subsidies are controversial for several reasons. First, what constitutes a subsidy can be the subject of much debate. Beneficiaries of alleged subsidies may argue that the economic or social benefits to society of their activity (e.g., small family farms or mining) outweigh the economic advantage of the government benefit they receive. Purchasers of public resources (e.g., timber or livestock forage) claim that the price they pay accurately reflects the value of the resources when the costs of extracting those resources and other costs of doing business are considered.

A second reason has to do with equity. Those businesses not subsidized by government cry foul at the advantage enjoyed by those who are; the unfairness is especially apparent where the two groups are competitors (for instance, livestock producers who enjoy federal grazing permits and those who operate on private lands). Moreover, few persons, if any, can claim that they do not receive government subsidies, whether in the form of public schools, highways, tax deductions, or assistance or preferential treatment in some form. Thus, when conservation groups decry the subsidies to public land ranchers, timber companies, or mining companies, those interests are likely to point out that most recreational use of public lands is free. The obvious counterargument in this example, of course, is that the commodity interests are using public lands for private profit, while most recreationists are engaged in a pastime, not a business endeavor. Nevertheless, the debate persists.

Although certain federal statutes, notably the Federal Land Policy and Management Act, declare that it is federal policy to obtain fair value for resources, the actual practice can be very different. A bill introduced by Congressman George Miller (D-CA) in 1997 (H.R. 919) would give teeth to these provisions by prohibiting the below-market sale or lease of federally owned natural resources, including minerals, livestock forage, and timber.

American agricultural policy continues to be rife with subsidies. The federal government provides price and income support for producers of food grains (wheat, rice), feed grains (corn, sorghum, barley, oats, rye), cotton, oilseeds, peanuts, sugar, milk, and tobacco. A 1995 *Wall Street Journal* editorial reported that farm subsidies (totaling $12 billion annually) have led to annual per capita payments ranging from $20,000 to corn farmers, $150,000 to rice growers, and $200,000 to cotton planters *not* to plant their crops. According to the writer, our farm program has induced American farmers to forgo income amounting to $65 billion a year; 40 percent of American farmers want to end these subsidies.

Sugar subsidies, in place since 1981, have survived perennial congressional termination attempts. These subsidies are blamed for the conversion of more than 500,000 acres of the Florida Everglades to sugarcane fields and pollution of this valuable ecosystem by fertilizers. Sugar refiners claim that current laws (which drive up the price of domestic raw sugar and restrict imports) are putting them out of business. They cite the closure of 12 of 22 plants since the law was passed. An effort to end the subsidy in 1996, in the Freedom to Farm bill, failed by five votes. Ironically, the Clinton administration's 1997 budget proposal recommended that $76 million of

Land and Water Conservation Fund monies be used to acquire land in the Everglades for inclusion in Everglades National Park.

See also **Below-Cost Timber Sales; Farm Bills; Range Reform.**

SUBSISTENCE HUNTING AND FISHING The harvest of fish and wildlife for meat and to provide for other basic needs and cultural uses. The term today applies almost exclusively to Alaska.

The Alaska Native Claims Settlement Act (ANCSA), passed in 1971, granted Natives and non-Natives in Alaska the right to engage in subsistence hunting and fishing on federal lands in the state. Prompted by the state and federal agencies' failure to adequately protect subsistence uses, Congress in 1980 passed the Alaska National Interest Lands Conservation Act (ANILCA), Title VIII of which requires that rural Alaskans' subsistence uses of public lands be accorded priority. ANILCA defined subsistence use as "the customary and traditional uses by rural Alaskans of wild, renewable resources for direct personal or family consumption as food, shelter, fuel, clothing, tools, or transportation," and gave priority to nonwasteful subsistence uses of natural resources by rural Alaskans. Subsistence uses must be compatible with maintaining healthy wildlife populations and fisheries, however. ANILCA also directed federal agencies to consider the effects of their management policies on subsistence uses, and authorized the state of Alaska to promulgate its own subsistence policy to implement the rural subsistence preference.

Anticipating Title VIII, Alaska had enacted such a law, and the Interior Department approved state management of subsistence uses. This state law was challenged, however, and the Alaska Supreme Court ruled it unconstitutional (essentially on equal protection grounds) because it allowed only rural Alaska residents to hunt or fish for subsistence. [*McDowell v. Alaska* (1989)] When the state legislature was unable to resolve the "rural" issue, the secretary of the interior rejected the state program and took over implementation of Title VIII, issuing rules to implement the subsistence preference. The rules established a Federal Subsistence Board, with the authority to manage fish and wildlife on public lands in Alaska.

The federal regulations provided that "navigable waters" generally are not included within the definition of "public lands" in Alaska, and hence the subsistence preference would not generally apply to such waters. These regulations were challenged by Alaska Natives who had fished in certain navigable waters for generations. The state of Alaska also challenged the federal subsistence program, contending that the United States had no right to manage fish and wildlife in Alaska at all. The cases were consolidated, and the litigation, which had a convoluted history, culminated with the Ninth Circuit's opinion in *State of Alaska v. Babbitt* (1995), which the U.S. Supreme Court declined to review.

The Ninth Circuit held (with one judge dissenting) that ANILCA's subsistence priority applies only to those navigable waters in which the United States has reserved water rights. It further ruled that the respective federal land management agencies are responsible for identifying these waters. The court admitted that its decision might be viewed by the parties as "unsatisfactory," and that it imposed "an extraordinary burden" on the federal agencies, but the court seemed to view its decision as a compromise between the extreme views of the parties, neither of which had any support in ANILCA or its legislative history. The court also believed that the issue raised by the parties "cries out for a legislative, not a judicial, solution." According to the court, the matter could and should be resolved either by Congress, amending ANILCA to redefine "public lands" and clarify which "waters" are included, or by Alaska, amending the state constitution or "otherwise comply[ing] with ANILCA's rural subsistence priority."

Unless either legislature heeds the Ninth Circuit's advice, implementing the rural subsistence fishing preference will depend on the federal agencies identifying which of Alaska's thousands of navigable waters are subject to a federal reserved water right. This will require determining where water is necessary to support the purposes of a federal reservation of land (e.g., a national park, preserve, or wildlife refuge). One such purpose that could necessitate a water right, of course, is the federal preference for subsistence fishing.

See also **Alaska National Interest Lands Conservation Act; Alaska Native Claims Settlement Act; Hunting; Navigable Waters; Reserved Rights Doctrine.**

SURFACE MINING CONTROL AND RECLAMATION ACT OF 1977 (SMCRA)

A complex and detailed federal statute that sets environmental protection performance standards and reclamation requirements for surface (or "strip") coal mines on private and public lands. SMCRA was initially resisted by states that had no reclamation standards and by some mining companies, but the U.S. Supreme Court held that the statute, on its face, is constitutional. [*See*, e.g., *Hodel v. Virginia*

Surface Mining and Reclamation Association (1981).] One court, however, has held that the act, as applied to a particular coal mine, effected a taking of the owner's property. [*Whitney Benefits, Inc. v. United States* (1991)] Very little SMCRA litigation has involved mining on public lands. Most western states (where the large public-land mines are located) had reclamation requirements in place when SMCRA passed, and they generally supported the statute.

SMCRA provides for direct federal regulation or for regulation by states once they develop and obtain approval for a state program. The secretary of the interior has approved state programs in 24 states, including all the major western coal-producing states. The state may even enter into a cooperative agreement with the Interior secretary to regulate coal mining on *public* lands. State courts have jurisdiction to enforce state-approved programs. SMCRA provides for several enforcement methods: permits, inspections, and civil penalties.

As applied to public lands, SMCRA requires that surface coal mines comply with all the act's regulatory requirements, including permitting and reclamation. The act also directed the secretary of the interior to determine which public lands are unsuitable for surface mining (for coal *or* other minerals) and to withdraw them or specify appropriate conditions in leases. SMCRA prohibited mining in national parks, wildernesses, wildlife refuges, and components of the wild and scenic river system, subject to "valid existing rights," a term that has posed interpretational problems for the agency. Surface coal mining may take place in national forests only if it would not be incompatible with other significant values or uses of the land.

The Office of Surface Mining Reclamation and Enforcement within the Department of the Interior oversees the administration of the statute. It conducts inspections, mostly of eastern mines, and imposes fines. The Bureau of Land Management oversees the mining unsuitability review process. The responsibilities of the federal government under SMCRA and the relationship of the federal government to the states have been the subject of several lawsuits, with inconclusive results.

See also **Mine Reclamation; Withdrawal.**

SUSTAINABLE DEVELOPMENT Definitions of this term vary. The definition used in the Brundtland Report (the 1987 Report of the UN World Commission on Environment and Development, named after the commission chair, Gro Harlem Brundtland, prime minister of Norway), which has been adopted by the President Clinton's Council on Sustainable Development, is: "Development that meets the needs of the present without compromising the ability of future generations to meet their own needs." The International Union for the Conservancy of Nature's 1991 *World Conservation Strategy* defines sustainable development as "improving the quality of human life while living within the capacity of supporting ecosystems."

Regardless of how it is defined, the concept of sustainable development embraces two fundamental principles: (1) the finiteness of world resources and the planet's limited ability to accommodate human population and industrial development, and (2) the current generation's ethical obligation to use natural resources so as not to deprive future generations of resources necessary to maintain a quality of life and environment. Sustainable development is a core principle of several international treaties and agreements—such as the Framework Convention on Climate Change, the Convention on Biological Diversity, and the Declaration on Principles of Rational Exploitation of Ocean Resources—and of certain international business agreements, such as the Business Charter for Sustainable Development, which has been signed by approximately 1,250 corporations since it was drafted in 1991.

The President's Council on Sustainable Development, which is attempting to devise a national sustainable development action strategy, consists of 25 representatives of industry, government, labor, environmental, and civil rights organizations. The group evaluates and develops policies to simultaneously encourage economic development, create jobs, and protect the environment and cultural heritages. It has formed eight issue-specific working groups. One of these, the Natural Resources Task Force, is developing a concept of what constitutes sustainability for U.S. natural resources, incorporating biodiversity, ecosystem, and watershed principles. In fact, the task force has set up three regional teams, each applying watershed principles in its investigations. The Western Team has conducted several workshops around the region, the Midwestern Team concentrates on the Mississippi River basin, and the Eastern Team uses three watersheds as case studies.

The Natural Resources Task Force is chaired by Richard Barth, president and CEO of Ciba-Geigy Corporation, and Ted Strong, executive director of the Columbia River Intertribal Fish Commission. Other members consist of three federal officials (including Interior Secretary Bruce Babbitt and EPA Administrator Carol Browner), an industry executive, and three national conservation organization officials.

Examples of our failure to ensure that development is sustainable are as diverse as definitions of the term. To illustrate: American farmers remove 20 billion more gallons of groundwater than is replaced by precipitation. All the world's major fishing areas are being harvested at or above sustainable levels, according to the United Nations, and per capita seafood supplies decreased by 9 percent from 1989 to 1994. Fossil fuel extraction and consumption are outstripping research and development in alternative fuels. Unacceptable rates of soil erosion mean that land productivity will continue to decline. Finally, the rate of loss of old-growth forests exceeds the rate at which they are being replaced. President Clinton has announced a goal of achieving sustainable forest management by the year 2000, but it is not known whether old-growth forests can be replicated.

A chief component of sustainable development is using renewable resources at rates that are sustainable, that is, maintainable indefinitely. This concept resembles the sustained-yield principle that is supposed to guide the use and management of federal public lands, particularly national forests and lands managed by the Bureau of Land Management.

See also **Biodiversity Conservation; Intergenerational Equity; Sustained Yield.**

SUSTAINED YIELD   This term is most often used in combination with the phrase "multiple use" to refer to the broad management philosophy that guides management of the federal public lands and national forests. The term is defined in the Multiple-Use, Sustained-Yield Act (MUSYA), which applies to national forests managed by the U.S. Forest Service, and in the Federal Land Policy and Management Act (FLPMA), applicable to lands managed by the Bureau of Land Management (BLM).

The definitions of sustained yield in these two statutes are almost identical: "'Sustained yield' means the achievement and maintenance in perpetuity of a high-level annual or regular periodic output of the various renewable resources of the [public lands and national forests] consistent with multiple use" [or "without impairment of the productivity of the land"]. (Each statute uses the phrase "without impairment of the productivity of the land" in its definition of multiple use.) In FLPMA, Congress indicated that both "multiple use" and "sustained yield" have traditional, accepted meanings. [See 43 U.S.C. § 1712(c)(1).]

Whether the Forest Service or BLM has provided for sustained yield of the various renewable resources, particularly timber and livestock forage, is a common challenge to the agencies' land-use plans, but courts are usually very deferential to such technical decisions by agencies possessing the relevant expertise. In fact, few courts have construed the terms "multiple use" and "sustained yield," and they have found "little law to apply."

On the other hand, both terms have been rather widely debated by legal scholars and the popular press. Most commentators seem to agree that the law is vague and provides little guidance to the agencies. Professors Coggins, Wilkinson, and Leshy (1993) wrote: "'Sustained yield' timber management is almost bereft of meaning as a management standard." In 1973 the Forest Service adopted as a policy "nondeclining even flow" (NDEF), the most conservative variation of sustained yield as applied to timber harvesting. In essence, this means cutting the same amount of timber *annually*, "in perpetuity." Recall that MUSYA calls for a "high-level annual *or regular* periodic output." Probably the most significant difference between the two approaches, as applied, is in old-growth forests. Because the volume of timber is so much greater in these ancient forests (especially in the Pacific Northwest) than in managed, second-growth timber stands, a much larger volume of timber could be cut annually until the old growth was liquidated. Then the annual cut would have to be reduced to reflect the typical conversion period (the time from one cut to the next) in managed forests, perhaps 100 years. If NDEF were applied to old growth, however, the early annual cuts would have to come down in order to meet the "annually in perpetuity" requirement.

Congress attempted to provide some guidance on this issue in section 13 of the National Forest Management Act of 1976. This complex provision starts out by requiring the Forest Service to "limit the sale of timber from each national forest to a quantity which can be removed from such forest annually in perpetuity on a sustained-yield basis." But the section goes on to include several conditions or exceptions. For instance, it allows deviations "within any decade," permits the combination of two or more forests if they contain little commercial forest land, and excludes "salvage or sanitation harvesting." These provisos complicate application of the NDEF requirement and do not clearly resolve the old-growth issue.

Several states also have requirements for sustained-yield harvesting of timber from state lands.

See also **Coggins, George Cameron; Federal Land Policy and Management Act; Multiple Use; Multiple-Use, Sustained-Yield Act of 1960; Salvage Logging; Wise Use Movement.**

SWAMPBUSTER One of two major agricultural wetland protection programs; the other is the Wetlands Reserve Program within the Conservation Reserve Program (CRP). The Swampbuster provisions of the 1985 Food Security Act were designed to protect wetlands by providing incentives to farmers not to convert wetlands to crops, by linking eligibility for federal farm program benefits, such as commodity price supports, to a producer's willingness to protect wetlands. By and large, these incentives have been successful. From the 1950s through the 1970s, nearly 15 million acres of wetlands were converted to agricultural use. The Swampbuster provisions have reduced the annual rate of wetlands loss to fewer than 80,000 acres.

The Regulatory Scheme

Swampbuster differs from the CRP's Wetlands Reserve Program in that it is voluntary and operates via incentives; under Swampbuster, farmers who convert wetlands are "punished" by losing their eligibility to participate in and receive payments under certain farm programs. Unlike Clean Water Act section 404, Swampbuster regulates *draining* of a wetland. Swampbuster restrictions apply only to wetlands that fall within the statutory definition and are delineated as such by the Natural Resources Conservation Service (NRCS). The Food Security Act defines a wetland as land that: (1) has a preponderance of hydric soils, (2) is inundated or saturated by surface or groundwater often enough to support a prevalence of hydrophytic vegetation that is typically adapted for life in saturated soil, and (3) under normal conditions does support a prevalence of such vegetation. A wetland can be dry much of the year, as long as these conditions are met. NRCS field staff visit the land in question; if they determine that the area meets the statutory definition, they identify the area as a wetland on an official NRCS map. (In light of the controversy over wetland delineation, the NRCS stopped making wetland determinations in 1995 except upon request. To date, only 2.6 million of 4 million tracts believed to contain wetlands have been field checked and mapped.) An amendment in the 1996 act provides landowners an opportunity to appeal a wetland delineation. Agricultural lands that could qualify as wetlands include cropland, pastures, grazing land, and tree farms. Thus, if a wetland that was formerly used as pasture or for growing trees is converted to commodity crop production, the farmer will likely be ineligible for farm benefit programs. (Commodity crops are defined as "any crop produced by the annual tilling of the soil or sugarcane.")

The Swampbuster program applies only to agricultural wetland conversions begun after 23 December 1985. A farmer who produces agricultural commodity crops on such lands cannot collect income support payments, Commodity Credit Corporation loans, federal disaster payments, or Farm Home Administration loans. Prior to the 1996 amendments to the Food Security Act, crop insurance was also among the benefits that farmers lost if they converted wetlands. Violators are ineligible for benefits in the crop year and in subsequent years; only one violation per ten years is allowed on a given parcel of land.

By regulation, certain agricultural wetlands are exempt from Swampbuster restrictions. Wetlands converted for use in producing fish, trees, vineyards, shrubs, or cranberries are exempt from Swampbuster restrictions, as are lands converted in the course of building and road construction. NRCS may also grant an exemption if it determines that conversion of the wetland or production of commodities on the wetland will have minimal environmental impact.

The 1996 Amendments

Although the 1996 Farm Bill generally maintained the Swampbuster wetlands protections, Congress also sought to provide the NRCS with greater enforcement flexibility. The original law allowed the agency to reduce a producer's ineligibility by "not less than $750 nor more than $10,000" if the violation was done in good faith, the producer was actively restoring the wetland at issue, and the land had seen no prior Swampbuster violations in the last ten years. A 1996 amendment allows the Secretary of Agriculture to impose ineligibility in proportion to the severity of the violation *or* to award a complete waiver of Swampbuster penalties, on a showing that the conversion was made in good faith and without intent to violate the law. It remains to be seen whether the NRCS will continue to rigorously enforce ineligibility penalties against farmers who have converted wetlands in violation of Swampbuster. Given the local nature of NRCS administration, this amendment could weaken the program's effectiveness.

Furthermore, prior to 1996, a producer who obtained a Clean Water Act section 404 permit to fill a wetland still had to comply with Swampbuster requirements, including mitigation, if he wished to continue to receive farm program benefits. The 1996 amendments exempt from Swampbuster requirements those wetland conversions authorized by a section 404 permit, provided that the conversion is accompanied by an adequate mitigation plan. The law also eliminated the requirement to consult with the U.S. Fish and Wildlife Service and created a pilot mitigation banking program (using the Conservation Reserve Program). The potential for increased wetland conversion under the 1996 amendments has been lessened somewhat by the U.S. Army Corps of Engineers' announcement in late 1996 that it was withdrawing nationwide permit #26, which authorized, on a regional basis, conversion of wetlands less than one acre in size.

Perhaps the most significant long-term change in the 1996 law is the provision for "freezing" prior converted croplands, exempting them indefinitely from Swampbuster. Until 1996, previously converted croplands that had returned to a wetland condition by either natural forces (usually neglect by the landowner) or affirmative action by the landowner were subject to Swampbuster regulation after five years in the renewed wetland state. Now the "prior converted" status of the land stays with the land. In addition, owners of wetlands that were converted *prior to 1985* (and thus, never subject to Swampbuster) can continue to avoid Swampbuster regulation if their lands return to a wetland condition. To preserve the parcel's exclusion from Swampbuster regulation, a landowner must notify the NRCS, which will document the landowner's intention to allow the land to return to a wetland but to maintain its exclusion from Swampbuster. The saving grace of this provision is that the NRCS must also document the land's existing wetland values and functions. Any reconversion of the land in the future must preserve the wetlands values and functions previously documented by the NRCS.

The potential harm to wetlands posed by the 1996 amendments will be clearer once the NRCS finalizes its new implementing regulations. For instance, categorical exemptions are the subject of required rule making under the 1996 amendments. These exemptions will vary from region to region and will likely be the target of litigation. In addition, as of this writing, NRCS rules concerning mitigation and other topics were broader than the statutory language, rendering court challenges to the rules almost certain.

See also **Clean Water Act Section 404; Conservation Reserve Program; Farm Bills; Mitigation; Natural Resources Conservation Service; Soil Erosion and Conservation; Wetland.**

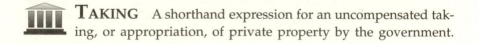**TAKE**   Section 9 of the Endangered Species Act of 1973 (ESA) makes it unlawful for any person to take an endangered species. The act defines "take" as "to harass, harm, pursue, hunt, shoot, wound, kill, trap, capture, or collect, or to attempt to engage in any such conduct." The U.S. Fish and Wildlife Service (USFWS), which administers the ESA, has extended this prohibition, by regulation, to all threatened species as well. Another USFWS regulation defines the word "harm" (used in the statutory definition of "take") to mean "an act which actually kills or injures wildlife. Such act may include significant habitat modification or degradation where it actually kills or injures wildlife by significantly impairing essential behavioral patterns, including breeding, feeding, or sheltering." The U.S. Supreme Court upheld the regulatory definition of "harm" against a challenge that it exceeded the USFWS's authority and improperly constrained private landowners' ordinary use of their property. [*Babbitt v. Sweet Home Chapter of Communities for a Great Oregon* (1995)] Thus, landowners may be subject to penalties under the ESA for taking a threatened or endangered species if they modify habitat (e.g., by cutting timber, cultivating the land, or developing it) in a way that would result in the death or injury of a threatened or endangered animal.

See also ***Babbitt v. Sweet Home Chapter of Communities for a Great Oregon* (1995); Endangered Species; Endangered Species Act of 1973; Incidental Taking; Threatened Species.**

TAKING   A shorthand expression for an uncompensated taking, or appropriation, of private property by the government.

Development of Takings Doctrine

"Takings law" is a branch of constitutional law that derives from the Fifth Amendment of the U.S. Constitution, which provides that private property may not be taken for public use without just compensation. In other words, governments are not prohibited from taking private property; they are only forbidden to appropriate property for a nonpublic use or without paying for it. This appropriation can occur as a direct occupation (invasion) or confiscation of the property, or it may result from a regulation that restricts excessively the use of the property. Physical invasions by government are more readily ruled takings than are restrictions on property *use* arising from "public program[s] adjusting the benefits and burdens of economic life to promote the common good." [*Penn Central Transportation Co. v. City of New York* (1978)] The latter category of takings is termed "regulatory takings"; such takings are a fairly recent development in our law. The notion that property could be taken without actually being invaded or confiscated by the government was first accepted by the U.S. Supreme Court in 1922 in *Pennsylvania Coal Co. v. Mahon.*

As the Supreme Court itself acknowledges, determining what constitutes an unconstitutional taking has "proved to be a problem of considerable difficulty." The Court has been "unable to develop any 'set formula' for determining when 'justice and fairness' require that the economic injuries caused by public action be compensated by the government, rather than remain disproportionately concentrated on a few persons." The Court undertakes "essentially ad hoc, factual inquiries" in analyzing takings claims, although it has "identified several factors that have particular significance to the inquiry." These include the "economic impact of the regulation on the claimant and, particularly, the extent to which it interferes with distinct, investment-backed expectations," and "the character of the government action." [*Penn Central*] This case-by-case analytical approach renders takings law difficult to summarize.

In *Pennsylvania Coal*, the Court said that, "while property may be regulated to a certain extent, if regulation goes too far it will be recognized as a 'taking.'" Some courts and commentators view this as a balancing process; that is, the court must weigh benefits to the public against the harm, or burden, of a land-use regulation on an individual property owner. This analysis can be very subjective. Only seven years before *Pennsylvania Coal*, the Court had upheld against a taking challenge a Los Angeles zoning ordinance that, according to the property owner, had reduced the value of his land 92 *percent* by forbidding him to continue his brick-making business there. [*Hadacheck v. Sebastian* (1915)] The Court has often said that "mere diminution in the value of property, however serious, is insufficient to demonstrate a taking." [*Concrete Pipe & Products v. Construction Laborers Pension Trust* (1993)]

The Supreme Court has developed one categorical test for determining when a regulation goes "too far." In *Lucas v. South Carolina Coastal Council*

(1992), the Court held that a government regulation that "deprives land of all economically beneficial use" effects a taking, *unless* the "proscribed use interests were not part of the [landowner's] title to begin with."

In *Lucas*, the state had enacted a law prohibiting building habitable structures on Lucas's (and others') beachfront property *after* Lucas had acquired his property. The Court had long recognized a "nuisance exception" to takings—that is, that private property rights are subject to the state's power to abate nuisances. The *Lucas* Court explained that this limit on private rights encompasses only those restrictions that inhere in the landowner's title. Thus, if the government prohibits some use or activity that has not traditionally been deemed a nuisance under the state's common law of nuisance, and such prohibition destroys the economic value of private property interests that predate the regulatory prohibition, the government must pay for the property "taken."

Most regulations, however, do not deprive landowners of *all* economic use of their property; these are the difficult cases. The U.S. Court of Appeals for the Federal Circuit, in *Florida Rock Industries v. United States* (1994), took up the issues of whether a regulation that "deprives the owner of a substantial part but not essentially all of the economic use or value of the property, constitute[s] a partial taking, and is it compensable as such." The case involved the U.S. Army Corps of Engineers' (Corps) denial of a limestone mining company's application for a Clean Water Act section 404 permit to conduct mining in a wetland. In 1972, Florida Rock paid an average of $1,900 per acre for 1,560 acres of wetlands on which it intended to mine limestone. After the Corps refused to issue a permit, the company sued. Evidence in the case showed that the property's remaining value ranged from "negligible" to $10,000 per acre; the company had received actual purchase offers of $4,000 per acre. (An assessor testified that these offers reflected the would-be buyers' lack of sophistication and their ignorance of the regulatory requirements.) The court held that a "partial regulatory taking" could occur where government regulation had destroyed less than the full value of property, but that the line between a *compensable* partial taking and a *noncompensable* "mere diminution [of value]" had not been resolved. The appeals court remanded the case (for the third time) to the Claims Court for additional factual determinations and for an "initial" ruling on the "partial taking" legal question.

Another difficulty in deciding takings claims is determining the relevant parcel or unit of property. (This is sometimes referred to as the denominator question.) According to the Supreme Court, takings law "does not divide a single parcel into discrete segments and attempt to determine whether rights in a particular segment have been entirely abrogated. In deciding whether a particular government action has effected a taking, [the] Court focuses rather...on the nature and extent of the interference with rights in the parcel as a whole." [*Penn Central*] For instance, if a landowner challenges a regulation that prevents her from building on two acres of an undivided ten-acre tract because of the presence of wetlands, a court presumably would examine not the reduced value of the two-acre portion, but the economic impact of the building prohibition on the entire ten-acre tract. This is the approach taken by most courts to date, but the Federal Circuit Court of Appeals recently viewed the matter differently.

In *Loveladies Harbor, Inc. v. U.S.* (1994), another wetlands case, the Federal Circuit considered whether a refusal by the Corps to issue a section 404 permit effected a taking of property. Loveladies had purchased 250 acres of shoreline property, 192.6 acres of which it had developed (before wetlands regulations were in place) and sold. In 1982, 51 undeveloped acres of the original 250 remained in Loveladies' ownership. In exchange for a state development permit, Loveladies had agreed to dedicate to New Jersey 38.5 of these 51 acres. But Loveladies was denied a section 404 permit to develop the remaining 12.5 acres.

The court was called upon to identify the relevant parcel of land for the takings analysis. It excluded the 199 acres developed before wetlands regulations were in place. It then excluded the 38.5 acres that had been promised to New Jersey. That left the 12.5-acre tract as the "relevant property for the takings analysis." The fair market value of this land prior to the permit denial was $2,658,000; after permit denial the value was $12,500. The court concluded that denial of the 404 permit had effected a taking. The court's decision has been criticized as ignoring the usual rule against "segmenting" property into individual parcels or units for purposes of the takings analysis.

Political Developments

Recent years have seen a dramatic increase in the number of property rights advocacy groups and growing criticism of what many perceive as overregulation by both state and federal governments. One consequence has been the proliferation of so-called "takings bills" introduced in Congress and state legislatures. As of 1996, takings bills or other property rights initiatives had been introduced or passed in 31 states. In addition, several bills were introduced in the 104th Congress, one of which passed the House of Representatives in 1995. The most extreme among them, introduced by

Senator Phil Gramm (R-TX), would have compensated private landowners whenever government regulations reduced property values by at least 25 percent, or $10,000. Other bills proposed higher thresholds, such as 30 or 50 percent. Such takings bills, if enacted, would simply provide a legislative-damages remedy to property owners impacted by government regulation. They would not amend constitutional law—only an amendment to the Constitution, enacted as provided in the Constitution itself, can do that. Nor would they alter the current judicial interpretation of what the Fifth Amendment requires. The U.S. Supreme Court has the final say on what the Constitution means, although any court may be asked to decide what the Constitution requires when applied to a new set of facts. (The two federal court cases, *Florida Rock* and *Loveladies Harbor*, for instance, could affect the future direction of takings law.)

Support for legislative takings measures seems to have waned, due at least in part to concern over the consequences to the government's ability to function and enforce existing laws, particularly environmental and health and safety regulations. Many feared that takings bills would halt numerous government programs if not actually bankrupt governments. Motivated by such concerns, voters in Arizona, for instance, rescinded by referendum a property rights bill passed by the prior session of the state legislature.

Senator Larry Craig (R-ID) told an audience at a Defenders of Property Rights conference in mid-1997 that passage of any stand-alone takings legislation by the 105th Congress was highly unlikely. Craig noted that the vast majority of Americans believe that environmental laws have been generally successful and were wary of efforts by Republicans in the 104th Congress to retreat from some of those protections. Craig noted, however, that the Senate could use the appropriations process to attempt to pass takings legislation by attaching riders to budget bills. According to him, Senate Appropriations Committee chair Ted Stevens was "very interested" in using that strategy.

See also **104th Congress; Scalia, Antonin; Wetland.**

TAYLOR GRAZING ACT (TGA) Federal statute governing grazing on lands managed by the Bureau of Land Management (BLM). The Taylor Act was the first federal legislation concerning grazing on the public domain. It is often said to have "closed the public domain," because it signaled the end of free grazing and most homesteading. Agreement was nearly universal in the 1920s and early 1930s that the public domain grazing lands were seriously overgrazed. Vegetation was depleted, watersheds eroded, reservoirs filling with silt, and flooding increasingly common and severe. The U.S. Forest Service had been exercising some control over grazing on national forests since 1905, but public domain grazing remained totally unregulated. After the failure of the Hoover administration's proposal to transfer federal grazing lands to the states, support for a federal leasing system grew, culminating with passage of the Taylor Act in 1934.

The act's three purposes, stated in its preamble, are: "To stop injury to the public lands by preventing overgrazing and soil deterioration, to provide for their orderly use, improvement, and development, and to stabilize the livestock industry, dependent on the public range, and for other purposes." The TGA authorized the Secretary of the Interior, at his discretion, to establish grazing districts on lands "which in his opinion are chiefly valuable for grazing and raising forage crops." This discretion was to be exercised "to promote the highest use of the public lands pending [their] final disposal." Section 2 of the act gave the secretary broad authority to regulate the "occupancy and use" of grazing districts, "to preserve the land and its resources from destruction or unnecessary injury, [and] to provide for the orderly use, improvement and development of the range." Section 7 directed the secretary to identify lands "more valuable or suitable" for uses other than grazing.

One effect of the act, as expanded by executive order and congressional amendment in 1936, was to withdraw from homesteading and other nonmineral entry all vacant and unreserved lands in the 12 western states until the lands could be classified as to their best use. Where grazing districts were set up, "preference" was to be given in the issuance of grazing permits to "those within or near a district who are landowners engaged in the livestock business, bona fide occupants or settlers, or owners of water or water rights." However, the act provided that a grazing permit was a revocable privilege that conveys no "right, title, interest, or estate in or to the lands." Congress amended the act again in 1939 and 1940 to officially recognize district and national grazing advisory boards.

The establishment of a grazing district had no effect on other existing rights in, or uses of, the public lands under any other laws. For instance, the act preserved existing rights to hunt and fish; the rights of settlers to use timber, stone, and other minerals; and rights under the mining laws. It also preserved limited opportunities for homesteading. These "savings" provisions are not equivalent, however, to the "multiple-use" authority later conferred on BLM by the Classification and Multiple Use Act of 1964, or by the Federal Land Policy and Management Act of 1976 (FLPMA).

The Taylor Grazing Act did not fully accomplish any of its purposes. Although it probably prevented the overstocking of, and competition over, the range from getting worse, it did not halt the declining trend of much of the range. Congress recognized this when it passed FLPMA in 1976 and the Public Rangeland Improvement Act in 1978. Grazing on BLM lands continues to be regulated under both the TGA and FLPMA.

See also **Federal Land Policy and Management Act; Public Domain; Public Rangelands Improvement Act; Range Reform; Tragedy of the Commons;** *United States v. Fuller* **(1973).**

TENNESSEE VALLEY AUTHORITY (TVA) An independent agency created by an act of Congress in 1933 that coordinates resource conservation and development in the Tennessee River Valley. The TVA was Congress's first attempt to establish a system for water resources planning and development for an interstate river basin. The agency manages 300,000 acres of public lands and the adjacent reservoir system (45 reservoirs), which provide flood control, promote navigation, and support multiple uses, including forestry and wildlife-related activities, in the 12 subwatersheds of the Tennessee River drainage. The agency also provides wholesale electrical power (hydro- or nuclear) to municipalities, cooperatives, federal facilities, and industry. Its headquarters are in Knoxville, Tennessee.

In the early 1990s TVA was one of 21 agencies selected to comply with the Government Performance and Results Act; it was subsequently recognized by the Office of Management and Budget as being among the top ten "Reinventing Government" models. Although one goal of the TVA had been to ensure that all Tennessee Valley waters are ecologically healthy and support their beneficial uses, the agency announced in 1996 that it planned to eliminate its environmental responsibilities. This led the organization American Rivers to include the Tennessee River in its 1997 list of the United States' ten most threatened rivers.

See also **Watershed.**

TENNESSEE VALLEY AUTHORITY V. HILL **(1978)** A landmark U.S. Supreme Court opinion, authored by former Chief Justice Warren Burger, that interpreted the Endangered Species Act of 1973 (ESA) as forbidding completion of a dam on the Tellico River in Tennessee because it would destroy the only known habitat of an endangered fish, the recently discovered snail darter. *TVA v. Hill* is one of the two most important Supreme Court cases concerning the ESA. The other is the 1995 case *Babbitt v. Sweet Home Chapter of Communities for a Great Oregon.*

The Facts and the Litigation

In *TVA v. Hill*, the Court was called on to construe federal agencies' obligations under the ESA to protect ESA-listed species and their critical habitat. The snail darter was first discovered and identified as a species during preparation of the environmental impact statement on the proposed Tellico Dam. As this was the only known population of the fish, it was subsequently listed as an endangered species, and the stretch of the Tellico River where it was found was designated critical habitat. Congress continued to appropriate funds for the project, however, and construction of the dam progressed—at an accelerated pace aimed at preempting any attempt under the ESA to halt the project. Everyone agreed that opening the dam would destroy the fish's habitat and, consequently, the snail darter itself.

The respondents (who had earlier petitioned the Interior secretary to list the snail darter as endangered) included a regional association of biologists, a Tennessee conservation group, and several individuals. They sued, asking the lower court for an injunction against completion of the dam. They argued that section 7 of the ESA forbids a federal agency (in this case, the Tennessee Valley Authority, created by federal law) to jeopardize the continued existence of any threatened or endangered species. Section 7 requires all federal agencies to "tak[e] such action necessary to insure that actions authorized, funded, or carried out by them do not jeopardize the continued existence of [listed species] or result in the destruction or modification of [their critical] habitat." The district court refused to enjoin the project, considering it "absurd" that a tiny fish could halt a public works project on which hundreds of millions of dollars had already been spent. The appellate court reversed, holding that only Congress could excuse TVA and the Tellico project from compliance with the ESA.

The Supreme Court, by a 6-3 vote, affirmed the appeals court. It held that in the ESA Congress had given endangered species the "highest of priorities" and that the subsequent appropriations bills could not repeal the mandate in the 1973 act. The Court also ruled that the only appropriate remedy was an injunction to stop work on the dam, explaining that it was not the Court's role to balance the harm (destruction of the fish) against the benefits to be achieved by the dam. Congress had made the policy choice in favor of species preservation, and the Court was not authorized to upset that choice, or, as the TVA urged, to exercise "common sense" in applying the law. According to the Court, only Congress could allow dam construction to go forward—by amending the law or exempting the Tellico Project.

The Aftermath

Congress did act to amend the ESA, but it did not change the substantive duties imposed on federal agencies in section 7. Rather, it adopted complex procedures for implementing section 7, including a final appeal to a new Endangered Species Committee, which is empowered to exempt a project from compliance with the ESA if it decides that the national or regional significance and benefits of that project outweigh the harm to the listed species or its habitat. The Endangered Species Committee has since become known as the "God Squad," reflecting its power to make "life or death" decisions about the continued existence of listed species. The new committee's first order of business was the Tellico Dam, but the committee surprised nearly everyone when it decided that the snail darter should take precedence over the uneconomic "pork barrel" TVA project. Shortly thereafter, however, the Tellico Project was exempted by Congress through a rider attached to an appropriations bill. The rider was not debated, and few who voted on the bill were even aware of its contents. President Jimmy Carter threatened to veto the bill because of the rider, but eventually and reluctantly signed it. The dam was completed in November 1979.

Although the Tellico River snail darter and its habitat were destroyed, the story had an unexpected happy ending. Several other populations of the species were later found in other Tennessee rivers, and the U.S. Fish and Wildlife Service eventually removed the snail darter from the list of endangered species.

The Case's Significance

TVA v. Hill is an important decision for at least two reasons. It is an unequivocal affirmation that the ESA commands federal agencies to conserve threatened and endangered species and to avoid any action that would threaten their continued existence. Moreover, because the provisions of the act that the Court construed remain in effect, the case continues to reflect the power of the Endangered Species Act. The case also stands for the proposition that social policy choices, such as those reflected in the ESA, are to be made by Congress, not the courts or the agencies. Just like private persons, agencies and courts must abide by the law as enacted by Congress. The remedy for an unwise law, or for an outdated policy choice, is through the political process, not judicial intervention.

See also **Critical Habitat; Endangered Species Act of 1973; Listing; Section 7 Consultation.**

THOMAS, JACK WARD Chief of the U.S. Forest Service (USFS) under President Bill Clinton from 1993 to 1996. Thomas was the first wildlife biologist ever to serve as chief, and the first chief who did not come from the upper ranks of USFS management.

Thomas is perhaps best known for his work on the northern spotted owl. He was centrally involved in USFS research in the Blue Mountains that led to the conclusion that logging in the Pacific Northwest would have to be substantially reduced to prevent extinction of the owl and perhaps several other species dependent on old-growth forests. He subsequently chaired the Interagency Scientific Committee (widely known as the Thomas Committee), which in 1990 made a number of recommendations for protecting owl habitat that critics claimed would result in the loss of thousands of timber jobs.

Thomas served as chief during an especially contentious period in the USFS and in environmental politics. A year after assuming the post, the Republican-dominated 104th Congress assumed power in Washington, complicating his job even further. Still, he was widely praised by environmentalists and industry officials alike for his integrity and his efforts to ensure that forest management is guided by science, not just politics. He is also largely credited for the USFS's adoption of ecosystem management principles in its land-use planning.

Thomas resigned in November 1996 to accept a position on the faculty at the University of Montana with the title of Boone and Crockett Professor of Wildlife Conservation. He was succeeded by Michael Dombeck, a former USFS fisheries biologist who had most recently served as acting director of the Bureau of Land Management.

See also **Dombeck, Michael; Northern Spotted Owl; U.S. Forest Service.**

THREATENED SPECIES The category of organisms considered at risk of becoming endangered and designated for protection by the Endangered Species Act of 1973 (ESA). The ESA defines a threatened species as "any species which is likely to become an endangered species within the foreseeable future throughout all or a significant portion of its range." "Species" is defined to include "any subspecies of fish or wildlife or plants, and any distinct population segment of any species of vertebrate fish or wildlife which interbreeds when mature." "Fish or wildlife," in turn, means "any member of the animal kingdom," including vertebrates (mammals, fish, birds, amphibians, and reptiles), invertebrates (mollusks, crustaceans, arthropods, etc.), and "any part, product, egg, or offspring thereof, or the dead body or parts thereof." A total of 114 fish and wildlife species endemic to the United States and 92 plants were listed as threatened in 1995; six other species were proposed for listing.

The ESA requires federal agencies to conserve threatened species and their critical habitats. It also authorizes the U.S. Fish and Wildlife Service (USFWS) to extend, by regulation, to threatened species any of the ESA's prohibitions (in section 9) against taking or engaging in commerce in endangered species. This gives USFWS more management discretion over threatened species (because the act does not *mandate* that the section 9 prohibitions apply to threatened species, only to endangered species). Nevertheless, regulations promulgated by the USFWS under this authority have conferred on threatened species essentially the same protections that endangered species enjoy.

In 1995, however, the USFWS proposed an amendment to these regulations that would exempt "certain small landowners and low impact activities that are presumed to individually or cumulatively have little or no lasting effect on the likelihood of survival and recovery of threatened species of fish and wildlife." The proposed rule would have applied to all species listed in the future, unless the USFWS determined in a particular case that the exemption was inappropriate. The rule also contained an exemption for activities "conducted in accordance with a State-authorized or -developed habitat conservation strategy for a threatened species," if the USFWS finds that it comprehensively addresses threats and promotes species recovery. In the agency's opinion, strictly prohibiting "isolated takings" associated with small landowners' and other low-impact land-use activities is not necessary in order to conserve *all* threatened species. Basically, the rule would have excused incidental takings occurring in connection with single household dwellings on five acres of land or less, low-impact activities by one landowner affecting less than five acres, and other activities that the USFWS finds to have negligible effects on threatened species. In each case, the exempted activity must be "otherwise lawful" (e.g., it must comply with all applicable water quality standards, requirements for pesticide use, and zoning laws). The rule was widely criticized, however, and was never formally promulgated. It reflects one of the many issues under discussion in Congress as ESA reauthorization efforts continue.

See also **Endangered Species; Endangered Species Act of 1973; Habitat Conservation Plan; Listing.**

TONGASS NATIONAL FOREST The nation's largest national forest (nearly 17 million acres) and one of two in Alaska. The Tongass National Forest was established by President Theodore Roosevelt in 1907. Comprising the bulk of southeast Alaska, it contains mountains, glaciers, more than a thousand islands and 11,000 miles of coastline, 10 million acres of official or de facto wilderness, and tremendous wildlife, fish, and timber resources. Only 59 percent of the Tongass is forested, however, and of that, only 34 percent is "productive," or commercial, forest. Only 4 percent of the forest contains old-growth timber.

Tongass timber harvesting policies have been controversial since the 1950s; four long-term (e.g., 50 years) contracts to sell huge volumes of timber led to a forest policy dominated by logging interests and local communities dependent on a steady supply of trees. Even the Alaska National Interest Lands Conservation Act of 1980 contained provisions protecting logging interests on the Tongass. Two of these contracts were in effect until 1994, when one was canceled due to a breach of contract by the company, Alaska Pulp Corporation. The remaining contract, with Ketchikan Pulp Company for 5 billion board feet of timber, is due to expire in 2004. (Both companies have histories of violating air and water pollution laws.) These long-term contracts have prevented smaller logging companies or more lucrative "value-added" operators from succeeding on the Tongass. In 1989 a congressional committee report called the Tongass the "most egregious example of below cost timber sales in the National Forest System."

Widespread concerns that the forest was being managed for timber at the expense of all other resources led to the Tongass Timber Reform Act of 1990 (TTRA). The TTRA was a compromise between the U.S. House—which wanted to cancel the long-term contracts, designate more wilderness, and make all provisions of the National Forest Management Act of 1976 applicable to the Tongass—and the Senate, which was more concerned about the effects of radical changes in forest policy on southeast Alaska communities. Still, the act mandated several significant changes in forest management and timber contract supervision, designated six wilderness areas and 12 protected roadless areas, and provided for auditing the forest's compliance with the act. At least one legal scholar argues that the U.S. Forest Service (USFS) has failed to live up to either the express requirements or the spirit of the TTRA, and in fact has proposed to increase logging even though timber sales are becoming increasingly unprofitable. [Daugherty 1994]

"Highgrading" is one example of the agency's failure to comply with the TTRA. The statute attempted to eliminate this practice of harvesting a disproportionate amount of high-volume, old-growth timber by requiring that the percentage of high-volume, old-growth timber logged not exceed the percentage of such timber existing in each management area. In its first lawsuit ever, the Wildlife Society, a professional organization of wildlife biologists, claimed that the Tongass was essentially continuing to highgrade old growth by virtue of the method being used to calculate the amount of timber available to cut. Courts generally defer to government agencies in management matters such as this, which require professional expertise and technical judgments, but in this case a federal court held in 1994 that the USFS's method of calculating the amount of high-volume, old-growth timber was arbitrary and capricious. The court agreed with the plaintiff that the agency's calculation of the *volume* of old growth available, based on *acreages* of timber types derived from aerial photos, was inaccurate. Furthermore, the TTRA's harvest provisions are stated in terms of "volume," not area. Thus, the USFS's methods were not only inaccurate but impermissible under the governing law.

Other infractions include the USFS's failure to implement the TTRA's provisions concerning purchaser road credits. According to the Government Accounting Office, this contributed to a loss of more than $64 million on the Tongass in 1992. The USFS also has violated the TTRA requirement that 100-foot vegetated buffers be retained along stream courses to protect water quality. Furthermore, the agency apparently used the TTRA-designated wilderness and protected areas as justification for not proposing any additional wilderness in its recently completed forest plan. (Yet nearly half of all wilderness-qualifying lands on the Tongass received no protection under the TTRA.)

The Alaska congressional delegation is notorious for pressuring the USFS to maintain timber harvest quotas on the Tongass to support the state's timber industry. Senator Ted Stevens, for instance, reportedly required *weekly* reports from the agency during the early 1990s. In August 1997, Republicans asked Congress to disapprove the recently completed Tongass forest plan under a provision in the Small Business Regulatory Enforcement Fairness Act (SBREFA), which permits Congress to review and disapprove major "rules" within 60 days. According to the federal Office of Management and Budget, a forest plan is a "rule." This new Tongass Plan sets an annual sale quantity (ASQ) of 220-267 million board feet of timber over the next ten years (enough to build 20,000 homes per year). Environmentalists say this is more than twice the sustainable harvest level on the forest, and the timber industry and Alaska delegation object that the ASQ is too low. The move under the SBREFA caused speculation—and concern—that Congress could invoke the SBREFA to easily reject any forest plan or resource management plan prepared by the Bureau of Land Management. Under the SBREFA, a congressional vote on a rule is subject to filibuster but not to a presidential veto. Whatever the outcome of this latest skirmish, forest management policies on the Tongass promise to be controversial for the foreseeable future.

See also **Below-Cost Timber Sales; Forest Plan; Old Growth; U.S. Forest Service.**

TRAGEDY OF THE COMMONS An expression coined by Garrett Hardin in a 1968 article by the same name in *Science* magazine. Where land or some other natural resource is freely available to all, every user has an incentive to get all he can before someone else does, leading eventually to overexploitation, waste, and even destruction of the resource. Hardin used a common-use grazing pasture to describe the phenomenon, explaining that each herdsman will continue to add animals to his flock in order to convert the free resource (forage) to his own benefit: Larger flocks mean greater prestige and greater wealth. Because every herdsman has the same idea, the pasture will be overused; overgrazing will result in "erosion and weed dominance." As Hardin put it: "Therein lies the tragedy. Each man is locked into a system that compels him to increase his herd without limit—in a world that is limited."

A similar situation exists in the national parks, Hardin said. The parks are a limited resource, but our population continues to grow. "Plainly,"

Hardin wrote, "we must soon cease to treat the parks as commons or they will be of no value to anyone."

More recently, the theory has been applied to explain the overexploitation of ocean fisheries. As with grazing, individual resource users do not have an incentive to limit catches to sustainable levels because there is no guarantee that other users will follow suit. Without a collective agreement to preserve the common resource or regulations limiting the size of the catch, each user has an incentive to take as much of the available resource as fast as possible. The demise of ocean fisheries threatens to become another common-resource conservation tragedy.

There are options, of course. Using the parks as an example, Hardin suggested various forms of government regulation of use, for example, setting an overall limit on visitation and then allowing visitors on a "first-come, first-served" basis, by a lottery system, or by auctioning off permits. Another alternative is to sell parks to the private sector. Hardin conceded that each option is objectionable, but warned that we would lose the parks as we know and value them unless we amend our management of them.

See also **National Park Service; Privatization.**

TRANSFERABLE DEVELOPMENT RIGHT (TDR) A legal mechanism for compensating a landowner deprived of the right to develop property by conferring development rights applicable to other property or properties. Also referred to as transferable development credits, TDRs have been called "an increasingly important tool" for dealing with land use and conservation issues.

TDRs provide a means of transferring development from a place where it is not desirable to a more acceptable location. The scheme involves designating certain areas for preservation in their current state (farmland, historic districts, or key watershed areas) and other areas that can sustain more intensive (higher density) development. These areas are sometimes called the transferor and transferee zones, respectively. Owners of land in the protected zone, whose rights to develop their land are restricted, are compensated with "credits" that they can sell to owners of land in the designated development zone (or apply to land that they themselves own in that zone). These credits authorize the purchasers to exceed the otherwise applicable density limits on property within the development zone. Examples of TDR schemes include New York City's program for protecting historic landmarks [*see, e.g., Penn Central Transportation Co. v. New York*

(1978)] and a public-private partnership in California designed to prevent development within the Santa Monica Mountains National Recreation Area.

A recent U.S. Supreme Court case involved a TDR system for protecting environmentally sensitive lands in the Lake Tahoe area in western Nevada. [*Suitum v. Tahoe Regional Planning Agency* (1997)] The scheme involves rating the suitability of property for development, denying construction permits to any parcels that do not earn a minimum score, and granting TDRs to owners of such parcels. The Court did not rule on the substantive merits of the scheme, only whether the property owner could, *prior to* attempting to sell the TDRs, challenge the scheme as an uncompensated taking of her private property. In other words, the issue was the ripeness of the plaintiff's claim. The Court decided that she could bring her claim, stating expressly that "we have no occasion to decide, and we do not decide, whether or not these TDRs may be considered in deciding whether there has been a taking in this case." In its 1978 decision in *Penn Central,* the Court decided that the New York landmark law effected no taking and thus it was not necessary to consider whether just compensation as required by the Fifth Amendment had been provided. The Court suggested that TDRs, which the law provided for, might be considered "compensation," had the issue been raised, but at least one commentator states that the *Suitum* decision implies that TDRs are not relevant to the takings issue.

See also **Land Trust; Ripeness; Taking; Zoning.**

TROUT UNLIMITED (TU) A nonprofit, tax-exempt organization, whose mission is to "conserve, protect, and restore North America's coldwater fisheries and their watersheds." Founded in 1959 in Grayling, Michigan, TU has 95,000 members and 455 state and local chapters nationwide. Long considered a leader in efforts to conserve trout and salmon and their habitats, its methods include grassroots organizing, lobbying, monitoring administrative agencies, and educating the public and its members through its magazine, *Trout,* and various reports. Recent state lobbying successes include Montana laws that allow leasing of water rights to provide instream flows and diversion of fishing license revenues into a habitat restoration program.

For the past few years, clean water has been identified as TU's top resource priority. In 1995 the organization was prominent among conservation groups that opposed H.R. 961, the so-called "Dirty Water Bill," which would have weakened many federal water programs, including wetlands protections. TU also fought other antiregulatory measures proposed by the 104th Congress; vigorously opposed the 1995 federal salvage logging law, which allows logging of old-growth timber in key salmon watersheds in the Pacific Northwest; and lobbied in support of reauthorization of the Endangered Species Act of 1973 (ESA).

In the mid-1990s, TU participated actively in the process of renewing Federal Energy Regulatory Commission (FERC) licenses for hydroelectric projects. These private dams are licensed for 30 to 50 years, and relicensing is subject to review under the National Environmental Policy Act (NEPA). TU and other conservationists have taken advantage of the NEPA environmental impact statement (EIS) process to influence the conditions of the renewed permits. Such conditions may include requiring the maintenance of minimum instream flows to protect fish populations or modifying facilities to allow fish passage around the dams. TU efforts led to settlements favorable to fish in more than 12 hydropower licensing cases in 1995 in Maine, Michigan, New York, and New Hampshire. Particularly noteworthy was a 1996 FERC EIS whose preferred alternative was to remove the Clyde River Dam in Vermont. A local TU chapter had been urging removal of the dam, which had eliminated a run of landlocked Atlantic salmon when constructed in 1957. After a portion of the dam was washed out by spring floods in 1994, juvenile salmon were once again seen in the river above the dam. The state of Vermont and certain federal agencies joined TU's campaign, which culminated in FERC's recommendation to remove the dam and restore fish populations. TU hopes to use this decision as a precedent in its efforts to get similar dams removed from the Elwha River in Washington and the Kennebec River in Maine. It is also working with a Washington hydropower utility, several years in advance of the relicensing decisions on two dams on the lower Clark Fork River in Idaho and Montana, to devise plans for protecting bull trout. Its attorney was invited to serve on an interagency panel to advise the congressional Office of Technology Assessment concerning fish passage at hydropower dams.

On other fronts, TU, the U.S. Forest Service (USFS), and the Bureau of Land Management launched in 1993 a joint program, "Bring Back the Natives," for enhancing native fish stocks on private and public lands. In 1995 alone, projects were conducted in 17 watersheds in several states. TU and the USFS have entered into other partnership agreements concerning public land issues, such as the effects of logging on brook trout habitat in West Virginia, the impacts of mining in Nevada on native cutthroat trout, and the effects of grazing on wild and native trout in New Mexico. The organization and the USFS also collaborated on a habitat restoration manual, *Saving a Stream*, in 1995.

When cooperation does not work, TU is willing to litigate, as it did against the USFS in Colorado to prevent the total dewatering of streams by irrigators and municipal water users. It has also gone to court to protect salmon in the Snake and Columbia Rivers: It sued the Northwest Power Planning Council, forcing it to adopt a new salmon restoration plan, and it sued the National Marine Fisheries Service to compel it to comply with the ESA. TU also participated as *amicus curiae* (friend of the court) in the landmark Supreme Court case *Babbitt v. Sweet Home Chapter of Communities for a Great Oregon* (1995).

In addition, TU engages in fisheries research. In 1996 it released a national assessment of whirling disease, a disease that infects hatchery fish and threatens native trout populations in several states. It has also studied agricultural nonpoint source pollution, acid mine drainage, restoration of Pacific salmon stocks, and instream flow needs on several rivers.

TU's work is financed by member dues, private donations, and foundation grants. Program services in 1995 were about $3.5 million, approximately 80 percent of total expenditures.

See also **Anadromous Fish.**

UDALL, STEWART Secretary of the Interior from 1962 to 1969 under Presidents John F. Kennedy and Lyndon B. Johnson. Udall served longer than any Interior secretary except Harold Ickes (under Franklin D. Roosevelt). Udall was elected to Congress in 1954 and served on the House Interior and Insular Affairs Committee. He is the author of *The Quiet Crisis* (1963) and its sequel, *The Quiet Crisis and the Next Generation* (1988).

Udall has been described as the "nation's last great secretary of Interior" and has received awards from national conservation organizations. During his tenure at Interior, nearly 4 million acres were added to the national park system and several important statutes were passed for which he deserves significant credit, including the Land and Water Conservation Act of 1964, the Wilderness Act of 1964, the 1966 Endangered Species Preservation Act, the Wild and Scenic Rivers Act of 1968, and the National Trails System Act of 1968. He was largely responsible for the creation of the Bureau of Outdoor Recreation, and his and First Lady "Lady Bird" Johnson's efforts led to passage of the Highway Beautification Act.

Udall has been a tireless campaigner for reform of federal mining law. As Interior secretary, between 1966 and 1968 he suspended the issuance of mineral patents in Alaska and then withdrew nearly all unreserved federal lands from entry or disposal. This action was designed to protect public lands in Alaska pending the resolution of state and native claims to the lands. Eventually, millions of acres of federal lands in the state were placed into one or more of the federal preservation systems by the Alaska National Interest Lands Conservation Act of 1980. Also in 1968 he withdrew 3 million acres in Colorado, Wyoming, and Utah from entry under the General Mining Law of 1872 (an action upheld by a federal court), and in the early 1960s he attempted to end the practice of patenting oil shale claims made under the same law by challenging all such claims. (Oil shale was made subject to leasing in 1920, but claims made prior to that date, under the 1872 hardrock law, were still potentially valid.) In 1988, Udall cofounded the Mineral Policy Center, an influential nonprofit organization dedicated to reforming federal mining law, on whose board he still serves. He also serves as a director of the Grand Canyon Trust. His brother Morris (Mo) Udall also served as congressman from Arizona and chaired the House Interior Committee.

See also **Land and Water Conservation Fund; Mineral Policy Center; Mining Law Reform.**

U.S. FISH AND WILDLIFE SERVICE (USFWS) An agency within the U.S. Department of the Interior that oversees the National Wildlife Refuge System, administers fish and wildlife research and habitat conservation activities, manages migratory bird hunting and conservation activities, and implements and enforces the Endangered Species Act of 1973 (ESA). The agency manages more than 91 million acres of land, including nearly 500 national wildlife refuges, 84 fish hatcheries, 111 research and field stations, and 75 wilderness areas (totaling nearly 21 million acres); it has more than 7,500 employees. The USFWS is responsible for consulting with the U.S. Army Corps of Engineers and the U.S. Environmental Protection Agency in dredge-and-fill permit decisions under Clean Water Act section 404, consulting with all federal agencies pursuant to the ESA, and providing comments on water projects under the Fish and Wildlife Coordination Act. The USFWS shares responsibility for anadromous fish conservation with the National Marine Fisheries Service in the Department of Commerce.

From 1993 to 1996, the USFWS was directed by Mollie Beattie, a forester by education and a former Forests, Parks, and Recreation commissioner for the state of Vermont. The first woman to serve as USFWS director, Beattie was appointed by President Bill Clinton. During her short tenure, Beattie was instrumental in the reintroduction of wolves to Idaho and Yellowstone National Park, the designation of 15 new national wildlife refuges, and the Clinton administration's habitat conservation planning activities. She died of brain cancer in 1996, and was succeeded in 1997 by another woman (also appointed by President Clinton), Jamie Rappaport Clark, former assistant director for ecological services at the USFWS. Clark holds a master's degree in wildlife biology and has extensive experience with the USFWS and other federal agencies on wetlands, fish and wildlife and land-use management, and recovery of natural resources.

See also **Anadromous Fish; Department of the Interior; Endangered Species Act of 1973; Habitat Conservation Plan; Listing; National Wildlife Refuge System; Wetland.**

🏛 U.S. FOREST SERVICE (USFS)

The nation's oldest and largest (35,000 employees) land management agency, established in 1905, responsible for managing approximately 140 million acres of national forests and 51 million acres of national grasslands. Its land holdings are second only to those of the Bureau of Land Management (BLM). The USFS is an agency within the U.S. Department of Agriculture.

Agency History and Personality

The nation's forestry program was initially housed in the Department of the Interior. Gifford Pinchot, the first USFS chief, was successful in getting it transferred to the Department of Agriculture. Occasionally over the years campaigns have been mounted to either move the agency to Interior or combine its functions with the BLM's in a new federal natural resources agency. The only such scheme to even get off the ground was President Ronald Reagan's proposed reorganization in 1984, in which the USFS and BLM would exchange certain lands in the western states; however, only a few areas under BLM control were ultimately transferred to the USFS.

Long noted for its professionalism and esprit de corps (due in large measure to the efforts and persona of Chief Pinchot), the agency has come under increasing scrutiny and criticism in recent years for overemphasizing commodity production, especially timber, and giving short shrift to other resources, including wildlife, recreation, and wilderness. Even Pinchot, the United States's first professionally trained forester, warned against what he called "lumbermanitis"—capture of the USFS by the timber companies that the agency was supposed to regulate. In the 1980s, discord within the agency's own ranks over this and other issues led to the formation of Forest Service Employees for Environmental Ethics.

Most observers agree that the policy attitudes of USFS officials have evolved significantly in the past 10 to 15 years, especially with regard to logging. Indeed, the appointment in 1993 of wildlife biologist Jack Ward Thomas as chief—he was the first nonforester ever to hold the position—itself signaled a change in the agency. (In 1997, Thomas was succeeded by former USFS fishery biologist Michael Dombeck.) In June 1994, USFS officials and scholars from a variety of disciplines met—fittingly, at Pinchot's former home—to discuss current efforts to "reinvent" the Forest Service. (All federal agencies undertook some sort of self-evaluation as part of President Clinton and Vice President Al Gore's "reinventing government" initiative.)

Although the agency encouraged recreational use of the national forests even in the 1920s, and some agency officials (notably Aldo Leopold and

Robert Marshall) called for preserving wilderness as early as the 1920s and 1930s, producing trees has long been considered the Forest Service's main business. A recent survey of USFS employees revealed that more than 60 percent believe that timber is the agency's most important objective. In a break from tradition, however, only 15 to 20 percent of these same employees think that timber *ought to be* the most important, and more than 70 percent of all employees surveyed believe that noncommodity uses (water, recreation, wildlife, and fish) should be more important uses of national forests. When asked to recommend the most important management change the agency should make, the following three responses occurred most frequently: (1) continue the trend toward emphasizing noncommodity, rather than commodity, uses; (2) continue to increase efforts to involve the public and respond to public needs; and (3) continue the agency's enhanced emphasis on ecology and environmental concerns. According to survey respondents, several factors frustrate agency attempts to reform itself, including increasing political pressure on the agency, interference from Congress and interest groups, loss of public support, inadequate funding, and job-related stress.

Shortly after Mike Dombeck took over as chief in 1997, a group of 170 USFS biologists and botanists from 30 national forests signed a letter to Dombeck, cautioning him that "many forests now find their fish, wildlife and botany programs in substantial trouble and facing serious problems." The group lamented recent budget cuts—cuts disproportionately directed toward their programs—warning that these funding reductions jeopardize the agency's conservation mission.

Agency Structure and Mission

The USFS is organized hierarchically. Its headquarters are in Washington, D.C., and the agency is organized into ten regions, each of which is headed by a regional forester and covers several national forests in one or more states. For instance, the Rocky Mountain Region (Region 2) encompasses Colorado, New Mexico, part of Wyoming, South Dakota, and Nebraska, while Region 9 covers all national forests in states east of the Mississippi River. The western regions, 1 through 6, consist of 44 forests. Within regions, individual national forests are administered by a forest supervisor; each forest is further subdivided into ranger districts headed by district rangers. Efforts to cut costs and improve efficiency in recent years have resulted in combining some forests so that two, or occasionally more, are managed out of a single supervisor's office. In addition, the USFS operates seven forest and range experiment stations, a forest products laboratory, and divisions that provide forestry assistance to states and nonindustrial private foresters as well as international assistance.

About one in 35 Forest Service employees is a line officer, that is, one having policy-making authority. Line officers include the chief, associate chief, deputy chiefs, regional foresters, deputy regional foresters, forest supervisors, deputy forest supervisors, and district rangers. Unlike other public land management agency heads, the USFS chief is not subject to Senate confirmation. However, a bill introduced recently by conservative Congresswoman Helen Chenoweth (R-ID), an outspoken critic of federal land policy, would change that. USFS staff employees include specialists and technicians in the various disciplines or resource categories, such as foresters, wildlife biologists, recreation and wilderness specialists, archaeologists, and range conservationists; operational employees, such as engineers and landscape architects; and those in personnel and clerical positions.

The USFS is a multiple-use land management agency governed by several statutes, notably the Organic Act of 1897, National Forest Management Act of 1976, Multiple-Use, Sustained-Yield Act of 1960, Federal Land Policy and Management Act, Forest and Rangeland Renewable Resources Planning Act (RPA), Wilderness Act of 1964, National Environmental Policy Act, and Endangered Species Act of 1973. In general, national forests are managed for multiple uses: outdoor recreation, grazing, timber, watershed, and wildlife and fish. Grazing occurs on more than 97 million acres of the 191 million managed by the agency; the only use more widespread is recreation.

Mineral development also occurs on forest lands. The USFS is responsible for ensuring that surface resources are protected, while the BLM regulates disposition of the minerals themselves: hardrock metals, oil and gas, coal, etc. The uses of specific areas, however—for instance, wilderness areas, research natural areas (a designation accorded certain areas possessing natural values or characteristics that are deemed worthy of special protection), or wild and scenic rivers—may be more restricted. The USFS manages 398 units (34.6 million acres) within the National Wilderness Preservation System, as well as 14 million acres of wetlands and riparian areas.

The Forest Service in the Courts

The first injunctions issued against the USFS occurred in the early 1970s, when federal courts forbade the agency from pursuing logging and road-building activities that would threaten the wilderness suitability of a Colorado roadless area and ordered it to stop illegal clear-cutting practices in West Virginia. Since then, the agency has been sued frequently by plaintiffs challenging environmental impact statements or forest plans, logging and road-building projects, grazing decisions, and other land-use proposals. Many of these suits were at least partially successful. Clear-cutting remains controversial, although the agency reports that it is shifting from its reliance on clear-cutting to more selective cutting methods. Clear-cut acreages decreased by 18 percent from 1992 to 1993. Today, lawsuits against the agency often involve claims under the Endangered Species Act of 1973 and the National Environmental Policy Act.

Future Directions

The agency's 1990 Strategic Plan (a long-term planning document required by the RPA and prepared every ten years) focuses on enhancing recreation and fish/wildlife resources, making commodity production environmentally acceptable, advancing scientific knowledge, and responding to global resource needs. Among the most important issues facing the agency, according to this plan, are clear-cutting, below-cost timber sales, old-growth logging, loss of biological diversity, effects of management actions on riparian areas, loss of threatened and endangered species, threats to wilderness areas, meeting recreational needs, and the condition of forest rangelands. In a draft of its *1995 Program for Forest and Rangelands Resource: A Long-Term Strategic Plan* (released in 1995), the agency adopted four goals: protect ecosystems, restore degraded ecosystems, provide multiple benefits within the sustainable capacities of ecosystems, and ensure the effectiveness of the organization.

The USFS and the BLM, both landlords of large holdings in the western United States, are often criticized for their efforts to implement the federal land laws. In recent years such criticism has taken the form of bombings and other terroristlike tactics, as well as less violent, but equally illegal conduct (e.g., unpermitted road construction in wilderness study areas and fencing of public land springs). Yet, at the same time, the agencies are also involved in many cooperative management ventures with private landowners, public land users, and other citizens. Which approach will eventually hold sway is yet to be seen.

See also **Below-Cost Timber Sales; Bureau of Land Management; Clearcutting; Department of Agriculture; Dombeck, Michael; Ecosystem Man-**

agement; Federal Land Policy and Management Act; Forest Plan; Multiple-Use, Sustained-Yield Act of 1960; National Forest Management Act of 1976; Old Growth; Organic Act of 1897; Thomas, Jack Ward; *United States v. New Mexico* (1978); Wise Use Movement.

UNITED STATES V. FULLER (1973)   An important U.S. Supreme Court decision concerning public land grazing and the value of a federal grazing permit. The case involved the condemnation by the federal government of a portion of ranchers' privately owned lands. The Fullers claimed that their permit to graze cattle on the nearby public lands made their own land more valuable than it would otherwise be; that is, used in conjunction with public land, their private lands could support more cattle. They argued that the government was required by the Fifth Amendment to the U.S. Constitution to compensate them for the portion of the land's value attributable to the federal grazing permit.

The ranchers conceded that, under the express terms of the Taylor Grazing Act, they had no private property interest in the public lands themselves. (The Taylor Act states that the issuance of a grazing permit does "not create any right, title, interest, or estate in or to the [federal] lands.") They claimed, however, that they *did* have a compensable interest in the enhanced value of their own private ranch lands that resulted from being able to use them in conjunction with their "permit lands."

A divided Court (5-4) rejected this argument. The majority held that, even though a buyer on the open market would pay more for the Fullers' property because of the federal grazing privileges attached to it, the government was not required to compensate the Fullers for this element of the land's value. The Court reasoned that "the Government as condemnor may not be required to compensate a condemnee for elements of value that the Government has created, or that it might have destroyed under the exercise of governmental authority other than the power of [condemnation]." By the latter, the Court was referring to the government's authority under the Taylor Act to revoke or terminate federal grazing privileges without paying compensation.

The Court explained that the result would be different in cases of condemnation of private property located near completed public works projects, such as a reservoir or highway, or near public lands open to the public at large. In these cases, as in *Fuller*, the lands are worth more because of their location, but, in contrast to *Fuller*, the element of value is not "revocable"—at least not in the same way as in the Fullers' situation. (The dissenters seemed not to understand this distinction, arguing that location value had always been considered in determining the fair market value of property value for purposes of compensation.) As the Court put it, given that Congress clearly intended permit holders to have no compensable property interest in federal grazing lands, it "would be unusual" if Congress "turned around and authorized compensation for the value added to [private] lands by their potential use in connection with permit lands."

Until such time as the Taylor Grazing Act and the Federal Land Policy and Management Act are amended to change federal grazing law, they and *Fuller* make clear that federal grazing permits create no compensable property interest in the permit itself, the permitted public grazing lands, or the value added to private ranch lands.

See also **Federal Land Policy and Management Act; Range Reform; Sagebrush Rebellion; Taking; Taylor Grazing Act.**

UNITED STATES V. LOCKE (1985)   A U.S. Supreme Court decision interpreting a Federal Land Policy and Management Act (FLPMA) requirement that hardrock miners file an annual notice with the Bureau of Land Management, "prior to December 31," of their intention to hold their mining claims. The Court held (by a vote of 6-3) that failure to meet the filing deadline, even by one day (as in the Lockes' case), works an *automatic forfeiture* of the miner's interest in his claim, without regard to whether he intended to abandon his claim.

The Court recounted the background of, and need for, the FLPMA filing requirement. Millions of mining claims had been staked on the public lands since the mid-1800s—many speculative, some entirely fraudulent—yet the federal government had no record of these claims nor any way of ascertaining their status. Even though the U.S. government retains the paramount interest in federal lands claimed by miners, including "substantial regulatory power over [the miner's] interests," the holders of valid mining claims possess a property interest in the minerals within their claims. The Court called this interest a "unique form of property." Thus, the millions of mining claims "clouded" the government's title to federal lands and interfered, at least potentially, with its ability to manage the lands for other uses.

The Court concluded that FLPMA's notice requirement was a reasonable response to the problem of outstanding claims, even though the statute acted retroactively, affecting rights established prior to FLPMA's passage in 1976. The filing requirement imposed a minimal burden on claim holders, the Court said, and they could protect their property interest simply by giving the required annual notice. Automatic forfeiture was not an unreasonable penalty for failing to file as required. Requiring the government to prove that a miner *intended* to abandon his claim before the claim could be forfeited would simply perpetuate the problem FLPMA was intended to resolve—millions of claims of unknown status on the public lands and no means of determining their viability. Although the Lockes lost their mining claims (worth millions of dollars) as a result of filing a day late, it had been within their power to avoid that result by following the law; the Court suggested that the Lockes should have sought better advice, perhaps from an attorney, or at least filed early. The law did not violate the Lockes' right to due process under the Constitution, nor did it take their property in contravention of the Fifth Amendment's requirement of just compensation.

Congress subsequently passed a private bill that restored the Lockes' claim, but it has not amended the FLPMA filing requirement. Public lands law scholar George Cameron Coggins has described *Locke*'s importance thus: "*Locke* expressly and implicitly recognizes that new public priorities demand new approaches, procedural as well as substantive. *Locke* sets the stage for modernization of obsolete laws governing allocation of public resources, 'vested rights' not withstanding." Although efforts to enact more substantive reforms of hardrock mining law have thus far failed, *Locke* lays to rest any doubt that Congress possesses the necessary authority—it need only muster the political will.

See also **Mining Law Reform; Multiple Use; Taking.**

UNITED STATES V. NEW MEXICO (1978)   An important federal reserved water rights decision. In this U.S. Supreme Court case, the U.S. Forest Service (USFS) argued that reservation of the Gila National Forest (in 1899) had impliedly reserved rights in the Rio Mimbres sufficient to maintain minimum stream flows for fish and wildlife and support aesthetic, recreational, and stock-watering purposes. By a 5-4 vote, however, the Court rejected the federal government's position. The Court held that the 1897 Organic Act reflected Congress's intent that national forests be reserved for only two purposes: "securing favorable conditions of water flows, and to furnish a continuous supply of timber."

Because the reserved water rights doctrine encompasses only the minimum amount of water necessary to satisfy the *primary* purposes of a reservation, the Court held, water is reserved when a national forest is established "only where necessary to preserve the timber or to secure favorable water flows for private and public uses under state laws." According to the Court, the act does not authorize the reservation of forests for aesthetic, recreational, or wildlife preservation purposes; hence, no water is reserved for these uses.

In a portion of the opinion considered dicta by the dissenters, the Court opined that the 1960 Multiple-Use, Sustained-Yield Act "was intended to broaden the purposes for which the national forests had been administered." But according to the majority, this statute established *secondary* purposes for the forests and thus did not expand the federal government's reserved water rights.

The dissenters criticized the majority for its narrow reading of the Organic Act, arguing that the act's language clearly embraces a third primary purpose, that is, "to improve and protect the forest." According to the dissent, forests consist not only of the trees that supply timber, but of all other plant species and the animals that inhabit the forest. For this reason, the federal government should have been entitled to a reserved water right sufficient to "sustain the wildlife of the forests, as well as the plants."

The Court did not define the statutory purpose, "securing favorable conditions of water flows," nor did it suggest how to quantify the water right that attaches to this purpose of a forest reservation. One state court has suggested that the water right might be quantified in terms of channel maintenance—the range of flows needed to maintain an efficient stream channel. The court pointed out that these flows can be determined scientifically, according to principles of fluvial geomorphology. [*United States v. Jesse* (1987)]

Most commentators view *United States v. New Mexico* as a very narrow view of the reserved water rights doctrine and of the purposes for which national forests were reserved. The USFS is not limited to the reserved rights doctrine to obtain water needed for administering the forests, however. The federal government may condemn water rights, acquire them as would any other applicant under state water law, or employ other mechanisms, such as exchanges or cooperative agreements with water rights holders. Federal agencies have not shown much activism in asserting reserved water rights, however, or in otherwise attempting to secure water rights to serve forest purposes.

See also **Multiple-Use, Sustained-Yield Act of 1960; Reserved Rights Doctrine; Watershed.**

🏛 UNITED STATES V. RIVERSIDE BAYVIEW HOMES, INC. (1985)

(1985) A significant U.S. Supreme Court decision concerning federal power to protect wetlands. Regulations of the U.S. Army Corps of Engineers (Corps) and the Environmental Protection Agency define broadly the federal Clean Water Act (CWA) term "waters of the United States" to include *virtually all* bodies of water, even seasonal and some man-made waters, as well as wetlands and wetlands adjacent to other waters. The regulations define a wetland as any area flooded or saturated with sufficient frequency to sustain "vegetation typically adapted for life in saturated soil conditions." These rules help define the scope of the Corps's authority to require CWA section 404 permits for discharges of dredged or fill material to wetlands.

The plaintiff developer in *Riverside Bayview Homes* challenged the Corps's authority to require a 404 permit to fill a wetland, but the Court easily upheld the Corps rules. The Court found that the Corps's interpretation of "waters of the United States" was supported by the language of the CWA itself and its purposes, and by the act's legislative history. In particular, the Court seemed persuaded by the need to protect waters at their source in order to achieve the CWA purpose of restoring and maintaining water quality. The Court discussed the ecological importance of wetlands in serving this purpose, and further noted that, in later amending the statute, Congress itself indicated approval of the Corps regulations by rejecting proposals to change the definition of "waters" legislatively.

The wetland at issue in *Riverside Bayview Homes* was adjacent to a perennial stream; thus, the Court was not required to decide whether "isolated wetlands" (those not adjacent to a stream or other "water of the United States") are also within the Corps's regulatory jurisdiction. This was an issue, at least implicitly, in *Hoffman Homes, Inc. v. Environmental Protection Agency* (1993). In *Hoffman Homes* the Seventh Circuit ruled that the Corps's (i.e., federal) jurisdiction encompasses *any* water that has a sufficient connection with interstate commerce.

See also **Clean Water Act Section 404; Corps of Engineers; Dredge and Fill;** *Hoffman Homes, Inc. v. Environmental Protection Agency* **(1993); Navigable Waters; Wetland.**

WALD, JOHANNA Senior attorney with the Natural Resources Defense Council (NRDC). Wald has worked for NRDC for more than 20 years. She represented the group in a landmark case in which the court ruled that the Bureau of Land Management must prepare environmental impact statements, as required by the National Environmental Policy Act, on all public land grazing decisions. [*Natural Resources Defense Council v. Morton* (1974)] She also represented *amici curiae* (friends of the court) in *Robertson v. Methow Valley Citizens Council* (1989).

Wald is a Pew Scholar in Conservation and the Environment. She writes and speaks widely on public land issues, particularly government subsidies and rangeland management concerns. While applauding the Clinton administration's early rangeland reform efforts, she contended the reforms did not go far enough. In her view, grazing of public lands should not be a foregone conclusion; grazing of some lands is simply inappropriate or is much less valuable than other uses, and Americans generally do not support subsidized public land ranching. She argues that protection of the land itself, not the private "interests that recklessly exploit it," should drive public land policy. Wald has advocated (sometimes jointly with Karl Hess of the conservative Cato Institute) terminating the "obsolete" federal subsidies to logging, mining, and grazing interests on the public lands; subjecting public-land ranching to market standards; and replacing the federal grazing preference system with competitive bidding for permits to federal forage, which would allow the recipient to either graze the land or implement conservation measures to protect it. She opposes privatization or local control of federal public land resources, pointing to the degraded condition of many private rangelands to support her concern about the likely effects on the environment.

See also **Natural Resources Defense Council.**

WASTE A term that connotes squandering of a resource, whose precise meaning depends on the context. Waste of several natural resources may be restricted by law. For instance, many western states prohibit the waste of water, and may impose specific requirements (such as lining or covering water delivery canals and ditches) designed to prevent waste. Oil and gas leases contain "conservation" conditions aimed at reducing production-related losses of minerals. State game and fish laws ordinarily prohibit the "waste of meat" to ensure against hunters harvesting animals solely for their head, hide, or other trophy body parts.

WATERSHED   A drainage area; a geographic area defined by topographic boundaries whose precipitation runoff is distinct from runoff from other, adjacent watersheds. "Watershed" is a geographic, ecological, and land-use management concept of increasing importance. Watersheds may be aggregated or subdivided; that is, the drainage area of a tributary stream may be considered separately from, or combined with, that of the larger stream it feeds. For instance, the Mississippi River watershed extends from Minnesota to the Gulf Coast and includes the drainages of all tributary streams, such as the Missouri. The Chesapeake Bay Watershed encompasses portions of five states and hundreds of rivers and streams.

Watershed also refers to the ability of land to absorb, filter, and regulate the runoff of precipitation. Watershed is one of the multiple uses of public lands. It is listed in the Multiple-Use, Sustained-Yield Act of 1960; Federal Land Policy and Management Act; and National Forest Management Act of 1976.

Geographic watersheds, especially larger or aggregated ones, often can be distinguished on the basis of their vegetation patterns, certain animal populations, soils, meteorology, and other biotic and physical factors. For these reasons, land and resource management agencies increasingly recognize that watersheds often describe more appropriate management units than do areas delineated by political boundaries, such as counties, national parks, or national forests.

The U.S. Environmental Protection Agency (EPA) cited protection of watersheds as one of its top regulatory priorities for 1997. The EPA has established a National Watershed Assessment Program, a partnership effort to evaluate the health of some 2,150 watersheds in the United States and begin the process of restoration. The approach's strength, the EPA believes, is in relying on teams of local stakeholders to make decisions about their watersheds. The agency concedes, however, that this approach to problem solving will require institutional and sometimes cultural changes.

The EPA also is developing a watershed approach to fulfilling its obligations under the Clean Water Act (CWA). Section 319 of the CWA expressly urges states to adopt a watershed approach for remedying problems of nonpoint source pollution. The EPA recognizes that a watershed approach will be required to carry out the total maximum daily load assessments required by CWA section 303. Deciding how much pollution a water body can tolerate, the sources of pollution that potentially impact it, and the best means of restoring degraded waters will obviously necessitate consideration of all sources within the respective watershed area.

The EPA publishes a quarterly newsletter, *Watershed Events*, in which it reports watershed-related activities and developments around the country and advertises publications, conferences, and other sources of information (increasingly abundant) for the public, agency professionals, scientists, and land managers.

A 1997 report by the Trust for Public Lands (TPL) urged protection of watersheds as a more effective and cost-efficient means of protecting public drinking water supplies. The group estimated, for instance, that New York City could save up to $8 billion in water treatment facility construction costs, plus $300 million in annual operating costs, by a one-time investment of $1.5 billion to conserve its watershed. Protecting watersheds offers the added benefits of conserving wildlife habitat and affording recreation opportunities. Protection of the Sterling Forest, a crucial part of New Jersey's watershed, is also conserving 15,000 acres of mature forest. The TPL advised purchase and ownership by the city or water supplier as the most effective way to provide long-term watershed protection.

Both private landowners and public agencies are beginning to adopt management strategies—for managing timber and grazing activities, regulating recreational use, and conserving soil and water quality—that are based on watershed boundaries. The success of such approaches depends on partnership agreements, memoranda of understanding, and other cooperative means, given that watersheds nearly always cross jurisdictional and ownership boundaries. The Chesapeake Bay, which supports one of the most productive and valuable estuarine fisheries in the world, is often cited as an example. Efforts in recent years to check pollution by agricultural runoff and treated sewage have begun to pay off, but many other threats to the bay remain, including urban runoff and sprawl. More than 90,000 acres of open space within the Chesapeake watershed are lost annually, and pollution in runoff from these developed lands is five to seven times higher than from forested land. Any effort to restore and protect estuarine resources that fails to account for all sources of impacts is doomed to fail.

See also **Ecosystem Management; Partnerships;** *United States v. New Mexico* **(1978).**

WETLAND An ecological community that performs critical ecological functions, including water purification and water storage (for flood control), and provides valuable wildlife and fish habitat. Wetlands also offer recreation opportunities, produce food and timber, and provide open space and venues for scientific research. More than half of the United States's original wetlands have been drained, converted to other uses, or otherwise destroyed. An estimated 220 million acres existed when Europeans first arrived in the continental United States; by 1980 that number had been reduced to 104 million. An estimated 100.9 million acres remain today. About 80 percent of all coastal wetlands lost were in Louisiana. In contrast, very little of Alaska's extensive wetlands have been lost. Wetlands were being destroyed in the 1970s at a rate of 500,000 acres annually, and despite an official federal regulatory policy of "no net loss of wetlands," wetlands continue to be destroyed. Estimates of the current rate of loss range from 80,000 to 135,000 acres or more of nonfederal wetlands per year, depending on the source and whether "restored" wetlands are considered. Most losses (about 80 percent) are agriculture-related.

In recent years, the value of wetlands has become more widely recognized and better understood, resulting in a proliferation of federal, state, local, and private protection programs. Several federal agencies, including the U.S. Army Corps of Engineers (Corps) and the Natural Resources Conservation Service (NRCS), are charged with implementing federal wetland programs. For instance, the Corps administers the Clean Water Act section 404 permitting program; the NRCS oversees Swampbuster and, in cooperation with the Farm Service Agency, the Wetlands Reserve Program; and the U.S. Fish and Wildlife Service (USFWS) administers the North American Wetland Conservation Fund and Partners in Wildlife program. Available evidence suggests that these efforts may be paying off. However, as development interests have come to understand that wetland protection programs, such as Clean Water Act section 404 and Swampbuster, are here to stay, they have redoubled their efforts to narrow the regulatory definition of "wetland."

Delineating Wetlands

Even those who recognize the importance of protecting wetlands find it difficult to agree on a definition. Wetlands scientists and wetlands regulators have different goals, which are reflected in their divergent definitions. Scientists view wetlands as intermediate zones between aquatic and terrestrial ecosystems. Because wetlands exhibit attributes of both systems, they provide unique habitats for plants and wildlife. The dynamic nature of wetlands further complicates their definition. Cyclical changes in the hydrology of wetlands may render them wetter during some periods and dry during others. Available evidence suggests that hydrology is the key component in any wetland. The hydrology of a wetland leads to the formation of hydric soils and the presence of hydrophytic plants (plants adapted to life in soils that are often saturated). Simply put, too little water may render a wetland an upland, while too much water may convert it into a lake, pond, or other purely aquatic ecosystem.

The most widely accepted scientific definition for wetlands, known as the Cowardin definition, was developed by an interdisciplinary team of biologists, ecologists, and geologists: Wetlands are lands transitional between terrestrial and aquatic systems where the water table is usually at or near the surface, or the land is covered by shallow water. Wetlands must have one or more of the following three attributes: (1) at least periodically, the land supports predominantly hydrophytes; (2) the substrate is predominantly undrained hydric soil; and (3) the substrate is nonsoil and is saturated with water or covered by shallow water at some time during the growing season each year. The goal of the scientists who developed this definition was to identify a particular habitat type.

By contrast, the Corps defines "wetlands," for regulatory purposes, as follows:

> Those areas that are inundated or saturated by surface or ground water at a frequency and duration sufficient to support, and that under normal circumstances do support, a prevalence of vegetation typically adapted for life in saturated soil conditions. Wetlands generally include swamps, marshes, bogs, and similar areas.

This definition is used by the Corps and the NRCS in identifying areas that are subject to regulation under Clean Water Act section 404 or Swampbuster. (NRCS is responsible for agricultural wetland determinations.) The scientific definition recognizes the indefinite nature of habitat delineation by using words such as "predominantly" and "periodically." The regulatory definition requires sufficient water to support the appropriate plants in saturated soil, and all three factors—hydrology, soils, and vegetation—must be present. However, the term "under normal conditions" affords the regulatory agencies some discretion in identifying wetlands.

Agencies charged with wetland regulatory responsibilities have developed procedures for delineating wetlands. Initially, each agency had its own manual, with slightly different definitions and delineation procedures, to be used by its field staff in identifying wetlands. As a result, an area that constituted a wetland for purposes of Swampbuster might not have been a wetland under the Migratory Bird Conservation Act. In an effort to resolve these inconsistencies, the Corps, Environmental Protection Agency, the USFWS, and the NRCS (then, the Soil Conservation Service) developed a joint delineation manual. The 1989 Joint Manual has been a focus of controversy within the executive branch and Congress and among the public because it was seen as expanding the regulatory definition of wetlands. Largely due to objections from the oil and home-building industries, this document was subsequently withdrawn, as were the Bush administration's 1991 revisions to the 1989 Joint Manual. In 1993 all agencies with wetland regulatory authority were directed to use only the 1987 Corps manual to delineate wetlands.

Consistent with the regulatory definition quoted above, the 1987 Corps manual requires field staff to examine an area for hydric soils, hydrology, and hydrophytic vegetation. Most disagreements over wetlands identification revolve around hydrology and vegetation characteristics. (Hydric soils may remain long after all other wetland indicators have disappeared, making them a less useful identifying factor.) The 1987 manual states that an area exhibits wetland hydrology if plants are saturated in major portions of the root zone (usually within 12 inches of the surface) during the growing season. The withdrawn 1989 manual designated as wetlands any areas whose soils within 6 to 18 inches of the surface were inundated or saturated for seven consecutive days. In other words, a site could lack wetlands hydrology for 51 weeks per year and still be regulated as a wetland.

With respect to vegetation, the 1987 manual relies on the percentage of "obligate" species (plants that survive only in wetlands), "facultative wetland" species (plants that usually occur in a wetland), and "facultative" species (plants that have an equivalent likelihood of occurring in a wetland or an upland setting). If 50 percent or more of the vegetation in an area is in one or more of these three categories, the area is designated a wetland.

Assessing Wetland Values

After the withdrawal of the 1991 manual revisions, Congress directed the National Research Council, an arm of the prestigious National Academy of Sciences (NAS), to study methods for delineating and characterizing wetlands. The NAS concluded that current regulatory efforts were scientifically sound and effective in most respects. Nevertheless, the group recommended changes directed at making wetlands determinations more uniform, credible, and accurate in a technical and scientific sense. Specifically, it concluded that a definition more closely resembling the Cowardin definition would lead to more accurate and scientifically defensible wetlands identification.

A significant conclusion of the NAS report was that no single system can accurately compare wetland functions and values. Agencies have long sought a comparison tool to help them decide which wetlands could be developed without real loss to the wetlands community and which should be protected or restored because of their ecological value. The relative value of wetlands is an issue in current congressional efforts to both reauthorize the Clean Water Act and pass a wetlands mitigation banking bill. Meanwhile, the Corps is in the midst of a staged process to develop the hydrogeomorphic approach (HGM) to assessing wetlands. According to the Corps, which formally announced the new approach (a "technical tool" that does not set policy) in mid-1997, HGM takes into account regional differences in wetland functions. Three factors are considered: the wetland's location in the landscape, the source of its water, and water flow and variation within the wetland. HGM is said to offer benefits for assessing the environmental impact of projects in wetlands and predicting the kind and amount of mitigation required. Full development of the approach is expected to take several years; the agency is currently developing regional models and guidebooks for using the method. Eventually, several federal agencies, including the Corps, EPA, USFWS, and NRCS, will use the new tool.

Reflecting both the increasing attention being given to wetlands and the ongoing controversy over identifying these important habitats, the U.S. Geological Survey published in 1997 a comprehensive *National Water Summary on Wetland Resources*. The book addresses technical aspects of wetland delineation, assessment, management, and restoration; wetland legislation; and the history of wetlands in the United States. In addition, the Environmental Law Institute maintains an electronic information service covering wetlands law, policy issues, science, and management. [To subscribe, send an e-mail message to majordomo@ige.org. The message should read: "subscribe eli-wetlands<*your e-mail address*>," or call (202) 939-3248.]

Wetland Conservation Programs

The two principal federal wetland conservation programs are the Wetlands Reserve Program (WRP), a 1990 expansion of the Conservation Reserve Program, and Swampbuster, established by the 1985 Farm Bill and amended by the 1990 and 1996 Farm Bills. WRP eligibility was initially limited to nine states, but has since been expanded. The U.S. Department of Agriculture is authorized to purchase easements from, or enter into cost-sharing agreements with, eligible landowners who agree to restore converted wetlands. Since its inception, 412,000 acres have been enrolled in the program. Many easements and agreements are now funded by nonfederal dollars, through partnerships and other arrangements. These acres are exempt from statutory acreage limitations. Under Swampbuster, farmers who convert wetlands to agricultural production lose eligibility for various farm program payments and benefits. The 1996 Farm Bill amended this program to provide the NRCS with greater enforcement flexibility. A goal of these programs is to help achieve the national goal of no net loss of wetlands. Many other federal, state, and private conservation efforts target wetlands. For instance, the USFWS reported in 1995 that it was restoring 300,000 acres of wetlands under 14,000 agreements with the private owners of these lands.

Both the Clean Water Act section 404 and Swampbuster programs provide for mitigating impacts to wetlands and restoring or creating wetlands to help achieve the federal "no net loss" policy. Whether it is actually possible to create wetlands that function ecologically as natural wetlands, however, is an important scientific and policy issue.

Property Rights

Nearly 75 percent of the remaining U.S. wetlands occur on private property. The section 404 program, which (with certain exceptions) prevents development of wetlands without a permit, gives rise to the concern that government regulation is taking private property for a public purpose without compensation. This concern plays an important role in the wetland delineation controversy, congressional debates over reauthorization of the Clean Water Act and passage of a comprehensive federal wetlands law, and court cases challenging the denial of section 404 permits.

See also **Clean Water Act Section 404; Conservation Reserve Program; Corps of Engineers; Dredge and Fill; Farm Bills; Mitigation; Mitigation Banking; Natural Resources Conservation Service; Swampbuster; Taking.**

WILD AND SCENIC RIVERS ACT OF 1968 (WSRA)

Set forth congressional policy concerning certain rivers that, "with their immediate environments, possess outstandingly remarkable scenic, recreational, geologic, fish and wildlife, historic, cultural, or other similar values," and which "shall be preserved in free-flowing condition and...protected for the benefit and enjoyment of present and future generations." As of 1993, the system contained 152 units and 10,503 river miles. Several new segments were added by the 104th Congress.

The WSRA designated the initial components of the system and established the criteria and procedures by which additional rivers and river segments could be added. Three designations were created (listed in order of decreasing stringency, or level of protection): wild, scenic, and recreational. The statutory scheme thus resembles that of the National Trails System Act, also enacted in 1968.

"Wild" rivers are "free of impoundments and generally inaccessible except by trail, with watersheds or shorelines essentially primitive and waters unpolluted." "Scenic" rivers differ from wild rivers only in that they may be accessible in places by roads. "Recreational" rivers, however, are "readily accessible by road or railroad," and "may have some development along their shorelines, and...may have undergone some impoundment or diversion in the past."

The secretaries of agriculture and interior are charged with studying rivers identified by Congress and recommending whether they should be included in the system. The act provides for public comment and state consultation in this process. Rivers may be designated by Congress, or may be included in the system if designated by state legislation, after review and approval of the Interior secretary in consultation with the heads of other federal departments.

The area included with the river designation usually extends one-quarter mile from the normal high-water line on each side of the river. The federal agencies are authorized to acquire lands within the boundaries of any designated river segment, subject to certain area limits and a limit on the use of the power to condemn. Lands may be acquired using Land and Water Conservation Fund monies or by exchange.

One of the WSRA's most important provisions is its restriction on water projects in or affecting designated river segments. The act prohibits the construction (and the federal government from assisting in the construction) of any dam, water conduit, or other water project "that would have a direct and adverse effect on the values for which the river was established." In addition, the Federal Energy Regulatory Commission is forbidden to license any water project on or directly affecting any of the rivers identified by Congress for study for possible inclusion in the system. Another significant provision is the withdrawal of all public lands within designated components "from entry, sale, or other disposition under the public land laws." Subject to valid existing rights, the lands within one-quarter mile of designated rivers are thereafter unavailable for mining. This means that miners may continue to develop valid claims (subject to regulation), but they cannot patent their claims unless they had already applied for a patent and met all the patenting requirements. Prospecting may also continue, also subject to regulations imposed by the land manager. The act provides that such regulations should safeguard against pollution and impairment of the scenery.

Components of the WSRA system are to be managed to protect the values for which they were designated. Land management agencies are directed to prepare management plans for rivers under their jurisdiction and manage them using their general statutory authorities (e.g., the National Park Service Organic Act of 1916 for the National Park Service). The act also specifies that federal agencies should pay "particular attention" to "timber harvesting, road construction, and similar activities which might be contrary to the purposes" of the WSRA.

Several recent court cases have examined some of these planning and management requirements. A federal court in Arkansas ruled that comprehensive management plans for rivers within national forests must contain management prescriptions for activities on all national forest lands that *may impact* designated river segments, not just areas actually within the designation boundaries. A federal judge in Oregon held that the Bureau of Land Management had violated substantive requirements of the WSRA by failing to provide, in a river management plan, for protection against the degrading effects of livestock grazing. The agency also should have examined in an environmental impact statement the effects of both grazing and planned road and parking improvements, the court said.

See also **Land and Water Conservation Fund; National Trails System Act of 1968; Withdrawal.**

WILD, FREE-ROAMING HORSES AND BURROS ACT (WFRHBA)

A federal statute passed in 1971 that protects wild horses and burros on public and private lands in the West and provides for their management. The statute defines "wild free-roaming horses and burros" as "all unbranded and unclaimed horses and burros on public lands of the United States." Wildlife biologists argue, however, that these animals are not "wildlife"; they are the feral offspring of once-domesticated mammals. Neither species is native to North America.

The WFRHBA was enacted by Congress after intense lobbying, including a massive letter-writing campaign by schoolchildren appalled by reports of the widespread slaughter of wild horses for use as dog food or to make other commercial products. The act has been controversial from the outset. One of its purposes was to increase wild horse and burro populations (Congress found that the animals were "fast disappearing from the American scene"), and in that respect it has been *too* successful. Most management problems—and litigation—involve allegations of overpopulations and the resulting conflicts with other uses of public rangelands, namely wildlife and livestock. Allocation of forage among the three categories of range users is an inevitable land-use planning issue in districts where the animals are found (horses, chiefly in Nevada and Wyoming; burros, in Arizona and New Mexico). In 1978, Congress amended the act (1) to clarify the balance that land managers are to establish in protecting these animals and providing for competing uses and (2) to provide for the immediate removal of "excess" horses and burros.

The act directs the secretaries of Interior and Agriculture to manage horses and burros "as components of the public lands," "in a manner that is designed to achieve and maintain a thriving natural ecological balance." The agencies are required to maintain inventories of these animals on public lands and national forests. The act specifies how, and on the basis of what information, surplus animals may be removed, and it directs the immediate removal of "excess" animals to restore ecological balance to the range and protect it from deterioration. The statute further provides for the adoption of surplus wild horses and burros by private individuals, sets forth requirements for the animals' care and maintenance, and establishes criminal penalties for violations of the act.

In *Kleppe v. New Mexico* (1976), the U.S. Supreme Court upheld the WFRHBA as a valid exercise of Congress's power under the Property Clause of the Constitution. The Court was persuaded by the extensive legislative history and the findings of the act itself, in which Congress declared that these animals are "an integral part of the natural system of the public lands." The Court ruled that Congress's "complete power" under the Property Clause "necessarily includes the wildlife living" on the public lands; thus, wild horses and burros fall within Congress's power to make all "needful Rules and Regulations respecting" the public lands. The Court further held that the New Mexico Estray Law was invalid and thus preempted to the extent that it conflicted with the WFRHBA. The Court did not rule that the federal government "owned" wild horses and burros, but rather that the act was a valid exercise of federal proprietary and sovereign power over the public lands. The Court was not called on to decide whether the statute was valid as applied to private lands. That issue was taken up in a later federal circuit court case, *Mountain States Legal Foundation v. Hodel* (1986), which held that the WFRHBA is "nothing more than a land use regulation." The Tenth Circuit (sitting *en banc*) upheld the statute against claims that it resulted in a taking of ranchers' property by protecting wild horses grazing on their private lands. The court explained that the WFRHBA is not unique among federal statutes; indeed, it is only one of many (such as the Endangered Species Act, Marine Mammal Protection Act, and Migratory Bird Treaty Act of 1918) in which Congress has acted to protect certain wildlife species.

After the national media in early 1997 reported widespread abuses and mismanagement of the BLM's wild horse adoption program—charges that the BLM denied or termed "distorted"—the agency transferred management of the program from its Nevada state office to Washington, D.C. Internal audits of the program and an investigation by the Department of Justice were also planned.

See also *Kleppe v. New Mexico* **(1976); Preemption; Property Clause; Taking; Wildlife Management.**

🏛 WILDERNESS A land designation authorized by the Wilderness Act of 1964 and defined as

> an area where the earth and its community of life are untrammelled by man, where man himself is a visitor who does not remain...an area of undeveloped Federal land retaining its primeval character and influence, without permanent improvements or human habitation, which is protected and managed so as to preserve its natural conditions, and which (1) generally appears to have been affected primarily by the forces of nature...; (2) has outstanding opportunities for solitude or a primitive and unconfined type of recreation; (3) has at least five thousand acres of land or is of sufficient size as to make practicable its preservation and use in an unimpaired condition; and (4) may also contain ecological, geological, or other features of scientific, educational, scenic, or historical value. [16 U.S.C. § 1131(c)]

Although wilderness areas are generally large (more than 5,000 acres), other qualities may outweigh an area's small size. Wisconsin Island in the Green Bay National Wildlife Refuge, for instance, is only two acres. Only Congress may designate a wilderness area; hence, what constitutes "wilderness" is a matter of congressional discretion.

The Wilderness Act of 1964 designated 9.1 million acres as "instant" wilderness areas; these were areas that had been designated administratively by the U.S. Forest Service (USFS) as wilderness, wild, or canoe areas. The act also provided for future designation of additional areas that qualified as wilderness. Specifically, it directed the USFS to study 5.4 million acres of primitive areas and the U.S. Department of the Interior to study roadless areas of more than 5,000 acres within the national wildlife refuge and national park systems. By 1995 an additional 95 million acres of lands had been added to the wilderness preservation system, bringing the total to 631 wilderness areas in 44 states. The California Desert Protection Act of 1994, which created 69 wilderness areas on Bureau of Land Management (BLM) lands, was the single largest expansion of the national wilderness preservation system since the addition of lands in Alaska in 1980 and the largest ever in the lower 48 states. Alaska contains more than 55 percent of designated wilderness (although only 17 percent of all national forest wilderness) and 37 percent of lands recommended for wilderness designation. Only Connecticut, Rhode Island, Iowa, and Kansas have no designated or recommended wilderness areas.

The Federal Land Policy and Management Act of 1976 called for a review within 15 years of BLM lands that possess wilderness potential. To date, 136 BLM wilderness areas have been established, comprising 5.2 million acres; approximately 600 study areas have yet to be either designated as wilderness or eliminated from consideration. BLM wilderness bills for Montana, Utah, and Idaho continue to be debated.

Since only Congress has the power to establish an official wilderness area, every wilderness area is subject to both the provisions of the Wilderness Act of 1964 and the specific legislation by which it is established. Wilderness proposals generally advance in Congress only if they have the support of the delegation of the state where the lands are located. In the case of Utah, however, such a split developed between the Utah delegation and the governor of Utah on one side, and environmentalists and many others around the country on the other, that considerable momentum has developed around a 5.7-million-acre wilderness bill supported by no member of the Utah delegation but by the 110 member organizations of the Utah Wilderness Coalition. The already hotly debated Utah wilderness issue was further inflamed by President Clinton's designation in 1996 of the Grand Staircase-Escalante National Monument. The monument encompasses 1.7 million acres of the environmentalists' 5.7-million-acre wilderness proposal. Resolution of wilderness issues by the 105th Congress was considered highly unlikely.

Another fairly recent development in the wilderness arena has been the introduction in Congress of regional rather than statewide wilderness proposals. A Northern Rockies wilderness bill, which would designate as much as 20 million acres of public lands in five western states, has been introduced in three Congresses, each time by a representative from an eastern state. In mid-1997, Representative James Hansen (R-UT) introduced a bill that would require the secretary of the interior to study the wilderness suitability of state, private, and federal lands in the *eastern* half of the country. Whether this move was simple retaliation for the perceived intervention by outsiders (i.e., Easterners) in western public lands politics, or as Hansen asserted, a legitimate effort to provide more readily accessible wilderness recreation opportunities to the heavily populated East, was a matter of debate.

See also **Alaska National Interest Lands Conservation Act; Clinton, William Jefferson; Roadless Area; Southern Utah Wilderness Alliance; Wilderness Act of 1964.**

WILDERNESS ACT OF 1964   Established the National Wilderness Preservation System, defined the qualities that characterize "wilderness," and provided for the management of certain federal lands as wilderness areas. The act conferred wilderness designation on 54 administratively identified national forest wilderness and primitive areas and provided for study and designation, by statute, of additional areas. The original National Wilderness Preservation System included 9.5 million acres; the system now encompasses more than 100 million acres.

The Wilderness Act provides that wilderness areas "shall be administered for the use and enjoyment of the American people in such manner as will leave them unimpaired for future use and enjoyment as wilderness" and to preserve "their wilderness character." Only Congress may establish wilderness areas. Each wilderness area is managed by the same federal agency that managed it prior to its designation as wilderness; the system encompasses lands managed by the U.S. Forest Service, Bureau of Land Management, National Park Service, and U.S. Fish and Wildlife Service.

Wilderness areas are generally roadless, and motor vehicles and commercial enterprises are usually prohibited. However, as discussed below, the act contains numerous exceptions to these requirements.

The Wilderness Act provides for protection of "existing private rights," such as roads or use of motorized vehicles (e.g., motorboats, airplanes, or snowmobiles), subject to the discretion of the managing agency. These uses have been permitted to continue in some wilderness areas, but are subject to regulation. The courts have held, however, that Congress may forbid motor vehicles or certain land uses on state or private lands located within wilderness areas. The managing agency has some discretion to use motorized equipment (e.g., chain saws) in wilderness areas where necessary to control fire, insects, or disease.

In general, mining and mineral leasing were allowed in wilderness areas through the end of 1983. Beginning 1 January 1984, only valid existing rights were recognized, although mineral prospecting was allowed to continue. Very little hardrock mining or mineral leasing activity has occurred in wilderness areas, and in 1987 Congress prohibited mineral leasing in wilderness study areas. The Wilderness Act's mining provisions apply only to national forest wilderness; mineral activities in wilderness areas established since 1964 are subject to provisions in the respective enacting legislation.

Water projects are allowed by the act, where authorized by the president, but the act's legislative history indicates that Congress contemplated only small-scale projects. Water rights and water development have been issues in the debates over numerous wilderness bills since 1964. Logging is not mentioned in the Wilderness Act, but commercial logging is effectively prohibited by the statute's bans on road construction, use of motorized equipment, and commercial enterprises. The act authorizes the land manager to permit livestock grazing to continue in wilderness areas, and grazing is allowed in many wildernesses. The act provides that it does not alter the authority of the states with respect to fish and wildlife; thus, hunting and fishing in wilderness areas remain subject to state regulation.

The Wilderness Act also contains provisions for state- and privately owned inholdings within designated wilderness areas. It specifies that these landowners shall be given adequate access to their property, or that their lands shall be exchanged for federal lands within the same state and of "approximately equal value." The statute does not specify whether the choice of remedy is left to the managing agency or to the inholder.

See also **Federal Land Policy and Management Act; Release; Reserved Rights Doctrine; Roadless Area; Southern Utah Wilderness Alliance; Wilderness.**

THE WILDERNESS SOCIETY (TWS) A nonprofit, tax-exempt, national environmental organization founded in 1935 by Robert Marshall and presently claiming more than 400,000 members. In addition to its headquarters, TWS staffs 15 regional offices—in Juneau and Anchorage, AK; San Francisco, CA; Portland, OR; Seattle, WA; Santa Fe, NM; Salt Lake City, UT; Denver, CO; Boise, ID; Bozeman, MT; Augusta, ME; Boston, MA; Atlanta, GA; and Miami and the Florida Keys, FL. Gaylord Nelson, former Wisconsin governor and senator and founder of Earth Day, serves as legal counsel to the organization. Its staff includes lawyers, foresters, ecologists, wildlife biologists, economists, and other professionals.

TWS is the only conservation organization whose activities relate exclusively to the federal public lands. Its programs include public education, lobbying, grassroots organizing, watchdogging federal agencies, and litigation. Although the organization was founded to promote the cause of wilderness preservation, an effort that culminated in passage of the Wilderness Act of 1964, it has expanded its work to encompass national parks and monuments, national forests, national wildlife refuges, and Bureau of Land Management lands. TWS works to protect endangered species, old-growth forests, rivers, coasts, and roadless areas, and to foster an American land ethic. It has been involved in scores of legal challenges to federal agency resource decisions, although it seldom is the lead plaintiff in these cases.

TWS publishes a quarterly magazine, *Wilderness*, and sponsors workshops and seminars on public land and resource topics.

WILDLIFE MANAGEMENT A field of applied science (some would say more an art than a science) generally considered to have been pioneered by Aldo Leopold. Wildlife management— sometimes considered to include fisheries management—embraces both the on-the-ground measures taken to regulate wildlife populations and protect or manipulate habitat, as well as the development of public policies for using and conserving wildlife and fisheries resources.

Wildlife management practices and policies are subject to both state and federal law. Under common law, states have principal authority for wildlife management. Unless state law has been preempted by federal statutes or regulations (for instance, the Endangered Species Act of 1973), states have primary wildlife management authority even on federal lands (with the exception of federal enclaves, such as some national parks). But it is often said that, on federal lands, the states manage the animals, and the federal government manages the habitat. That is, federal land management agencies have authority over wildlife, chiefly via their ownership of the habitat and authority to regulate the use of the land. For example, the U.S. Forest Service and Bureau of Land Management each has a multiple-use mandate for managing its lands that includes fish and wildlife. In addition, the U.S. Fish and Wildlife Service has statutory responsibilities for migratory species, threatened and endangered species, and national wildlife refuges.

The principal state mechanisms for managing populations of game species are hunting and trapping. State wildlife management agencies regulate who may take game animals and under what circumstances; this includes setting hunting seasons and "bag limits." Nongame species can be regulated by direct control of their populations by the state agency, by controlling populations of other animals (e.g., predators or competitors) through hunting seasons or direct control measures, and by cooperative programs with landowners. Still, habitat is the primary determinant of wildlife populations. Thus, landowners, whether private, state, or federal, play an important role in managing wildlife, directly or indirectly.

The public generally and conservation organizations in particular play active roles in wildlife management issues; avenues of participation include lobbying, litigating, testifying at public hearings, commenting on federal agencies' land use plans and environmental impact statements, and promoting the use of partnerships and conservation easements. Recently, citizen initiatives have had a significant influence on the development of wildlife management laws.

See also *Clajon Production Co. v. Petera* (1995); *Hughes v. Oklahoma* (1979); **Hunting;** *Kleppe v. New Mexico* (1976); **Nonresident License; State Ballot Initiatives**.

WILKINSON, CHARLES F. Scholar of public land law, water law, and Indian law. Professor Wilkinson holds the Moses Lasky distinguished chair at the University of Colorado School of Law. He has authored numerous books and law review and popular articles on western public land and natural resource topics, notably *Crossing the Next Meridian: Land, Water, and the Future of the West* (Island Press 1992) and "The Law of the American West: A Critical Bibliography of the Nonlegal Sources," *Michigan Law Review* 85 (1987): 953. He is also coauthor of the leading law school casebooks on public natural resources law and Native American law. He has written on the public trust doctrine; the National Forest Management Act of 1976; western water law, including the prior-appropriation doctrine; and mining law. Despite Wilkinson's stature as a legal scholar, his writing is highly accessible to nonlawyers. He lectures widely on public land and natural resource issues to students, conservation organizations, and professionals.

Wilkinson is a cofounder of the Native American Rights Fund, based in Boulder, Colorado, and continues to serve on its board of directors. He is also a director of The Wilderness Society. In 1989 he received the National Wildlife Federation's National Conservation Achievement Award for outstanding contributions to the wise management of natural resources. He is credited as the principal author of the presidential proclamation designating the Grand Staircase–Escalante National Monument.

WISE USE GROUPS More than 250 groups joined in 1988 to form the coalition known as the Wise Use Movement. Among the founding organizations were the American Mining Congress, National Rifle Association, American Motorcyclists Association, and National

Cattlemen's Association. Other supporters and cosponsors of subsequent Wise Use conferences include the American Farm Bureau Federation, National Association of Manufacturers, United 4-Wheel Drive Association, National Forest Products Association, and National Association of Mining Districts. Although some have adopted "green" populist names such as Citizens for the Environment and Citizens for Sensible Control of Acid Rain, many Wise Use groups actually have very close ties to industry. The Oregon Lands Coalition was initially housed in the offices of the Association of Oregon Industries. The Society of the Plastics Industry, Inc., was the parent organization to the Wise Use group Council for Solid Waste Solutions. Similarly, the National Wetlands Coalition, ostensibly concerned with the problems of small landowners, is in fact largely funded by the oil and gas industry, including Amoco, BP, Chevron, Exxon, and Marathon Oil. People for the West! was founded by the chief executive officer of Pegasus Gold and continues to be heavily funded by mineral and petroleum companies.

See also **Wise Use Movement.**

WISE USE MOVEMENT Closely related to the Sagebrush Rebellion of the 1970s and early 1980s and to the current County Supremacy Movement, this grassroots effort is centered in the rural West. It emerged on the national scene following the 1988 Multiple Use Strategy Conference, and consists of a coalition of hundreds of groups and organizations, including private property rights advocates, extractive natural resource industries, trade associations, and conservative political interest groups. The Wise Use Movement is well funded by industry groups, including the American Mining Congress, American Farm Bureau Federation, United 4-Wheel Drive Association, National Cattlemen's Association, and National Forest Products Association. The movement's agenda tends to be corporate-friendly, emphasizing consumptive uses of the public lands, with an accompanying decrease in the regulatory role of the federal government. In its own words, it has "declared war" on environmentalism. Movement spokespersons, such as Chuck Cushman, founder of the National Inholders Association, typically frame Wise Use issues in terms of the environment versus jobs.

Participants in the 1988 conference developed a set of 25 goals, most of which related to public land commodity use and development. They advocated extending the General Mining Law of 1872 to all wilderness areas and national parks, making grazing the principal use of public rangelands, and recognizing private property rights in mining claims, timber contracts, and grazing permits. Other agenda items include clear-cutting old-growth forests, developing wilderness off-road vehicle trails, and repealing landmark environmental statutes, such as the Endangered Species Act of 1973.

Wise Use groups are loosely organized and affiliated; representative organizations include People for the West!, Alliance for America, and the National Inholders Association. Their principal strategies have been to oppose laws and policies backed by environmental groups, although they became more activist during the 104th Congress. Thus far, Wise Use interests have not generally called for privatization of federal lands and resources; instead, they lobby for more liberal treatment of commodity interests under current laws and regulations.

See also **County Supremacy Movement; Multiple Use; Sagebrush Rebellion; Wise Use Groups.**

WITHDRAWAL Traditionally, a legislative or executive action that designated public lands as unavailable for certain kinds of uses (e.g., mining) or for sale or other forms of disposition (e.g., homestead entry). Reservations of land (e.g., for Indian reservations, wilderness, national parks, or wildlife refuges) typically include withdrawals from other uses that would interfere with accomplishment of the particular purposes of the reservation.

Prior to 1976, no prescribed procedures governed executive withdrawals. While Congress's power (under the Property Clause of the Constitution) to withdraw lands was never questioned, the absence of express executive authority occasionally raised doubts as to the source and extent of presidential withdrawal authority. Congress attempted to clarify matters in the Federal Land Policy and Management Act (FLPMA), passed in 1976. FLPMA establishes specific procedures for, and defines the limits of, executive withdrawals. FLPMA defines "withdrawal" more broadly than its historical sense: "withdrawal" now includes "withholding an area of Federal land from settlement, sale, location, or entry, under some or all of the general land laws," "reserving the area for a particular public purpose or program," and "transferring jurisdiction" over federal land from one agency or bureau to another. [43 U.S.C. § 1702(j)]

Under FLPMA, executive withdrawals may now be made only by the secretary of the Interior and certain other presidential appointees within his office. [43 U.S.C. § 1714(a)] Withdrawals of lands not administered by the Department of the Interior (for instance, national forest lands) may be made only with the consent of the respective agency head. Withdrawals of less than 5,000 acres may be for an indefinite duration if deemed "desirable for a resource use," and for limited time periods (not more than 5 or 20 years) if done for other purposes (e.g., administrative or "proprietary" purposes or to preserve an area under consideration by Congress for special designation). Withdrawals of 5,000 acres or more may be made for not more than 20 years, but are subject to rejection by either house of Congress. FLPMA outlines procedures that apply to each category of withdrawal. Emergency withdrawals, which are not subject to the usual withdrawal procedures, may be made by the secretary on his own motion or at the direction of the House Resources Committee or Senate Energy and Natural Resources Committee, whenever the secretary or one of the committees determines that "extraordinary measures must be taken to preserve values that would otherwise be lost." [43 U.S.C. § 1714(e)] Emergency withdrawals are limited to three years.

FLPMA required that the secretary review all withdrawals existing as of October 1976 and report to Congress his decision whether to extend or terminate those withdrawals. The actions of the Bureau of Land Management (within the Department of the Interior) in carrying out this provision were the subject of litigation in *Lujan v. National Wildlife Federation* (1990). The statute calls for public hearings on all new withdrawals, and it makes clear that the secretary may not modify or revoke any withdrawal executed by Congress.

FLPMA's provision for review and disapproval of an executive withdrawal by one house of Congress raises constitutional questions. Some scholars and courts believe that this and similar provisions of FLPMA allow a "legislative" action to be taken without compliance with all constitutionally required procedures for enacting legislation, specifically, the requirements for bicameral approval and presentment to the president for his signature. A few lower federal courts have disagreed on the issue; the U.S. Supreme Court has not addressed it. Litigation can be expected in the event of some politically popular (or unpopular) secretarial withdrawal that is ultimately vetoed by one house of Congress.

See also *Lujan v. National Wildlife Federation* (1990); **Property Clause**; **Reservation**.

WOLF REINTRODUCTION The objective of various programs, coordinated by the U.S. Fish and Wildlife Service (USFWS),
to reestablish wolves in portions of their historical range. Many years after
having been extirpated from the vast majority of their former range, three
subspecies of wolves were listed as endangered under the Endangered
Species Act of 1973 (ESA). The gray wolf (*Canis lupus*) in Minnesota was
listed as threatened; gray wolves in Alaska are not protected under the act.
The first reintroduction efforts were releases of captive red wolves (*Canis
rufus*) in the Alligator River National Wildlife Refuge in North Carolina in
1986 and in Great Smoky Mountains National Park in North Carolina and
Tennessee in 1991. In 1994-1996, following an extensive planning process
under the ESA and the National Environmental Policy Act (NEPA), wild
gray wolves from Canada were transplanted to sites in Yellowstone National Park and central Idaho. An effort to return Mexican wolves (*Canis
lupus mexicanus*) to parts of New Mexico and Arizona began in early 1998.

In each case, the USFWS exercised its authority under section 10(j) of
the ESA to designate the reintroduced animals as a "nonessential experimental population," thus affording greater flexibility in managing the new
populations by dispensing with certain ESA protections to which the animals would otherwise be entitled, such as section 7 consultation requirements and the full range of prohibitions (e.g., against taking an endangered
animal) under section 9. For instance, the experimental population status
of wolves reintroduced to Yellowstone and Idaho allows the USFWS to
relocate or remove problem animals and further allows a rancher to kill
any wolf caught in the act of preying on livestock. ("Nonessential experimental population" status was also given to a group of endangered California condors released in northern Arizona in 1996.)

The Yellowstone wolf reintroduction effort received nationwide public-
ity. Preparation of the environmental impact statement (EIS) was controversial and occasionally acrimonious. Before issuing the final EIS, the
USFWS held more than 30 open houses and public meetings in the region
and received 160,000 comments. Most opposition came from ranchers concerned about livestock loss to predation, but some hunters objected to
wolves on similar grounds. They claimed that wolf predation on big game
would force the game and fish agencies of the three states (Wyoming, Montana, and Idaho) to curtail hunting seasons and/or numbers of permits or
licenses sold in the areas colonized by wolves. Some objected on more general grounds, that the program involved excessive interference by the federal government in state affairs, that species protections under the ESA

would result in restrictions on private property owners' use of their land, or that federal funds would be better spent on other matters.

Yet another objection to the Yellowstone reintroduction led to a ruling by a Wyoming federal court in late 1997 that the program is illegal. Several plaintiffs, including the National Audubon Society and certain individuals, claimed that wolves, while rare, already existed in the transplant areas, and thus reintroduction violated the requirement in ESA section 10(j) that the experimental population be "wholly separate geographically from nonexperimental populations of the same species." These groups are concerned that wolves already present, which are entitled to full protection as an *endangered* species, would receive less protection as a result of the transplant because they would be indistinguishable from the "nonessential experimental" animals. They further fear that the genetic diversity of local wolves will be diluted by interbreeding with the Canadian animals. The federal judge agreed with the plaintiffs, but stayed his order, pending completion of any appeal. The ruling has been appealed by other environmental groups. If the district court's order is affirmed, it would require the federal government to remove all wolves from the Yellowstone ecosystem. At least one USFWS official has said that this could be accomplished only by killing the wolves—a proposal that would inevitably trigger more lawsuits.

The EIS estimated the total cost of the Yellowstone reintroduction at $6 million, while predicting revenues of $23 million from visitors attracted to the Yellowstone area by the wolves. In fact, park visitation in 1995 was even higher than anticipated, and biologists involved in the project were surprised that wolves were sighted frequently by visitors.

Livestock losses attributable to wolf releases have been minimal. Only about 20 calves were killed by red wolves in the vicinity of Great Smoky National Park from 1987 through 1995. Losses since the Idaho and Yellowstone releases have also been infrequent and low; the USFWS policy is to move to a remote area any wolf that preys on livestock, and to destroy it on its second offense. The environmental organization Defenders of Wildlife maintains a fund that reimburses livestock owners for any documented losses of cattle or sheep to wolf predation.

According to the USFWS, wolf reintroduction efforts have been biological successes. Nevertheless, local resistance to the programs persists. In the East, lawsuits have been threatened, and two counties have passed antiwolf ordinances. In the West, both livestock interests and environmental plaintiffs sued in 1995—the former to prevent the first Yellowstone-Idaho transplant, the latter to force the USFWS to give the released animals full protection under the ESA. Although these suits were unsuccessful, several parties filed suit again the following year, challenging the second transplant. The outcome of that suit, as described above, is still uncertain.

Members of western congressional delegations have held field hearings on the issue and attempted to remove funding for the wolf reintroduction program. Resistance from livestock groups is also expected as efforts proceed to reestablish the Mexican wolf in the Southwest. In Wyoming, the state assessed public views concerning whether the state should participate in wolf management and, if so, in what form. A series of public meetings around the state and a written comment period revealed such polar views on the issue that the state Game and Fish Commission announced that Wyoming would not participate in wolf management until the animal was removed from the list of endangered species.

See also **Endangered Species Act of 1973; Take; U.S. Fish and Wildlife Service; Wildlife Management.**

YOUNG, DON Republican congressman from Alaska. Young chairs the House Resources Committee, and was responsible for deleting the word "Natural" from the committee's name when he ascended to the chair in 1995. As this move suggests, Young is an ultraconservative who favors commercial/commodity uses of the public lands. Young has long supported drilling in the Arctic National Wildlife Refuge and staunchly opposes wilderness designation for the area. In 1997 he introduced legislation that would limit the area that could be designated as biosphere reserves and restrict the secretary of the interior's authority to place lands on the World Heritage List. Young was a target of a 1997 Wilderness Society petition drive aimed at removing him as chair of the Resources Committee and replacing him with a less conservative Republican.

ZONING

ZONING The principal tool by which local governments (e.g., county or municipal) plan for and control the use of land. Zoning is often implemented by an ordinance that enacts all or some portions of a comprehensive land-use plan for the area, along with means for enforcing it. To be valid, zoning ordinances must be authorized by state law. Comprehensive zoning ordinances in the United States date to 1916 (in New York City). The U.S. Supreme Court first upheld comprehensive zoning in *Euclid v. Ambler Realty Co.* (1926) against claims by a landowner that a zoning ordinance violated his due process rights and constituted a taking of his property by disallowing the more lucrative development he had planned for it. Most zoning ordinances in the United States are patterned on or at least bear similarities to the Standard Zoning Enabling Act, developed by the U.S. Department of Commerce in the 1920s. (This is a "model" act, not legislation.)

Zoning ordinances commonly consist of a written text and a map. They may specify any or all of the following: types and intensities of permissible land use (e.g., residential or commercial; single- versus multifamily dwellings; etc.), building area and height limitations, setback requirements from streets or sidewalks, percentage of lots that may be occupied by buildings, requirements for subdividing, etc. The zoning ordinance usually makes provisions for nonconforming uses, such as an existing commercial establishment in an area now zoned residential. Commonly, nonconforming uses are amortized over a specified period of years, at the end of which the use must be discontinued. Finally, zoning ordinances specify procedures for amending the zoning classification, petitioning for variances or special exceptions, and appealing decisions by the zoning authority. In most jurisdictions, a land-use plan itself is not enforceable, but zoning or other ordinances that implement the plan can be enforced.

Zoning is an important weapon against sprawl, which is a growing problem in certain areas of the country and on the outskirts of many metropolitan areas. Sprawl poses numerous dilemmas for cities and counties, including how to finance and maintain needed infrastructure, such as roads and utilities, provide services, and deal with the concomitant outmigration from and decay of older or inner-city neighborhoods. Sprawl also contributes to a variety of environmental and ecological problems, including air pollution and energy consumption from increased motorized vehicle use, loss of open space (often agricultural land) to development, and fragmentation of wildlife habitat. Sprawl is occurring in many rural areas of the West, a result of in-migration of people seeking an improved quality of life (less congestion, better air and water quality, less crime). These areas often have no zoning system in place, and residents discover belatedly that no mechanism for controlling this unexpected growth is readily available to them.

Zoning classifications have been challenged on numerous constitutional grounds—as takings of private property without compensation or without due process (*see Euclid*, cited above), infringing on the right to free speech (e.g., restrictions on the location of adult theaters or bookstores), or infringing on the free exercise of religion (e.g., restricting churches to only one or a few zones). The courts have established tests for potential problems such as these and have only rarely found zoning schemes constitutionally flawed.

See also **Land-Use Planning; Taking; Transferable Development Right.**

Bibliography

Adams, David A. *Renewable Resource Policy: The Legal-Institutional Foundations*. Washington, DC: Island Press, 1993.

Adler, Robert. "Addressing Barriers to Watershed Protection." *Environmental Law* 25 (1995): 973–1106.

Baker, Katherine K. "Consorting with Forests: Rethinking Our Relationship to Natural Resources and How We Should Value Their Loss." *Ecology Law Quarterly* 22 (1995): 677–728.

Battle, Jackson, and Maxine Lipeles. *Environmental Law*. Vol. 2: *Water Pollution*. Cincinnati: Anderson Publishing Co., 1993.

Bean, Michael, and Melanie J. Rowland. *The Evolution of National Wildlife Law*. 3d ed. Westport, CT: Praeger Publishers, 1987.

Bosselman, Fred. "Four Land Ethics: Order, Reform, Responsibility, Opportunity." *Environmental Law* 24 (1994): 1484–1511.

Braddock, Theda. *Wetlands: An Introduction to Ecology, the Law and Permitting*. Rockville, MD: Government Institutes, 1995.

Brown, Lester R. *State of the World, 1996: A Worldwatch Institute Report on Progress toward a Sustainable Society*. New York: W. W. Norton & Co., 1996.

Brubaker, Sterling, ed. *Rethinking the Federal Lands*. Washington, DC: Resources for the Future, Inc., 1984.

Center for Wildlife Law and Defenders of Wildlife. *Saving Biodiversity: A Status Report on State Laws, Policies, and Programs*. July 1996.

Chereb, Sandra. "Extremists Blamed in Van Bombing." *Chicago Sun-Times*, 6 August 1995, p. 22.

Clawson, Marion. *The Federal Lands Revisited*. Washington, DC: Resources for the Future, Inc., 1983.

Clementine. Newsletter published by the Mineral Policy Center, Washington, DC.

Coggins, George Cameron. "The Law of Public Rangeland Management IV: FLPMA, PRIA, and the Multiple Use Mandate." *Environmental Law* 14 (1983): 1–131.

————. "Of Succotash Syndromes and Vacuous Platitudes: The Meaning of 'Multiple Use, Sustained Yield' for Public Land Management." *University of Colorado Law Review* 53 (1980): 229–283.

————. "Overcoming the Unfortunate Legacies of Western Public Land Law." *Land and Water Law Review* 29 (1993): 381–389.

Coggins, George C., and Robert L. Glicksman. *Public Natural Resources Law.* 3 vols. Deerfield, IL: Clark Boardman Callaghan, 1990 & Release 1996.

Coggins, George C., Charles F. Wilkinson, and John D. Leshy. 3d ed. *Federal Public Land and Resources Law.* Westbury, NY: Foundation Press, Inc., 1993.

Coppelman, Peter D. "The Federal Government's Response to the County Supremacy Movement." *Natural Resources & Environment* 12 (Summer 1997): 30–33, 79–80.

Culhane, Paul. *Public Lands Politics: Interest Group Influence on the Forest Service and the Bureau of Land Management.* Baltimore: Johns Hopkins University Press, 1981.

Daugherty, Stephen A. "The Unfulfilled Promise of an End to Timber Dominance on the Tongass National Forest: Forest Service Implementation of the Tongass Timber Reform Act." *Environmental Law* 24 (1994): 1573–1632.

Echeverria, John D., and Raymond Booth Eby, eds. *Let the People Judge: Wise Use and the Private Property Rights Movement.* Washington, DC: Island Press, 1995.

Fairfax, Sally K. "Thinking the Unthinkable: States as Public Land Managers." *West-Northwest* 3 (1996): 249–263.

Fairfax, Sally K., and Caroline Yale. *Federal Lands: A Guide to Planning, Management, and State Revenues.* Washington, DC: Island Press, 1987.

Findley, Roger W. "Symposium: Sustainable Development in Latin American Rainforests and the Role of Law." *Texas International Law Journal* 32 (1997): 1–15.

Fink, Richard J., ed. *The Natural Resources Law Manual.* Chicago: American Bar Association, 1995. (Publication of ABA Section on Natural Resources, Energy, and Environmental Law.)

Freyfogle, Eric T. "Owning and Belonging: The Private Landowner as Ecosystem Member." *Sustain* 1 (Spring 1996): 16–23. (A publication of the Kentucky Institute for the Environment and Sustainable Development.)

General Accounting Office. *Report to Congress: Preserving America's Farmland—A Goal the Federal Government Should Support.* 20 September 1979.

Glicksman, Robert L., and George Cameron Coggins. *Modern Public Land Law*. St. Paul, MN: West Publishing Co., 1995.

Gore, Albert, Jr. *Earth in the Balance: Ecology and the Human Spirit*. New York: Houghton Mifflin, 1992.

"Graham County Bulldozes Rare Fish's Habitat." *Arizona Daily Star*, 23 April 1995, p. 7B.

Grossman, Margaret Rosso, and Thomas G. Fischer. "Protecting the Right to Farm: Statutory Limits on Nuisance Actions against the Farmer." *Wisconsin Law Review* 1983: 95–165.

Grumbine, R. Edward. "What Is Ecosystem Management?" *Conservation Biology* 8 (1994): 27–38.

Hager, Alan V. "State School Lands: Does the Federal Trust Mandate Preservation?" *Natural Resources & Environment* 12 (Summer 1997): 39–45, 80.

Hand, Jacqueline P. "Right-To-Farm Laws: Breaking New Ground in the Preservation of Farmland." *University of Pittsburgh Law Review* 45 (1984): 289–350.

Hardin, Garrett. "The Tragedy of the Commons." *Science* 162 (1968): 1243–1248.

Henry, Robert S. "The Railroad Land Grant Legend in American History Texts." In *The Public Lands: Studies in the History of the Public Domain*, edited by Vernon Carstensen. Madison: University of Wisconsin Press, 1963, p. 121.

High Country News. Biweekly Rocky Mountain regional newspaper, published by High Country Foundation, 119 Grand Avenue, Paonia, CO 81428.

Hinchman, Steve. "Developer's Ploy: Letting Wilderness Slip through Loopholes." *Los Angeles Times*, 12 January 1993, p. A5.

Hungerford, Andrea. "'Custom and Culture' Ordinances: Not a Wise Move for the Wise Use Movement." *Tulane Environmental Law Journal* 8 (1995): 457–503.

Keller, Richard. "Buying Recycled: Investing Dollars To Close the Loop." *World Wastes*, 1 January 1994, pp. 38–48.

Keystone Center. *Biological Diversity on Federal Lands: Report of a Keystone Policy Dialogue*. April 1991.

———. *The Keystone National Policy Dialogue on Ecosystem Management*. October 1996.

Knickerbocker, Brad. "Sagebrush Rebels Take on Uncle Sam." *Christian Science Monitor*, 3 January 1996, pp. 1, 10–11.

Land Letter. Newsletter published by Environmental and Energy Study Institute, 122 C Street, NW, Washington, DC 20001.

Larsen, Erik. "Unrest in the West." *Time,* 23 October 1995, pp. 52–66.

Lavelle, Marianne. "'Wise Use' Movement Grows." *National Law Journal,* 5 June 1995, p. A1.

Leopold, Aldo. "The Land Ethic." In *A Sand County Almanac,* p. 243. Sierra Club/Ballantine Books, 1974.

Leshy, John D. *The Mining Law: A Study in Perpetual Motion.* Washington, DC: Resources for the Future, 1987.

Lueck, Dean. "Property Rights and the Economic Logic of Wildlife Institutions." *Natural Resources Journal* 35 (1995): 625–670.

McBeth, Daryn. "Wetlands Conservation and Federal Regulation: Analysis of the Food Security Act 'Swampbuster' Provisions as Amended by the Federal Agricultural and Improvement and Reform Act of 1996." *Harvard Environmental Law Review* 21 (1997): 201–263.

McCoy, Charles. "Cattle Prod: Catron County, N.M., Leads a Nasty Revolt over Eco-protection." *Wall Street Journal,* 3 January 1995, p. 1.

Mitsch, William J., and James Gosselink. *Wetlands.* 2d ed. New York: Van Nostrand Reinhold, 1993.

Musgrave, Ruth, and Mary Anne Stein. *State Wildlife Laws Handbook.* Rockville, MD: Government Institutes, 1993.

Nash, Roderick. *Wilderness and the American Mind.* 3d ed. New Haven, CT: Yale University Press, 1983.

National Agricultural Lands Study, Final Report. 1981. (Jointly sponsored by the U.S. Department of Agriculture and the President's Council on Environmental Quality.)

National Research Council. *Setting Priorities for Land Conservation.* Washington, DC: National Academy Press, 1993. (Prepared by the Committee on Scientific and Technical Criteria for Federal Acquisition of Lands for Conservation.)

National Wetlands Newsletter. Bimonthly newsletter published by Environmental Law Institute. 1616 P Street, S.W., Washington, D.C. 20036.

National Wildlife Federation. *Conservation Directory: A List of Organizations, Agencies, and Officials Concerned with Natural Resource Use and Management.* 37th ed. Washington, DC: 1996.

Newkirk, Ingrid. *Save the Animals! One Hundred Easy Things You Can Do.* New York: Warner Books, 1990.

Noss, Reed F., and Allen Y. Cooperrider. *Saving Nature's Legacy: Protecting and Restoring Biodiversity.* Washington, DC: Island Press, 1994.

O'Toole, Randal. *Reforming the Forest Service.* Washington, DC: Island Press, 1988.

Payne, Neil F. *Techniques for Wildlife Habitat Management of Wetlands.* New York: McGraw-Hill, 1994.

Pearson, Mark. "The Private Parts of Paradise: 'Inholdings' and the Integrity of Wilderness." *Wilderness* (Spring 1993), pp. 20–27.

Public Land Law Review Commission. *One Third of the Nation's Lands.* Washington, DC: U.S. Government Printing Office, 1970. (A report to Congress.)

Public Lands News. Biweekly newsletter published by Resources Publishing Co., 1010 Vermont Avenue, Suite 708, Washington, DC 20005.

"Recycling." *Waste Information Digests.* n.p., 1 June 1994.

Reed, Scott W. "The County Supremacy Movement: Mendacious Myth Marketing." *Idaho Law Review* 30 (1993/1994): 525–553.

Regan, Tom. "Progress without Pain: The Argument for Humane Treatment of Research Animals." *St. Louis University Law Journal* 31 (1987): 513–542.

Reisner, Marc. *Cadillac Desert: The American West and Its Disappearing Water.* New York: Penguin Books, 1987.

"Resource Guide: Public Lands." *West-Northwest* 3 (1996): 265-271.

Restatement (Second) of Torts § 821B(1). American Law Institute, 1977.

Richardson, Valerie. "No-Nonsense Idaho Sheriff Tells Federal Law Officers To Steer Clear." *Washington Times,* 27 August 1995, p. A1.

Schmahmann, David R., and Lori J. Polacheck. "The Case against Rights for Animals." *Boston College Environmental Affairs Law Review* 22 (1995): 747–781.

Seigel, Barry. "A Lone Ranger; U.S. Forest Service Ranger Guy Pence Is a Persistent and Passionate Defender of Public Lands. Is That Why Someone Bombed His Office and His Home?" *Los Angeles Times Magazine,* 26 November 1995, p. 20.

Sheldon, Karin P. "Harvesting." In *Sustainable Environmental Law,* edited by Celia Campbell-Mohn, et al. § 6.2. 1993.

Sheridan, David. *Desertification of the United States.* Washington, DC: Council on Environmental Quality, 1981.

Simon, David J., ed. *Our Common Lands: Defending the National Parks.* Covelo, CA: Island Press, 1988.

Singer, Peter. *Animal Liberation.* Rev. ed. New York: Avon, 1991.

Small, Stephen J. *Preserving Family Lands.* Boston: Landowner Planning Center, 1992.

————. *Preserving Family Lands: Book II; More Planning Strategies for the Future.* Boston: Landowner Planning Center, 1997.

Snape, William J., III, ed. *Biodiversity and the Law.* Washington, DC: Island Press, 1996.

Souder, Jon A., and Sally K. Fairfax. *State Trust Lands: History, Management, and Sustainable Use.* Lawrence: University of Kansas Press, 1996.

Southern Utah Wilderness Alliance. Newsletter and other publications. 1471 S. 1100 E., Salt Lake City, UT 84105.

Stapleton, Richard M. "Greed vs. Green." *National Parks,* November/December 1992, pp. 32–37.

Stone, Christopher D. "Should Trees Have Standing? Toward Legal Rights for Natural Objects." *Southern California Law Review* 45 (1972): 450–501.

Strand, Margaret. *Wetlands Deskbook.* Washington, DC: Environmental Law Institute, 1993.

————. "Recent Developments in Federal Wetlands Law: Part I." *Environmental Law Reporter* 26 (June 1996): 10283–10295.

————. "Recent Developments in Federal Wetlands Law: Part II." *Environmental Law Reporter* 26 (July 1996): 10339–10357.

————. "Recent Developments in Federal Wetlands Law: Part III." *Environmental Law Reporter* 26 (August 1996): 10399–10410.

Sugg, Ike C. "Caught in the Act: Evaluating the Endangered Species Act, Its Effects on Man and Prospects for Reform." *Cumberland Law Review* 24 (1993-1994): 1–78.

Sullivan, Dan. "Retiree Finds Niche Protecting Lands." *Denver Post,* 2 January 1997, p. A1.

U.S. Army Corps of Engineers. "Wetland Delineation Manual." In *Wetlands Deskbook,* by Margaret Strand. Washington, DC: Environmental Law Institute, 1993.

U.S. Bureau of Land Management. *Public Lands Statistics.* 1996.

Wald, Patricia M. "Environmental Postcards from the Edge: The Year that Was and the Year that Might Be." *Environmental Law Reporter* 26 (1996): 10182.

Weiss, Edith Brown. *In Fairness to Future Generations: International Law, Common Patrimony, and Intergenerational Equity.* Dobbs Ferry, NY: Transnational Publishers, 1989.

————. "Our Rights and Obligations to Future Generations for the Environment." *American Journal of International Law* 84 (1990): 198–207.

————. "The Planetary Trust: Conservation and Intergenerational Equity." *Ecology Law Quarterly* 11 (1984): 495–581.

Weizer, William. "International Status of Plastics Recycling." *Chemistry and Industry*, 18 December 1995, p. 1013.

Wilkinson, Charles F. *Crossing the Next Meridian: Land, Water, and the Future of the American West*. Covelo, CA: Island Press, 1992.

———. "The Law of the American West: A Critical Bibliography of the Nonlegal Sources." *Michigan Law Review* 85 (1987): 953–1011.

———. "The National Forest Management Act: The Twenty Years Behind, and the Twenty Years Ahead." *University of Colorado Law Review* 68 (1997): 659–682.

Williams, Florence. "Sagebrush Rebellion II." *High Country News*, 24 February 1992, p. 1.

Williams, Rolla. "Report Shoots Down Anti-hunters; 50 Years after Pittman-Robinson Act." *San Diego Union-Tribune*, 25 May 1986, p. H17.

Wilson, Edward O. *The Diversity of Life*. Cambridge, MA: Harvard University Press, 1992.

Wilson, James A. "A Test of the Tragedy of Commons." In *Managing the Commons*, edited by G. Hardin and J. Baden. San Francisco: W. H. Freeman, 1977, p. 97.

Table of Cases

Table of Statutes

Note: The date indicated in parentheses following each statute's citation indicates the date the act was passed. Statutes cited to "U.S.C." (the U.S. Code) can be located in any version (annotated or official) of the U.S. Code. Statutes cited by "Stat." or their Public Law number can be found in the U.S. Statutes at Large or the U.S. Code Congressional and Administrative News.

Administrative Procedure Act
5 U.S.C. §§ 551–559, 701–706, *et seq.* (1946, as amended)

Alaska National Interest Lands Conservation Act
16 U.S.C. §§ 3101–3233 (1980, as amended)

Alaska Native Claims Settlement Act
43 U.S.C. §§ 1601–1624

Antiquities Act
16 U.S.C. §§ 431–433 (1906, as amended)

Beachfront Management Act
1988 S.C. Act No. 634, S.C. Code Ann. §§ 48–39-10 to -360

California Comprehensive Land Use Plan
Cal. Gov't Code §§ 65300–65307 (1965, as amended)

California Desert Protection Act
16 U.S.C. §§ 410aaa-1 to -83 (1994)

Clean Air Act
42 U.S.C. §§ 7401 *et seq.* (1970, as amended)

Clean Water Act
33 U.S.C. §§ 1251–1387 (1972, as amended)

Coastal Zone Act Reauthorization Amendments
Pub. L. No. 101-508, title VI, subtitle C, §§ 6201–6217 (5 November 1990)

Coastal Zone Management Act
16 U.S.C. §§ 1451–1464 (1972, as amended)

Common Varieties Act
30 U.S.C. §§ 601–604 (1947, as amended)

Comprehensive Environmental Response, Compensation, and Liability Act
42 U.S.C. §§ 9601–9675 (1980, as amended)

Conservation Reserve Program
16 U.S.C. §§ 3831, 3835 (1985, as amended)

Endangered Species Act
16 U.S.C. §§ 1531–1543 (1973, as amended)

Energy Policy Act
Pub. L. No. 102-486, 106 Stat. 2776 (1992)

Federal Agricultural and Improvement and Reform Act
Pub. L. No. 104-127, 110 Stat. 888, 986–992 (1996)

Federal Aid in Fish Restoration Act (Dingell-Johnson Act)
16 U.S.C. §§ 777–777k (1950, as amended)

Federal Aid in Wildlife Restoration Act (Pittman-Robinson Act)
16 U.S.C. §§ 669–669j (1937, as amended)

Federal Land Policy and Management Act
43 U.S.C. §§ 1701–1784 (1976, as amended)

Federal Onshore Oil and Gas Leasing Reform Act
Pub. L. No. 100-203, title V, subtitle B, §§ 5101–5113 (22 December 1987)

Federal Water Pollution Control Act Amendments
Pub. L. No. 92-500 (18 October 1972)

Fish and Wildlife Conservation Act
16 U.S.C. §§ 2901–2911 (1980)

Fish and Wildlife Coordination Act
16 U.S.C. §§ 661–667 (1934, as amended)

Food, Agriculture, Conservation, and Trade Act
Pub. L. No. 101-624 (28 November 1990)

Food Security Act
16 U.S.C. §§ 3821–3823 (1985, as amended)

Forest and Rangelands Renewable Resources Planning Act
See Resources Planning Act.

General Mining Law
30 U.S.C. §§ 21–42 (1872, as amended)

Geothermal Steam Act
30 U.S.C. §§ 1001–1025 (1970, as amended)

Government Performance and Results Act
Pub. L. No. 103-62, 107 Stat. 285 (3 August 1993)

Highway Beautification Act
Pub. L. 89-285, 79 Stat. 1028 (22 October 1965)

Knutson-Vandenberg Act
16 U.S.C. §§ 576–576b (1930, as amended)

Lacey Act
16 U.S.C. §§ 667e, 701, 3371–3378, 18 U.S.C. §§ 42–44 (1900, as amended)

Land and Water Conservation Act
16 U.S.C. §§ 460l-4 to 460l-11 (1964, as amended)

Magnuson Fishery Conservation and Management Act
16 U.S.C. §§ 1801–1882 (1976, as amended)

Marine Mammal Protection Act
16 U.S.C. §§ 1361–1362, 1371–1384, 1401–1407 (1972, as amended)

Migratory Bird Conservation Act
16 U.S.C. §§ 715–715s (1929, as amended)

Migratory Bird Hunting Stamp Act
16 U.S.C. §§ 718a–718j (1934, as amended)

Migratory Bird Treaty Act
16 U.S.C. §§ 703–711 (1918, as amended)

Mineral Leasing Act
30 U.S.C. §§ 181–287 (1920, as amended)

Multiple-Use, Sustained-Yield Act of 1960
16 U.S.C. §§ 528–531 (1960)

National Environmental Policy Act
42 U.S.C. §§ 4321–4370d (1969, as amended)

National Forest Management Act
16 U.S.C. §§ 1600–1614 (1976, as amended)

National Park Service Organic Act
16 U.S.C. §§ 1–18f (1916, as amended)

National Trails System Act
16 U.S.C. §§ 1241–1249 (1968, as amended)

National Wildlife Refuge Administration Act
16 U.S.C. §§ 668dd–668ee (1966, as amended)

National Wildlife Refuge System Improvement Act of 1997
Pub. L. No. 105-57, 111 Stat. 1252 (9 October 1997)

New Mexico–Arizona Enabling Act
Act of 20 June 1910, 36 Stat. 557, as amended

Oregon and California Revested Lands Management Act
43 U.S.C. §§ 1181a–1181f (1937, as amended)

Organic Administration Act (Forest Service)
16 U.S.C. §§ 472–482, 551 (1897, as amended)

Pacific Northwest Electric Power Planning and Conservation Act
16 U.S.C. §§ 839–839h (1980, as amended)

Public Rangelands Improvement Act
43 U.S.C. §§ 1901–1908 (1978)

Refuge Protection Act
16 U.S.C. §§ 460k-460k-4 (1962, as amended)

Resource Conservation and Recovery Act
42 U.S.C. §§ 6901-6992k (1976, as amended)

Resources Planning Act
16 U.S.C. §§ 1601–1613 (1974, as amended by National Forest Management Act of 1976)

Rivers and Harbors Appropriation Act
ch. 425, 30 Stat. 1121 (3 March 1899)

R.S. 2477
Act of 26 July 1866 (repealed 21 October 1976)

Safe Drinking Water Act
42 U.S.C. §§ 301f *et seq.* (1974, as amended)

Small Business Regulatory Enforcement Fairness Act
Pub. L. No. 104-21, 5 U.S.C. §§ 801–808, 15 U.S.C. § 657 (1996)

Soil and Water Resources Conservation Act
Pub. L. No. 95-192, 16 U.S.C. §§ 2001 *et seq.* (1977)

Surface Mining Control and Reclamation Act
30 U.S.C. §§ 1201–1328 (1977, as amended)

Surfaces Resources Act
30 U.S.C. §§ 611–615 (1955, as amended)

Taylor Grazing Act
43 U.S.C. §§ 315–315r (1934, as amended)

Tongass Timber Reform Act
Pub. L. No. 101-626, 104 Stat. 4426 (28 November 1990)

Union Pacific Act of 1 July 1862
ch. 120, 12 Stat. 489 (as amended)

Unlawful Inclosures Act
43 U.S.C. §§ 1061–1066 (1885, as amended)

Wild and Scenic Rivers Act
16 U.S.C. §§ 1271–1287 (1968, as amended)

Wild, Free-Roaming Horses and Burros Act
16 U.S.C. §§ 1331–1340 (1971, as amended)

Wilderness Act
16 U.S.C. §§ 1131–1136 (1964, as amended)

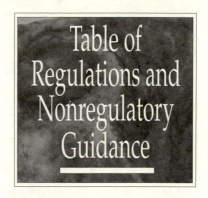

Table of Regulations and Nonregulatory Guidance

Bureau of Land Management, Grazing Administration, 43 C.F.R. Part 4100

Bureau of Land Management, Minerals Management, 43 C.F.R. Parts 3000–3809

Bureau of Land Management, Planning, Programming, and Budgeting, 43 C.F.R. Part 1600

Bureau of Land Management, Rights-of-Way, 43 C.F.R. Part 2800

Clean Water Act Section 404 Permit Public Interest Review, 33 C.F.R. § 320.4(a)

Clean Water Act Section 404 Permit Regulatory Policies, 33 C.F.R. Parts 320, 323, 328–330

Clean Water Act Section 404(b) Guidelines, 40 C.F.R. Part 230

Coastal Zone Management Program Regulations, 15 C.F.R. Part 923

Conservation Reserve Program Appeal Procedures, 7 C.F.R. Part 614

Council on Environmental Quality Regulations for Implementing the National Environmental Policy Act, 40 C.F.R. Part 1500

Endangered and Threatened Wildlife and Plants, 50 C.F.R. Part 17 (definition of harm, 50 C.F.R. § 17.3)

Endangered Species Act, Interagency Cooperation, 50 C.F.R. Part 402.

Federal Aid in Fish Restoration and Federal Aid in Wildlife Restoration Acts, Administration Requirements, 50 C.F.R. Part 80

Federal Consistency with Approved Coastal Management Programs, 15 C.F.R. Part 930

Fish and Wildlife Conservation Act, Administration Requirements, 50 C.F.R. Part 83

Highly Erodible Land and Wetland Conservation, 7 C.F.R. Part 12 [commodity crops, 7 C.F.R. § 12.2.(a)(1) (definition)]

349

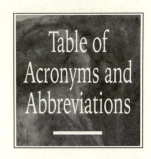

Table of Acronyms and Abbreviations

ADC	Animal Damage Control
ANCSA	Alaska Native Claims Settlement Act
ANILCA	Alaska National Interest Lands Conservation Act
ANWR	Arctic National Wildlife Refuge
APA	Administrative Procedure Act
ASQ	allowable sale quantity
bbf	billion board feet
BLM	Bureau of Land Management
BMP	best management practice
BOR	Bureau of Reclamation
CEQ	Council on Environmental Quality
COE	Corps of Engineers
CRP	Conservation Reserve Program
CWA	Clean Water Act
CZARA	Coastal Zone Act Reauthorization Amendments
CZMA	Coastal Zone Management Act
DOI	Department of the Interior
DOW	Defenders of Wildlife
EBAM	Ecosystem-based approaches to management
EDF	Environmental Defense Fund
EIS	environmental impact statement
ELI	Environmental Law Institute
EPA	Environmental Protection Agency
ESA	Endangered Species Act
FLPMA	Federal Land Policy and Management Act
FONSI	finding of no significant impact
FY	fiscal year
GIS	geographic information system
HCP	habitat conservation plan
IBLA	Interior Board of Land Appeals
LRMP	Land and Resource Management Plan (or forest plan)

LWCF	Land and Water Conservation Fund
mbf	million board feet
MBTA	Migratory Bird Treaty Act
MMPA	Marine Mammal Protection Act
MSLF	Mountain States Legal Foundation
MUSYA	Multiple-Use, Sustained-Yield Act
NDEF	nondeclining even flow
NEPA	National Environmental Policy Act
NFMA	National Forest Management Act
NIPF	Nonindustrial private forest
NPCA	National Parks and Conservation Association
NPS	National Park Service
NRCS	Natural Resources Conservation Service
NRDC	Natural Resources Defense Council
NWF	National Wildlife Federation
NWPS	National Wilderness Preservation System
NWRS	National Wildlife Refuge System
OCS	Outer Continental Shelf
ORV	off-road vehicle
PRIA	Public Rangelands Improvement Act
PUD	planned unit development
RAC	Resource Advisory Council
RMP	Resource Management Plan
SCLDF	Sierra Club Legal Defense Fund
SMCRA	Surface Mining Control and Reclamation Act
TDR	transferable development right
TMDL	total maximum daily load
TNC	The Nature Conservancy
TTRA	Tongass Timber Reform Act of 1990
TU	Trout Unlimited
TVA	Tennessee Valley Authority
TWS	The Wilderness Society
USDA	U.S. Department of Agriculture
USFS	U.S. Forest Service
USFWS	U.S. Fish and Wildlife Service
WFRHBA	Wild, Free-Roaming Horses and Burros Act
WRP	Wetlands Reserve Program
WSRA	Wild and Scenic Rivers Act

Directory of Organizations

Following are addresses, and, when available, websites for the conservation-related organizations that appear as entries in this dictionary.

AMERICAN RIVERS
1025 Vermont Avenue, NW, Suite 720, Washington, D.C. 20005. Phone: (202) 547-6900. Website: amrivers.org/amrivers/

BUREAU OF LAND MANAGEMENT (BLM)
1849 C Street, N.W., Washington, D.C. 20240. Phone: (202) 208-3801 (director), (202) 208-3171 (public information).

BUREAU OF RECLAMATION (BOR)
1849 C Street, N.W., Washington, D.C. 20240. Phone: (202) 208-4291.

CORPS OF ENGINEERS (CORPS)
Casimir Pulaski Building, 20 Massachusetts Avenue, N.W., Washington, D.C. 20314-1000. Phone: (202) 761-0660.

DEFENDERS OF WILDLIFE (DOW)
1101 14th Street, NW, Suite 1400, Washington, D.C. 20005. Phone: (202) 682-9400. Internet address: http://www.information@defenders.org

EARTH JUSTICE LEGAL DEFENSE FUND
See Sierra Club Legal Defense Fund, Inc.

ENVIRONMENTAL DEFENSE FUND (EDF)
257 Park Avenue S., New York, NY 10010. Phone: (212) 505-2100, (800) 684-3322. Website: http://www.edf.org

ENVIRONMENTAL LAW INSTITUTE (ELI)
1616 P Street, NW, Washington, D.C. 20036. Phone: (202) 328-5150, (202) 328-5002.

ENVIRONMENTAL PROTECTION AGENCY (EPA)
401 M Street, S.W., Washington, D.C. 20460. Phone: (202) 260-2090. Website: http://www.epa.gov

FOREST SERVICE EMPLOYEES FOR ENVIRONMENTAL ETHICS (FSEEE)
P.O. Box 11615, Eugene, OR 97440. Phone: (541) 484-2692.

FRIENDS OF THE EARTH (FOE)
The Global Building, 1025 Vermont Avenue, NW, Suite 300, Washington, D.C. 20005. Phone: (202) 783-7400.

FUND FOR ANIMALS
200 W. 57th Street, New York, NY 10019. Phone: (212) 246-2096.

GREATER YELLOWSTONE COALITION (GYC)
P.O. Box 1874, Bozeman, MT 59771. Phone: (406) 586-1593. Website: http://www.desktop.org/gyc

GREENPEACE
1436 U Street, NW, Washington, D.C. 20009. Phone: (202) 319-2444. Internet address: greenpeace.usa@green2.greenpeace.org

LAND TRUST ALLIANCE (LTA)
1319 F Street, NW, Suite 501, Washington, D.C. 20004-1106. Phone: (202) 638-4725.

LEAGUE OF CONSERVATION VOTERS (LCV)
1707 L Street, NW, Suite 750, Washington, D.C. 20036-2266. Phone: (202) 785-8683. Website: http://www.econet.org/lcv

MINERAL POLICY CENTER
1612 K Street, NW, Washington, D.C. 20006. Phone: (202) 887-1872. Website: http://www.mineralpolicy.org

MOUNTAIN STATES LEGAL FOUNDATION (MSLF)
707 17th Street, Suite 3030, Denver, CO 80202. Phone: (303) 292-1980.

NATIONAL AUDUBON SOCIETY
700 Broadway, New York, NY 10003. Phone: (212) 979-3000. Website: http://www.audubon.org/audubon/

NATIONAL BIOLOGICAL SERVICE (NBS)
U.S. Geological Survey-Division of Biological Resources, U.S. Geological Survey National Center, 12201 Sunrise Valley Drive, Reston, VA 22092. Phone: (703) 648-4000.

NATIONAL MINING ASSOCIATION (NMA)
1130 17th Street, NW, Washington, D.C. 20036. Phone: (202) 463-2625.

NATIONAL PARKS AND CONSERVATION ASSOCIATION (NPCA)
1776 Massachusetts Avenue, NW, Washington, D.C. 20036. Phone: (202) 223-6722.

NATIONAL WILDLIFE FEDERATION (NWF)
1400 Sixteenth Street, NW, Washington, D.C. 20036-2266. Phone: (202) 797-6800. Website: http://www.nwf.org/nwf.

NATURAL RESOURCES DEFENSE COUNCIL (NRDC)
40 West 20th Street, New York, NY 10011. Phone: (212) 727-2700. Website: http://www.nrdc.org.

THE NATURE CONSERVANCY (TNC)
International headquarters: 1815 North Lynn Street, Arlington, VA 22209. Phone: (703) 841-8745, (800) 628-6860. Website: http://www.tnc.org.

ROCKY MOUNTAIN ELK FOUNDATION (RMEF)
2291 W. Broadway, Missoula, MT 59802. Phone: (406) 523-4500, (800) CALL-ELK.

SIERRA CLUB
730 Polk Street, San Francisco, CA 94109. Phone: (415) 776-2211. Website: http://www.sierraclub.org.

SIERRA CLUB LEGAL DEFENSE FUND, INC. (SCLDF)
180 Montgomery Street, Suite 1400, San Francisco, CA 94104. Phone: (415) 627-6700. Fax: (415) 627-6740.

SOUTHEAST ALASKA CONSERVATION COUNCIL (SEACC)
419 Sixth Street, Suite 328, Juneau, AK 99801. Phone: (907) 586-6942. Website: http://www.Juneau.com/seacc.

SOUTHERN UTAH WILDERNESS ALLIANCE (SUWA)
1471 S. 1100 E., Salt Lake City, UT 84105. Phone: (801) 486-3161.

TROUT UNLIMITED (TU)
1500 Wilson Boulevard, Suite 310, Arlington, VA 22209-2404. (703) 522-0200 or (888) 221-2137. Website: http://www.tu.org/trout/.

U.S. FISH AND WILDLIFE SERVICE (USFWS)
1849 C Street, N.W., Washington, D.C. 20240. Phone: (202) 208-5634. Website: http://www.fws.gov.

U.S. FOREST SERVICE (USFS)
P.O. Box 96090, Washington, D.C. 20090-6090. Phone: (202) 205-0957.

THE WILDERNESS SOCIETY (TWS)

900 Seventeenth Street, NW, Washington, D.C. 20006. Phone: (202) 833-2300. Internet address: tws@tws.org.

Index

Debra L. Donahue is associate professor of law at the University of Wyoming. Her prior legal experience includes private practice and serving as staff counsel for the National Wildlife Federation. She was also environmental coordinator for a gold mining company, executive director of a statewide conservation organization, and served three land management agencies in several capacities.